Masks of Fiction in
DREAM OF THE RED CHAMBER
Myth, Mimesis, and Persona

MONOGRAPHS OF THE ASSOCIATION FOR ASIAN STUDIES

Published by and available from: The University of Arizona Press
Box 3398, Tucson, Arizona 85722

XXVIII.   *Masks of Fiction in DREAM OF THE RED CHAMBER,* by Lucien Miller. 1975. $7.95 cloth; $3.95 paper.

XXVII.   *Politics and Nationalist Awakening in South India, 1852–1891,* by R. Suntharalingam. 1974. $7.95 cloth; $3.95 paper.

XXVI.   *The Peasant Rebellions of the Late Ming Dynasty,* by James Bunyan Parsons. 1970. $7.50.

XXV.   *Political Centers and Cultural Regions in Early Bengal,* by Barrie M. Morrison. 1970. $7.50.

XXIV.   *The Restoration of Thailand Under Rama I: 1782–1809,* by Klaus Wenk. 1968. $7.50.

XXIII.   *K'ang Yu-wei: A Biography and a Symposium,* translated and edited by Jung-pang Lo. 1967. 541 pp. $14.50.

XXII.   *A Documentary Chronicle of Sino-Western Relations (1644–1820),* by Lo-shu Fu. 1966. xviii + 792 pp. $14.50.

XXI.   *Before Aggression: Europeans Prepare the Japanese Army,* by Ernst L. Presseisen. 1965. O. P.

XX.   *Shinran's Gospel of Pure Grace,* by Alfred Bloom. 1965. $2.50 paper.

XIX.   *Chiaraijima Village: Land Tenure, Taxation, and Local Trade, 1818–1884,* by William Chambliss. 1965. $5.00.

XVIII.   *The British in Malaya: The First Forty Years,* by K. G. Tregonning. 1965. O. P.

XVII.   *Ch'oe Pu's Diary: A Record of Drifting Across the Sea,* by John Meskill. 1965. $4.50.

XVI.   *Korean Literature: Topics and Themes,* by Peter H. Lee. 1965. O. P.

XV.   *Reform, Rebellion, and the Heavenly Way,* by Benjamin B. Weems. 1964. $3.75.

XIV.   *The Malayan Tin Industry to 1914,* by Wong Lin Ken. 1965. $6.50.

Earlier-published AAS Monographs

XIII.   *Conciliation and Japanese Law: Tokugawa and Modern,* D. F. Henderson. Univ. Washington Press, 1965. $15.00.

XII.   *Maharashta Purana,* E. C. Dimock, Jr., and P. C. Gupta. East-West Center Press, 1964. O. P.

XI.   *Agricultural Involution: The Process of Ecological Change in Indonesia,* C. Geertz. Univ. California Press, 1963. $7.00 c; $2.45 p.

X.   *Bangkhuad: A Community Study in Thailand,* H. K. Kaufman. J. J. Augustin, 1959. O. P.

IX.   *Colonial Labor Policy and Administration, 1910–1941,* J. N. Parmer. Augustin, 1959. $6.00.

VIII.   *A Comparative Analysis of the Jajmani System,* T. O. Beidelman. Augustin, 1959. $2.50.

VII.   *The Traditional Chinese Clan Rules,* Hui-chen Wang Liu. Augustin, 1959. $5.50.

VI.   *Chinese Secret Societies in Malaya,* L. F. Comber. Augustin, 1959. $6.50.

V.   *The Rise of the Merchant Class in Tokugawa Japan: 1600–1868,* C. D. Sheldon. Augustin, 1958. O. P.

IV.   *Siam Under Rama III, 1824–1851,* W. F. Vella. Augustin, 1957. O. P.

III.   *Leadership and Power in the Chinese Community of Thailand,* G. W. Skinner. Cornell Univ. Press, 1958. O. P.

II.   *China's Management of the American Barbarians,* E. Swisher. Far Eastern Pubs., Yale, 1951. O. P.

I.   *Money Economy in Medieval Japan,* D. M. Brown. Far Eastern Pubs., Yale, 1951. O. P.

The Association for Asian Studies: Monograph No. XXVIII
Edgar Wickberg, *Editor*

Masks of Fiction in
Dream of the Red Chamber
Myth, Mimesis, and Persona

Lucien Miller

 Published for the Association for Asian Studies by
THE UNIVERSITY OF ARIZONA PRESS
Tuscon, Arizona

About the author . . .

Lucien Miller received his doctorate in Comparative
Literature at the University of California, Berkeley.
He teaches Comparative Literature and Chinese at the
University of Massachusetts, Amherst.

The publication of this volume
has been financed from a revolving
fund that was initially established
by a generous grant from the
Ford Foundation.

THE UNIVERSITY OF ARIZONA PRESS

For the unborn
living
and
dead

Acknowledgments

I should like to express my profound gratitude to the following individuals:

to Professors Warren Anderson, Cyril Birch, Philip Damon, and Wolfram Eberhard for the time they so freely gave to careful reading and thoughtful criticism;

to Professors Ch'ing-mao Cheng, Angela Jung Palandri, and Mr. Richard Kunst for their invaluable help with critical, textual, and translation problems;

to Professor Lewis Lancaster for translations of Buddhist terminology;

to my colleague, Professor Alvin Cohen, for many perceptive suggestions and for his excellent notes and translation of chapter 1 of Hung-lou meng based on the Kao E text of 1792;

to Professor Joanna Handlin for the generous loan of her personal copy of the chia-hsu manuscript of the Chih-yen Chai annotated Shih-t'ou chi;

to Ms. Anne Souza for the gift of her talents in doing layout and graphic work;

to Ms. Sandy Milliken for typing this book with diligence and grace;

to Ms. Rosa Yang for her excellent work as calligrapher.

Finally, I should like to remember especially my lao-shih, the late Shih-Hsiang Chen. He suggested this study and guided it from its inception. Had he lived, this would have been a better book.

Whatever the merits of the present work, they are due to the aid and encouragement of these persons. The faults and errors, of course, are my own.

Contents

all commentary is allegorical interpretation

Northrop Frye

CLCHCYCCPSTC   Ch'ien-lung chia-hsu Chih-yen Chai ch'ung-
p'ing Shih-t'ou chi 乾隆甲戌脂硯齋
重評石頭記 . Hu Shih 胡適 , ed.
2 vols. Taipei: Shang-wu yin-shu-kuan, 1961.

CYCCPSTC   Chih-yen Chai ch'ung-p'ing Shih-t'ou chi 脂
硯齋重評石頭記 . 2 vols. Peking:
Wen-hsueh ku-chi k'an-hsing she, 1955.

CYCHLMCP   Chih-yen Chai Hung-lou meng chi-p'ing 脂
硯齋紅樓夢輯評 . Yu P'ing-po 俞
平伯 , ed. Revised edition. Shanghai:
Chung-hua shu-chu, 1963.

HLMPSHCP   Hung-lou meng pa-shih hui chiao-pen 紅樓
夢八十回校本 . Yu P'ing-po 俞平
伯 ed. Peking: Jen-min wen-hsueh ch'u-pan
she, 1958.

Note on Wade-Giles Romanization
For purposes of typographical simplicity, the letter u appears without
umlaut marks in this book.

Masks of Fiction in
DREAM OF THE RED CHAMBER
Myth, Mimesis, and Persona

Introduction

Over two hundred years ago, a then obscure Chinese author named Ts'ao Hsueh-ch'in began to circulate among his intimate friends and relatives chapters of an imaginative work he was writing. It depicted the adolescent world of a young boy and his female cousins who lived together in a garden paradise. As this intriguing piece of fiction was passed from hand to hand, members of the small band of admirers would insert their personal views in margins and between the lines of the text. From this marginal and interlinear commentary which exists in extant manuscript versions of the novel, we know that Ts'ao Hsueh-ch'in's first readers were deeply moved by what we wish to suggest is one of the most exquisite examples of fictional art in world literature. After the death of the author, his work appeared in printed versions under the title of Dream of the Red Chamber.[1] The posthumous publication of Ts'ao Hsueh-ch'in's novel gave rise to a popular acclaim and a scholarly attention which have not been surpassed by any other piece of Chinese ver-

----

[1] Hung-lou meng 紅樓夢 . Throughout this study we use Dream of the Red Chamber (Hung-lou meng) because the work is more widely known under this name in both Chinese and in translations. For a discussion of the various titles of the novel, see below, pp. 30ff.

nacular fiction over the course of two centuries.

In a review of the standard bibliography of Dream of the Red Chamber,[2] Wu Shih-ch'ang observes that it lists the following works published up to October, 1954: thirty-three manuscript versions of the novel of which six are annotated; seventy-two printed editions of which forty-five are with commentaries; thirteen translations into foreign languages; thirty continuations or sequels to the novel and twenty-one imitations of the novel; eighty-six works and one hundred and ninety articles (in newspapers and periodicals); twenty pictorial albums and twenty-five compendia of literary games based on the novel; sixty-two works commenting on the novel in verse, varying from a few to two hundred poems; dramatizations of stories in the novel in three hundred and thirty-nine works varying from one scene to a full play, mostly in local operas; three film scenarios; four re-written stories and seven serialized pictorial illustrations.[3] As our own bibliography indicates, since 1954 interest in Dream of the Red Chamber has continued to increase so that today it is easy to surmise that China's most widely acclaimed novel is also the one which has been subject to the most thorough scholarly attention.

Despite the extensive number of materials on the novel, most of them have been devoted to questions of authorship, dates, and text, with the result that there have been few literary studies. While we cannot accept the popular view that there is nothing in hung-hsueh[4] which helps one to appreciate Dream of the Red Chamber, we might suggest that, with the exception of the work of Wang Kuo-wei and

----

2Hung-lou meng shu-lu 紅樓夢書錄, ed. I-su 一粟 (Ch'ien Hsing-ts'un 錢杏邨), Shanghai, Ku-tien wen-hsueh ch'u-pan she, 1958.

3Wu Shih-ch'ang 吳世昌 , see his review in Revue Bibliographique de Sinologie, IV (1958), 348-349.

4hung-hsueh 紅學 , i.e., mainly native Chinese textual, biographical, or bibliographical studies of Dream of the Red Chamber, sometimes translated as "Redology". Wu Shih-ch'ang cites the Record of Painters in the Eight Banners, 八旗畫錄, by Li Fang 李放 (in the Yun-tsai shan-feng ts'ung-shu, p. 33), as evidence that the term, "hung-hsueh", or, "Redology", was coined by scholars in Peking around 1875. See Wu's On the Red Chamber Dream, Oxford, 1961, p. 4.

some comments by Hu Shih,[5] we find few examples of literary analysis until recently.[6] The following pages represent our modest
attempt to consider Dream of the Red Chamber as a literary work of
art. Through a close textual analysis of Yu P'ing-po's collated
edition of Dream of the Red Chamber,[7] we shall try to arrive at an
understanding of the aesthetic appeal of this novel. If we are successful, we shall have helped to correct the erroneous view (fostered
largely, we believe, by readers who know the novel mainly in translation) that Dream of the Red Chamber lacks a definable style,
structure, and organizing principle, or that, in the words of one
Western commentator, it is a "bedside book" for "adolescent boys
and girls".[8]

In order to assess Ts'ao Hsueh-ch'in's artistry and to identify many
of the unique features of Dream of the Red Chamber, we invite the
reader to embark with us upon a study which is, at least in its initial
stages, mildly revisionist. There is one school of late nineteenth
and early twentieth century critics of the novel--now largely ridi-
culed or ignored--whose view indirectly suggests and confirms our
approach to Dream of the Red Chamber through myth, mimesis, and
persona. The members of this group, whom for want of a better term

----

[5]Wang Kuo-wei 王國維 , "Hung-lou meng p'ing-lun"
紅樓夢評論 , in Hung-lou meng chuan 紅樓夢卷 ,
vol. I (Peking, 1963), pp. 244-265. Hu Shih "胡適, Hung-
lou meng k'ao cheng 紅樓夢考證 , Taipei, Yuan-tung
t'u-shu kung-ssu, 1961.

[6]See especially, C.T. Hsia's essay, "Dream of the Red Chamber",
in his work, The Classic Chinese Novel, New York & London, 1968,
pp. 245-297. Hsia himself believes that native Chinese criticism
fails to elucidate the novel. See "Love and Compassion in Dream
of the Red Chamber", Criticism, V: iii (Summer, 1963), 262.

[7]Hung-lou meng pa-shih hui chiao-pen 紅樓夢八十回校本
(hereafter HLMPSHCP), ed. Yu P'ing-po 俞平伯 , Jen-min wen-
hsueh ch'u-pan she, Peking, 1958. For our reasons for the choice
of this text and for a discussion of the text and the textual critics of
Dream of the Red Chamber, see Appendix A.

[8]Odile Kaltenmark, Chinese Literature, trans. from French by
Anne-Marie Geoghegan, New York, 1964, p. 128. (First published as La Littérature Chinoise; English translation contains new
material.) Kaltenmark's view that the novel has been very popular
among Chinese adolescents is only partially true, for this view ignores the novel's wider appeal.

we shall call the "Allegorists",[9] base their investigations on the
following sentence from the so-called "Preface"[10] to Dream of the
Red Chamber:

> The author relates that he once passed through a dream-vision
> and afterwards he hid the real affairs therein and composed
> the book.[11]

Endeavoring to bring out that which is "hidden" and to guess the
real purport of the novel, the Allegorists variously interpret Dream
of the Red Chamber as a political satire, an imperial love story,

----

[9]Yuan Sheng-shih 袁聖詩 has outlined the development of
this school in his article, "Hung-lou meng yen-chiu" 紅樓夢研究,
Tung-fang tsa-chih 東方雜誌, XLIV:xi (Nov., 1948), 49.
  According to Wu Shih-ch'ang, this school emerged in the late
nineteenth century and enjoyed a strong following until 1922, when
Hu Shih published his theory that Dream of the Red Chamber is
Ts'ao's autobiography. See Wu, On the Red Chamber Dream, pp.
4-5. For Hu Shih's autobiographical theory, see Hung-lou meng
k'ao cheng, pp. 1-42, 48-57.
  The term "allegory" is particularly difficult to translate into
Chinese. The following are suggestions: P'an Ch'ung-kuei
notes Hu Shih's use of ying-shu 影書 ; P'an himself uses the
phrase, 隱含特殊意義的小說, and says that it is appli-
cable to half of the critical views of Dream of the Red Chamber
(see P'an's "Hung-hsüeh wu-shih-nien" 紅學五十年, in
Hsin-ya shu-yuan Chung-kuo wen-hsüeh hsi nien-k'an 新亞書院
中國文學系年刊, IV (June, 1966), 4.
  P'ei-chih 佩之 uses the phrase 神祕派的小說. Perhaps
"mystical" fiction might be construed to mean "allegoric" fiction.
See P'ei-chih's article, "Hung-lou meng hsin-p'ing"紅樓夢新評,
Hsiao-shuo yüeh-pao 小說月報, XI:vii (July, 1920), 11.
  [10]For our discussion of the Preface and its importance in Dream
of the Red Chamber, see "Persona" chapter.
  [11]We translate here from a reprint of the so-called chia-hsu annotated manuscript of the novel. Ch'ien-lung chia-hsu Chih-yen Chai
ch'ung-p'ing Shih-t'ou chi, 乾隆甲戌脂硯齋重評石頭記
(hereafter CLCHCYCCPSTC), Hu Shih, ed., Taipei, Shang-wu yin-
shu kuan, 1961, vol. 1, p. 31, life 5ff. (we use Hu Shih's pagination): 作者自云因曾歷過一番夢幻之後故將真事隱去
而撰此石頭記一書也。

and a patriotic dirge to the fallen Ming dynasty.[12] Developers of
the allegorical approach such as Ts'ai Yuan-p'ei, Chang Hsin-chih,
Yao Hsieh, Hung Ch'iu-po, and Sun Ch'u-fu,[13] argue that the
novel is a ying-shu, or "shadow-book", and that every character
is a ying-tzu, "reflection", or "shadow" of another.[14] Even
those who react most strongly against the era of "riddle mongering"
and the school of Allegorists, such as Hu Shih and Yu P'ing-po,
adopt interpretive allegory in their studies of Dream of the Red
Chamber.[15] Yu tries to prove that the hidden theme of the novel

----

[12]General reviews of Dream of the Red Chamber criticism may
be found in the following:

Chen-fu 振甫 , "T'ung-kuo tui Hung-lou meng yen-chiu te p'i-
p'an lai jen-shih yueh-tu ku-tien tso-p'in" 通過對紅樓夢
研究的批判來認識閱讀古典作品 , Yu-wen hsueh-hsi
語文學習, no. 40 (Jan., 1955), 7-13.

Chou Ch'i 周琪 ,"P'ing Hung-lou meng chung kuan-yu shih-erh
ch'ai te miao-shieh" 評紅樓夢中關於十二釵的描寫 ,
Wen-hsueh p'ing-lun 文學評論 , 4 (Aug., 1964), 80-90.

Hu Shih, Hung-lou meng k'ao-cheng (in the 1921 Ya-tung t'u-shu
kuan edition of Hung-lou meng), pp. 6-11, 87-93.

Li Wei-ch'iu 李未秋 , "Hung-lou meng yu T'ai-wan" 紅樓
夢與臺灣, T'ai-wan feng-wu 臺灣風物, X:iv (April,
1960), 13.

Lu Hsun 魯迅 , A Brief History of Chinese Fiction, Yang Hsien-
yi and Gladys Yang, trans. Peking, 1964, pp. 309-312.

P'an Ch'ung-kuei 潘重規, "Hung-hsueh wu-shih-nien", 1-13.
"Chih-erh hung-hsueh" 今日紅學 , Hung-lou meng yen-chiu
chuan-k'an 紅樓夢研究專刊 , (ed. by the
Research Group on the Hung-lou meng, Chinese Department, New
Asia College, Hong Kong Chinese University), No. 7 (Jan., 1970),
111-117.

Wu Shih-ch'ang, On the Red Chamber Dream, pp. 1-11.

Yuan Sheng-shih 袁聖世 , "Hung-lou meng yen-chiu", 49.

[13] 蔡元培; 張新之 ;姚燮 ;洪秋蕃源渠甫
Names cited by Chou Ch'i, ibid., 84.

[14]ying-shu 影書 ; ying-tzu 影子 . See note 9.

[15]Chou Ch'i, "Ping Hung-lou meng chung kuan-yu shih-erh
ch'ai te miao-hsieh", 84, points out that while Yu rejected the old
school of Allegorists, he still accepted the "character reflection"
theory.

is that life is an illusory dream.[16]   According to Hu Shih's "autobiography" theory, characters, events, and places in Dream of the
Red Chamber are hua-shen, "transformations", or ying-tzu, "reflections", of characters, events, and places in Ts'ao Hsueh-ch'in's
life.[17]   Dream of the Red Chamber is based on real life experience,
of course, but Hu Shih's attempt to bridge reality and fiction is a
study in allegorical technique.

While the Allegorists are so attracted by the author's enigmatic
statement about hiding real affairs that they abandon the novel to
seek its meaning everywhere but in the text, Communist critics in
mainland China are so repelled by the implicit allegory of the framework that they ignore the latter altogether. Both deliberate abandonment and chosen ignorance[18] may be attributed partly to the
iconoclastic reaction to the old Chinese literary tradition, partly to
the desire to apply the correct line of Marxism-Leninism in assessing
literature, and partly to the enormous influence of Western realistic
fiction and socially conscious critical theory. After reading nearly
all of the mainland criticism on Dream of the Red Chamber, we feel
that many contemporary Chinese are made self-conscious and embarrassed by old beliefs in the machinations of fate and the predominance

----

[16]Yu's view originates in his Hung-lou meng pien 紅樓夢辨,
Shanghai, Ya-tung t'u-shu-kuan, 1923. In Hung-lou meng yen-
chiu 紅樓夢研究, Shanghai, T'ang-ti ch'u-p'an she, 1952,
Yu revises his earlier views: he considers the novel to be an autobiographical lament, a love confession, and a biography of the
Twelve Hairpins. In his more recent publications, Yu has dropped
the autobiographical theory.

[17]hua-shen 化身. P'an Ch'ung-kuei observes that there is
much of this sort of allegorizing in the conclusion to Hu Shih's Hung-
lou meng k'ao cheng. See P'an, "Hung-lou meng wu-shih-nien", 4.

[18]Chosen ignorance sometimes results in inadvertent humor.
Thus, the title of an article by the novelist, Lao She 老舍, is,
"Hung-lou meng ping pu-shih meng" 紅樓夢並不是夢
("Red Chamber Dream Really is Not a Dream"), Jen-min wen-hsueh
人民文學, No. 62 (Dec., 1954), 1-3. Lao She's title is especially ridiculous, since nothing is said in his article about the novel's
dream motif. He simply informs us that from his viewpoint as an
experienced author, the "realistic" language of the novel proves it
is not a dream, but reality.

of chance. The majority of the mainland commentators debunk the
dominating presence of the supernatural in traditional fiction and
they celebrate Dream of the Red Chamber solely as a work of socialist realism which attacks the values of an aristocratic society.
Ts'ao is hailed as a revolutionary who writes out of sympathy for the
proletarian masses. The prevailing view among those readers who
do take cognizance of such features in Dream of the Red Chamber
as myths, dream visions, and marvellous events, is that these are
vestiges of a "feudal" world which reflect the superstitious beliefs
of Ts'ao's social class.[19]

----

[19]Examples of mainland ideological criticism are:
Chang Tai 張戴 , "Lun Hung-lou meng te shih-tai pei-ching ho
Ts'ao Hsueh-ch'in te ch'uang tso ssu-hsiang", 論紅樓夢的時
代背景和曹雪芹的創作思想, in Hsin-chien-she 新
建設, 3 (March, 1955), 32-37, esp. 37.
Chiang Ho-sen 蔣和森 , Hung-lou meng lun kao 紅樓夢論稿
Jen-min wen-hsueh ch'u-pan she, Peking, 1959.
Li Shi-fan 李希凡 and Lan Ling 藍翎 , "Kuan-yu Hung-lou
meng chien-lun chi ch'i-t'a" 關於紅樓夢簡論及其他 ,
Wen-shih-che 文史哲, 9 (Sept., 1954), 22.
Li Hsi-fan and Lan Ling, Hung-lou meng p'ing-lun chi 紅樓夢
評論集 , Tso-chia ch'u-pan-she, Peking, 1957, passim.
P'eng Hui 彭慧 , "Lun Hung-lou meng te jen-min-hsing ho t'a
shih-fou shih 'shih-min wen-hsueh' wen-t'i, 論紅樓夢的人民
性和它是否市民文學的問題 , Jen-min wen-hsueh, No. 83
(Sept., 1956), 117-126.
Shan-tung ta-hsueh shih-sheng chi-t'i t'ao-lun 山東大學師生
集體討論 , "Wo-men tui Hung-lou meng te ch'u-pu k'an-fa"
我們對紅樓夢的初步看法, Jen-min wen-hsueh, 人民
文學, No. 64 (Feb., 1955), 111-121.
Teng T'o 鄧拓, "Lun Hung-lou meng te she-hui pei-ching ho
li-shih i-i" 論紅樓夢的社會背景和歷史意義, Hsin-hua
yueh-pao, No. 64 (Feb., 1955), 269-274.
Yang Hsiang-k'uei 楊向奎 , "Ts'ao Hsueh-ch'in te ssu-hsiang"
曹雪芹的思想 , Wen-shih-che 文史哲,3 (March, 1955),
36-40.
Ying Pai 映白 and Sun Chen-chih 孫慎之 , "Kuan-yu Hung-
lou meng so piao-hsien te mao-tun te hsing-chih wen-t'i" 關於紅樓
夢所表現的矛盾的性質問題 , Wen-shih-che 文史哲,
4 (April, 1955), 38-45.

The major reason why there is such a widespread misunderstanding
of the novel is not merely ideological, but rather is owing to a
predilection for "realistic" fiction among Communist critics --a bias
unfortunately shared by many Western readers of Dream of the Red
Chamber. This predilection is actually a limitation of perspective,
and leads to the inability to perceive that it is the interplay between the mythic, mimetic, and narrative modes of the framework
which creates the brilliant illusion that the closely detailed description of daily life at the heart of the novel is "realistic".[20]
Arthur Waley's reservations about the framework in traditional
Chinese fiction and in Dream of the Red Chamber are instructive.
In his Preface to Chi- chen Wang's translation of Dream of the Red
Chamber, Waley alludes to what he finds to be the distasteful usage
of the didactic framework by Chinese story-tellers and novelists.
He notes that:

> Even the most licentious of Chinese novelists did indeed make
> some show of pointing a moral, but the pretence is usually
> carried out in such a way as to irritate those who read for
> pleasure without appeasing those who read for improvement.[21]

An exceptionally fine article is Ho Ch'i-fang's 何其方 "Lun
Hung-lou meng" 論紅樓夢   , Wen-hsueh yen-chiu chi-k'an
文學研究集刊, 5 (May, 1957), 28-148. Ho is critical of
other Communist critics who say that the love tragedy of Pao-yu
and Tai-yu is due simply to their being rebels against feudal society.
Like many mainland readers, however, Ho believes that myths and
dreams are of minor importance in the novel. He takes the author's
statement about hiding real affairs (noted above) to mean that while
Ts'ao bases his novel on his own experience and life, he uses his
imagination to write fiction. See esp. pp. 34 and 108.

[20]We ought to remember in this connection that "The Great
Debate" over the meaning of Dream of the Red Chamber which took
place in mainland China roughly between 1954 and 1958 centered
on the meaning of realism. The debate resulted in a host of articles
which take the novel to be a work of socialist realism and a portrayal of the corruption and imminent decline of "feudal" society.
For a listing of the available materials on "The Great Debate" and
the names of the leading participants, See Appendix A. The articles in note 19, above, should be included also.

[21]Dream of the Red Chamber, trans. C. C. Wang, First Edition,
Doubleday, Garden City, New York, 1929, p. viii.

To Waley, Chinese fiction has a "moralizing tendency" and "is always on the defensive-- is always, with an eye on official Puritanism,
trying to prove that, like serious and approved literature, it has a
'message'".22 On those rare occasions when the story-teller wants
to tell a new story, says Waley, "either he sets it in the framework
of a familiar theme . . . or else he encloses his perhaps quite realistic and everyday subject in a strong casing of supernatural . . . ."23
  As Chinese fictional art gradually evolves from its oral origins,
this supernatural casing ceases to be merely a matter of embellishing
the usual with the unique. Yet, according to Waley, Dream of the
Red Chamber, like its predecessors, contains the unhappy mixture
of the natural and the supernatural. Comparing Ts'ao Hsueh-ch'in's
novel with All Men Are Brothers, Monkey, and Romance of Three
Kingdoms, he states:

> It has their inordinate length . . . their lack of faith
> in the interestingness of the everyday world, leading to the
> conviction that a realistic story must necessarily be set in a
> supernatural framework.24

The only saving grace in Ts'ao's subjection to "the rigid framework
imposed by tradition" is that it probably prevented the author from
committing "the error of transcribing with too careful a fidelity the
monotonies of actual life".25
  Every reader of Dream of the Red Chamber surely is aware that the
novel is set in the framework of a familiar theme-- that of mutability
and the vanity of human desire-- and that the realistic story of Pao-
yu and the Chia clan is enclosed in a supernatural casing-- the creation myth and the story of the Stone discarded by the goddess Nu-kua.
But what many readers fail to realize, and perhaps Waley should be
included among them, is that the reason why the so-called "realistic
story" must be set within a "supernatural framework" is because
Ts'ao Hsueh-ch'in's imaginative vision and polysemous style insist
upon it. Instead of opting for one world over another, the artist
presents, through a variety of styles, a unified vision in which the
supernatural and the natural cohere in a work of mythic, rather than
"realistic", fiction.
  As for a "message", there is no doubt that Dream of the Red Chamber has one, despite the fact that, as we shall note in "Persona",

----

22ibid., p. xi.
23ibid., p. ix.
24ibid., p. x.
25ibid., p. xi.

various readers of the novel such as the Reverend Taoist Kosmo Kosmos[26] complain about the absence of a conventional moral. The complex "message" of Dream of the Red Chamber naturally forms a part of our subject--the meaning which flows from the interplay of form and content. In our study of the latter two entities we hope to identify the particular quality of Ts'ao Hsueh-ch'in's didacticism. For the present, suffice it to say that didacticism is not necessarily a negative feature in literature. As Robert H. Brower and Earl Miner observe, the absence of didactic verse in the Japanese tradition is a distinct limitation:

> Didactic poetry has been in bad odor for so long that some people may find Japanese poetry well off without it. We cannot agree, for after one has exluded the poems of Juvenal, Lucretius, and Milton, many of the best poems of Dryden and Pope, and a good deal of French poetry, the Western world is considerably impoverished of many of its character-istic works. Moreover, many Western works not primarily didactic--and by now it should be clear that we do not con-sider didactic poetry to be filled with tedious sententiousness, but to be poetry in which the poet informs or "teaches"--are characteristically Western in that they have didactic elements unknown, or at least unused, by Japanese poets. If one takes the "teaching" or serious moral purpose out of Dante, Milton, and Wordsworth, hell loses its terrors and Tintern Abbey its significance.[27]

Neither didacticism nor the marvellous is inimical to literature, yet it remains true that their presence in Chinese fiction is nearly always cited as a fault by both Chinese and Western critics because these features do not meet with the requirements of formal realism.[28] One point we believe our study will make clear is that Dream of the Red Chamber is not a work of realistic fiction. Ts'ao Hsueh-ch'in's use of the supernatural and of improbable events reminds us that Hawthorne treats similar materials in his fiction. Because of these materials, and because of an interest in the problem of the relation between the real and the ideal (an interest of the New England

----

[26]K'ung-k'ung tao-jen 空空道人. Our translation will be explained in "Myth".

[27]Japanese Court Poetry, Stanford, 1961, p. 441.

[28]For a definition of formal realism, see Ian Watt, The Rise of the Novel, Berkeley and Los Angeles, 1962, pp. 30-34.

transcendentalists which Ts'ao Hsueh-ch'in would share), Hawthorne states in his Preface to The House of the Seven Gables that he prefers to use the term "romance" rather than "novel" in describing his works. Using Hawthorne's example, we suggest that Dream of the Red Chamber might be more accurately identified as a romance. The point is that, as Henry Nash Smith has observed, "realistic" novels are created through the use of literary conventions, as are "psychological" novels, "naturalistic" novels, "scientific" novels, "historical" novels, "philosophical" novels, "stream of conscious- ness" novels, and, for that matter, "romances". A "realistic" mode of writing is no more "true to life" than any other.[29] It is Ts'ao Hsueh-ch'in's skillfully combined use of several modes which makes Dream of the Red Chamber China's most credible work of fiction. To single out the realistic style and to ignore the allegoric or the narrative is a form of enervating criticism which can only debilitate Ts'ao's magnificent achievement.

In Dream of the Red Chamber, we are concerned with a work in which the framework appears to function as a disturbing negative commentary on an otherwise sympathetic treatment of romantic love. When we look at other examples of Chinese and Western love lit- erature, we find that there are various explanations for the presence of the framework. The framework both satirizes and stimulates the reader's erotic sensibilities. Our response to the religious dimen- sion in erotic tales from Boccaccio's Decameron, Chaucer's Canter- bury Tales, or Feng Meng-lung's Ku-chin hsiao-shuo, for example, may be one of both dismissal and delight: dismissal, because of an inability to take the religious motifs seriously; delight, because ribald humor is enhanced when the protagonists in love affairs are monks and nuns--whether Christian, Buddhist, or Taoist. Perhaps, as in Defoe's Moll Flanders and the anonymous "moral-erotic" Chinese novel, Prayer Mat of Flesh, the authors' moralizations in introductions and epilogues actually serve the spurious objective of placating censors while disguising the scatological, although this

----

[29]Our understanding of Hawthorne is based on Professor Smith's lectures in his course on the American novel, University of Cali- fornia, Berkeley. He further noted that today it is difficult to appreciate Hawthorne's romances because we are still part of a "realistic" intellectual climate which began in the era of William Dean Howells. The works of Hawthorne, along with those of Mel- ville, belong to "pre-realistic" fiction.

seems extremely unlikely.[30] A late sixteenth century translation
of Ovid's Metamorphoses by the Puritan, Arthur Golding, provides
us with a different reason why the moral framework may be necessary. Golding himself established such a framework for the Metamorphoses by means of a prefatory verse-epistle to the Earl of
Leicester in which he explains that licentious literature, like the
Metamorphoses, is really a vehicle of religious didacticism:

> For sure theis fables are not put in writing to th' entent
> To further or allure to vice, but rather this is meant,
> That men, beholding what they be when vice doth reign instead
> Of virtue, should not let their lewd affections have the head.[31]

Or the framework may offer the reader a means of escape from the
tedium of daily life while providing the author a method by which
he can liberate his creative imagination. A presently popular
viewpoint insists that the reader must sever the religious-moral framework from the body of a work, as the former only serves to invali-
date the intention and effect of the latter.

When we examine the relation between mystical faith and romantic love in Dream of the Red Chamber, we find that the erotic
element is less deliberately exploited, and none of the above explanations is sufficient. Our dissatisfaction with both traditional
and modern responses on the part of Chinese and Western critics has
led to the present study. We hope that it will enable the reader to
perceive that Pao-yu's abandonment of the Red Dust represents a
brilliant and natural evolution of the style and structure set forth in
the novel's framework and developed in the main body of the narrative. In this connection we recall a comment by Charles Muscatine
on Chaucer's Troilus and Criseyde:

> To dwell at length on the attractiveness of earthly love and
> then to repudiate all in a palinode is neither philosophical
> nor artistic. But to present secular idealism as a beautiful
> but flawed thing, and to present practical idealism as an ad-
> mirable but incomplete thing, to present them, indeed, as
> antithetical and incongruous to each other, is by implication

----

30肉蒲團.Jou P'u T'uan: The Prayer Mat of Flesh, trans.
Richard Martin, New York, 1966. For reference to the history of
Dream of the Red Chamber censorship, see Appendix A.
　　31From the Verse-Epistle, lines 121-124, in, The Renaissance in
England, eds. Hyder E. Rollins and Herschel Baker, Boston, 1954,
p. 542.

to present a third view, higher and more complete than either. This philosophical third view hovers over every important sequence in the Troilus, and is made explicit in the epilogue.[32]

Like Dream of the Red Chamber, Troilus and Criseyde is a story of human passion in which the hero attains a kind of ultimate enlightenment in the divine sphere after a tragic experience on earth. Structurally, the poem is set against, or, leads toward, the backdrop of a religious or philosophical "framework", that is, the palinode. While this structural parallel reflects a remarkable similarity of artistic vision, it also delineates a major difference between the two writers. Chaucer "sees in turn the whole sphere of human experience against eternity", and in the light of divine perfection, "he sees the imperfection inherent in any mode of life . . . wherein the end itself is earthly joy . . . ."[33] On the other hand, Ts'ao Hsueh-ch'in finds the divine sphere to be equally imperfect—it is this fact which drives the heaven-bound Stone to seek liberation in earthly joy—and thus we discover that the author's vision undercuts the sacred and the profane with equanimity. The final revelation of Dream of the Red Chamber is unique. Pao-yu's forsaking of the world is not a reflection of unrequited love or a reaction against human passion, but rather, it symbolizes his discernment of two myths, only one of which is ultimately true to him, but both of which appear equally fictitious to Ts'ao Hsueh-ch'in. In order to give meaning to the facts of life, "facts" here being the beauty of women and the joy of youth, Pao-yu has been faithful to a myth of timelessness in a mutable world. The abandonment of that myth cannot but lead him to the acceptance of another myth which spellbinds him with the promise of eternity.

The problem of nearly all of the interpreters of Dream of the Red Chamber is their tendency to seek the significance of the novel in Ming dynastic history, Ch'ing politics, Ts'ao clan documents, or a Chinese "feudal" society, rather than in the text of the novel itself. Our reading of Dream of the Red Chamber suggests to us that its meaning is much too complex to be understood in terms of the facts of history, politics, biography, or dialectical materialism. We should like to avail ourselves of the Allegorists' belief in the

---

[32]Charles Muscatine, Chaucer and the French Tradition, Berkeley and Los Angeles, 1964, p. 132.
[33]ibid., p. 132.

author's obscure statement that he has taken true affairs and hidden them. But rather than seek that hidden meaning somewhere other than in the novel, we suggest that we look for it in the inter-relation he builds between mystical faith and human passion within the confines of the text. The hidden beauty of Dream of the Red Chamber is not merely a matter of content, but rather one of style and structure. To understand Ts'ao Hsueh-ch'in's imaginative presentation of this relationship and the power he exerts over his reader, we believe that the traditional Chinese allegorical approach to this "shadow-book", Dream of the Red Chamber, must be re-formulated in terms of three of the primary literary modes in which the novel is written.[34]

----

[34]Recent native Chinese criticism has pointed to a re-formulation in terms of symbolism, but no one, to my knowledge, has pursued it.
As early as 1920, P'ei-chih wrote of the concept of chen-chia 真假 in Dream of the Red Chamber. That which is "true" and that which is "false" exist within one another and each produces its opposite. This theme may be seen as a corollary to Yu P'ing-po's se-k'ung 色空 theory ("form-emptiness", "conditioned-unconditioned", "desire-non desire"). Both belong to the novel's allegory. (See P'ei-chih's article, "Hung-lou meng hsin-p'ing", 11-12). However, P'ei-chih does not recognize that chen-chia is part of the basic symbolic style. In fact, he sees the novel's creation myth, its allegory, and the author's use of the supernatural to be major defects.
Yuan Sheng-shih observes that previous allegorical interpretation was justified (although the particular theories were not) because of the line in chapter 1 referred to above, "he hid the real affairs therein", and because the novel is full of symbols. "Hung-lou meng yen-chiu", p. 49.
Ch'en Yu-p'i 陳毓羆 and Li Ch'i 李祁 have studied, respectively, the mythic beginnings of the novel and the mythic origins of some of the principal characters. Ch'en, "Hung-lou meng shih tsen-yang k'ai-t'ou te" 紅樓夢是怎樣開頭的, in Wen-shih 文史, 3 (Oct., 1963), 333-338; Li, "Lin Tai-yu shen-hua te pei-ching" 林黛玉神話的背景, in Ta-lu tsa-chih 大陸雜誌, XXX:x (May, 1965), 1-4.

Myth:
the Allegoric Mode

To many readers of <u>Dream of the Red Chamber</u>, the creation myth[1] of chapter 1 is a superficial allegorical veneer which bedecks a gleaming body of pure realistic fiction. They are charmed by the tale of the Stone[2] discarded by the goddess Nu-kua,[3] the miraculous appearance of Buddhist and Taoist celestial clerics,[4] and the legend of the Divine Crystal Page and the Crimson Pearl Sylph

----

[1]The creation myth is found in the Huai-nan tzu 淮南子 , Lan Ming 覽冥 , and in the <u>Shih Chi</u> 史記, Pu San-Huang pen-chi 補三皇本記.

[2]Shih-t'ou 石頭 .

[3]Nu-kua 女媧 , also known as Kua Huang 媧皇 or Nu Huang 女皇 "Empress". Goddess of Go-betweens, sister of the legendary Emperor Fu Hsi 伏羲 . A mythic source for marriage and courtship regulations. Ts'ao uses the legend that Nu-kua melted stones to repair the vault of heaven which fell when the feudatory prince Kung Kung 共工 pulled down one of eight supporting pillars. See Werner, <u>Dictionary of Chinese Mythology</u>, New York, 1961, pp. 334-335.

[4] 一僧一道 (茫茫大士,渺渺真人).

Herb,5 but while the simple apologue is found entertaining, its
very thinness seems to suggest that the realistic mode is Ts'ao Hsueh-
ch'in's paramount concern. Thus, for example, the first person in
the West to write a critique of the novel, Karl A. F. Gutzlaff,
records his impatience by drawing a parallel between the then anonymous author of Dream of the Red Chamber and Washington Irving:

> The author, after making many protestations of his inability
> to do justice to the subject, which indeed is the only truth
> in the book, commences his story, like the History of New
> York, with the creation of the world.6

Gutzlaff's entire essay represents a mistaken, and oftentimes inadvertently humorous, view of the novel,7 but he is by no means the

----

5The Divine Crystal Page 神瑛侍者 , the mythic name of
Pao-yu. The Crimson Pearl Sylph Herb 絳珠仙草, the mythic name
of Tai-yu. Li Ch'i 李祁, "Lin Tai-yu shen-hua te pei-ching"林
黛玉神話的背景, Ta-lu tsa-chih 大陸雜誌 XXX:x (May,
1965), 1-4, studies the origins of Tai-yu's various mythic names
and observes how very carefully Ts'ao selects names and epithets
for his characters. Mythic origins partially account for the unique
characters of leading "real world" protagonists.

6"Hung Lau Mung or Dreams in the Red Chamber", Chinese
Repository, XI (May, 1842, Canton), 266. The actual report does
not name Gutzlaff as the author; the editor of the Chinese Repository simply says, "Noticed by a Correspondent". Wu Shih-ch'ang,
On the Red Chamber Dream, p. 2, note 3, says Gutzlaff was the
first Westerner to discuss Dream of the Red Chamber.

7Here are a few of Gutzlaff's entertaining notions of the novel.
On the ladies: "They seem to be after all the most trivial beings,
chattering like magpies . . . ." (p. 268)
On the setting: "There is no end to finery, gewgaws, knicknacks
and dress . . . ." (p. 268)
He speaks of Pao-yu as though the hero is a woman: "the lady
Pauyu". (p. 268). "The leading character amongst the inmates of
Ka's (Chia) family, was a very petulant woman, who committed
many freaks which involved herself as well as the others in consid-
erable difficulties". (p. 270)
He finds the ladies "when left to their own society become very
tiresome to their friends as well as to themselves" (p. 270), and he
notes, finally, "Having brought this tedious story to a conclusion,
in expressing our opinion about the literary merits of the performance,

only person who is unwilling to give serious consideration to the mythic mode.

Chinese Communist critics, such as Mao Hsing,[8] insist that episodes about the Great Void Illusion Realm[9] (chapters 5 and 116) and otherworldly figures such as the Reverend Taoist Kosmo Kosmos[10] (chapter 1 and 120) are not important since Dream of the Red Chamber is a work of socialist realism. As a brilliant flower of literature, the novel is rooted in the earth. Naturally its leaves bear some dust from the author's class and era--that is, "myth", but the latter is merely a vestige of eighteenth century "feudalism". Any critic who emphasizes the metaphysical vision of the novel is one who takes one of these dusty leaves in his lily-white hands and proclaims the meaning of the flower.[11] A few other readers, including the

----

we may say that the style is without any art, being literally the spoken language of the higher classes in the northern provinces. Some words are used in a sense different from that in ordinary writings, and others are formed for the occasion, to express provincial sounds. But after reading one volume, the sense is easily understood, and whosoever wishes to familiarize himself with the manner of speaking the northern court dialect, may peruse the work with advantage". (p. 273)

8 毛星.

9 太虛幻境.

10K'ung-k'ung tao-jen 空空道人 . Other translations might be: the Taoist Emptiness of Emptiness, sūnyata-sūnyata, the fourth of the 18 kinds of emptiness (十八空) in Buddhism (from Lewis R. Lancaster, "Lists of Buddhist Terms", unpublished); the Ku Klux Taoist, from the Greek, kyklos, "circle" (thus conceiving of a circle as an ideal form); the Taoist Pure Purity (since k'ung-k'ung tao-jen is a purist in search of the Tao--and is naive); the Taoist Ideal Idealist; the Taoist Ethereal Ether; the Reverend Taoist Sphero Spheroid (i.e., not quite a perfect sphere, like the earth). Wu Shih-ch'ang, On the Red Chamber Dream, p. 262, suggests "the Taoist Priest the Reverend Void".

11Mao Hsing 毛星 , "P'ing Yu P'ing-po hsien-sheng te 'se-k'ung' shuo" 評俞平伯先生的色空說,in Jen-min wen hsueh 人民文學 , No. 63 (Jan., 1955), 58-64. See especially, pp. 59, 60, 64. The passage referred to is on p. 64. Mao, p. 60, notes that whenever a girl in the novel takes up a life as a Buddhist nun, it is a symbol of tragedy, and thus, Ts'ao cannot be celebrating a Buddhist view.

redoubtable Chao Kang, believe that the emphasis in the novel on allegorical dreams, the illusoriness of love and the return to the Stone myth in chapter 120, is due to the commentary of Chih-yen Chai.[12] Others, such a Yu P'ing-po and Wu Shih-ch'ang, attri-

----

Chang Tai 張戴 and Chiang Ho-sen 蔣和森 , as well as Ho Ch'i-fang 何其方 likewise feel that the mythic, fatalistic, and dream episodes in the novel reflect Ts'ao's feudal background and that they are exceptional. See Chang Tai, "Lun Hung-lou meng te shih-tai   pei-ching ho Ts'ao Hsueh-ch'in te ch'uang tso ssu-hsiang" 論紅樓夢的時代背景和曹雪芹的創作思想, in Hsin chien-she 新建設, 3 (March, 1955), 37; Chiang Ho-sen, "Hung-lou meng ai-ch'ing miao-hsieh shih-tai i-i chi ch'i chu-hsien" 紅樓夢愛情描寫時代意義及其局限, in Wen-hsueh p'ing-lun 文學評論, 6 (Dec., 1963), 20-44; Ho Ch'i-fang, "Ts'ao Hsueh-ch'in te kung-hsien" 曹雪芹的貢獻, in Wen-hsueh p'ing-lun 文學評論, 6 (1963), 15; Ho Ch'i-fang, 何其方, "Lun Hung-lou meng" 論紅樓夢 , in Wen-hsueh yen-chiu chi-k'an 文學研究集刊, 5 (May, 1957), 34, 37, 108, 109.
       [12]Throughout this study, I use "Chih-yen Chai commentary" in its collective sense as referring to the composite work of the several commentators found in various 80 chapter manuscripts of the novel. There is little agreement among scholars as to the identities of authors of individual (unsigned) comments. Chao Kang 趙岡 and Ch'en Chung-i 陳鍾毅 identify Chih-yen Chai 脂硯齋 as Ts'ao T'ien-yu 曹天祐 , the posthumous son of Ts'ao Yung 曹顒, and the grandson of Ts'ao Yin 曹寅 . After Ts'ao Yung's death, Ts'ao T'ien-yu lived with the family of his cousin, Ts'ao Hsueh-ch'in. The two boys were approximately the same age and were raised together (biographical information which accounts for the intimate relation between the author and commentator in the novel). Chao Kang and Ch'en Chung-i theorize that Ts'ao T'ien-yu (Chih-yen Chai) completed parts of the novel when Ts'ao Hsueh-ch'in died. Another commentator, Chi-hu 畸笏 , (whom Chao and Ch'en identify as Ts'ao Fu 曹頫 , the father of Ts'ao Hsueh-ch'in), took over Chih-yen Chai's task after the latter died. See Hung-lou meng hsin-t'an 紅樓夢新探 , Hong Kong, 1970, pp. 153-164, 206-211. As John Wang of Stanford University notes, Chao Kang's identifications are the most plausible we have, but are still lacking in positive evidence. (Through the courtesy of Professor Wang, I have obtained a copy of his article, "The Chih-

bute the supernatural events and figures in the last forty chapters of
the novel to the editor, Kao E.[13] Referring to Pao-yu's loss of his
jade talisman, his visit to the Great Void Illusion Land, and the
visitation of an immortal monk (chapters 115 and 116), Wu remarks:

> All these jejune, superstitious, absurd stories were designed
> to fill up space which would otherwise have to be filled with
> grander, more tragic and complicated episodes as those drafted
> by Ts'ao Chan and revealed in Chih-yen's commentary.[14]

----

yen Chai Commentary and the Dream of the Red Chamber: A Literary
Study", prior to its publication). For further reference to the identities of commentators, see Ch'en Ch'ing-hao 陳慶浩 ,
"Hung-lou meng Chih-p'ing chih yen-chiu" 紅樓夢脂評之
研究, in Hung-lou meng yen-chiu chuan-k'an 紅樓夢研究專
刊, Nos. 5 & 6 (Jan., July, 1969).
For the view that Chih-yen Chai is responsible for the novel's emphasis on the Stone myth, dreams, fate, and illusory love, see:
Chao Kang, "Chih-yen Chai yu Hung-lou meng" 脂硯齋與
紅樓夢 , Ta-lu tsa-chih 大陸雜誌 , XX:iv
(Feb., 1960), 28-29; Ch'en Yu-p'i 陳毓羆 , "Hung-lou meng
shih tsen-yang k'ai-tou te" 紅樓夢是怎樣開頭的 , Wen-shih
文史, 3 (Oct., 1963), 337; Li Hsi-fan 李希凡 and Lan Ling
藍翎 , Hung-lou meng p'ing-lun chi 紅樓夢評論集 ;
Mao Hsing, "P'ing Yu P'ing-po hsien-sheng te 'se-k'ung' 'shuo'", 59.
      13 高鶚 .
   14On the Red Chamber Dream, p. 282.
   In an article, "History of The Red Chamber Dream", Chinese
Literature, no. 1 (1963), p. 99, Wu Shih-ch'ang says that Kao E
excised from chapter 1 of the novel Ts'ao's moral and social satire
and added a Buddhist "twist".
   Yu P'ing-po 俞平伯 states that Kao E was one who believed in
the idols of ghosts and spirits. Yu records episodes from chapters 94,
101, 103, 104, 108, 111, 112, 114, 115, 116, and 120, which he
believes reveal that Kao emphasized the supernatural. Yu differen-
tiates these chapters from Ts'ao's "spirit" passages (e.g., chapters
1, 5, etc.) which he says are mere addenda. These are parables,
allegories, or else comic instances of Ts'ao's burlesque humor. Thus
Yu endeavors to distinguish between what he believes to be Kao's
superstitious viewpoint and Ts'ao's imagination. The distinction
remains obscure. See Yu's Hung-lou meng yen-chiu 紅樓夢研
究 , Shanghai, T'ang-ti ch'u-pan she, 1952, pp. 54, 55, 147.

After drawing up a list of stories in the last forty chapters which he dislikes, Wu comments:

> These stories are obviously too superstitious to be convincing. They are hardly relevant to the central theme of the novel or to other stories. Even if they are well written, so many of them must be boring to any reader; and the great space they occupy in the last forty chapters does little justice to the novel or to its reader. They look like grotesque buildings artificially scattered in one-third of a well-designed garden, neither serving any useful purpose nor adding any pleasant sight for the visitor.[15]

Our own reading of Dream of the Red Chamber reveals to us that many, though not all, of the stories which Wu types as "jejune" and "superstitious" are entirely convincing because they belong to the mythic framework and are one with the style and theme therein set forth. Wu, like many critics who view Dream of the Red Chamber as a work primarily of either socialist or psychological realism, is aware of the mythic mode and its concomitant allegory and symbolism, but dismisses such features because they do not meet with contemporary criteria for "life-like" fiction. C.T. Hsia admits that the novel is "allied to the modes of poetry and allegory", but he does not examine the significance of this fact.[16] He objects to what he feels to be an unpleasant strain of didacticism found in the allegory, and he believes, therefore, that the reader must distinguish the intention of the work from the intention of the author.[17] Professor Hsia compliments Ts'ao's use of myth and allegory only when the author is about to discard them. Remarking on Pao'yu's dream visit to the Great Void Illusion Realm in chapter 5, Hsia says:

> Ts'ao Hsueh-ch'in, however, is too good a psychologist to be a thoroughgoing allegorist. The didactic dream is immediately followed by a scene of realism which places the allegory in an ironic perspective.[18]

Elsewhere he observes that the same scene appears to be didactic:

> . . . but by and large it is safe to maintain that none of these assertions have received fictional and philosophical corrobora-

----

[15]On the Red Chamber Dream, pp. 308-309.
[16]The Classic Chinese Novel, p. 261.
[17]"Love and Compassion in 'Dream of the Red Chamber'", Criticism, V:iii (Summer, 1963), 263.
[18]The Classic Chinese Novel, p. 264.

tion in the far richer and more sympathetic realistic narrative.[19]
One might feel that Professor Hsia's remarks point to the conventional credibility gap of the supernatural in Chinese fiction. Allegoric fiction is a contradiction in terms. What, then, about mythic fiction? Hsia himself, in his study of Monkey[20], writes about the mythic mode and calls for a general reappraisal of this mode in Chinese fiction.[21] The problem we encounter in his foregoing remarks is the word "realism", for it is most difficult to apply such a term to Dream of the Red Chamber unless its definition includes myth, allegory, symbols, dreams, and even "superstitious" visitations. Even didactic allegory is assimilated in the narrative. The symbolic significance of the allegorical frame, for example, envelops the "realism" of the novel and renders it meaningful. To reverse Professor Hsia's own terms, the fictional and philosophical corroboration of allegory through the mythic frame is precisely what enriches the closely textured presentation of daily life and makes it "real". We find in Dream of the Red Chamber what is perhaps a unique union in literature of the didactic and the ironic, the mythic and the mimetic, rather than, as Professor Hsia indicates, a separation between modes.

To depict Dream of the Red Chamber as a work of realistic fiction and realistic characterization is then, in our opinion, a misrepresentation. In our Introduction to this study, we noted that in the late Ch'ing period there were several early studies of the novel which sought to uncover its hidden or allegoric meaning. There was some consideration of the beginning chapters but no effort was made to discover the relation between the framework and the body of the novel. Nearly seventy years ago, Herbert A. Giles made an important observation on the supernatural in Dream of the Red Chamber which seems to have gone unnoticed:

> The opening chapters, which are intended to form a link between the world of spirits and the world of mortals, belong to the supernatural; after that the story runs smoothly along upon earthly lines, always however, overshadowed by the near presence

----

[19] "Love and Compassion", p. 263.
[20] Hsi-yu chi, 西遊記.
[21] "Monstrous Appetite: Comedy and Myth in the Hsi Yu Chi", in Wen-Lin: Studies in the Chinese Humanities, ed. Chow Tse-tung, Madison, Milwaukee, London, 1968, pp. 229-239.

of spiritual influences.[22]

Giles was not aware, apparently, of the dominant role played by myth in Dream of the Red Chamber, but at least he did observe that there may be some relation between the opening chapters of the novel and the story proper.

The framework is beginning to receive the attention it deserves, as in the excellent study by Mr. Richard Kunst,[23] although there has been some brief mention of its importance in relatively recent investigations.[24] Two comments in an essay by Frederick P. Brandauer are of special interest here, as they contrast vividly to several of the conventional responses we have observed in our survey of Chinese and Western critical views of the mythic framework. Speaking of the hidden meaning of the novel, Brandauer says:

> This framework is highly significant and cannot be ignored, for it serves not only as a source of continuity in the novel but also provides a clue to the underlying meaning the author seeks to convey through the novel.

He further observes the unifying power of the framework:

> Now it is important to notice that throughout the entire novel the author never loses sight of his mythological setting. It becomes a unifying factor. It is like a thread which is drawn through the novel from beginning to end.[25]

22Herbert A. Giles, "Hung Lou Meng", in A History of Chinese Literature, Book VIII, chap. 1, p. 356 (London, 1901).

23"The Beginning and Ending of The Dream of the Red Chamber", M.A. thesis in Oriental Languages, University of California, Berkeley, 1969. Richard Kunst's presentation is especially fine in two distinct areas: Ts'ao's concept of literature, and the texts of the novel.

24See Chuang Hsin-cheng, "Themes of Dream of the Red Chamber: a Comparative Interpretation", unpublished Ph.D. dissertation, Indiana University, 1966, p. 138; Mary Gregory Knoerle, S.P., The Dream of the Red Chamber: A Critical Study, Bloomington & London, 1972, p. 25; Knoerle, "A Critical Analysis of the Dream of the Red Chamber in Terms of Western Novelistic Criteria", Ph.D. dissertation, Indiana University, 1966, pp. 34 & 39: See too an earlier doctoral thesis by Kuo Lin-ko 郭麟閣 (French romanization, Kou Lin Ke), "Essai sur le Hong Leou Mong (Le Rêve dans le Pavillon Rouge, celebré roman chinois du xviiie siecle), University of Lyon, 1935, pp. 7 & 11.

25"Some Philosophical Implications of the Hung Lou Meng", Ching Feng, IX: iii (1966), 15 & 19.

In our study of the mythic, mimetic, and narrative layers, we shall
attempt to demonstrate in what sense the framework reveals the
unity, continuity, and meaning of Dream of the Red Chamber.[26]
   As we begin our textual discussion, we might suggest that we follow
Jaroslav Průšek's plea to expand the meaning of the term, "reality",
so that if we are to apply it to Chinese fiction we might understand
it to include the whole region of man's spiritual life as well as his
"outer" reality.[27] With such a broader concept in mind, we may

----

   [26]Yuan Sheng-shih 袁聖時 , "Hung-lou meng yen-chiu" 紅
樓夢研究) , Tung-fang tsa-chih 東方雜誌 XLIV: xi
(Nov., 1948), 47-48, finds that the framework forms a unit. The
ending where Pao-yu returns to the stone world of chapter 1 and
becomes a monk Yuan believes to be appropriate and inevitable,
as indicated by the first chapter. In contrast to Wu Shih-ch'ang,
Yuan holds that the structure and style are the same in the last forty
chapters as they are in the first eighty. Ts'ao completed the novel
in rough draft, for no man could so successfully imitate another as
Kao E is claimed to have imitated Ts'ao.
   In comparing the Wang and Kuhn-McHugh translations of the novel,
Anthony West observes: "And it is impossible not to feel when one
is reading the Kuhn-McHugh version that the concluding chapters
relate organically to the rest of the book and that the inexorable
chain of logic connecting all its parts, which are in any case linked
by an unbroken emotional tension, must have been created by a
single mind". "Through a Glass, Darkly", New Yorker Magazine
(Nov. 22, 1958), 228.
   Even Wu Shih-ch'ang, after reconstructing the Roster of Lovers
and the ending of the novel on the basis of the Chih-yen Chai commentary, agrees that Ts'ao intended "a truly grand project that
attempted to merge the mundane with the other world without lessen-
ing his realistic effect in the main plot and ideology of the novel".
On the Red Chamber Dream, p. 157. See too pp. 158-160.
   Kunst, "The Beginning and Ending of The Dream of the Red Chamber", p. 41, notes that the mythic level of the prologue of chapter
1 is a "testing ground" for themes which reappear later in the novel,
and p. 51, he observes that in the body of the novel, the Stone
comments on its own story.
   [27]"Reality and Art in Chinese Literature", Archiv Orientalni,
XXXII (1964), 605.

share Prŭšek's appreciation of Ts'ao Hsueh-ch'in's imagination:
> Here lyrical sensibility, which inspired the greatest works of
> Chinese literature, permeates the epic structure, giving to
> it that soaring quality, that weightlessness in which the
> gravitational drag of life's grey uniformity is no longer opera-
> tive, possessed by only the greatest achievements of world
> literature . . . . Moreover, the stressing of the imaginatively
> inventive element, as opposed to the emphasis on the noetic,
> intellectual values more commonly associated with the pro-
> duction of the literati . . . is observable already in the
> introduction to this novel, the author presenting his story as
> a mythological fable . . . .[28]

While the lyricism Prŭšek observes in Ts'ao is an imaginative syn-
thesis of folk tradition and originality, mythic and realistic modes,
his technique is deliberative and noetic. Our endeavor will be to
identify that technique and thus to define the power of his imagination.

When we examine the structure of chapter 1 of Dream of the Red
Chamber, we discover that it consists of nine layers, or episodes,
which belong to three dominant literary modes of the novel: the
mythic, the mimetic, and the narrative. Chapter 1 is prefaced by
a lengthy autobiographical comment attributable to Ts'ao Hsueh-
ch'in.[29] The chapter proper begins with the Nu-kua creation myth
which introduces the story of the Stone the goddess rejects in her
repairment of Heaven and includes a conversation between the Stone
and two Immortals, a Buddhist monk and a Taoist, in which the
Stone expresses its desire to be reborn on earth and to experience
the pleasures of the Red Dust. In the next episode, we discover
the Stone after its return to Heaven. Countless years have passed
since its original creation and its earthly adventures are inscribed
upon its surface. Here a critical conversation occurs between the
Stone and the Reverend Taoist Kosmo Kosmos concerning the nature
of the Stone Record. Kosmo Kosmos becomes convinced of the
value of the inscribed tale, and he agrees to copy it for the benefit
of other readers. Brief mention is made of an editor of the novel,
one Ts'ao Hsueh-ch'in.

----

[28]ibid., 616-617.
[29]For a discussion of the Preface and its place in the novel, see
"Persona" chapter, pp. 206-223.

There follows an account of Chen Shih-yin,[30] a gentleman of
modest means who lives a quiet exemplary life in Soochou, one of
the wealthiest regions of the Red Dust. In a dream-vision, Chen
encounters two otherworldly figures, the Buddhist and Taoist of the
original creation myth, through whom he learns of the Divine
Crystal Page (Pao-yu) and the Crimson Pearl Sylph Herb (Tai-yu).
Immediately upon his awakening, Chen is again visited by a
Buddhist and a Taoist, who now appear crippled and dishevelled,
and who attempt to take away his infant daughter. The narrative
then turns to a description of the relations between Chen and his
neighbor, Chia Yu-ts'un,[31] and then finally closes with the visit
of an otherworldly Taoist.

The preceding summary gives the false impression that the various
episodes of chapter 1 form a continuous narrative. In fact, Ts'ao
Hsueh-ch'in blends three modes with the result that he establishes
the polysemous form of Dream of the Red Chamber and disorientates
his reader. The Preface, presented as the author's statement of
why he chose to write together with an account of his vision of fiction, bears little relation to the mythic origins of the novel. As
we shall note in our discussion of the content and style of the Preface ("Persona" chapter), there is some ambiguity as to whether the
author speaks in direct or indirect quotation, or whether his statement is made by someone else. The abrupt transitions between
sections add to our confusion. The Preface begins with the line:

This is the first chapter that begins the book.[32]

It ends with:

Reader firmly remember this.[33]

After a poem summarizing the arduous task of writing, the narrative appears to begin again with the following question and answer:

Dear Reader, do you ask where this book came from?
Although the account of its origin borders on the fantastic,
once you are familiar with the details, you will find it
utterly fascinating. Allow me humbly to elucidate the back-

---

30 甄士隱.

31 賈雨村.

32Hung-lou meng pa-shih hui chiao-pen 紅樓夢八十回校本,
(hereafter HLMPSHCP), ed. Yu P'ing-po 俞平伯 , Peking: Jen-
min wen-hsueh ch'u-pan she, 1959.

33ibid., line 10: 閱者切記之 .

ground, for then you will not have any misgivings.[34]
There follows the story of the goddess Nu–kua and the two Immortals
who discover the discarded Stone. Clearly, we are in the divine
sphere and the world of myth. The passage ends abruptly when the
Stone asks the Buddhist monk what characters the latter is going to
engrave on it and where it is going to be carried:

> "You had best not ask. You naturally will understand later".
> And speaking thus and with the Stone within his sleeve, he
> wafted off with his companion Taoist to an area and a
> dwelling we know not where.[35]

The episode which follows is not introduced by any statement which
would inform the reader that the Stone has now experienced life in
the Red Dust and has returned to its place of origins. We only are
told that untold generations have passed when the Reverend Taoist
Kosmo Kosmos happens upon a curious stone with characters incised
upon its surface.[36] We immediately lose perspective due to the
sudden transition, the long elapse of unexplained time, and the un-
certainty of our geographical location. The Reverend Taoist discovers the stone beneath Blue–Channel Peak at Incredible Cliff on
Mt. Fantasia.[37] That is, we are seemingly still within the heavenly
realm of the goddess Nu–kua. But according to the narrative,
Kosmo Kosmos is the earthly scribe who reads the complete Stone
Record and:

> . . . copies it down from top to bottom so as to inform the
> world and pass on the rare.[38]

34ibid., p. 2, lines 2-3: 列位看官你道此書何來,説起
根由雖近荒唐,細按則深有趣味,待在下將此來
歷註明,方使閱者了然不惑.
35ibid., p. 3, lines 6-7: 你且莫問,日後自然明白的.
説者便袖籠了這石,同那道人飄然而去,竟不知投
奔何方何舍.
36ibid., lines 7-9: 後來又不知過了幾世幾刧,因有個
空空道人訪道求仙,從這大荒山無稽崖青埂峯下經
過,忽見大塊石上字跡分明,編述歷歷.
37Blue-Channel Peak 青埂峯 ; Incredible Cliff 無稽崖 ;
Mt. Fantasia 大荒山 . These titles are explained in the notes
to our complete translation of this passage below.
38HLMPSHCP, chap. 1, p. 5, line 2: 方從頭至尾抄錄回
來,問世傳奇 ....

One of his criticisms of the tale he peruses is that it lacks the kind
of information and characterization conventionally given in literature: there are no dynasty names, no dates are given, and there
are no distinguished bureaucrats or court figures.[39] In other words,
Kosmo Kosmos demands evidence of the "real" world. He also
serves as a kind of transitional figure between the divine and human
spheres, like Chen Shih-yin.[40] In chapter 1 he converses with the
mythic Stone and passes the Stone Record down to earthly creatures
for editing, and in chapter 120, after that Record is truly completed,
he tries to prevail upon both Chia Yu-ts'un and Ts'ao Hsueh-ch'in
to transmit the finished text.

After listening to the arguments both pro and con between the
Stone and the Reverend Taoist concerning the merits of the Stone
Record, we sense some relief when we learn of the work of the
"editor", Ts'ao Hsueh-ch'in, for perhaps now the novel will begin
in earnest. Ts'ao, however, is glossed over as a pedant who labored
on the novel for ten years, emended it five times, and gave it a
table of contents and chapter divisions. His only original contribution was to entitle his work, Twelve Hairpins of Chin-ling,[41] a
title which did not endure.

Following this brief allusion to Ts'ao Hsueh-ch'in, a new and different statement indicates a new and different beginning:

With the origins now clear, let us see what story is on the
Stone. According to the writings on the Stone, it is related
that . . . .[42]

These words serve to introduce the narrative of Chen Shih-yin and
seemingly divide the mythic from the real world. Yet the origins
of the Stone are not now entirely clear, and in the real world of
Chen we shall learn more about the mythic Stone. When Chen hears
of the Divine Crystal Page and the Crimson Pearl Sylph Herb in his
dreams, we realize that Ts'ao interweaves the mythic and mimetic

----

[39]ibid., p. 3, lines 15-16: 無朝代年紀可考⋯無大賢
大忠理朝廷治風俗的善政⋯⋯

[40]A complete discussion of Chen Shih-yin occurs in our chapter
called "Mimesis".

[41]For the description of Ts'ao, see HLMPSHCP, chap. 1, p. 5,
lines 3-4: 後因曹雪芹於悼紅軒中披閱十載,增刪五次,
纂成目錄,分出章回,則題曰金陵十二釵.

[42]ibid., line 7: 出則既明,且看石上是何故事按那
石上書云⋯⋯

modes and that statements of clarity, such as the one above, represent deliberate pretense. The statement appears to indicate the start of Dream of the Red Chamber, yet Chen Shih-yin is a very minor figure. Furthermore, no sooner are the briefest facts given about his name, birthplace, and family, than we return to the mythic world:

> One long intensely hot summer's day, Shih-yin was leisurely sitting in his study . . . . [he] began to doze, until before he knew it, he had fallen asleep. He arrived somewhere in a dream, but he could not identify the location. Suddenly he glimpsed in one direction a Buddhist Monk and a Taoist coming along and chatting together.[43]

Again, the transition between worlds is almost too rapid for the reader to become aware of a change. As Chih-yen Chai remarks, the Stone passes from the mythic world of Blue-Channel Peak to the world of Chen Shih-yin's dreams without a trace of its origins.[44]

The mythic and real worlds become one when Chen awakes from his dream only to be visited by the Buddhist and Taoist. But Chen has forgotten his dream and is unable to recognize the two Immortals. He is only aware that they have some lai-li, "background", which would explain their mysterious actions.[45] Chia Yu-ts'un then appears on the scene and there begins the story of a young scholar who seeks to pass the Civil Service Examinations. Again, as in the case of Chen Shih-yin, we have a figure who rarely appears during the course of the novel. Moreover, soon after the friendship of Chen Shih-yin and Chia Yu-ts'un begins to unfold, the former disappears in the company of an otherworldly Taoist.

Further evidence of distortion is found in the various names of the novel and the ambiguity of its setting. One title is found in the first lines of the Preface to Chapter 1:

> The author relates that he once passed through a dream-vision, and afterwards he hid the real affairs therein and, availing

---

43ibid., lines 12-13: 一日,炎夏永晝,士隱於書房閒坐…伏几少憩,不覺朦朧睡去,夢至一處,不辨是何地方.忽見那廂來了一僧一道,且行且談.

44Chih-yen Chai Hung-lou meng chi-p'ing 脂硯齋紅樓夢輯評, (hereafter CYCHLMCP). ed. Yu P'ing-po, Shanghai, 1963, chap. 1, p. 11, chai-hsu chia-p'i: 是方從青埂峯袖石而來也.

45The dominant interest in lai li 來歷 is discussed in "Mimesis".

himself of what is called, 'Penetrating the Numinous', he composed the Stone Record.[46]
The two Immortals in the creation myth give no name to the inscriptions they place on the Stone, but when the Reverend Taoist Kosmo Kosmos discovers the Stone, he takes its name for the title of its story:

> . . . he took the Stone Record and once again read it through carefully.[47]

Chih-yen Chai comments on this line, "basic name", or, "original name",[48] meaning, according to the first of the General Editorial Principles[49] found in the Preface to chapter 1 (chia-hsu pen), that Stone Record is a metaphor for the adventures inscribed on the mythical Stone.[50] The Reverend Taoist is so entranced with the romantic emotions depicted in the Story he reads that he changes his name to "Bonze of Love", Ch'ing Seng,[51] and gives the Stone Record the new title, Memoirs of the Bonze of Love. [52] This significant metamorphosis will be examined in our discussion of Ts'ao's concept of fiction in our "Persona" chapter. Following Kosmo Kosmos, one K'ung Mei-hsi[53] (identified by Hu Shih and Wu Shih-ch'ang as Ts'ao Hsueh-ch'in's younger brother Ts'ao T'ang-

----

[46]HLMPSHCP, chap. 1, p. 1, line 1: 作者自云，因曾歷過一番夢幻之後，故將真事隱去，而借「通靈」之説，撰此石頭記一書也。
"Penetrating the Numinous" for t'ung-ling 通靈 is the suggestion of my colleague, Professor Alvin Cohen.

[47]HLMPSHCP, chap. 1, p. 4, line 15: 將這石頭記再細閱一遍....

[48]CYCHLMCP, chap. 1, p. 7, chia-hsu chia-p'i: 本名.
Noting that Chih-yen Chai uses the title Shih-t'ou chi (Stone Record) in his commentary on the 80 chapter manuscripts of the novel, David Hawkes gives this title to his recent complete translation. See The Story of the Stone, Penguin Books, 1973, p. 18.

[49]fan-li 凡例.

[50]CYCHLMCP, chap. 1, p. 1, chia-hsu pen fan li: 又曰石頭記，是自譬石頭所記之事也.

[51] 情僧.

[52]HLMPSHCP, chap. 1, p. 5, line 3: 遂易名為情僧，改石頭記為情僧錄.

[53] 孔梅溪.

ts'un)[54] entitles the novel, Precious Mirror of Wind and Moon.[55]
According to the first General Editorial Principle, this title suggests
the novel is a cautionary tale which warns against precipitous
love.[56] Thus the title becomes a stern warning against sexual fantasies in chapter 12. Exactly one year after Chia Jui's[57] frustrated
attempt to seduce Wang Hsi-feng,[58] he is visited by a lame Taoist
who brings a magic double sided mirror with the title, Precious
Mirror of Wind and Moon, inscribed on the front side. Chia Jui is
warned to look only at the back side of the mirror, but when he
sees a horrible image of a skeleton there (himself), he turns to the
front side and a lovely image of Wang Hsi-feng, and has intercourse
with her repeatedly until he finally dies in a pool of semen.[59]
According to the Chih-yen Chai commentary to the catalogue of
titles in chapter 1, Ts'ao once wrote a book called Precious Mirror
of Wind and Moon (this was one of the earlier titles of Dream of
the Red Chamber) with a Preface by his brother, T'ang-ts'un.[60]
    After these various titles are given in the Kosmo Kosmos episode of
chapter 1, an "editor", Ts'ao Hsueh-ch'in, calls the novel Twelve
Hairpins of Chin-ling.[61] In the General Editorial Principles there
is speculation that this title must be an allusion to the Twelve Maidens of Chin-ling, that is, the heroines of the novel.[62] The title,

----

54 曹棠村.
Hu Shih Wen-ts'un 胡適文存, vol. III (Shanghai, 1930), p.
571; Wu, On the Red Chamber Dream, p. 63.
55 風月寶鑑.
56CYCHLMCP, chap. 1, p. 1, chia-hsu pen fan-li: 又曰風月
寶鑑,是戒妄動風月之情.
57 賈瑞.
58 王熙鳳.
59HLMPSHCP, chap. 12, p. 124, lines 10-11:象人上來看看,已
沒了氣,身子底下,冰涼漬濕一大灘精.
60CYCHLMCP, chap. 1, p. 8, chia-hsu mei-p'ing:雪芹舊有風
月寶鑑之書,乃其弟棠村序也.今棠村已逝,余覩新懷舊,故
仍因之.
61 金陵十二釵.
62CYCHLMCP, chap. 1, p. 1, chia-hsu pen fan-li:然此書又名
曰金陵十二釵,審其名則必係金陵十二女子也.然通部細
搜檢去,上中下女子豈止十二人哉.若云其中自有十二個,則
又未當指明白係某某.

Dream of the Red Chamber (Carmine Tierem Dream)[63] does not appear in chapter 1 among the list of titles we have noted in the printed editions of the novel, such as the two edited by Ch'eng Wei-yuan[64] and Kao E,[65] nor does Dream of the Red Chamber appear in chapter 1 of Yu P'ing-po's collated edition (HLMPSHCP). However, as the General Editorial Principles indicate, chapter 5 contains songs with this title,[66] and the chapter title of chapter 120 indicates that Chia Yu-ts'un returns to conclude the Dream of the Red Chamber.[67] This title does appear in chapter 1 of the chia-hsu manuscript in between the titles Memoirs of the Bonze of Love and Precious Mirror of Wind and Moon.[68] It is a title which is said to be given the novel by one Wu Yu-feng,[69] a name which is possibly another pseudonym, like Chi-hu, for Ts'ao Fu, the father of Ts'ao Hsueh-ch'in.[70] Another curious feature of the chia-hsu manuscript not found in printed editions of the novel is that after the list of various titles is given, it is mentioned that when Chih-yen Chai commented on the manuscript he continued the use of the title, Stone Record.[71]

Such a high degree of distortion cannot be accidental. Ts'ao is not merely being faithful to Chinese novelistic conventions when he fails to mention that he is the author of the novel. The ambiguity created by five distinct titles (none of them definitive) and the question of authorship (we know only the names of editors and late

----

[63]Hung-lou meng. We borrow here the name in the Russian translation of the novel for ladies quarters: tierem. A pseudo-philological translation might be: Dreams in the Vermillion Red Second Story Loft Building Gynaeceum!

[64] 程偉元.

[65] 高鶚.

[66]CYCHLMCP, chap. 1, p. 1, chia-hsu pen fan-li: 如寶玉作夢,夢中有曲,名曰紅樓夢十二支,此則紅樓夢之點睛.

[67]The chapter titles of chapter 120 are the following: 甄士隱詳說太虛情　賈雨村歸結紅樓夢.

[68]See the chia-hsu manuscript, p. 9a, line 9, for mention of the title Hung-lou meng given by Wu Yu-feng.

[69] 吳玉峰.

[70]See Chao Kang and Ch'en Chung-i, Hung-lou meng hsin-t'an, pp. 206-212.

[71]See chia-hsu manuscript, p. 9b, line 3.

redactors and the titles they make up to agree with their readings
of the novel) are indications of the meaning of Dream of the Red
Chamber. The author changes the reader's concept of convention
and enlarges his sense of reality. To struggle with Ts'ao's original
and imaginative claim that his work has no identifiable author, no
certain beginning, no established name,[72] no definite dynastic
time[73] or geographical location,[74] is to be drawn into the mythic

----

[72]The first of the General Editorial Principles says that the
theme of the novel is "the red-chamber dream". CYCHLMCP, chia-
hsu pen fan li, chap. 1, p. 1: 紅樓夢旨義 ⋯⋯ 口口紅樓夢,是
總其全部之名也.
Yu P'ing-po, Hung-lou meng yen-chiu, pp. 245-251, surveys the
various names for the novel, and, referring to Chih-yen Chai commentary, decides that Dream of the Red Chamber is the "true name"
正名. When in chapter 5 of the novel, Pao-yu visits the Great
Void Illusion Land in a dream-vision, and is told that bewitching
dancers and singers will perform for him the "twelve songs of Dream
of the Red Chamber" (HLMPSHCP, chap. 5, p. 48, line 8), Chih-
yen Chai remarks: 點題.蓋作者自云所歷不過紅樓一夢耳.
(CYCHLMCP, chap. 5, p. 82, chia-hsu chia-p'i). The title,
Dream of the Red Chamber, refers to Ts'ao's own description of his
past in a dream-vision in the Red Loft Building 紅樓.
There is a constant emphasis in the novel on its being a work of
dream literature (thus pointing to the correctness of the title, Dream
of the Red Chamber). In chapter 48, for example, Pao-ch'ai 寶釵
remarks that she composes poetry in her dreams. Chih-yen Chai
here remarks that much in the novel originates in dreams and therefore it is called Dream of the Red Chamber. He adds that even his
criticism originates in dreams. CYCHLMCP, chap. 48, p. 463,
keng-ch'en: 一部大書,起是夢,寶玉情是夢,賈瑞淫是夢,秦之
家計長策又是夢,今作詩也是夢,一柄風月鑑亦從夢中所有,
故紅樓夢也.余今批 評在夢中,特為夢中之人,特作此一大夢
也.脂硯齋.
[73]Ts'ao makes no mention of the dynastic setting of the novel.
In fact, one of his narrative techniques is deliberate obscurity.
This is noted in the second, third, and fourth of the anonymous
General Editorial Principles.
As Kosmo Kosmos complains, the Story of the Stone has no verifiable dynasty or date. HLMPSHCP, chap. 1, p. 3, line 15: 無朝代
年紀可考 ⋯
[74]For discussion of the ambiguous location of the novel, and

world of <u>Dream of the Red Chamber</u> where the reader is continually
lost between two reflecting surfaces: the dream-vision and waking
reality.

As the <u>Stone Record</u> unfolds in chapter 1, admittedly our impression is one of dazzled bewilderment. Initially, the lines are clearly
drawn between the heavenly and earthly realms, between the dream
state and consciousness, and between mythic beauty and mundane
reality. Gradually, these lines blur, and we wonder if Ts'ao Hsueh-
ch'in has not lost control of his text, just as all those who encounter
the <u>Stone Record</u>, such as the Reverend Taoist Kosmo Kosmos and
Chen Shih-yin,[75] become numb and confused even as they are
converted to a new and altogether unconventional perception of
reality. If our criterion for the beginning of a novel is the introduction of a major figure, then we shall have to wait until chapter
3 when we meet Pao-yu and Tai-yu.

In fact, any usual sense of a beginning simply does not apply to
<u>Dream of the Red Chamber</u>, partly because Ts'ao obviously tries to
disorientate the reader and to thwart his conventional expectations.
We soon discover ourselves to be enchanted by the pretense that
<u>Dream of the Red Chamber</u> originates in myth and therefore has no
known author and no certain beginning. This is, indeed, the
allegorical meaning of the creation myth--an enchantment which
results from what we might call Ts'ao's "conversion technique".
Critical judgment causes us to admit what Ts'ao's narrative technique indicates: namely, each episode in the first chapter, whether
it be about a goddess, a divine Buddhist, a mundane Taoist, a
gentleman, or a scholar, is a beginning. Each piece of the narrative represents another starting thread. Taken together, they constitute the start of the novel, so that we have to talk about the
"beginnings" of <u>Dream of the Red Chamber</u>, rather than about a

----

especially of the identity of the Ta-kuan Yuan 大觀園, "Grand
View Garden", see Yu P'ing-po, <u>Hung-lou meng yen-chiu</u>, pp.
129-139; Wu Shih-ch'ang, On the Red Chamber Dream, pp. 137-
144, 64, 114, 120-121, 177, 215; Jonathan Spence, <u>Ts'ao Yin
and the K'ang-hsi Emperor: Bondservant and Master</u>, Appendix,
New Haven, 1966: Chao Kang and Ch'en Chung-i, <u>Hung-lou
meng hsin-t'an</u>, pp. 185-187.

[75]The conversion of these two figures and the significance of
that conversion in Ts'ao's concept of fiction will be discussed in
"<u>Persona</u>".

"beginning".

Our assessment of these beginnings--taken in the order in which they appear--reveals that perplexity about the nature of reality as well as the nature of the novel results from Ts'ao Hsueh-ch'in's narrative technique. We shall examine that technique more fully later in the present essay. We might observe here that by the end of chapter 1 we are no longer concerned about our earlier loss of perspective. Rather, we have entered into Ts'ao's vision of reality. According to this vision and our experience in reading, the world of myth and every-day reality, the events and figures in dreams and the conscious state, are one. Through this shared experience, we realize a new orientation, an orientation which insists that, on the philosophical level, human suffering results from the willful division of life into distinct categories and that, in the realm of fiction, critical misunderstanding originates in the mistaken separation of literary modes.

It must be part of Ts'ao Hsueh-ch'in's intended irony that in order to understand the style of Dream of the Red Chamber, we must distinguish the various literary modes before we can appreciate their unity. In the preceding general discussion of the beginnings of the novel, we have seen that the structure of chapter 1 is one of designed ambiguity. We refer the reader to our essay in Chapter II of this study on the story of Chen Shih-yin and Chia Yu-ts'un for a detailed discussion of the mimetic layer of the framework. We now begin our close examination of the contribution of the mythic layer of chapter 1 to the style and meaning of Dream of the Red Chamber with the following translation:

Dear Reader, do you ask where this book came from? Although the account of its origin borders on the fantastic, once you are familiar with the details you will find it utterly fascinating. Allow me humbly to elucidate the background, for then you will not have any misgivings.

Now once upon a time, when the goddess Nu-kua was refining stones to patch the Firmament of Heaven, she refined 36,501 plain stone slabs[76] at Incredible Cliff on Mt.

----

[76]wan shih 頑石, "plain stone slabs". Wan 頑 in the sense of "merely" stone, i.e., to begin with, there is nothing special about the stones until they are refined. Wan 頑, interchangeable with wan 玩, "play", probably indicates a sense of irony. The Stone is playful, stubborn, and obstinate. Professor Wolfram

Fantasia which were 120 feet high by 240 feet square. As
she only had use for 36,500 slabs,[77] there was one left over,[78]
so she discarded it at the base of Blue-Channel Peak. Now
who would have known that this single Stone, after being
wrought and refined, thence imbued with a divine spiritual
nature, would blame and pity itself, and wail and moan night
and day, when it saw that the mass of stone slabs had all been
utilized and that it alone was unworthy of selection?

One day while it was moaning and groaning, it happened
to glimpse from afar a Buddhist and a Taoist[79] coming along
of unusual carriage and extraordinary spiritual aspect. Now
speaking, now smiling, they arrived at the base of Blue-
Channel Peak, sat themselves down beside the Stone, and
began to chat in a gay bantering fashion. At first they spoke
of 'Cloud and Mountain', 'Fog and Sea', 'Divinity and Sylph',
'Mystery and Illusion'; later they came to 'Splendor and
Riches' among mortals of the Red Dust. As the Stone listened,
worldly desires were unconsciously aroused, and it longed to
go among mortals to savor their splendor and riches. While it
regretted being a coarse fool, it nevertheless could not resist
sputtering out human words:

"Great Master!", said the Stone to the Monk, "I am a foolish
thing that doesn't know its manners. I happened to overhear
you both discussing the magnificence and luxuries of the mortal
world and my heart is filled with yearning. Although in substance I am only a coarse fool, my nature partakes of some
spirituality--upon seeing the divine forms and immortal bodies
of you two Masters, I became certain you are uncommon.

Eberhard informs me that ch'ih-wan 癡頑 often is applied to boys
who dally with girls and suggests that wan 頑 may be equivalent
to wan 玩. The description of the Stone thus appears as a reference to Pao-yu. In chapter 2, Chia Yu-ts'un repeatedly uses wan
頑 (see his conversation with Leng Tzu-hsing) to describe bad
types of boys.

[77] chih yung 只用, "only had use for". The "only" is an obvious
example of irony. It emphasizes the uselessness of the Stone which
will become the hero of the novel.

[78] chih tan-tan-te 只單單的. Again emphasis on the isolation
of the Stone.

[79] i-Seng i-Tao 一僧一道. Archetypal figures which appear in
myths, dreams, and everyday experiences.

Surely you have the material to patch Heaven and to regulate
Earth, and the virtue to benefit all things and to save men.
Should you show some compassion and carry me to the Red Dust
where I may enjoy myself for several years in the realm of
wealth and in the homeland of soft, warm affection, I would
cherish forever your vast favor and not forget you for myriad
ages".

When the two Divines heard this, they both giggled like
idiots. "Bless you! Bless you!", they exclaimed. "There
actually are some happy affairs in the Red Dust, it's just that
one cannot depend on them forever. Then again, there is
'discontent within bliss, numerous demons in auspicious affairs',
a phrase of eight words all of which belong tightly bound
together. In the twinkling of an eye, sorrow is born of utter
happiness, men are no more, and things change. In the last
analysis, it's all but a dream and the myriad realms return to
nothingness--really, it's better not to go at all!"

But the Stone was already aflame with worldly desire. How
could it obey such advice? It began to plead pitifully again
and again. The two Immortals realized there was no forcing
the Stone:

"This too is a destiny of non-being giving birth to being,
and a situation where, when quietude reaches an extreme,
thought of action arises", they said with a sigh. "Since that's
how it is, we will carry you to enjoy yourself--but when you
become dissatisfied--absolutely no later regrets!"

"Naturally", replied the Stone. "Naturally".

The Buddhist then spoke again: "One may say your nature
partakes of a divine spirit, yet you are also a plain fool.
Moreover, there is nothing about you which would indicate
you are rare or precious--you're just a stepping stone, and
that's about it![80] Well then, now I shall display the Buddha

----

80 如此也只好踮脚而已」 . Chih-yen Chai's ob-
servation here suggests that the Immortals are aware of the fact that
even after the Stone is refined by Nu-kua, and thus endowed with
a divine nature, it will be regarded by mortals as a mere stepping
stone. Without learning (the incised characters on the Stone will
symbolize knowledge) the Stone's true preciousness will go unrecognized on earth. What can a mortal do without learning?
CYCHLMCP, chap. 1, p. 4, chia-hsu chia-p'i: 煅煉過尚與人
踮脚,不學者又當如何.

Dharma and help you a bit. When the kalpa ends you will be returned to your original substance and your case would be settled--what would you say to that?"81

When the Stone heard this, it could not thank the Immortals enough.

The Monk then chanted incantations and wrote charms, unfurled his magic arts, and in an instant the slab of stone became a piece of lovely jade, fresh and lustrous, gleaming and pure.82 Moreover, it shrank into the size of a fan pendant which could be worn or carried. The Monk placed it in his palm and smiled:

"You have become a precious thing in form, but you still lack any genuine sign of merit. Several characters must be incised upon you so that as soon as people see you they will know you are rare and marvelous. After that we shall bear you to a prosperous realm of abundance,83 a cultured clan of successive ranks,84 a fecund soil of blooming luxuriance,85 and a rich homeland of soft, warm affection.86 There you

----

81 我如今大施佛法助你一助,待刼終之日,復還本質
This line points to the theme of retribution in the novel and Pao-yu's return to his original substance after his earthly experience.

82 將一塊大石登時變成一塊鮮明瑩潔的美玉····
The archetype of the jade gem is thus introduced. It is described in terms of purity and lustre, words which weave a theme through the novel.

83 昌明隆盛之邦···· Alludes to a great capital, such as Ch'ang-an. That is, Peking. CYCHLMCP, chap. 1, p. 5, chia-hsu chia-p'i: 伏長安大都.

84 詩禮簪纓之族. Alludes to the Jung-kuo branch of the great Chia clan. CYCHLMCP, chap. 1, chia-hsu chia-p'i: 伏榮國府. Tsan-ying 簪纓 "hair-pins and cap tassels", a metaphor for high officials. We translate as "successive rank" as the metaphor, when applied to the Chia clan, seems to imply a family of several generations of officials.

85 花柳繁華也···Alludes to the Ta-kuan Yuan, the "Grand View Garden". Hua-liu 花柳, "blooming luxuriance", frequently refers to sex life.

86 溫柔富貴鄉···· Alludes to the Tzu-yun Hsuan 紫芸軒, Purple-Rue Pavilion. CYCHLMCP, chap 1, p. 5, chia-hsu chia-p'i: 伏紫芸軒.
Possibly there is an allusion to Ch'in K'o-ch'ing 秦可卿, through

shall settle and enjoy your lot".[87]

As the Stone listened, its delight grew boundless. Whereupon it asked: "I do not know what unique signs you are to engrave on me,[88] nor where I am to be carried. How about an explanation so that I may have no misgivings?"

----

whom (in a dream-vision visit to the Great Void Illusion Realm) he has his first sexual experience, for in chapter 5 the Matriarch of the Chia clan observes that K'o-ch'ing is: 行事又溫柔和平 (HLMPSHCP, chap. 5, p. 46, line 6). Because of such associations with love, and because the phrase wen-jou 溫柔 often refers to sexual intercourse, we have translated the phrase 溫柔富貴鄉 as "a rich homeland of soft, warm affection".

Nearly the same phrase is used by Chen Shih-yin in chapter 120 when he asks Chia Yu-ts'un if the latter knew of one Chia Pao-yu in "that land of warm, soft affection, and of wealth?" 豈不知溫柔富貴鄉中有一寶玉乎? (HLMPSHCP, chap. 120, p. 416, line 10). An excellent instance of framework unity.

87 安身樂業. "Lot", literally, "patrimony", perhaps meaning the inheritance Pao-yu will enjoy through the offices of the Immortals.

Chih-yen Chai suggests that a phrase be added to this one: "and select a paragon of beauty for your love". CYCHLMCP, chap. 1, p. 5, chia-hsu chia-p'i: 何不再添一句云, 擇個絕世情癡作主人.

In an upper margin comment, Chih-yen Chai playfully records his envy of the Stone, and he notes the parallel story of the Taoist military figure Chang Liang 張良 of Han (T. Tzu-fang 子房), who, when he visited Huang Shih-kung 黃石公 through whom he had mastered military skills, he found that the latter had turned into a stone. Chang Liang regretted that he could not follow Shih-kung (the "stone"). CYCHLMCP, chap. 1, p. 5, chia-hsu mei-p'i: 昔子房後謁黃石公惟見一石, 子房當日恨不隨此石去, 余亦恨不能隨此石而去也, 聊供閱者一笑.

88 不知賜了弟子那幾件奇處. Chih-yen Chai here engages in a little psychological commentary. The Stone wants to know in what way it will be unique and precious on earth, and therefore wants to know what words the Monk is going to inscribe. But one must be unconscious of one's qualities. If one is conscious of them, he is no longer really a unique person. CYCHLMCP, chap. 1, p. 5, chia-hsu chia-p'i: 可知若果有奇貴之處, 自己亦不知者. 若自以奇貴而居, 究竟是無真奇貴之人.

The Monk laughed and said: "You had best not ask. You naturally will understand later".

And speaking thus and with the Stone within his sleeve, he wafted off with his companion Taoist to an area and a dwelling we know not where.[89]

We discuss in our "Persona" chapter the subsequent passage in which the Reverend Taoist Kosmo Kosmos discovers the Stone upon its return to the base of Blue-Channel Peak following its experience in the Red Dust. Further knowledge of the Stone and the mythic origins of the lovers, Chia Pao-yu and Lin Tai-yu, is presented in chapter 1 in Chen Shih-yin's dream-vision:

One long intensely hot summer's day, Shih-yin was leisurely sitting in his study. When his fingers felt weary, he shoved aside his books and began to doze, until before he knew it, he had fallen asleep.[90] He arrived somewhere in a dream, but he could not identify the location. Suddenly he glimpsed in one direction a Buddhist Monk and a Taoist coming along and chatting together. He overheard the Taoist say:

"This Foolish Thing you have in your grasp--which way do you intend to take it?"

The Monk said with a smile: "Do not trouble yourself. Now here is a ready case of passion which happens to need settlement. As there is a group of Fated Lovers who have yet to be reincarnated into the world, I shall avail myself of this opportunity and locate this Foolish Thing among them, thus causing it to live and learn".[91]

"So once again these lovers fated for retribution will pass through the world and meet with ordeals? But whereabouts will their area and location be?"

"This affair is a laughable story to tell", smiled the Monk. "Why it is one of those oddities you would not hear of in a thousand ages! On the bank of Numinous River in the Western

----

[89]The preceding section of translation is from HLMPSHCP, chap. 1, p. 2, line 2, to page 3, line 7. Chinese text begins on p. 47.

[90] 不覺朦朧睡去 ···· A rhetorical expression in Dream of the Red Chamber. Mystical experiences and unique perceptions are frequently prefaced by such phrases as pu chueh 不覺 "unconsciously", "without realizing it".

[91] 經歷經歷 ···· "Live and learn", that is, to experience the sorrows of the Red Dust.

Regions, and at the side of Tri-Births Stone, there was the
Crimson Pearl Sylph Herb. Because the Divine Crystal Page
of the Carmine Jade Palace nurtured it daily with sweet dew,
the Crimson Pearl Sylph Herb was able to grow. Later on, it
received the sacred quintessence of Heaven and Earth, and
the nourishment of rain and dew. Accordingly, it shed its
plant shape and foliage form for that of a human--though it
could be but moulded into the body of a woman. For whole
days she would wander beyond the confines of the Heaven
of Parting Sorrow. When hungry, she would dine on Bice
Colored Honey-Fruit for her victuals; when thirsty, she would
imbibe Nourishing Melancholia Sea Water for her beverage.
And because she had not yet requited the Divine Crystal Page
for the favor of watering, her longing would not be extin-
guished, even if her five viscera had been wrapped into a
knot. It happens that recently this Divine Crystal Page,
suddenly burning with earthly desire, longs to take advantage
of the prosperity and tranquility of the present dynasty[92]
and descend into the world so as to pass through illusory
involvement. It has already registered before the Bureau of
the Beware Illusion Fairy.

"When the Beware Illusion Fairy inquired whether the watering
love-debt had been requited--for this opportunity could be used
for settlement--the Crimson Pearl Sylph Herb said: 'Indeed I

---

92 乘此昌明太平朝世‧‧‧‧ A formulaic cliché which
sounds politically condescending. Wu Shih-ch'ang, On the Red
Chamber Dream, pp. 258-266, argues that Kao E excised and
added sections to Ts'ao's original work for political reasons. Kao
softened the "social significance" of Dream of the Red Chamber,
its "educative purpose", and its "attacks on the evils" of Ts'ao's
times (Wu, pp. 262-263).
However, the above phrase could not be by Kao E as it is found
in the chia-hsu pen, p. 10b, line 8. The exact political significance of Dream of the Red Chamber remains unclear. The comments
in the General Editorial Principles and in the conversation between
the Stone and Kosmo Kosmos in chapter 1 (discussed in "Persona"
chapter) to the effect that the novel has no political content seem
to argue indirectly that the novel does indeed have political significance. Otherwise, such protestations would be unnecessary.

have no liquid that could repay his kindness of sweet dew. If
he descends into the world as a mortal, I too shall descend
and return to him an entire lifetime of tears--this should be
sufficient requitement'. Because of this affair, several Fated
Lovers have been led out to accompany them so as to settle
this case".

"Odd indeed!", said the Taoist. "Why never before have I
heard of 'Repaying with Tears'. I imagine that this story,
compared to all the 'Wind and Moon' romances up to this date,
is even more detailed and refined".

"Of the past figures of romance", replied the Buddhist Monk,
"all that is related is a general outline together with poems,
lyrics, and essays, and that's that. Nothing is recorded about
how they wine and dine in the ladies boudoir. Furthermore,
in most of the 'Wind and Moon' romances, all you get is:
'Pilfering Perfume', 'Snatching Jade', 'Evening Tryst', and
'Secret Runaway'.93 Never is there leaked even a hint or
two of the genuine emotions of the lovers. I believe that what
is told of this group who are about to enter the world--the
foolish lovers, the wanton devils, the wise and the naive as
well as the degenerate--will be different from that which has
been narrated before".

"Why don't you and I take advantage of this opportunity and
also descend into the world and redeem a few?", asked the
Taoist. "Would not this be an act of merit?"

"Exactly what I was thinking. But first go with me to the
Palace of the Beware Illusion Fairy to hand over this Foolish
Thing so that it might be cleared. We shall wait until those
Fated Ghosts of Love Retribution descend into the world, then
you and I shall go. Though already half of them have fallen
into the Red Dust, as yet they have not gathered together".

"Fine", said the Taoist, "since such is the case, let me
accompany you".94

Now let us tell that although Shih-yin had heard everything
clearly, as yet he did not know what that "Foolish Thing" was

----

93 偷香竊玉暗約私奔而已.
Clichés for romantic literature.

94The passage which follows is translated and discussed in our
"Mimesis" chapter. We include the translation here, with the
addition of a few footnotes, to complete the myth paradigm.

they had discussed. He could not resist[95] coming forward and
making a courteous sign. He said with a smile: "Greetings
two Immortal Masters!"

The Buddhist Monk and the Taoist responded in kind. Shih-
yin said therefore: "I just happened to hear the Immortal
Masters talking about Cause and Effect--something which is
rarely heard of in the actual human world--but due to my
simpleton muddlement I cannot fathom the whole. Should I
be given liberation from my silly dullness and explication in
fine of that which I have just heard, I would wash my ears and
listen. Then I would be somewhat aware of my faults and I
could avoid sinking into the bitter underworld".

The two Immortals laughed: "This in fact is Penumbra
Mechanics,[96] the secret of which may not be leaked in advance.
When you arrive at the moment of crisis, just do not forget us
two, for then you may jump out of the fire pit".

Shih-yin understood. It would be inopportune to inquire
further. Thus he smiled and said: "Penumbra Mechanics may
not be leaked in advance, but whatever that 'Foolish Thing'
is which was just discussed--how about a glimpse?"[97]

----

95 遂不禁上前施禮....
A repeated formula. Chen Shih-yin cannot help himself. He must
talk to the Immortals. Similarly, the Stone cannot resist questioning the Immortals. In chapter 120, Kosmo Kosmos pesters Chia
Yu-ts'un after the latter's enlightenment. Mortals insist on knowing.

96Hsuan chi 玄機 . Hsuan means "dark", "mysterious",
"mystical", "arcane", "unknown", "ineffable". We use "penumbra"
to describe those shaded areas of human experience Ts'ao is referring to which cannot be illuminated solely through rational thought.

Edward H. Schafer in, "Thoughts About a Students' Dictionary of
Classical Chinese", Monumenta Serica, XXV (1966), pp. 202-3,
gives the following terms for chi 機 : "fundamental machine,
esp. loom; trigger mechanism; source of energy, secret faculty".
Alvin Cohen suggests "Key to the Arcane" for hsuan chi. Chen
Shih-yin is denied that key.

97 或可一見否?
The "glimpse" formula. Enlightening experiences always begin
with a "single glimpse" in the novel, but the subsequent experience
is usually baffling in its initial stages.

The Buddhist Monk replied: "This thing you ask about--it happens that in fact you are fated to see it once". And as he spoke he took it out and handed it to Shih-yin. The latter received it and looked it over. He discovered it to be in fact a lovely luminous jade gem. On the front surface the etching of characters was clearly visible--four words were inscribed: 'Precious Jade for Penetrating the Numinous'.98 On the back surface there were also several lines of small characters. Just when he wanted to look closely, the Buddhist Monk said they had already arrived at Illusion Realm and he forcefully snatched away the jade from Chen's hand. The Monk and the Taoist then went past a great stone stele, and in fact, the four characters written on top were: 'Great Void Illusion Realm'. One the two sides there was also a couplet which said:
'When the Unreal is conceived as the Real,
   the Real is simultaneously Unreal;
Where Non-Being is taken for Being,
   Being turns into Non-Being'.99
Shih-yin also longed to pass and to accompany them, but just as he started to take a step he suddenly heard a thunderous

----

98原來是塊鮮明美玉,上面字跡分明鐫著「通靈寶玉」四字.
Here the jade gem reappears, as lovely and luminous as before, but now with the addition of written words.
Chih-yen Chai tabulates the mysterious reappearances of the jade. CYCHLMCP, chap. 1, p. 13, chia-hsu chia-p'i:凡三四次始出明玉形,隱屈之至.
99In Chinese Buddhism, yu 有 is a Chinese translation for the Sanskrit term, bhava, "becoming", that desire to be born which causes you to be re-born. Bhava is the tenth of the Twelve Links of Conditioned Co-production (pratīya-samutpāda). See Lancaster, "Lists of Buddhist Terms". The sense of yu as the desire to be born which causes you to be re-born applies to the heavenly Stone which, because of its mundane desire, "becomes" part of the Red Dust. However, the opposite of yu, wu 無 "non-becoming", is practically meaningless in English. Professor Alvin Cohen notes that, while there is no notion of "being" or "non-being" in pre-Buddhist Chinese, Buddhism, with its Indo-European linguistic heritage, brought such concepts to China. Therefore we render yu as "being" and wu as "non-being".

roar as though mountains were crumbling and the earth collaps-
ing. He screamed in terror, then blinked his eyes for a better
look. He perceived but the fierce burning of the sun and the
gracefullness of the banana tree and half forgotten were the
events of his dream.[100]
This pretty little story set forth in the creation myth and the dream-
vision of Chen Shih-yin quite obviously serve to introduce a hero
and heroine of the novel, Chia Pao-yu and Lin Tai-yu, and form a
supernatural setting in which their romantic passion unfolds.
Prettiness, however, is deceptive, for the mythic layer of the framework contains much of the style and meaning of the novel.[101] As
Mark Schorer observes, myths are what give meaning to the facts
of life.[102]
Let us begin by examining the myth at its simplest level of meaning. The "once upon a time" narrative originates in a never-never
land of allegorical names, occult numerology, and divine machinery. It is an absurd world which is enlivened by a rhythmic contrast
between moral dogmatism and ironic humor. Yet, while the setting
is fantastic, it is also meant to contain a sense of reality. We note
that the first words of the narrative are yuan-lai,[103] "as a matter
of fact", which we translate as, "once upon a time", to convey the
Chinese concept that the myth is both timeless and true.
The hidden meaning of the allegorical names is one indication of
the relevance of the myth to the novel. The goddess Nu-kua refines

----

[100]The preceding passage, Chen Shih-yin's dream-vision, is
translated from HLMPSHCP, chap. 1, p. 5, line 12, to p. 7, line
7. The Chinese text may be found on pages 50 and following.

[101]The late Professor Shih-Hsiang Chen noted that through this
Chinese myth Ts'ao presents a vision of humanity. Like the Stone,
man is an outcast from heaven, but there remains to him a touch of
the divine. Man's sorrow originates in the contradiction between
those divine origins and his longing for human experience. The
Stone's salvation results when it passes through human emotions and
becomes a Stone of feeling. It discovers that every form of passion
is a kind of suffering, and in the process it becomes purged of its
emotions and returns to its original stone state. (Alvin Cohen note,
from class taught by Professor Chen.)

[102]William Blake: The Politics of Vision, New York, Vintage
Books, 1959, p. 25.

[103] 原來.

第一回　甄士隱夢幻識通靈　賈雨村風塵懷閨秀

　二

有情癡抱恨長。字字看來皆是血，十年辛苦不尋常。

列位看官，你道此書何來，說起根由雖近荒唐，細按則深有趣味，待在下將此來歷註明，方使閱

者了然不惑。

原來女媧氏煉石補天之時，於大荒山無稽崖煉成高經十二丈，方經二十四丈頑石三萬六千五百零

一塊。媧皇氏只用了三萬六千五百塊，只單單的剩了一塊未用，便棄在此山青埂峰下。誰知此石自經煅

煉之後，靈性已通，因見眾石俱得補天，獨自己無材不堪入選，遂自怨自歎，日夜悲號慚愧。一日正當嗟

悼之際，俄見一僧一道遠遠而來，生得骨格不凡，丰神迥別，說說笑笑來至峰下，坐於石邊，高談快

論。先是說些雲山霧海神仙玄幻之事，後便說到人間紅塵中榮華富貴。此石聽了，不覺打動凡心，想要

到人間去享一享這榮華富貴，但自恨粗蠢，不得已便口吐人言，向那僧說道：「大師，弟子蠢物不能

見禮了。適聞二位談那人世間榮耀繁華，心切慕之。弟子質雖粗蠢，性卻稍通，況見二師仙形道體，

定非凡品，必有補天濟世之材，利物濟人之德，如蒙發一點慈心，攜帶弟子得入紅塵，在那富貴場中

溫柔鄉裏受享幾年，自當永佩洪恩，萬劫不忘也。」二仙師聽畢，齊憨笑道：「善哉，善哉。那紅塵

中卻有些樂事，但不能永遠依恃；況又有『美中不足，好事多魔』八個字緊相聯屬，瞬息間則又樂極

悲生，人非物換，究竟是到頭一夢，萬境歸空，倒不如不去的好。」這石凡心已熾，那裏聽得進這話

去，乃復苦求再四。二仙知不可強制，乃歎道：「此亦靜極思動，無中生有之數也。既如此，我們便

攜你去受享受享，只是到不得意時，切莫後悔。」石道：「自然，自然。」那僧又道：「若說你性靈，

卻又如此質蠢，並更無奇貴之處，如此也只好踮腳而已。也罷，我如今大施佛法助你一助，待劫終之

日，復還本質，以了此案。你道好否？」石頭聽了，感謝不盡。那僧便念咒書符，大展幻術，將一塊大

石登時變成一塊鮮明瑩潔的美玉，且又縮成扇墜大小的可佩可拿。那僧托於掌上，笑道：「形體倒也

是個寶物了，還只沒有實在的好處，須得再鐫上數字，使人一見便知是奇物方妙；然後攜你到昌明隆

盛之邦，詩禮簪纓之族，花柳繁華地，溫柔富貴鄉去安身樂業。」石頭聽了，喜之不盡，乃問道：「不

知賜了弟子那幾件奇處，又不知攜了弟子到何地方，望乞明示，使弟子不惑。」那僧笑道：「你且莫

問，日後自然明白的。」說著便袖了這石，同那道人飄然而去，竟不知投奔何方何舍。後來又不知

過了幾世幾劫，因有個空空道人訪道求仙，從這大荒山無稽崖青埂峰下經過，忽見大塊石上字跡分明，

編述歷歷。空空道人乃從頭一看，原來就是無材補天，幻形入世，蒙茫茫大士渺渺真人攜入紅塵，歷

盡離合悲歡炎涼世態的一段故事，後面又有一首偈云：

　『無材可去補蒼天，枉入紅塵若許年。

　　此係身前身後事，倩誰記去作奇傳。』

詩後便是此石墜落之鄉，投胎之處，親自經歷的一段陳跡故事。其中家庭閨閣瑣事以及閒情詩詞倒還

全備，或可適趣解悶，然朝代年紀地與邦國，卻反失落無考。空空道人遂向石頭說道：「石兄，你這

一段故事，據你自己說有些趣味，故編寫在此，意欲問世傳奇。據我看來，第一件無朝代年紀可考，

第二件並無大賢大忠理朝廷治風俗的善政，其中只不過幾個異樣女子，或情或癡，或小才微善，亦無

第 一 回　甄士隱夢幻識通靈　賈雨村風塵懷閨秀

三

第一回　甄士隱夢幻識通靈　賈雨村風塵懷閨秀

班姑蔡女之德能。我縱抄去，恐世人不愛看呢。」石頭笑答曰：「我師何太癡也！若云無朝代可考，今我師竟假借漢唐等年紀添綴，又有何難。但我想歷來野史皆蹈一轍，莫如我不借此套者反倒新奇別致，不過只取其事體情理罷了，又何必拘拘於朝代年紀哉！再者，市井俗人喜看理治之書者甚少，愛看適趣閒文者特多。歷來野史，或訕謗君相，或貶人妻女，姦淫凶惡不可勝數；更有一種風月筆墨，其淫穢污臭，荼毒筆墨，壞人子弟，又不可勝數。至若佳人才子等書，則又千部共出一套，且其中終不能不涉於淫濫，以致滿紙潘安子建西子文君，不過作者要寫出自己的那兩首情詩艷賦來，故假擬出男女二人名姓，又必旁出一小人其間撥亂，亦如劇中之小丑然，且鬟婢開口，即者也之乎，非文即理。故逐一看去，悉皆自相矛盾大不近情理之說，竟不如我半世親睹親聞的這幾個女子，雖不敢說強似前代所有書中之人，但事跡原委亦可以消愁破悶，也有幾首歪詩熟詞可以噴飯供酒，至若離合悲歡，興衰際遇，則又追蹤躡跡，不敢稍加穿鑿，徒為供人之目而反失其真傳者。今之人，貧者日為衣食所累，富者又懷不足之心，縱一時稍閒，又有貪淫戀色好貨尋愁之事，那裏有工夫去看那理治之書。所以我這一段故事，也不願世人稱奇道妙，也不定要世人喜悅檢讀，只願他們當那醉淫飽臥之時，或避事去愁之際，把此一玩，豈不省了些壽命筋力，就比那謀虛逐妄，卻也省了口舌是非之害，腿腳奔忙之苦。再者亦令世人換新眼目，不比那些胡牽亂扯，忽離忽遇，滿紙才人淑女子建文君紅娘小玉等，通共熟套之舊稿。我師以為何如？」空空道人聽如此話，思忖半晌，將這石頭記再檢閱一遍，因見上面雖有些指奸責佞貶惡誅邪之語，亦非傷時罵世之旨，乃至君仁臣良父慈子孝，凡倫常所關之處，皆是稱功

四

頌德存仁無窮，竟非別書之可比。雖其中大旨談情，亦不過實錄其事，又非假擬妄稱，一味淫邀艷約，私討偷盟之可比。因毫不干涉時世，方從頭至尾抄錄回來，問世傳奇；因空見色，由色生情，傳情入色，自色悟空，遂易名為情僧，改『石頭記』為『情僧錄』。東魯孔梅溪則題曰『風月寶鑑』。後因

曹雪芹於悼紅軒中披閱十載，增刪五次，纂成目錄，分出章回，則題曰『金陵十二釵』。並題一絕云：

『滿紙荒唐言，一把辛酸淚。

都云作者癡，誰解其中味。』

出則既明，且看石上是何故事。按那石上書云：當日地陷東南，這東南一隅有處曰姑蘇，有城曰閶門者，最是紅塵中一二等富貴風流之地。這閶門外有個十里街，街內有個仁清巷，巷內有個古廟，因地方窄狹，人皆呼作葫蘆廟。廟旁住着一家鄉宦，姓甄，名費，字士隱。嫡妻封氏，情性賢淑，深明禮義。家中雖不甚富貴，然本地便也推他為望族了。因這甄士隱稟性恬淡，不以功名為念，每日只以觀花修竹酌酒吟詩為樂，倒是神仙一流人品。只是一件不足，如今年已半百，膝下無兒，只有一女，乳名英蓮，年方三歲。一日，炎夏永晝，士隱於書房閒坐，至手倦拋書，伏几少憩，不覺朦朧睡去，夢至一處，不辨是何地方。忽見那廂來了一僧一道，且行且談。只聽道人問道：『你攜了這蠢物，意欲何往？』那僧笑道：『你放心，如今現有一段風流公案正該了結，這一干風流冤家尚未投胎入世，趁此機會就將此蠢物夾帶於中，使他去經歷經歷。』那道人道：『原來近日風流冤孽又將造劫歷世去不成。但不知落於何方何處？』那僧笑道：『此事說來好笑，竟是千古未聞的罕事。只因西方靈河岸上三生石畔有

第一回　甄士隱夢幻識通靈　賈雨村風塵懷閨秀

六

絳珠草一株，時有赤瑕宮神瑛侍者日以甘露灌溉，這絳珠草始得久延歲月。後來既受天地精華，復得雨露滋養，遂得脫卻草胎木質，得換人形，僅修成個女體，終日遊於離恨天外，飢則食蜜青果為膳，渴則飲灌愁海水為湯；只因尚未酬報灌溉之德，故甚至五內便鬱結着一段纏綿不盡之意。恰近日這神瑛侍者凡心偶熾，乘此昌明太平朝世，意欲下凡，造歷幻緣，已在警幻仙子案前掛了號。警幻亦曾問及灌溉之情未償，趁此倒可了結的。那絳珠仙子道：「他是甘露之惠，我並無水可還。他既下世為人，我也去下世為人，但把我一生所有的眼淚還他，也償還得過他了。」因此一事，就勾出多少風流冤家來，陪他們去了結此案。」那道人道：「果是罕聞，實未聞有還淚之說。想來這一段故事比歷來風月故事更加瑣碎細膩了。」那僧道：「歷來幾個風流人物，不過傳其大概以及詩詞篇章而已，至家庭閨閣中一飲一食總未述記，再者，大半風月故事，不過偷香竊玉，暗約私奔而已，並不曾將兒女之真情發洩一二。想這一干人入世，其情癡色鬼賢愚不肖者，悉與前人傳述不同矣。」那道人道：「趁此何不你我也去下世度脫幾個，豈不是一場功德。」那僧道：「正合吾意。你且同我到警幻仙子宮中將這蠢物交割清楚。待這一干風流孽鬼下世已完，你我再去。如今雖已有一半落塵，然猶未全集。」道人道：「既如此，便隨你去來。」那僧道也答禮相問。士隱因說道：「適聞仙師所談因果，實人世罕聞者，但弟子愚濁不能洞悉明白，若蒙大開癡頑，備細一聞，弟子則洗耳諦聽，稍能警省，亦可免沉淪之苦。」笑問道：「二仙師請了。」二仙笑道：「此乃玄機不可預洩者，到那時只不要忘了我二人，便可跳出火坑矣。」士隱聽了，不便再問，因笑道：『玄機不可預洩，但適云蠢物不知爲何，或可一見否？』那僧道：『若問此物，倒有一面之緣。』說着，取出遞與士隱。士隱接了看時，原是塊鮮明美玉，上面字跡分明，鐫着「通靈寶玉」四字，後面還有幾行小字。正欲細看時，那僧便說已到幻境，便強從手中奪過一大石牌坊，上書四個大字乃是「太虛幻境」，兩邊又有一副對聯，道是：

『假作真時真亦假，無爲有處有還無。』

士隱意欲也跟了過去，方舉步時，忽聽一聲霹靂，有若山崩地陷。士隱大叫一聲，定睛一看，只見烈日炎炎，芭蕉冉冉，夢中之事便忘了對半。又見奶母正抱了英蓮走來。士隱見女兒越發生得粉裝玉琢，乖覺可喜，便伸手接來，抱在懷中，鬥他頑耍一回，又帶至街前，看那過會的熱鬧。方欲進來時，只見從那邊來了一僧一道，那僧則癩頭跣腳，那道則跛足蓬頭，瘋瘋顛顛，揮霍談笑而至。及到了他門前，看見士隱抱着英蓮，那僧便大哭起來，又向士隱道：『施主，你把這有命無運累及爹娘之物，抱在懷內作甚！』士隱聽了，知是瘋話，也不去睬他。那僧還說：『捨我罷，捨我罷！』士隱不耐煩，便抱女兒撤身要進去，那僧乃指着他大笑，口內念了四句言詞道：

『慣養嬌生笑你痴，菱花空對雪澌澌。

好防佳節元宵後，便是煙消火滅時。』

士隱聽得明白，心下猶豫，意欲問他們來歷，只聽道人說道：『你我不必同行，就此分手，各幹營生去罷。三劫後，我在北邙山等你，會齊了，同往太虛幻境銷號。』那僧道：『最妙，最妙。』說畢，二

第一回　甄士隱夢幻識通靈　賈雨村風塵懷閨秀

stones at Ta-huang Shan,[104] "Mt. Fantasia". We translate thus because, as Chih-yen Chai remarks, the name of the mountain means
huang-t'ang, "absurd", or, "fantastic".[105] Obviously, Ts'ao is
punning on his opening statement that the origin of his story borders
on the huang-t'ang.[106] The Stone Record is "fantastic", huang-
t'ang, while the Stone itself is created near Mt. Fantasia, Ta-
huang Shan (alternative translations: "Great Fantasy Mountain",
"Magic Mountain", "Mythic Mountain", "Mt. Nonsense", "Mt.
Absurd").[107] Huang-t'ang is a phrase which reappears throughout
the novel. In Chen Shih-yin's song commentary to the "Sweeter-
Over Song" (Hao-liao Ko), for example, he describes the vain worldly pursuits of mortals as, shen huang-t'ang, "what insanity!"[108]
The first step Ts'ao takes to establish his position that Dream of the
Red Chamber is mythic fiction is to place its origins in the absurd.[109]
We note in this connection that Nu-kua also works in the neighbor-
hood of Wu-chi Ai,[110] "Incredible Cliff". Wu-chi is a phrase
which is commonly applied to those matters which cannot be verified
or investigated. Perhaps what is suggested in this name is a phenomenon which recurs in the novel whenever human figures find themselves confronted by the mysterious. Thus in the above translation,
Chen Shih-yin beats a hasty retreat when he discovers that his
questions are touching upon the ineffable hsuan chi, "Penumbra

----

104 大荒山.

105CYCHLMCP, chap. 1, chia-hsu chia-p'i: 荒唐也.
Another source for the meaning and presence of this phrase in Dream
of the Red Chamber is the legend of Nu-kua. When she gathered
the ashes of reeds to stop a flood on earth caused by the crack in
the vault of heaven, her action was considered "absurd" 荒唐不經
huang-t'ang pu-ching.

106 說起根由雖近荒唐.

107Huang 荒 alone means "barren".

108 甚荒唐. For discussion of "Sweeter-Over Song", see
Mimesis", pp. 96-108.

109Chih-yen Chai marvels that at the beginning of the novel,
the author places the novel in the absurd. His comment suggests
that the reader should not be surprised by or complain about the
later presence of myth in the novel. CYCHLMCP, chap. 1, p. 2,
chia-hsu chia-p'i: 自占地步,自首荒唐,妙.
In the poem which closes the Preface to chapter 1, we find the
line: 'A perennial dream, all is absurdity'. 古今一夢盡荒唐.

110 無稽崖.

Mechanics". Similarly, in chapter 120, Chia Yu-ts'un refrains from questioning Chen Shih-yin about the whereabouts of Chia Pao-yu when he realizes that the answers have to do with the "Divine Unknown", hsien chi.[111]

Other titles and phrases have simple allegorical significance. The stones which are 12 by 24 chang[112] in size (120 feet by 240 feet) are references to the Twelve Hairpins of Chin-ling, that is, the maidens in the novel.[113] The 36,500 stone slabs Nu-kua uses are probably allusions to the fairy palace she built at Chung-huang Shan,[114] allegedly in Honan,[115] which was surrounded on all sides by a wall and a moat. Chih-yen Chai notes that 36,500 was the number of stones used to encircle heaven.[116] The Western Region[117] where the Crimson Pearl Sylph Herb lives may be the Western Paradise of the Buddhist Pure Land sect, but it is doubtful that Numinous River, Ling-ho,[118] is of any geographical significance (the ling[119] may imply the association between Tai-yu and Pao-yu, for the latter's jade amulet is inscribed, t'ung-ling pao-yu,[120] "Precious Jade for Penetrating the Numinous"). The Tri-

----

[111] HLMPSHCP, chap. 120, p. 417, line 3: 雨村聽著卻不明白了, 知仙機也不便問‥‥.

[112] 丈.

[113] CYCHLMCP, chap. 1, p. 2, chia-hsu chia-p'i: 總應十二釵. A second symbolism the size of the stones may represent is the twelve months and twenty-four solar stations of the year, that is, the "time" and "seasons" in general.

[114] 中黃山.

[115] 河南.

[116] This is the prototype of Chinese walled cities. See Werner, Dictionary of Chinese Mythology, p. 335. CYCHLMCP, chap. 1, p. 2, chia-hsu chia-p'i: 合週天之數. 36,500 is a very interesting number here: the civil Chinese year has 354 or 384 (sometimes 355 and 385) days, but the "astronomical" Chinese year, as determined by the solar stations, has 365 days. The "astronomical year" is the absolute year, the "civil" year is the one used in our floating life.

[117] 西方.

[118] 靈河.

[119] 靈.

[120] 通靈寶玉.

Births Stone[121] allusion suggests a destined affinity between Pao-yu and Tai-yu.[122] The ch'ing-keng[123] of Ch'ing-keng Feng,[124] "Blue-Channel Peak", is a homophone for ch'ing-ken,[125] "root of love". Because the Stone is cast at the base of Blue-Channel Peak, it symbolically falls to the very root of human emotions.[126] The mythic name for Tai-yu, "Crimson Pearl Sylph Herb", signifies the color red and the tears of blood (the suffering of love) she sheds for Pao-yu.[127] In Pao-yu's mythic name, "Divine Crystal Page",[128] we find an emphasis on the character jade, and thus a hint of the hero. The name of the place where he serves, "Carmine Jade Palace",[129] denotes both jade and the color carmine, and in addition, the fact that the jade is "diseased".[130] The exotic names

----

[121] 三生石.

[122]Chih-yen Chai notes that the allusion to the Tri-Births Stone is from a poem by the T'ang monk, Yuan Kuan. CYCHLMCP, chap. 1, p. 11, chia-hsu chia-p'i: 妙, 所謂「三生石上舊精魂」也.

Yuan Kuan 圓觀 and his friend, Li Yuan 李源, were once on an excursion to the San Hsia 三峽 (commonly identified with 瞿塘峽, 巫峽, 西陵峽), when Yuan Kuan spotted a woman carrying water. He announced to Li Yuan that this was the place of his re-birth. That night he died. As Yuan Kuan predicted, Li Yuan met him again twelve years later. The spot of their alleged meeting is called Tri-Births Stone, and symbolizes a fated friendship or love.

San-sheng, "Tri-Births", may also be an allusion to the three worlds of Buddhism: our world, the world of hells, and the world of heavens. 青埂.

[123] 青埂.
[124] 青埂峰.
[125] 情根.

[126]Interestingly, Chih-yen Chai's commentary suggests that because of this entanglement with love, the Stone is of no use when it comes to repairing heaven. CYCHLMCP, chap. 1, p. 3, chia-hsu mei-p'i: 妙, 自謂落墮情根, 故無補天之用.

[127]CYCHLMCP, chap. 1, p. 11, chia-hsu chia-p'i: 點紅字. 細思绛珠二字豈非血淚乎.

[128] 神瑛侍者.

[129] 赤瑕宮.

[130]On 神瑛侍者 : CYCHLMCP, chap. 1, p. 12, chia-hsu chia-p'i: 單點玉字二.

of food and drink which the Crimson Pearl Sylph Herb enjoys, such as "Bice Colored Honey-Fruit"[131] and "Nourishing Melancholia Sea Water",[132] imply that she is a creature of unique background.[133]

Despite the simplicity of these allegories, they serve several useful purposes. They provide a background to the novel which is both exotic and universal, and they hint towards the appearance of the major figures of Dream of the Red Chamber and tell us something of their characters. But their chief function is to create a medium through which some of the basic themes of the novel may be plainly stated and in which divine machinery may be set in motion.

One example of a firm assertion of the divine vision occurs when the Stone asks to be taken to the Red Dust:

> When the two Divines heard this, they both giggled like idiots. "Bless you! Bless you!", they exclaimed. "There actually are some happy affairs in the Red Dust, it's just that one cannot depend on them forever. Then again, there is 'discontent within bliss, numerous demons in auspicious affairs', a phrase of eight words all of which belong tightly bound together. In the twinkling of an eye, sorrow is born of utter happiness, men are no more, and things change. In the last analysis, it's all but a dream and the myriad realms return to nothingness--really, it's better not to go at all!"[134]

The obvious meaning of this passage does not lessen its importance in Dream of the Red Chamber. Chih-yen Chai finds it to be a general summary.[135] In the "Sweeter-Over Song" and Chen Shih-

----

On 赤瑕宮 : CYCHLMCP, chap. 1, p. 12, chia-hsu mei-p'i: 按瑕字, 本注玉小赤也, 又玉又病也, 以此命名恰極. Hsia 瑕 is jade with flaws or blemishes in it.

[131] 蜜青果.
Other editions of the novel say that Tai-yu eats 秘情果 which may be considered more apt, for it is an exact parallel with 灌愁水. Thus, she eats "Fruit of Hidden Love", and drinks "Nourishing Melancholia Sea Water".

[132] 灌愁海水.

[133] Again, these titles which denote love food, serve to point to the uniqueness of Tai-yu. CYCHLMCP, chap. 1, p. 12, chia-hsu chia-p'i: 飲食之名奇甚, 出身履歷更奇甚, 寫黛玉來歷自與別個不同.

[134] For text, see p. 47.

[135] CYCHLMCP, chap. 1, p. 3, chia-hsu chia-p'i: 四句乃一部之總綱.

yin's song commentary on the "Sweeter-Over Song" (discussed in "Mimesis"), we find repeated the ideas which are here set forth in the mythic realm: everything produces its opposite; the human condition is mutability; life is but a dream. What is interesting is the way in which these themes are stated. The Immortals are dogmatic, it is true, but they are also playful, one might almost say, satirical. They begin with the pretense that the Red Dust is not all that bad, it's just that it's undependable and mutable. They end by seeming to discover that human experience is an illusion and that there is nothing good about it. The Immortals are authoritative, but not authoritarian. They are archetypal figures who bear witness to the truth, but they are unable to control human desire. Their view that bliss and discontent are bound together[136] can only appear to the Stone to be a priori theorizing.

The Stone, an image of man, advances through inductive reasoning and remains immune to the deductive arguments of the Buddhist Monk and the Taoist. To the Immortals, however, the Stone's stubbornness is due to a combination of fate and what a few modern theologians might call, "situation ethics":

"This too is a destiny of non-being giving birth to being, and a situation where, when quietude reaches an extreme, thought of action arises", they said with a sigh.[137]

According to divine understanding, the Stone cannot help itself, for even its mortal desires are objects of predestination and the inevitable rhythm of the law of opposites. Thus, the Immortals play on the idea of wu,[138] "non-being", or "absence", creating yu,[139] "being", or "presence". We are reminded that when Chen Shih-yin visits the Great Void Illusion Land in a dream-vision, he sees

---

136 美中不足,好事多魔,八個字緊相聯屬.... Joy and sorrow are one, and are always producing their opposites. Mortals never remember these facts.

Later in chapter 1 when it is noted that Chen Shih-yin has no son, Chih-yen Chai applies the phrase 美中不足 to Chen. CYCHLMCP, chap. 1, p. 11, chia-hsu chia-p'i:所謂美中不足也. In other words, Chen appears to lead a happy peaceful life with his wife and daughter, but at the center of that life is sorrow, for he has no male heir.

137For text, see p. 47.

138 無.

139 有.

the couplet:
    'When the Unreal is conceived as the Real,
       the Real is simultaneously Unreal;
     Where Non-Being is taken for Being,
       Being turns into Non-Being'.[140]
Because of the fated movement of opposites, the very situation of
calmness in which the Stone exists demands that it thrust itself into
the state of active desire. The final irony of the situation is the
lack of awareness of Immortals and mortals alike. The re-birth of
the Stone and its subsequent experience of suffering in the Red Dust
are inevitable, yet the Stone must plead its case and the two Divines
must argue against it.[141]
    Just as a moral and philosophical world view is directly delineated
in the mythic realm, so too the action of Dream of the Red Chamber
is matter-of-factly explained through an appeal to divine machinery.
In its simplest variety, the latter takes the form of magic, and here
we have another touch of irony. When the Buddhist Monk declares
that he will help the Stone by "displaying the Buddha Dharma",
the reader is hardly prepared to find that the phrase means wizardry.
The re-birth of the Stone in the form of the hero, Pao-yu, is ac-
acounted for through the use of magic spells, incantations, and
charms.[142] We shall have occasion to comment on the significance
of this satire further on in our discussion. Here we should make one

----

[140]For text, see p. 52.
When Pao-yu visits the same place in a dream in chapter 5, he too
sees this couplet. See HLMPSHCP, chap. 5, p. 48, line 11.
    [141]Perhaps the commentary to the above couplet should be
applied to the conversation between the Stone and the Immortals.
The commentators observe that the couplet described the natural
rhythm of the conditioned and the unconditioned, being and non-
being, the true and the false, and Immortals may also follow such
natural patterns. CYCHLMCP, chap. 1, p. 13, chia-hsu chia-p'i:
甚用真假有無字,妙 . ibid., yu cheng:無極太極之輪
轉,色空之相生,四季之隨行,皆不過如此.
    [142] 大展幻術. Chih-yen Chai frequently points to Ts'ao's
delineation of magic and delusion. Thus he says of this phrase:
明點幻字好. CYCHLMCP, chap. 1, p. 4, chia-hsu chia-p'i.
Popular or folk Buddhism is to a large extent, of course, magical.

further point about this section of the myth. When the Monk remarks:
> "Now I shall display the Buddha Dharma and help you a bit.
> When the kalpa ends you will be returned to your original
> substance . . . ."[143]

Chih-yen Chai observes:
> Marvelous! If the Buddha Dharma must be indemnified, how
> much more the debts of mortals![144]

The commentator is always aroused when he sees an example of
retribution mechanics in the mythic realm to draw a comparison
between it and the theme of unrequited love in the mortal world.
Thus when he reads that:
> . . . because she had not yet requited the Divine Crystal Page
> for the favor of watering, her longing could not be extinguished,
> even if her five viscera had been wrapped into a knot.[145]

he marvels that if conditions are this difficult in the "Western
Regions", that is, the Buddhist paradisiacal realm, how much more
difficult they are on earth.[146] Chih-yen Chai's observation brings
out a forboding aspect of this supposed romance of the Red Chamber.
According to the workings of divine mechanics, love cannot attain
fulfillment, either in heaven or on earth.

We note here in passing the possibility that the tears of the Crimson Pearl Sylph Herb and the sighs of the Stone may have an autobiographical significance. The decision of the Herb to descend into
the world to accompany the Divine Crystal Page is a matter of
supernatural machinery which supposedly accounts for the reason why

----

[143]For text, see p. 48.
[144]CYCHLMCP, chap. 1, p. 4, chia-hsu chia-p'i (Yu P'ing-po
emendation): 妙, 佛法亦須償還, 況世人之償 (疑債字) 乎.
[145]For text, see p. 51. There is a possibility that these lines,
together with the statement, ". . . the Divine Crystal Page . . .
nurtured it daily with sweet dew . . . ." are archetypal expressions
of sexual relations. Wolfram Eberhard, Guilt and Sin in Traditional
China, Berkeley & Los Angeles, 1967, p. 12, notes that Chinese
characters associated with sexual activity commonly have water
radicals. Needless to say, any hint of such activity in the divine
realm does not apply to Pao-yu and Tai-yu.
[146]CYCHLMCP, chap. 1, p. 12, chia-hsu chia-p'i: 妙極. 恩
怨不清, 西方尚如此, 況世之人乎? 趣極緊甚.

Tai-yu is always weeping over Pao-yu:[147]

"Indeed I have no liquid that could repay his kindness of sweet dew. If he descends into the world as a mortal, I too shall descend and return to him an entire lifetime of tears--this should be sufficient requitement".[148]

To Chih-yen Chai, this passage also represents an ultimate expression of Ts'ao Hsueh-ch'in's personal sorrow, a sorrow which the commentator shares.[149] When the Reverend Taoist Kosmo Kosmos observes that, "the Stone in fact lacked talent to repair the Firmament and had entered the world in a transitory form",[150] Chih-yen Chai notes that the eight words, "lacked talent to repair the Firmament and had entered the world in a transitory form", are an expression of Ts'ao's regret over his life.[151] Such confessional, self-pitying language combined with Chih-yen Chai's commentary is a major source of the theory that the novel is autobiographical.

Chih-yen Chai notes still another statement of possible autobiographical significance in the Monk's address to the Stone:

"You have become a precious thing in form, but you still lack any genuine sign of merit".[152]

These words, says the commentator, exemplify the author's own sense of shame.[153] It is not enough for the Stone (and by extension, Pao-yu and Ts'ao Hsueh-ch'in) to have a divine inner nature and a precious gem form, its uniqueness will only be known to men if such is literally spelled out on its surface through the written word. If we follow the autobiography theory, we should argue that Ts'ao is hoping here that the failure of his life will be rectified by his Stone Record.

----

[147]The psychological reasons are much more complex, and have been explored by C.T. Hsia, The Classic Chinese Novel, pp. 169-278.

[148]For text, see p. 51.

[149]CYCHLMCP, chap. 1, p. 13, chia-hsu mei-p'i: 知眼淚還債人天都作者一人耳.余亦知此意,但不能說得出.

ibid., chia-hsu chia-p'i: 觀者至此,請掩卷思想,歷小說可曾有此句,千古未聞之奇文.

[150]HLMPSHCP, chap. 1, p. 3, line 9: 原來就是無材補天,幻形入世.

[151]CYCHLMCP, chap. 1, p. 5, chia-hsu chia-p'i: 八字便是作著一生慚恨.

[152]For text, see p. 48.

[153]CYCHLMCP, chap. 1, p. 4, chia-hsu chia-p'i: 自愧之語.

The language which sets the supernatural machinery in motion is partly legalistic and partly opportunistic. From the Immortals' point of view, the Stone Record is a collection of tales about fated lovers whose "cases" "need to be settled". The Divines are quite fond of such legalistic formulae. Speaking of the foolish Stone, the Buddhist Monk tells the Taoist: "Now here is a ready case of passion which happens to need settlement". Several Fated Lovers will accompany the Divine Crystal Page and the Crimson Pearl Sylph Herb on their journey in the Red Dust so as to "settle this case". The Divine Crystal Page is reported to have "registered before the Bureau of the Beware Illusion Fairy" in fulfillment of a legal requirement. The Beware Illusion Fairy is the Keeper of Lovers' Records. After lovers pay their love debts in the Red Dust, they must return to the palace of the Fairy and have their names checked off in order to balance her Registry of Lovers.[154]

Ts'ao creates a humorous image of the Immortals by having them refuse to leave everything to either fate or the law. It happens, the Buddhist Monk reports, that some lovers are about to be re-born into the world, and that he will "take advantage of this opportunity" to teach the stupid Stone a lesson. Not to be outdone, the Taoist replies to the Monk in the following terms:

"Why don't you and I take advantage of this opportunity and also descend into the world and redeem a few? Would not this be an act of merit?"[155]

Again we note the formulae of an opportunist. The Keeper of Lovers' Records uses nearly identical language:

". . . the Beware Illusion Fairy inquired whether the watering love-debt had been requited--for this opportunity could be used for settlement . . . ."[156]

----

[154]Chih-yen Chai records the legal role of the Beware Illusion Fairy. CYCHLMCP, chap. 1, p. 13, chia-hsu chia-p'i: 又出一警幻皆大關鍵處. The actions of the Fairy exemplify Ts'ao's concept of opposites. The Fairy warns against every kind of human passion, yet it is she who first brings Pao-yu to sexual experience in a dream-vision (chap. 5), supposedly with the idea that this enlightening experience will remove his desire. The "opposite" occurs, of course.

[155]For text, see p. 51.

[156]For text, see p. 51.

The preceding review reveals that the simple allegorical level of the myth has a rather negative appeal. We are not moved by mechanical explanations of human behavior, or dogmatic assertions of philosophical viewpoints encountered in the creation myth and Chen Shih-yin's dream-vision, and while the goddess Nu-kua, the Beware Illusion Fairy, and the two Immortals are entertaining, their motivations appear unexemplary and unattractive. We suggest that the reader is partially the victim of Ts'ao's irony, and that his dissatisfaction is part of Ts'ao's "hidden" intention. The quite simple lesson of the pretty little creation myth and the fable of the Divine Crystal Page and the Crimson Pearl Sylph Herb is that we are foolish to expect that divinity and perfection are synonymous. At the very moment we are solely in the mythical realm, its world view appears utterly fragmented and hallucinatory.

Before we can appreciate this mythic experience, we must turn to the appropriate Chih-yen Chai commentary on the style of the mythic mode and then examine Ts'ao Hsueh-ch'in's narrative technique.[157] Chih-yen Chai reinforces our conception that Dream of the Red Chamber is in part a work of mythic fiction.[158] The commentator contends that Ts'ao is being slightly playful in his use of the creation myth,[159] but that for the most part his intention is

----

[157]Further discussion of style will be found in our study of the Preface to chapter 1 and the conversation between the Stone and Kosmo Kosmos (see "Persona" chapter).

[158]There are certain obvious features which the commentator notes, as, for example, the fact that the exotic foods the Crimson Pearl Sylph Herb eats are meant to hint towards the eccentric and unique character of Lin Tai-yu, or that the discarded Stone serves to introduce various stories in the body of the novel. We have previously noted Chih-yen Chai's observation that Ts'ao Hsueh-ch'in's first step in writing Dream of the Red Chamber is to place it in the absurd world of myth. As the novel begins, a "fantastic" (huang-t'ang) tale unfolds at the base of "Mt. Fantasia" (Ta-huang Shan). See: CYCHLMCP, chap. 1, p. 12, chia-hsu chia-p'i: 飲食之名奇甚, 出身履歷更奇甚, 寫黛玉來歷自與別個不同.
ibid., chap. 1, p. 2, chia-hsu chia-p'i: 剩了一塊便出這許多故事.
ibid., chap. 1, p. 2, chia-hsu chia-p'i: 自占地步, 自首荒唐, 妙.

[159]Ts'ao casually uses common expressions such as, "to refine stones and to repair the Firmament". That is, he uses popular myths for his own purposes. CYCHLMCP, chap. 1, p. 2, chia-hsu chia-p'i: 補天濟世, 勿認真用常言.

serious. Chih-yen Chai's comments are sometimes interpolations of
Ts'ao's text, rather than explications, and his stress on the didactic
value of the novel tends to be somewhat traditional.160 Thus, he
elaborates on the line in the creation myth describing the origin of
the Stone, "there was one left over":

> Even though the Stone was not used <u>that</u> <u>day</u> to repair the
> Firmament of Heaven, it is fitting that it went to repair the
> <u>sloping</u> earth so as to make it even and smooth. But then,
> we would not have had this mythic story.161

In other words, the Stone has some sort of mission to fulfill on earth
which, according to the commentary, is out of order. Just what
that mission is remains unclear, however, for the human condition
is not altered by the appearance of the Stone, and Pao-yu, while
he does come to a personal enlightenment, is not entirely successful

----

The phrase, 補天濟世 originates in the Nu-kua legend as
given in the Shih Chi.

160Another example of Chih-yen Chai's habit of reading <u>Dream</u>
<u>of the Red Chamber</u> as a moral <u>exemplum</u> is found in his comment on
the phrase, "You have become a precious thing in form, but you
still lack any genuine sign of merit". Chih-yen believes when
hypocrites see this phrase they will be unhappy, for in their external
form they appear worthy, while internally they are in fact corrupt.
The Stone in its present appearance will remind such persons of
themselves. CYCHLMCP, chap. 1, p. 4, chia-hsu chia-p'i:妙極,
(今)之金玉其外敗絮其中者,見此不觀喜.
(今 before 之 is an emendation added from the chia-chen mss.,
as a character is apparently missing in the chia-shu pen).

In another comment on the passage, "Well then, now I shall display the Buddha Dharma and help you a bit. When the kalpa ends
you will be returned to your original substance . . . ," Chih-yen
Chai notes an instance of satire directed against those who think
they can escape their debts. CYCHLMCP, chap. 1, p. 4, chia-
hsu chia-p'i:妙,佛法亦須償還,況世人之償(疑債字)乎.近
之賴債者來看此句,所謂游戲筆墨也.
161CYCHLMCP, chap. 1, p. 2, chia-hsu chia-p'i:使當日雖不
以此補天,就該去補地坑陷,使地平坦,而不得有此一部鬼話.
"Sloping earth" for 地坑陷 is our interpolation, rather than
the more correct "earth crater" as we are trying to make our English
consistent with 陷 "sloped" in the next quoted passage.

in illuminating the lives of those around him.[162]

Two clues to Chih-yen Chai's understanding are found in his use of the word hsien[163] and the phrase tang-jih.[164] Surely he is thinking ahead at this point in the narrative to the line with which the story of Chen Shih-yin begins:

> With the origins now clear, let us see what story is on the Stone. According to the writings on the Stone, it is related that: On that day the earth sloped towards the south-east . . . .[165]

Just as there is a crack in the Firmament of Heaven, so too there is a slope or crater in the earth crust, each defect representing the imperfection of the divine or human realm. Chih-yen Chai perhaps detects, then, the slight touch of irony in the use of hsien, for he links his comment (thereby linking heaven and earth) to the Chen Shih-yin story by the use of tang-jih. The Stone was not used on "that day", and on "that day" the earth sloped towards the south-east. He must also be aware that the word hsien recalls an episode from the original creation myth. When Kung Kung (see note 3) broke one of the eight pillars holding up the canopy of heaven, it fell and sloped downward in its southern section. The mountain on which the pillar rested also caved in on its southern slope (symbolizing the giving way of a corner of the earth). The creation myth is thus a tale telling of the imperfection of heaven and earth (the mountain is named Pu-chou Shan, "Imperfect Mountain").[166]

As the commentary indicates the word hsien and the phrase, "to refine stones and to repair the Firmament", are convenient ploys Ts'ao borrows from Chinese mythology to begin his narrative.

Chih-yen Chai's awareness of the mythic layer of Dream of the Red Chamber is underscored by his scorn for those who read the novel solely on the mimetic "realistic" level. When it is written

----

[162]The significance of Pao-yu's pilgrimage will be discussed later. Suffice it to say now that his role as a missionary figure will have to be severely qualified.

[163] 陷.

[164] 當日.

[165]HLMPSHCP, chap. 1, p. 5, line 7: 出則既明,且看石上是何故事. 按那石上書云:當日地陷東南 ‥‥ Italics are added in the above translations.

[166] 不周山.

Werner, Dictionary of Chinese Mythology, pp. 334-335.

that the Stone "could not resist sputtering out human words", the commentator adds:

And yet there are those who ask, 'Where does the Stone's mouth come from?' Their lack of feeling is extremely laughable and reprehensible.[167]

In other words, it is hardly surprising that the Stone speaks in human language in the world of myth. "Realists" will miss the meaning of Ts'ao's art. Chih-yen Chai appears to be continually concerned with the question that Ts'ao raises, what is reality? Periodically he seems to claim that Ts'ao's vision of myth is one with that which is real and that "mythic" means "true". When Chen Shih-yin sees in his dream-vision a Buddhist and a Taoist "of unusual carriage and extraordinary spiritual aspect", Chih-yen Chai comments: "These are real images, not mirages".[168] Immortals cannot look ordinary, of course, but Chih-yen Chai's point is to note the relation between these figures and reality. The sense in which these figures are real and true is clarified by another of Chih-yen Chai's comments. When the same two Immortals make a "real-life" appearance to Chen Shih-yin following his dream-vision, and try to take away his daughter from him, they are described as being scabby headed and lame footed; at which point, Chih-yen Chai remarks that this is a "mirage" or an "illusion".[169] The idea here is not merely that mortals are not enlightened enough to be aware of the presence of Immortals, but that divine beauty, reality, and truth make human physical perfection irrelevant. Buddhist monks have "scabby" shaven heads, Taoists prize physical imperfections. We are reminded of Yeats' line, "in dreams begins responsibility".

Despite the transparency of dream-visions and the simplicity of mythic allegories, they are true visions of reality, or, as Chia Pao-yu remarks to an image of himself he encounters in a dream, the experience is "more true than truth itself".[170] Ts'ao's very style

----

[167]CYCHLMCP, chap. 1, p. 3, chia-hsu chia-p'i: 竟有人問口生於何處,其無心肝,可笑可恨之極.

[168]CYCHLMCP, chap. 1, p. 3, chia-chen: 這是真像,非幻像也.

[169]CYCHLMCP, chap. 1, p. 14, chia-hsu chia-p'i:此門是幻像

[170]HLMPSHCP, chap. 56, p. 620, line 16: 真而又真. Chia Pao-yu denies that his encounter with this image of himself is a dream experience, but it is. The episode is analyzed in "Mimesis", pp. 165-166.

illustrates that as we approach the world of myth, we find it is
really true. An example occurs when Chen Shih-yin is about to
look closely at the jade amulet which is inscribed: "Precious Jade
for Penetrating the Numinous". The Buddhist Monk snatches away
the piece of jade and makes the offhand comment that they have
arrived at "Illusion Realm":[171]

> The Monk and the Taoist then went past a great stone stele,
> and in fact, the four characters written on top were: 'Great
> Void Illusion Realm'.[172]

Through the use of nai,[173] "and in fact", Ts'ao marks the transition from a rumored name to an actual location. How can there be
such a strange-sounding place as "Illusion Realm"? And yet there
it is before one's very eyes.

This stress on the mythic level of Dream of the Red Chamber is
further revealed by Chih-yen Chai's continued citation of the word
huan[174] (variously translated as "illusion", "delusion", "transitory") whenever he finds it in the text. Thus he records the use of
huan in the phrase, huan yuan, "illusory involvement".[175] He
remarks that the Buddhist Monk's use of magic is a manifestation of
this word.[176] The four words on the top of the stele, 'Great Void
Illusion Realm',[177] he finds to be really worth thinking about.[178]
Perhaps his most important observation occurs at the point where the
Monk announces to the Taoist that they have arrived at "Illusion
Realm":

> Here again is delineated the character, huan. This means that
> the narrative has entered into the realm of illusion.[179]

----

171 幻境.
172 For text, see p. 52.
173 乃.
174 幻.
175 Huan yuan 幻緣 . Yuan here represents the ill-fated
relations between lovers, or their painful involvement with one
another. The Monk uses huan to characterize the unreality of human
love. CYCHLMCP, chap. 1, p. 12, chia-hsu chia-p'i: 點幻字.
Huan, "illusion", can also have undertones of "cosy", denoting
sexual situations.
176 CYCHLMCP, chap. 1, p. 4, chia-hsu chia-p'i: 明點幻
字好.
177 大空幻境.
178 CYCHLMCP, chap. 1, p. 13, chia-hsu chia-p'i: 四字可思.
179 CYCHLMCP, chap. 1, p. 13, chia-hsu chia-p'i: 又點幻字,
云書已入幻境矣.

This comment marks an important point of demarcation in the novel and we might speculate that Chih-yen Chai intends two possible meanings. Immediately after the Monk's announcement, Chen Shih-yin awakens from his dream and is confronted by the two Immortals, now appearing dirty and dishevelled, who demand his daughter. There is no transition clearly drawn between the mythic vision and waking reality, and the passage is an instance of Ts'ao's habit of deliberate obfuscation we discussed at the beginning of this essay. We have entered into the Red Dust, that is, the world of reality and the mimetic layer of the novel and--from the Immortals' viewpoint--we have arrived at "Illusion Realm". At the same time, we must not forget that the Immortals have taken very deliberate steps to sever their relation with Chen Shih-yin. It is they who are going to enter into "Illusion Realm" and he cannot, despite his strong desire, accompany them. The point here is that "Illusion Realm" also means the world of myth and the mythic layer of Dream of the Red Chamber, the Great Void Illusion Realm, which envelops the mimetic layer, the "imitation of reality", like a glittering cover of foil.

In the preceding review of the Chih-yen Chai commentary on the creation myth and the dream-vision of Chen Shih-yin, we have noted the commentator's awareness of the mythic style of Dream of the Red Chamber.[180]   Let us develop Chih-yen Chai's suggestive emphasis on language as we turn to examine the narrative techniques Ts'ao uses in the mythic mode.

The creation myth is preceded by a traditional address to the reader:

> Dear Reader, do you ask where this book came from?
> Although the account of its origin borders on the fantastic,
> once you are familiar with the details you will find it utterly
> fascinating. Allow me humbly to elucidate the background,
> for then you will not have any misgivings.[181]

This beginning has a conventional character which belies a greater significance. The narrator brings the reader into his confidence by posing for him a very simple question: what is the origin of this book? In fact, this is an act of deliberate subterfuge, for there

----

[180]For an excellent review of the commentary on Ts'ao's literary technique, see the forthcoming article by John Wang, "The Chih-yen Chai Commentary and the Dream of the Red Chamber; a Literary Study".

[181]For text, see p. 47.

really is no answer to the reader's supposed question. There is of
course a fantastic tale about a silly block of stone and the details
are entertaining, but as we noted earlier in our review of the beginnings of Dream of the Red Chamber, there is an insistence that
the time, location, and authorship of the novel are unknown.
Ts'ao Hsueh-ch'in plays with conventional storyteller language and
formulae in this paragraph and, indeed, throughout the mythic
mode. He uses ordinary phraseology of traditional fiction to set
forth his unique vision of mythic experience. Besides the expression, "fantastic", which we discussed previously, the key words in
the above paragraph are "background", "misgivings", "details",
and "fascinating".

In the emphasis on "background", lai li, the author introduces a
false conception which dominates the minds of his protagonists.[182]
As we shall observe in our "Mimesis" chapter, there is the mistaken
notion that one only has to know the background story of a person
or event in order to fully understand. This is why persons such as
Chia Yu-ts'un develop all sorts of elaborate theories to establish
the causes of events. But just as knowledge of the origins of the
Stone does not explain Dream of the Red Chamber, the same knowledge does little to help us interpret the character of Chia Pao-yu.
Indeed, mythic information is true to its nature. That is, it per-
forms a service which is the reverse of illumination: in entertaining
us it leads us astray. As we become enamoured with the details of
the Stone Record, we completely forget the question of the origins
of the novel.

These formulaic expressions ought to be understood in terms of their
interrelationships. Huo,[183] "misgivings", is another word relating
to the theme of illusion (huan). We note that the conversation between the Stone and the Immortals ends with the Stone's question:
"I do not know what unique signs you are to engrave on me,
nor where I am to be carried. How about an explanation so
that I may have no misgivings?"[184]
The Stone's foolish blindness is exemplified in its desire to be re-
born on earth. But it cannot become enlightened (its huo cannot

----

[182]For a full discussion of lai li 來歷 and the views of Chen
Shih-yin, Chai Yu-ts'un, Leng Tzu-hsing, Chia Pao-yu, and Chen
Pao-yu, see "Mimesis" chapter, pp. 132-137, 145.
[183] 惑 or "doubts", "uncertainties", "suspicious".
[184]For text, see p. 48.

be assuaged) until it passes through earthly experience. Likewise,
the reader will be full of huo, "misgivings", until he is thoroughly
"familiar with the details" of the "fascinating" Dream of the Red
Chamber. He may be attracted by the entertaining notion that a
mythic account of background will give him an objective understanding of fiction, but critical enlightenment will not result until
he is intimate with every turn of phrase in Dream of the Red Chamber.
"Once you are familiar with the details you will find it utterly
fascinating"[185] is a statement of a constantly recurring theme in
the novel: interest and its concomitant, wisdom, result from the
intimate knowledge which flows from the experience of living (as
in the case of the Stone) or the experience of reading (as in the
case of the reader).

This pattern recurs in the denial of Chen Shih-yin's plea that he
might receive "explication in fine",[186] that is, that he might be
taught about "Cause and Effect", yin-kuo.[187] Here we gain insight into the meaning of hsuan chi, "Penumbra Mechanics", "the
secret of which may not be leaked in advance". Chen Shih-yin and
the Stone are rather similar in their impossible desires. The Stone
wishes to be informed of its experiences prior to its sojourn in the
Red Dust. Chen's request is ridiculous: he wants to be taught experience; but as the Immortals quite simply insist, he cannot know
what suffering is until he suffers.

In the address to the reader, which is the first paragraph of the
novel proper, the author introduces the mythic mode through a
special emphasis on ordinary storyteller language. Since the storyteller idiom is a basic part of the mythic mode, an appreciation of
its usage helps us understand the meaning of Dream of the Red
Chamber. We have observed the repetitious use of common words
such as "slope", hsien, "that day", tang-jih, and "misgivings",
huo. We have also noted the importance to the mythic mode of
"absurdity", huang-t'ang, and "background", lai li. In the
creation myth and the dream-vision of Chen Shih-yin, there are
other words and phrases which at first glance appear to be adventi-
tious but which, upon closer scrutiny, prove to be basic to Ts'ao's

----

185 細按則深有趣味.
186 備細一聞.
187 因果. The Buddhist principle of moral causality.

deliberate mythic technique.[188]

One example is the otherwise innocuous word, hsi,[189] meaning,
"to carry in the hand", "to take in hand", "to lead by the hand".
In the course of the conversation between the Buddhist Monk and
the Stone, this word appears repeatedly. The Stone initially pleads
to be "carried by the hand into the Red Dust".[190] The Immortals
agree to "carry [the Stone] by hand" so that it might enjoy itself on
earth,[191] and they promise to "carry [the Stone] by hand" to an
area of wealth and abundance.[192] Finally, the Stone requests
further information about where it is to be "carried by hand".[193]
It is not, of course, unusual that the word hsi is used since the
Stone is shrunk into the size of a fan pendant and quite naturally has
to be "carried by hand". It is, however, rare for such a consummate
stylist as Ts'ao Hsueh-ch'in not to vary his vocabulary. When we
ask ourselves what is the point of this somewhat boring repetition,
we discover that it has a stylistic and a thematic significance. The
very first sentence that Chen Shih-yin overhears the Taoist speak in
his dream-vision contains the "carry by hand" motif:

> "This Foolish Thing you have in your grasp--which way do
> you intend to take it?"[194]

We have noted that Ts'ao avoids directly drawing parallels between
episodes and he refuses to make transitions clear. However, by
the insertion of the word hsi in the sentence above the author indirectly reminds us of the origins of the Stone and the relation between the dream-vision and the creation myth. Through the casual
repetition of words Ts'ao lends muscularity and unity to his polysemous structure.

----

[188]Many other repetitious phrases may be meaningless, of course.
For example, the phrase, ". . . smiled and said", 笑道 hsiao
tao, which prefaces so much of the conversation in the mythic
passages, is usually little more than formulaic politeness. Such a
phrase does not necessarily tell us about the mood of the speaker,
although it can convey the weight of the statement which follows.

[189] 攜.

[190] 攜帶…得入紅塵.

[191] 我們便攜你去受享受享.

[192] 攜你到昌明隆盛之邦.

[193] 不知攜了弟子到何地方.

[194]For text, see p. 50.

There is also a thematic significance to the rhetorical expression, "hold in the hand", as evidenced in certain passages. After the Buddhist unfurls his magic arts and makes the slab of stone into a jade pendant, he places it in his palm and smiles.195   As in the Hebrew vision of God in the Book of Genesis, the Immortal pauses and contemplates his handiwork. This pause and the smile which ensues mark the supreme moment of Immortal condescension towards mortals in the novel.   The Stone must be handed over to the Beware Illusion Fairy in order that it may be cleared for its earthly sojourn.196 With such an emphasis on the omnipotence of the divinities, one may question whether even such an innocuous phrase as, "with the Stone within his sleeve",197 is fortuitous. While it is true that there are whole chapters in Dream of the Red Chamber which appear to be totally removed from myth, and while we have tried to indicate the limitations of that realm and some of the satire Ts'ao directs against it, the style of the mythic mode suggests the illimitable control and influence of the unknown. The force of this statement--and its ultimately positive significance--is brought home at the end of Dream of the Red Chamber when hsi becomes an image of reconciliation and harmony between the enlightened and the un-enlightened: Chen Shih-yin and Chia Yu-ts'un go off together "hand-in-hand" to contemplate the meaning of the novel.198

If we consider the Stone as a prototype of man, that is, as an original which is imitated in the figure of Pao-yu, we find that the creation myth presents a sardonic vision of humanity. Again, the language is deceptively simple:

One day while it was moaning and groaning, it happened to glimpse from afar a Buddhist and a Taoist coming along of unusual carriage and extraordinary spiritual aspect.199

We shall have occasion to comment on this sentence more fully later in our discussion. Our present interest is in the word "glimpse", chien.200 Momentous occasions, such as this one, typically begin with just such a casual glance. In chapter 1, the Reverend

195 那僧托於掌上, 笑道 ….
196HLMPSHCP, chap. 1, p. 6, lines 11-12: 你且同我到警幻仙子宮中將這蠢物交割清楚.
197 袖籠了這石.
198HLMPSHCP, chap. 120, p. 416, line 7: 兩人攜手而行.
199For text, see p. 47.
200 見.

Taoist Kosmo Kosmos happens to see the Stone beneath Blue-Channel Peak.[201] In chapter 120, Chia Yu-ts'un happens to glimpse his old friend, Chen Shih-yin, and this leads to a deep philosophical discussion.[202] Again in chapter 120, Kosmo Kosmos accidentally views the Stone beneath Blue-Channel Peak and thus learns of the ending of the Stone Record.[203] He also glimpses Ts'ao Hsueh-ch'in after learning of the latter through Chia Yu-ts'un and thus through a casual glimpse he finds an editor for the novel.[204]

The above quoted phrase recurs in Chen Shih-yin's dream encounter with the two Immortals in chapter 1:

> Suddenly he glimpsed in one direction a Buddhist Monk and
> a Taoist coming along and chatting together.[205]

The glimpse formula is, of course, a very regular narrative device and represents typical storyteller language. We draw attention to the expression because, in the mythic mode, Ts'ao appears to use this ordinary phrase frequently as a preface to a situation which tells us something about the nature of man. This is exemplified in Chen Shih-yin's plea to the Monk:

> "Penumbra Mechanics may not be leaked in advance, but
> whatever that 'Foolish Thing' is which was just discussed--
> how about a glimpse?"[206]

Chen is careful not to tread on the toes of Immortals by asking questions that are too fundamental. At the same time, he is naive enough to think that a "single glimpse"[207] of a divine symbol will be an enlightening experience. In fact, as in the case of all the above noted examples, the experience which follows the "glimpse" formula is as baffling as it is illuminating. In the brief glimpse which is allowed him, Chen only sees the enigmatic phrase written on the Stone: "Precious Jade for Penetrating the Numinous", and he arrives at the gateway of the Great Void Illusion Land before he can read the small print.

----

[201]HLMPSHCP, chap. 1, p. 3, line 8: 忽見大塊石上字跡分明⋯⋯

[202]ibid., chap. 120, p. 416, line 2: 只見一個道著.

[203]ibid., chap. 120, p. 418, line 5: 見那補天未用之石.

[204]ibid., chap. 120, p. 418, line 16, to p. 419, line 1: 見那曹雪芹先生.

[205]For text, see p. 50.

[206]For text, see p. 52.

[207]一見.

The Stone and Chen Shih-yin are similar in their accidental
visions of the divine. They are also parallel models of human behavior in their inability to control themselves in an encounter with
the supernatural. The narrator notes of the Stone:

> While it regretted being a coarse fool, it nevertheless could
> not resist sputtering out human words . . . .[208]

And of Chen Shih-yin he says:

> He could not resist coming forward and making a courteous
> sign.[209]

It is true, as we have just noted, that Chen changes his approach
when he learns that he is drawing near the sacred territory of
"Penumbra Mechanics":

> Shih-yin understood. It would be inopportune to inquire
> further.[210]

Nevertheless, what is important to observe is that he finds the opportunity to gain divine knowledge to be irresistible. The difference between his behavior and that of the Stone lies in Chen's
judicious application of that which he knows best, the code of
courtesy, to gain what he desires.

If Chen is a wiser figure than the Stone it is because he is about
to part from the Red Dust while the Stone is just beginning to yearn
for an experience of the same. Perhaps this fact explains why the

----

[208]For text, see p. 47.
Perhaps there is a touch of humor in the phrase, 不得已便口吐人言,
for Ts'ao may intend some irony in the fact that communication
between mythic beings is always relegated to human language. The
word t'u 吐 , "to spit", when combined with yen 言 , simply
means "to speak", but in the present context may have a slightly
ironical significance.
[209]For text, see p. 51.
[210]For text, see p. 51.
As we have noted earlier, in chapter 120 Chia Yu-ts'un withdraws
a similar question in his discussion with Chen Shih-yin about the
whereabouts of Pao-yu when Chia perceives that the answer to his
question would lead to the "Key of Transcendence" or the "Key to
Sylphdom", 仙機   hsien chi. Mortals like Chen Shih-yin and
Chia Yu-ts'un must refrain from approaching the "trigger mechanism"
(the key) to arcane knowledge.
HLMPSHCP, chap. 120, p. 417, line 3: 雨村···知仙機也不
便問.

Stone cannot help speaking--any words at all will do--while Chen is very perspicacious. At any rate, what we have in the Stone's garrulousness and Chen Shih-yin's reticence is an accent on what we might call the "human language" theme in the novel, a theme which is introduced in the Preface of chapter 1 in which the author elaborates on the chapter heading of chapter 1.[211]

A final example of the repetition of language in the mythic mode is found in the following passage in which the Stone's distinctive desire for pleasure is identified:

As the Stone listened, worldly desires were unconsciously aroused, and it longed to go among mortals to savor their splendor and riches.[212]

The words fan hsin, "mortal thoughts", "common desires", or "worldly desires"[213] and hsiang, "to savor" or "to enjoy",[214] reappear in the creation myth. The Stone tells the Immortals it wishes to "enjoy" itself for several years in the Red Dust.[215] And when they realize that it is aflame with "worldly desire", they know they must bear it to the Red Dust "to enjoy" itself.[216] In Chen Shih-yin's dream-vision, the Buddhist Monk tells of the Divine Crystal Page[217] who is burning with "worldly desire" to be reborn in the Red Dust.

In addition to these recurring phrases, actions, and ideas of a simple variety (see Appendix B for a survey of Formulaic Narrative

----

[211]That heading, which appears to mean, "Mr. Chia Yu-ts'un, Fallen on Evil Days, Longs for Boudoir Beauty", actually puns with the literal meaning, "Mr. Fictive Language and Vulgar Words, in Wind and Dust, Longs for Boudoir Beauty". For a full explanation of this heading, see Preface discussion in "Persona" chapter, pp. 208-217.

[212]For text, see p. 47.

[213] 凡心.

[214]An interesting phrase when one speculates that in the classical language, hsiang 享 is frequently linked with imperial activity, as in hsiang kuo 享國 .

[215] 受享幾年. Perhaps pointing to the few short years Pao-yu has in the Red Dust.

[216] 受享受享.

[217]Ts'ao leaves vague the connection between the Stone and the Divine Crystal Page.

Patterns and Narrative Techniques in Dream of the Red Chamber), [218]
there are two major formulaic elements introduced in the mythic
mode of chapter 1 which dominate the novel: synchronicity and
the fool.

"Synchronicity" is a perception of time which the psychologist
C.G. Jung finds in the I Ching, the Book of Changes. According
to Jung, synchronicity is:

> . . . a concept that formulates a point of view diametrically
> opposed to that of causality. Since the latter is a merely
> statistical truth and not absolute, it is a sort of working hypo-
> thesis of how events evolve one out of another, whereas
> synchronicity takes the coincidence of events in space and
> time as meaning something more than mere chance, namely, a
> peculiar interdependence of objective events among them-
> selves as well as with the subjective (psychic) states of the
> observer or observers. [219]

We wish to adapt Jung's theory of synchronicity to help us be aware
of the stress on acausal relationships in Dream of the Red Chamber.
Thus, we identify synchronicity as "meaningful chance": the vital
stylistic and thematic feature of the novel whereby the coincidental
juxtaposition of seemingly unrelated states is significant.

Before undertaking to demonstrate how Ts'ao Hsueh-ch'in uses
narrative formulae to embody this concept of time, we might point
out that there has been some confusion among readers concerning
time in Dream of the Red Chamber, with the result that the novel is
sometimes mistakenly considered to be loosely organized. In drawing comparisons between Ts'ao Hsueh-ch'in's work, the fiction of
Galsworthy and Dickens, and various western episodic novels of
manners of the eighteenth century, one critic has recently suggested
that in certain respects "The Dream of the Red Chamber is one of

----

[218]Other repeated motifs: ch'i 奇, "rare", applied to the jade
gem or to the Stone Record; chen-chia 真假, "true" and "false";
huan 幻, "illusion"; kan ching 乾淨, the theme of "purity";
pao-wu 寶物, a "treasure" such as Pao-yu.

[219]See Jung's Foreword to The I Ching, trans. Richard Wilhelm,
Third Edition, Princeton, 1967, p. xxiv. See too, "Synchronicity:
An Acausal Connecting Principle", The Structure and Dynamics of
the Psyche, in The Collected Works of C.G. Jung, Sir Herbert
Read, Michael Fordham, Gerhard Adler, eds. R.F.C. Hull, trans.
vol. 8. New York, 1960. pp. 417-519.

those 'large, loose baggy monsters' that Henry James decried."220
We hope that our study of myth, mimesis, and persona demonstrates
that Dream of the Red Chamber ought not to be classed with "large
loose, baggy monsters" and that indeed the style, structure, and
themes of the novel form together an unmistakable aesthetic pattern.
However, it is possible to ignore the latter if one fails to trace the
"by chance" formula in Dream of the Red Chamber.221
    Several passages in the creation myth and the dream-vision of
Chen Shih-yin reveal the dominance of circumstance and the importance of the acausal relationship between chance events. "Who
would have known", asks the anonymous narrator of the creation
myth, that the Stone would "wail and moan night and day?" In
fact, anyone would expect the Stone, "imbued with a divine spiritual nature", to feel remorse over its rejection. These lines remind
us of Ishmael's statement in the first chapter of Moby Dick that
when he looked ahead life was all a matter of free will, but when

----

220Mary Gregory Knoerle, SP, The Dream of the Red Chamber,
p. 53. See too Sister Knoerle's dissertation,"A Critical Analysis
of the Dream of the Red Chamber in Terms of Western Novelistic
Criteria", p. 161.
    Chuang Hsin-cheng, "Themes of Dream of the Red Chamber: A
Comparative Interpretation", p. 138, finds a varied use of time in
the novel: it stands still; it is whiled away; each individual has
his own concept of time; there is recurring time in the many festivals and birthdays which repeat themselves; time is deliberately
obscured to hide autobiographical features; finally, there is a
sense of timelessness and a correspondent lack of suspense.
    However, if the dominant role of the framework were understood,
this variety of "times" would be seen to fall into a consistent pattern of synchronicity.
    221To dismiss the importance of circumstance in the lives of
others is to forget its importance in one's own life. P'an Ch'ung-
kuei somewhat humorously notes that Hu Shih insisted that Ch'eng
Wei-yuan and Kao E were lying when they claimed to have discovered, "by chance", lost manuscripts of an 120 chapter text of
Hung-lou meng in marketplaces, but Hu Shih himself enjoyed "by
chance" discoveries of several manuscripts of Chinese literature
likewise in market places! See P'an Ch'ung-kuei, "Hung-hsueh
wu-shih-nien", p. 7.

he looked back he saw that it was all predestination. An analogous, but by no means identical, viewpoint recurs in Dream of the Red Chamber. An event which initially appears to have fortuitously developed and to possess an autonomous freedom is subsequently discovered to be rooted in destiny. The unexpected desire of the Stone for earthly reborn is the fated fulfillment of its divine origins.

Other words and phrases beside "who would have known" are clues to the hidden significance of circumstantial occurances.[222] The Stone "happens suddenly to glimpse"[223] the two Immortals one day and thus is luckily "rescued" from its lamentable plight. It "happens to overhear"[224] the conversation between the Buddhist and Taoist with the result that it learns of the Red Dust and its desire is aroused. Again this seems to be part of a divine plan. The Stone ought not to yearn for the Red Dust, but once it "accidentally" overhears the conversation of Immortals, desire is doomed to be insurmountable.

Similarly profound events take place in the life of Chen Shih-yin in a similarly haphazard fashion. He happens to be in his study on a hot summer's day, so quite naturally he becomes drowsy and falls asleep. But naturalness is only a surface appearance, and the reader of Dream of the Red Chamber is well prepared for the fact that a mystical experience and a unique perception are about to occur, for Chen's dream is prefaced by the phrase, "unconsciously" ("before he knew it").[225] That is, he accidentally slips into his dream-vision without being aware. The day is innocently described as being, "one long intensely hot summer's day", but as Chih-yen Chai notes, this is really an exceptional day, for "hot days are not many".[226] Like the Stone, Chen Shih-yin happens to "suddenly see"[227] two Immortals in his dream-vision and to overhear their conversation and thus he accidentally gains access to divine information.[228]

----

[222]shei chih 誰知 . The use of this narrative cliché reflects the author's desire not to make a situation too clear--not to spell out the meaningfulness of coincidence and chance.

[223]o chien 俄見 .

[224]shih wen 適聞 .

[225]pu chueh 不覺 .

[226]CYCHLMCP, chap. 1, p. 11, chia-hsu chia-p'i: 熱日無多.

[227]hu-chien 忽見 .

[228]After listening for a long time to the two Immortals, Chen Shih-yin admits to them that he "happened to overhear" their conversation, 適聞 shih wen.

In the story of the Divine Crystal Page and the Crimson Pearl
Sylph Herb which unfolds in Chen Shih-yin's dream-vision, we find
that the same sort of language is used to characterize accidental
change which is fraught with significance. Thus, just at the moment
when the Crimson Pearl Sylph Herb is longing to requite the Divine
Crystal Page, the latter affords the former an opportunity when it
"luckily"[229] and "accidentally",[230] as it were, desires to be born
in the Red Dust.

In our "Mimesis" chapter, we shall observe that the "realistic"
layer of Dream of the Red Chamber is rich with allusions to the relation between circumstances and destiny.[231]   Nearly every event
in the lives of Chen Shih-yin and Chia Yu-ts'un, Chen Pao-yu and
Chia Pao-yu, is prefaced by some word or phrase which stresses the
element of chance, luck, or surprise.[232]   Ts'ao Hsueh-ch'in presents his sense of time by embodying it within a specific stylistic
pattern.   Protagonists suffer because their destinies always appear
in the guise of chance while readers are mesmerized by the language
of chance into believing that Dream of the Red Chamber lacks a
coherent form and style.   Actually, synchronicity is a key unifying
device in the novel and serves to establish the theme of complementary opposites.[233]   A "by chance" sentence or an offhanded
remark is usually a clue that a situation is important or that it will
gain importance at some point later in the novel.   As Chih-yen Chai
notes of the union of Chiao-hsing[234] (a servant girl of Chen Shih-
yin) and Chia Yu-ts'un, it is the chance glance of the maid which
leads to her marriage with an official.[235]

----

[229]ch'ia 恰.
[230]ou 偶.
[231]See "Mimesis" for a review of "by chance", especially in
chapter 103 of the novel.
[232]For an outline of examples of synchronicity--"meaningful
chance"--throughout the novel, see Appendix C.   Terms such as,
"by chance", "who would expect", etc., are common in numerous
other novels, dramas, and ballads, and in narrative literature in
general.   Our view is that Ts'ao uses ordinary phraseology in a
subtle and unique manner in Dream of the Red Chamber.
[233]The Theme of complementary opposites is discussed at length
in "Mimesis".
[234] 嬌杏.
[235]CYCHLMCP, chap. 2, p. 25, chia-hsu chia-p'i:僥倖也. 託
言當日了頭回顧,故有今日,亦不過偶然僥倖耳,非真實
得塵中英傑也.

Another formulaic feature which deceives the reader by appearing
to have merely a casual significance is the fool symbol. In "Mimesis",
we shall give some attention to Chen Shih-yin's use of the vocabulary of foolishness to characterize himself--such usage indicates his
self-awareness and symbolizes his need for spiritual enlightenment.
The Stone is also cognizant of its foolishness, but in an entirely different sense. Because it is rejected by Nu-kua, it is embarrassed to
address the Buddhist Monk and it regrets being a "coarse fool".[236]
When the Stone does speak to the Immortal, it calls itself a "foolish
thing".[237]   Immediately, however, it makes a humorous attempt
to qualify this epithet:

"Although in substance I am only a coarse fool, my nature
    partakes of some spirituality".[238]

The words "substance", chih,[239] "coarse", ts'u,[240] and "some",
shao,[241] are both used and abused by the Monk in his reply to the
Stone:

"One may say your nature partakes of a divine spirit, yet
you are also a plain fool. Moreover, there is nothing about
you which would indicate you are rare or precious--you're

The story is that one day while Chia Yu-ts'un is visiting Chen Shih-
yin, the maid happens to glance at Chia. Her face is thus accidentally inscribed in his memory. One day some time later, and
after he has passed the Civil Service Examinations, it is his turn to
"happen to glance" at the maid while she is buying thread. While
she is no longer at Chen Shih-yin's home, Chia happens to recognize her. He subsequently procures her as his concubine, and when
his first wife dies, the maid becomes Chia's wife. As Chih-yen
Chai observes, the present day good fortune originates in the glance
of a former day.
    236 粗 蠢.
    237 蠢 物.
    238 弟子質雖粗蠢, 性卻稍通.
Chen-yeh Chai here remarks: "How dare? How dare?" For text
see p. 47. CYCHLMCP, chap. 1, p. 3, chia-hsu chia-p'i. The
Stone is not talented enough to repair heaven, nor should it talk
with Immortals, but it does so anyway.
    239 質.
    240 粗.
    241 稍.

just a stepping stone, and that's about it!"[242]
In these two passages we have an instance of Ts'ao's impish humor
which pervades the mythic mode. Whether the Immortals are talking with the mythical Stone or with Chen Shih-yin, everyone is
overly polite with the result that everyone is insulting. Here the
Buddhist Monk is careful not to use the word shao, "slightly", in
speaking of the Stone's nature: he pretends to give the Stone full
credit for being a "divine spirit", whereas the Stone only says it is
"slightly" imbued with spirituality. Yet the Monk cannot help remarking that the Stone is "also a plain fool" and a "stepping stone".
Note too that the Monk adds another satirical touch by giving chih
an epithetical usage. Thus he changes the Stone's "although in
substance I am only a coarse fool", to an adjectival expression,
"you are also a plain fool". By using chih as an adjective,[243] in
the sense of "plain", the Monk appears to ignore the Stone's meaning of chih, "substance" or "essence". Here we should also observe
that in Chen Shih-yin's dream-vision the Immortals humorously re-
vert to using the self-deprecating vocabulary the Stone originally
used in speaking of itself. The Taoist asks the Monk about "this
Foolish Thing"[244] he is carrying, that is, the Stone. But in this
instance the Immortals are talking about the Stone rather than to it,
and so they have temporarily abandoned their code of courtesy.

Whenever we find an Immortal in Dream of the Red Chamber making a special effort to pun on a particular word, we are usually
correct to assume that that word is of special significance. We may
expand our understanding of chih by remarking upon another one of
the Monk's disparaging comments made in reference to the Stone
even after the latter had become a jade gem:

   "You have become a precious thing in form, but you still
   lack any genuine sign of merit. Several characters must be
   incised upon you so that as soon as people see you they will
   know you are rare and marvellous".[245]
Several words of symbolic significance are brought together in this
passage. The jade is a pao-wu, "precious thing",[246] an epithet

---

242For text see pp. 47 - 48.
   243An alternative grammatical analysis: 質 蠢 "by nature
foolish", 性 急 "by temperament panicky".
   244 這 蠢 物.
245For text, see p. 48.
   246 寶 物.

which is commonly applied to Pao-yu, who is regarded by his grandmother and others as a pao-wu, "precious thing" or "precious treasure". The question which this passage suggests is: what really is a
pao-wu? An important phrase is, then, shih-tsai,[247] here translated as "genuine", but which implies that which is "really", "in
fact", or "actually" so. At this point in the myth, the Stone has a
"substance", chih, which is "coarse" and "foolish", if not down-
right "plain", and a "nature", hsing,[248] which is "slightly" imbued
with spirituality. And now after the Monk displays his magic arts
and transforms the Stone, it has a precious gem "form", hsing.[249]
It is vital that we observe that all three elements are in some sense
imperfect or found wanting.

In this combination of significant terminology we have Ts'ao's
comment on the nature of man together with a criticism of divinity.
Without the engraved characters, the Stone is "really" of a divine
nature and a precious form. But this is only in the divine realm.
Only with the incised writing will the Stone appear to mortals to be
"really" of merit.[250] Ironically, the substance, nature, and form
which originate in heaven are found imperfect by the divinities who
dwell there, and, at the same time, the divinities realize that these
same elements would not be appreciated on earth. In other words,
in what sense does the divine realm represent the ideal in the novel?

The mythic world is full of all sorts of imperfections, many of
which we have already observed. It is true that at the end of the
novel, Chen Shih-yin reports that the jade (Pao-yu) has parted

----

247 實在.
248 性.
249 形.

250The phrase, "as soon as people see you they will know you
are rare and marvellous", 使人一見便知是奇物方妙,
according to Chih-yen Chai raises the theme of "true" and "false".
The world only values or accords with that which is actually unreal or untrue. Chih-yen Chai finds very believable the popular
saying that one may sell three thousand falsehoods in a single day,
but not be able to sell one truth in three days. CYCHLMCP,
chap. 1, p. 4, chia-hsu chia-p'i: 世上原宜假,不宜真也.
諺曰:一日賣了三千假,三日賣不出一個真.信哉.
Apparently, the allegorical meaning of the phrase is that without
the written Stone Record, the meaning of the Stone will go unnoticed.

from the world and that "form and substance have returned to their unity".[251]   Here we interpret hsing to mean the manifestation of the pure Stone spirit in the body of Pao-yu, and chih to mean the original essence of Pao-yu in the spirit of the Stone. But such a metaphysical construct is but another example of supernatural machinery. It does not inform us about Ts'ao's view of the nature of man or the nature of divinity.

In the trinity of heavenly elements one feature is yet missing: the bodily form of Pao-yu, the "precious jade" of Dream of the Red Chamber. One might easily argue that all the imperfections of that form are inherent in the fusion of the three divine ingredients. Like the Stone, the most common epithets applied to Pao-yu are words meaning "foolish", "crazy", "silly", "naive", and "idiotic".[252]   And like the Stone, his idiocy is the key to his glory, as well as to his shame.

One indication of the limitations of the mythic world is the humor that is directed against it. While the divinities do "giggle like idiots"[253] at the foolishness of the Stone (and thus partake of the "idiot" symbolism), they themselves are not paradigms of self-control. When they first enter the mythic world, they are described in the following terms:

Now speaking, now smiling, they arrived at the base of
Blue-Channel Peak, sat themselves down beside the Stone,
and began to chat in a gay bantering fashion.[254]

Their light easy manner is an attribute of those who are enlightened and readily contrasts to the Stone's anxious desire for experience.[255] At the same time, enlightenment does not protect them from the manipulations of others. The Stone pretends that it "doesn't know its manners",[256] but if anything, it is excessively polite. "Surely", it remarks to the two Immortals, "you have the material to repair Heaven".[257]   Its courtesy is both extreme and humorous. The

----

[251]HLMPSHCP, chap. 120, p. 416, line 14: 形質歸一．
[252]癡；蠢；傻；獃；瘋；
[253]戀敢．
[254]For text, see p. 47.
[255]For a similar example of a contrast in mood and manner between the enlightened and the unenlightened, see our analysis of the meeting between Chen Shih-yin and Chia Yu-ts'un (chapter 103) in "Mimesis".
[256]For text, see p. 47.
[257]For text, see p. 47.

highest compliment it can pay to the Immortals is to tell them that they can do what it cannot--repair heaven. But this is a task which the Stone is entirely willing to leave to someone else, as it is now interested in enjoying the earth. While the Stone's praise is silly-- the Immortals express no interest in the condition of the Firmament-- it is also effective, for it succeeds in getting the divinities to carry it to the Red Dust. Here the phrase "to repair Heaven",[258] is an example of Ts'ao's style whereby a repeated cliché takes on a new meaning with a shift of context. Originally the phrase signifies to the Stone its frustrations in heaven; in this new context it signifies its earthly ambition. Similarly, the initially relaxed manner and mood of the Immortals ("the two Immortals realized there was no forcing the Stone") disappear momentarily in the dream-vision when Chen Shih-yin starts to read what is inscribed on the jade gem:

> Just when he wanted to look closely, the Buddhist Monk said they had already arrived at Illusion Realm and he forcibly snatched away the jade from Chen's hand.[259]

In a pinch, Immortals can act all too humanly.

Clearly, while human nature and the divine character are some-times lightheartedly indulged in the mythic mode, its meaning is radically ironic.[260] There is a crack in the firmament of heaven and the Stone of divine origins is imperfect. The refining processes of heaven are not sufficient. Like Pao-yu and Tai-yu and their mythic counterparts, the Divine Crystal Page and the Crimson Pearl Sylph Herb, the Stone must undergo the searing experience of the Red Dust before it will be "pure", kan ching.[261] There is no happiness in the divine realm. The Stone wishes to be taken to the mortal world, the Divine Crystal Page longs to pass through "illusory involvement", huan yuan,[262] while the Crimson Pearl Sylph Herb is fond of wandering beyond the protective confines of the Heaven

----

258 補天.

259For text, see p. 52.

260The word pu is interestingly ambiguous. Kao E is said to have pu, "repaired", the unfinished novel for publication purposes. As C.T. Hsia, observes, pu may also mean "to emend and redact" or "to complete". Classic, The Classic Chinese Novel, p. 367, note 13. Therefore, does pu t'ien 補天 in the Nu-kua myth mean "to repair", "to emend and redact", or "to complete" Heaven?

261 乾淨.

262 幻緣.

of Parting Sorrow. Were it not for the fact that the Herb is nour-
ished by the dew of the Page, it would die.

If the divine realm is defective, the Immortals are bound to be
less than ideal forms. The Buddhist Monk needs magic to convert
the raw material of a stone block into a jade gem. He and the
Taoist are extremely opportunistic and, like mortals, they are subject to volatile emotions such as desire and contempt.[263] While
they deride the Stone's longing for re-birth and they sigh over its
importunity, they are unable to deny it the experience it desires.
Their limitations are indicated by their lack of influence. The
Stone of divine origins is not at all interested in hearing a discussion
about esoteric subjects such as "Cloud and Mountain", "Fog and
Sea", "Divinity and Sylph", "Mystery and Illusion". What really
attracts it is the "Splendor and Riches" which mortals enjoy in the
Red Dust.

With so much trouble in paradise, the question with which the
creation myth begins can only be rhetorical:

> Now who would have known that this single Stone, after
> being wrought and refined, thence imbued with a divine
> spiritual nature, would blame and pity itself, and wail and
> moan night and day, when it saw that the mass of stone
> slabs had all been utilized and that it alone was unworthy
> of selection?[264]

The phrase, "imbued with a divine spiritual nature", ling-hsing i-
t'ung,[265] reminds us of the four characters engraved upon the jade
pendant which hangs from Pao-yu's neck, "Precious Jade for Penetrating the Numinous", t'ung-ling pao-yu.[266] In heaven the Stone
is t'ung, "pervaded by", "penetrated with", or "imbued with"
ling, "divine nature", thus allowing Pao-yu (symbolized in the jade
pendant) to t'ung ling, "penetrate the numinous".[267] In other
words, as we noted earlier in our discussion of meaningful chance,

----

263The Taoist asks the Monk: ". . . which way do you intend
to take it [the Stone]?"--thus suggesting divine desire to manipulate
the Stone.

264For text, see p. 47.

265 靈性已通，

266 通靈寶玉，

267Chih-yen Chai's commentary calls attention to the ineffable
nature of this spirituality. CYCHLMCP, chap. 1, p. 3, chia-hsu
chia-p'i: 煅煉後性方通，甚哉人生不能學也。

everyone should expect the Stone to feel keenly its rejection. Only Immortals anticipate that the Stone should stay forever in the state of wu,[268] "non-being" or "non-becoming", at the base of Blue-Channel Peak in the heavenly realm. They do not perceive that once perfection is unrecognized, the divine spirit of the Stone can only be subject to yu,[269] "being" or "becoming", that is, the desire to be born which causes rebirth .[270]

We have observed that the supposedly "superficial allegorical veneer" of the creation myth and the dream-vision is a literary mode which is complex in style and varied in meaning. The Allegory of the Stone engenders a number of "beginnings" in chapter 1 which in turn establishes the polysemous structure of Dream of the Red Chamber. At its simplest level, the mythic mode provides a fairy tale background replete with mysterious names, divine machinery, didactic moral views, wizardry, and magical events. This world is complicated by the presence of otherworldly figures who act in a strangely legalistic and opportunistic fashion. Stranger still, as the ubiquitous commentator, Chih-yen Chai points out, this simple apologue may also be read as a symbolic autobiography of Ts'ao Hsueh-ch'in. When we proceed beyond the simple casual tone of surface appearance to the intention of the mythic mode, we find that the style is no longer dogmatic or flippant. We come to consider the novel as mythic fiction and we discover the unifying power and figurative configuration of narrative formulae, synchronic time, and symbols. Improbable magic machinery evolves into a satire directed against the world and an ironic vision of heaven and man.

Perhaps the true thrust of the mythic mode is best revealed in the rhetorical question cited above. Ts'ao does not really intend for myth and allegory to resolve problems but to present them. We find that many of the questions posed are not answerable in terms of myth, and where the attempt is made, we remain dissatisfied with the solution. Thus, for example, when the two Immortals agree to carry the Stone to the Red Dust and warn it not to complain when it becomes dissatisfied, it replies, "naturally, naturally", tzu-jan, tzu-jan.[271] This expression is a rhetorical formula in Dream of the Red Chamber which invariably has an ambiguous meaning. The question

---

268 無 .

269 有 .

270See note 99, above, for a reference to the translation of wu and yu.

271 自然 自然 .

is, what is "natural"? The Stone seems to mean that he will "naturally" be grateful to the Immortals for helping him to get to the
Red Dust, and if things turn out badly, there will be no regrets. It
is "natural" to be grateful. But in the light of the fact that everything produces its opposite (see "mimesis"), tzu-jan could mean
that the Stone is aware its enjoyment will "naturally" turn to pain,
and "naturally" one must be stoical about the inevitable. In
"Persona" we shall note that in the final chapter of the novel, Chia
Yu-ts'un asks Chen Shih-yin whether the futures of the Ning-kuo
and Jung-kuo mansions will be happy, and Chen replies that good
and bad fortune follow a given pattern. He predicts that the Chia
family will be restored, and that this is "natural law".[272]   But
Chen does not mean that "natural law" is necessarily a positive
good for man, for after restoration decline "naturally" follows. The
perennial problem of mortals in the novel (from the view of Immortals) is that they continually take "natural" for "good".[273] Again,
when the Stone inquires what characters are to be incised upon itself, the Immortals evade the question by answering that soon the
Stone will "naturally understand". This brief but ambiguous phrase
actually points to the entire process of enlightenment in the novel.
One will "naturally" understand, that is, only after one has passed
through the "natural" pattern of mutability in the Red Dust, and
only if one is endowed with supernatural sensitivity.
     The fundamental irony of the mythic mode is the contradiction
between form and content. Surface appearances not withstanding,
and understanding of the former does not help us to account for the
latter. Earlier we observed that a knowledge of "background",
lai li, does not render a satisfactory explanation of the origins of
Dream of the Red Chamber or of the character of Pao-yu. What do
myth and dream really tell us of origins? We learn that the Stone
is somehow imperfect, the Crimson Pearl Sylph Herb is unhappy, the
Divine Crystal Page wishes to be re-born on earth, and that lovers
must suffer, but we are never told why. By suggesting through the
mythic mode that imperfection, unhappiness, desire, and suffering
are "natural", that is, both inevitable and unaccountable, and by
denying any normal sense of "real", Ts'ao Hsueh-ch'in creates the
painful vision that both the heavenly and the human condition are
ultimately meaningless and absurd.

----

272 也是自然的道理.
273See HLMPSHCP, chap. 120, p. 417, line 8.

Mimesis:
the Realistic Mode

We now turn to the mimetic mode of Dream of the Red Chamber which is first presented in the framework story of Chen Shih-yin[1] and Chia Yu-ts'un.[2]   While these characters play significant roles in a mere seven of the one hundred and twenty chapters of the novel,[3] Ts'ao Hsueh-ch'in sets forth and develops his theme of "opposites" through their contrary personalities.   In the interplay between "Mr. True (Chen Shih-yin) and "Mr. False" (Chia Yu-ts'un), and the homophones chen[4] and chia,[5] "true" and "false", "real" and "unreal", we discover the symbolic meaning of Dream of the Red Chamber.   A knowledge of this mimetic level is indispensable to an understanding of the form and content of the novel.

At the outset of our discussion we need to point out that Ts'ao

----

1 甄士隱.

2 賈雨村.

[3]Chen Shih-yin is of central importance in chapters 1, 103, and 120. He appears briefly in chapter 104. Chia Yu-ts'un plays a major role in chapters 1, 2, 3, 4, 103, 104, and 120. He is briefly mentioned in chapters 32, 33, 48, 72, 82, 92, and 107.

4 真.

5 假.

Hsueh-ch'in qualifies the "realistic" mode of the novel by juxtaposing it to the mythic and narrative modes. We have identified
Chen Shih-yin and Chia Yu-ts'un as belonging to the mimetic mode
because they are the first individuals we meet in the novel who may
be called "true to life", that is, in this world, life-like, non mythic
characters. By giving the reader detailed factual information about
the biographies and lives of these characters, Ts'ao attempts to
make them "mimetic", that is, faithful imitations of reality.
    At the same time, as the following discussion will make clear,
there is no character and no moment in Dream of the Red Chamber
which can be identified as belonging wholly to a single mode.
While Chen Shih-yin and Chia Yu-ts'un are presented on the realistic level, they are directly linked with the philosophical and religious layers of the novel so that they may be equally considered to
be archetypal or symbolic characters. Furthermore, their meaning
is completely understood only when they are viewed in relation to
the personae of the narrator which make up the narrative mode of
Dream of the Red Chamber. We should keep in mind that in the
last pages of the novel, the final history of the Stone Record is af-
fected by the relationship between Chen Shih-yin, Chia Yu-ts'un,
the Reverend Taoist Kosmo Kosmos, and Ts'ao Hsueh-ch'in. In
other words, in chapter 120, we find a union of the mythic, mimetic,
and narrative modes.
    The reader of our "Myth" chapter will recall that Ts'ao Hsueh-
ch'in does not present the mythic layer of the novel in a continuous
narrative. Since the mimetic mode is similarly and deliberately
fragmented, a brief review of the Chen Shih-yin Chia Yu-ts'un plot
should prove helpful for discussion.
    The whole of Chen Shih-yin's life prior to his religious enlighten-
ment unfolds in chapter 1. He is a minor gentry gentleman[6] of
fifty years age who leads a quiet simple life with his wife and three
year old daughter, Ying-lien,[7] in the area of the wealthy southern
city of Su-chou.[8] Next door to Chen Shih-yin is the Bottle-Gourd

----

6 鄉官.
7 英蓮 is her "milk name", 乳名.
[8]HLMPSHCP, chap. 1, p. 5, reads: 有處曰姑蘇, 有城曰
閶門, that is, Ku-su refers to Su-chou (Wu-hsien) and the city
gate mentioned is the northwestern gate of Su-chou, the center of
city life.

Temple[9] in which dwells the impoverished would-be literocrat, Chia Yu-ts'un.[10] When Chen learns of Chia's scholarly ambitions, he gives the latter financial assistance, thus enabling Chia to travel to the Capital to take the imperial Civil Service Examinations. While Chia Yu-ts'un is away, Chen Shih-yin's life undergoes drastic change. In a dream, he learns of the existence of a jade stone which has been discarded from heaven and which contains secrets for the avoidance of suffering. He receives little enlightenment from his dream and when he awakes, he is further troubled by the presence of a Buddhist monk and a Taoist who warn him that his daughter is ill-fated. Later, during the Lantern Festival[11] (in mid-autumn), Ying-lien is kidnapped. Two months later, the Bottle-Gourd Temple burns to the ground and with it the home of Chen Shih-yin. Thenceforth he suffers poverty and ill health until just before his death he is enlightened about the vanity of human existence by another limping, mad Taoist who is hardly distinguishable from the one who appeared earlier. As chapter 1 closes, Chen Shih-yin and the Taoist vanish together. He does not appear again in the novel until chapters 103, 104, and 120, where he serves as a medium of enlightenment for Chia Yu-ts'un.

In chapter 2, Chia Yu-ts'un returns to Ku-su (Su-chou) and takes a servant of Chen Shih-yin as his concubine. Chia has received an official appointment as a result of his success in the Capital Examinations, but he is soon dismissed because of a charge of corruption. He then becomes the tutor of Lin Tai-yu. During a country excursion, Chia meets Leng Tzu-hsing,[12] a shop owner from the Capital, from whom he learns about his illustrious distant "relatives", the Chia clan and its branches, the Ning-kuo[13] and the Jung-kuo.[14]

In chapter 3, when Tai-yu's mother dies, her father bids Chia Yu-ts'un to take Tai-yu to live with her mother's relatives, who are

----

[9]hu-lu miao 葫蘆廟 . This may refer to the hu-lu, attribute of one of the Pa-hsien (Eight Immortals). See Richard Wilhelm, Chinesische Märchen, Düsseldorf-Köln, 1958, p. 71.

[10]Chia Yu-ts'un is first described in HLMPSHCP, chap. 1, p. 8. "Literocrat" was coined by C. C. Wang, "Chinese Literature", Chambers' Encyclopedia, III (New York, 1950), p. 491.

11 團圓之節.
12 冷子興.
13 寧國.
14 榮國.

members of the same Chia clan about whom Chia Yu-ts'un has already heard. It happens that the Emperor has decided to pardon all
officials formerly removed from office. Chia Yu-ts'un uses his new
freedom and the occasion of his visit to the Chia household to secure
a government position through the auspices of Chia Cheng,[15] scion
of the Jung-kuo branch of the Chia family and the father of Pao-yu.

We next encounter Chia Yu-ts'un in chapter 4. There he acts as
judge in the murder trial of Hsueh P'an,[16] the brother of Hsueh
Pao-ch'ai,[17] the maiden whom Pao-yu eventually marries. Hsueh
P'an has killed a man named Feng Yuan[18] in a dispute over buying
Ying-lien (Chen Shih-yin's daughter has been kidnapped and is now
a slave girl). Since the Hsueh family members are guests and also
relatives of the Jung-kuo branch of the Chia family, Yu-ts'un ex-
onerates Hsueh P'an, who is guilty of homicide, in an effort to
curry favor with Chia Cheng.

After this episode, Chia Yu-ts'un does not make an appearance in
the novel until chapter 103, although occasional references are
made to him in some six chapters.[19] In chapter 103 he meets a
Taoist monk in a dilapidated temple whom he believes is his old patron, Chen Shih-yin, but the latter replies to Chia's pedestrian
questions with enigmatic mystical jargon. When Chia leaves the
temple, it suddenly catches fire and no trace of Chen can be found
in the ashes. This is a minor incident, but since it directly relates
to the final chapter of the novel, chapter 120, we may regard chapter 103 as part of the framework of Dream of the Red Chamber.

In chapter 120, the narrative returns to the story of Chia Yu-ts'un
and Chen Shih-yin and the framework of the novel is complete.
Once again Chia meets Chen at the site where they met previously
(in chapter 103), the ford of Rapid Flow River.[20] Now Chen has
become a saintly otherworldly figure from whom Chia seeks instruc-

----

15 賈政.
16 薛蟠.
17 薛寶釵.
18 馮淵.
[19] Brief references to him occur in chapters 32, 33, 72, 82, 92,
104, and 107.
20 急流津. 急流 is from the familiar idiom, 急流勇退
"courageous retreat while in rapid flow", meaning the sudden awareness or enlightenment that is accomplished with courageous effort.

tion. Chen proceeds, again using enigmatic language, to lecture
on tao, karma, love and illusion, reality and unreality. He links
the hero Pao-yu with the precious jade stone which the goddess
Nu-kua discarded when she was repairing the vault of heaven.
This final episode serves as a summary of the plot of the novel and
as a kind of philosophical commentary on its content. In its otherworldly mystical content, it is a palinode to a story of romantic
passion. It represents one of the most exquisite moments in Dream
of the Red Chamber and will receive our close consideration.

   With the preceding outline in mind, we may examine Ts'ao Hsueh-
ch'in's imaginative presentation of his theme through a close textual
analysis of the mimetic story of Chen Shih-yin and Chia Yu-ts'un.
As we initiate our study, we recall that that story begins immediately
after the mythic account of the origins of the Stone and the Stone
Record in chapter 1:

   With the origins now clear, let us see what story is on the
   Stone. According to the writings on the Stone, it is related
   that 21

Ts'ao proceeds to introduce first Chen Shih-yin, and later in the
same chapter, Chia Yu-ts'un. The author thus deliberately marks
the beginning of the mimetic layer of the novel. In this "imitation
of reality", we encounter the first earthly figures in Dream of the
Red Chamber. Ts'ao may have an ironic intention in using Chen
Shih-yin to establish the realistic layer of the novel, for Chen is
the archetype in the novel of the earthbound human figure who experiences the painful vicissitudes of the Red Dust and who then
abandons his loved ones to be reborn as an enlightened being. In
other words, while Chen is an in-this-world, non-mythic character,
he is also a symbolic figure who is translated from the secular to the
religious, and from the terrestrial to the celestial. His family's
decline represents a paradigm which the Chia families of the Ning-
kuo and Jung-kuo mansions will repeat, and, in his transcendence
over the Red Dust, Chen Shih-yin prefigures a positive pattern
which Pao-yu will unknowingly imitate.22

   21For text, see p. 50.
   22Yu P'ing-po, Hung-lou meng yen-chiu, p. 108, notes that
Chen is an image of what Pao-yu will become in the closing chapters. Like Chen, Pao-yu suffers, becomes enlightened, and abandons the world to become an otherworldly figure.
   Is this ending appropriate? Yu accords with his friend, Ku Chieh-

Chen Shih-yin represents, then, the ideal individual who is ready to receive enlightenment. We use "to receive" advisedly, because, as we shall see, enlightenment in Dream of the Red Chamber is not by any means identical with Christian salvation which is attained through faith, works, or God's special election. For Chen Shih-yin, Chia Pao-yu, and even Chia Yu-ts'un, enlightenment is fortuitous and is not consciously sought. There is no doubt, of course, that Chen is an exemplary character. His spirituality is identified by a lack of interest in worldly fame and an exterior and interior simplicity. The pleasures of daily life are gardening, chatting with friends, and reciting poetry:

    . . . really he is a man carefree like the Divine Immortals.[23]

A major sign of Chen Shih-yin's coming sanctification is his dream-vision[24] in which he discovers the two Immortals and learns

----

kang 顧頡剛 , that the ending is by the editor of the 1791 and 1792 printed editions of the novel, Kao E, and that it is appropriate. Ku believes that Pao-yu is probably a parallel to Chen, and therefore it is fitting that Pao-yu proceeds from a high position to a low one, and goes off with the Taoist and Buddhist otherworldly figures at the end of the novel. Enlightenment means unconcern for worldly affairs. Yu, p. 148.

[23]HLMPSHCP, chap. 1, p. 5, line 11: 倒是神仙一流人. "Carefree" because of the preceding line: 每日只以觀花修竹 酌酒吟詩為樂 . The epithet of immortality is an important mark of excellence in the novel. When, for example, Chia Pao-yu first meets Chen Pao-yu, he flatters the latter with what he considers to be the highest type of praise: "Long revering thy fragrant name, but lacking cause for intimacy. Today thy countenance is beheld--truly a creature belonging to the Banished Sylphs". See HLMPSHCP, chap. 115, p. 355, line 10-11. "Sylph" for hsien 仙 is a translation popularized by Professor Edward Schafer, meaning both "slender girl" and "soulless immortal" who inhabits the air. We find "sylph" particularly appropriate for the effeminate Chen Pao-yu. "Banished", i.e., polite complimentary language (you are in the class of immortals who are unexpectedly on earth). 謫仙 is the hao of the poet, Li Po.

[24]Chih-yen Chai underscores the uniqueness of Chen Shih-yin's dream-vision by noting that it occurs on an exceptionally hot day. "Hot days are not many", he states. CYCHLMCP, chap. 1, p. 11, chia-hsu chia-p'i: 熱日無多.

of the "Foolish Thing", the discarded Stone, and of its silly desire
to visit the mortal world. Ts'ao Hsueh-ch'in thus makes Chen Shih-
yin the medium through which the mythic mode is transposed onto
the mimetic and the allegoric Stone becomes the terrestrial Pao-yu.
However, as we learn when Shih-yin addresses the Immortals, while
the myth of the Stone serves Shih-yin as a moral exemplum, his
knowledge is only partial:

"I just happened to hear the Immortal Masters talking about
Cause and Effect--something which is rarely heard of in the
actual human world--but due to my simpleton muddlement,
I cannot fathom the whole. Should I be given liberation from
my silly dullness and explication in fine of that which I have
just heard, I would wash my ears and listen. Then I would be
somewhat aware of my faults and I could avoid sinking into
the bitter underworld".

The two Immortals laughed: "This in fact is Penumbra Mechanics, the secret of which may not be leaked in advance".[25]
Chen Shih-yin's worthiness is indicated by his longing for understanding and immortality. His progress towards salvation begins
with the questions he asks about Cause and Effect[26] and Penumbra
Mechanics.[27] In this regard, he exemplifies the pilgrim spirit
which is to be revealed in Pao-yu. In this episode, he foreshadows
Pao-yu in two other respects. Both Chen Shih-yin and Chia Pao-
yu reach towards spiritual understanding through dreams, but dreams
are always either only partially revelatory or else are forgotten
immediately after they occur. Pao-yu's early adolescent dreams,
such as his dream visit to the Great Void Illusion Land (chapter 5),
merely serve to trouble him and to cause him to ask questions.
Such dreams do not change his life until nearly the end of the novel.
Thus Ts'ao Hsueh-ch'in undermines a prime source of illumination
(the dream). An ingredient is missing from Chen's dream, which
we might call "active" suffering. For Chen Shih-yin as for Chia
Pao-yu, and indeed, as the author insists, for the reader too, a
full reading of the Stone Record is not possible until the pilgrim experiences both joy and sorrow, and embraces them with equanimity.
We note in the above passage that another important feature of

----

[25]For text, see p. 51.
[26]yin-kuo 因果 . Moral causality.
[27]hsuan chi 玄機 . For an explanation of this phrase, see
"Myth" chapter, note 96.

the Chen Shih-yin paradigm is self-awareness. Chen speaks of his
"simpleton muddlement", yu cho,[28] and his "silly dullness", ch'ih
wan.[29] In his words we find two of the most important symbols of
the novel: contamination and foolishness. Chen's use of cho,
"mud", "sordid", "sullied", or "impure", as an epithet is also reminiscent of the Pao-yu who feels cho, "sullied", whenever he sees
males, and who is obsessed with becoming spiritually pure.[30] In
the dream, Chen is aware that he is a foolish naive simpleton, if
only for the fact that he cannot escape the Red Dust through an
individual act of the will and cannot understand the enlightening
words he is so privileged to hear.
    The painful dilemma of being a fool bent on enlightenment is
symbolized in the act by which the Buddhist Monk allows Chen Shih-
yin to look at the Foolish Thing, ch'un wu,[31] the discarded Stone
upon which is engraved: "Precious Jade for Penetrating the Numinous":

    The Buddhist Monk replied: "This thing you ask about-- it
    happens that in fact you are fated to see it once". And as
    he spoke he took it out and handed it to Shih-yin. The
    latter received it and looked it over. He discovered it to
    be in fact a lovely luminous jade gem. On its front surface
    the etching of characters was clearly visible--four words
    were inscribed: 'Precious Jade for Penetrating the Numinous'.[32]
To mortals, this inscription may indeed appear flattering. The incarnation of the Stone in Pao-yu's person makes him "Precious
Jade" to his family in the dusty world; and the phrase, "Penetrating
the Numinous", because of the Stone's divine origin, makes Pao-
yu different from other mortals. But to the Immortals, the Stone is
a Foolish Thing because of its vain desire to be born among men in
the illusory world of the Red Dust. Likewise, Chen Shih-yin is a
fool to think that a mortal can be "instructed" about immortality.
Ironically, the Immortals only permit Chen to read these few words,

----

28 愚濁.
29 癡頑.
30Tai-yu and the nun, Miao-yu, also suffer from a cleanliness
complex. Cho is one of the many words in the sexual sphere which
is associated with water and which identifies sex as "dirty".
31 蠢物.
32For text, see p. 52.

"Precious Jade for Penetrating the Numinous", lest he have too much insight into the meaning of Cause and Effect, Penumbra Mechanics, and his own destiny:

> On the back surface there were also several lines of small characters. Just when he wanted to look closely, the Buddhist Monk said they had already arrived at Illusion Realm and he forcefully snatched away the jade from Chen's hand.[33]

We cannot be certain of Ts'ao's meaning here, although it is clear that Chen has to endure life and its ordeals and perchance become enlightened. The Immortals are afraid, of course, of a simple breach of celestial security and also that Chen may be moved to interfere with an immutable process. It is obvious that they feel Chen is interpreting the little he reads correctly--indeed, he needs no instructions from them--and this too is what they fear. At least we might suggest what it occurs to us Ts'ao may be suggesting: we do not perceive correctly and we need to look about us with a new sort of awareness, but the second and third glance and the understanding which ensues may be more damaging than our original blindness.

Immediately after his quickly forgotten dream, Chen Shih-yin experiences suffering. Significantly, as our above observations indicate, that experience follows a pattern that is delineated in terms of the vocabulary of foolishness. He takes his baby daughter out to the street to observe the busy life that is passing by. Suddenly a scabby headed Buddhist monk and a club footed Taoist[34] pass by and confront Chen with the prediction that his daughter will be "so fated as to be without luck".[35] Chen is certain this is but "foolish talk",[36] and so he disregards these degenerate clergy.[37] When he refuses to give his daughter to the mangy Buddhist despite the latter's adamant demands, the monk chants a lyric[38] which begins: "I laugh at your foolishness".[39] Perhaps the reader may feel that this example of an inability to communicate simply reflects

----

[33]For text, see p.52.
[34]The former may be identified with Pu-tai ho-shang, the latter reminds us of Li T'ieh-kuai.
[35] 有命無運.
[36] 知是癡話.
[37]HLMPSHCP, chap. 1, p. 7, line 11.
[38]tz'u 詞.
[39]HLMPSHCP, chap. 1, p. 7, line 13: 笑你癡.

a typical pattern in the novel: when the representatives of the divine and secular poles of the novel confront one another, they view their opposites as fools. What we should observe, however, is that at this point in the narrative Chen Shih-yin is not dreaming. His awareness of his own foolishness and ignorance is only apparent to him in dreams. The two visitants are, of course, transposed Immortals from Chen's dream-vision, but the latter does not, in his unenlightened "awake" state, make the connection. As the late Shih-Hsiang Chen once suggested, the Immortals appear to be mal-formed to Chen Shih-yin because the latter, being mortal, is blind to the divine dimension.[40]

The prediction of the Buddhist and Taoist proves to be correct, for at the end of chapter 1 Chen's daughter, Ying-lien, is kidnapped, and Chen and his wife are stricken in their middle years with un-bearable grief. Two months after the loss of Ying-lien, the Bottle-Gourd Temple catches fire and many homes in the area, including that of Chen Shih-yin, burn to the ground. Chen sells some coun-try property he has remaining to him and he and his wife go to live with his father-in-law. The latter dislikes having two more depend-ents live in his house and does all he can to make Chen's life miser-able. Gradually, Chen suffers extreme poverty and poor health.

Nearly two years after his dream-encounter with the Immortals, Shih-yin lies near death. Suddenly one day, a club footed Taoist, who is "crazed, wild, and unrestrained",[41] comes down Chen's street singing a tune which he calls the "Sweeter-Over Song", Hao-liao Ko:[42]

Mortals consider sainthood sweeter
  but rank and fame
  their hearts can't get over
Where are the generals and ministers of yore?
  'neath reedy graves
  they are no more

Mortals consider sainthood sweeter
  but gold and silver
  their hearts can't get over

----

[40]An observation gleaned from the classroom notes of Professor Alvin Cohen. Chih-yen Chai observes that the two monks are huan hsiang, like figures in a mirage. CYCHLMCP, chia-hsu chia-p'i; chap. 1, p. 14: 此門是幻像.
[41] 瘋狂落拓.
[42] 好了歌.

A lifetime of avarice and greed for store
  when at last there's plenty
  you die and see no more

Mortals consider sainthood sweeter
  but adorable wives
  their hearts can't get over
When you're alive they're love and charms
  but upon your death
  they're in another man's arms

Mortals consider sainthood sweeter
  but sons and grandsons
  their hearts can't get over
Foolish fond parents of old are many
  but a filial descendant
  has there been any?[43]

Chen has endured suffering and he is approaching death. At this critical moment, he is touched by the mention of mortal foolishness for the first time in his conscious life. By the end of chapter 1, he joins the ranks of the crazy Taoist and thus abandons his secular foolishness to become a religious fool. The prelude to his conversion is a comical exchange over the meaning of the Taoist's "Sweeter-Over Song":

Having listened to this lyric, Shih-yin then went forward and greeted the Taoist saying: "What is this your mouth is full of? All I hear is "sweeter-over", "sweeter-over".

The Taoist said with a courteous smile: "If you heard the two words, 'sweeter-over', then I take it that you understand: you know that of the myriad earthly things that which is 'sweeter' is when it is 'over', and that which is 'over' is then 'sweeter'. If it is not 'over', then it is not 'sweeter'; if you want it 'sweeter', it must be 'over'. So my song is named: 'Sweeter-Over Song'".

Shih-yin was one of natural sensitivity--no sooner did he hear these words than his mind was already enlightened. Accordingly, he said with a courteous smile: "But stop! How would it be if you allow me to take this 'Sweeter-Over Song' of yours and add my commentary?"

----

[43]HLMPSHCP, chap. 1, p. 12, lines 2-9. For text, see p. 98.

第一回　甄士隱夢幻識通靈　賈雨村風塵懷閨秀

落拓，麻屣鶉衣，口內念著幾句言詞道：

「世人都曉神仙好，惟有功名忘不了，
古今將相在何方，荒塚一堆草沒了。

世人都曉神仙好，只有金銀忘不了，
終朝只恨聚無多，及至多時眼閉了。

世人都曉神仙好，只有嬌妻忘不了，
君生日日說恩情，君死又隨人去了。

世人都曉神仙好，只有兒孫忘不了，
癡心父母古來多，孝順兒孫誰見了。」

士隱聽了，便迎上來道：「你滿口說些什麼？只聽見些『好』『了』『好』『了』。」那道人笑道：「你若果聽見『好』『了』二字，還算你明白。可知世上萬般，『好』便是『了』，『了』便是『好』；若不『了』，便不『好』，若要『好』，須是『了』。我這歌兒便名『好了歌』。」士隱本是有宿慧的，一聞此言，心中早已微悟，因笑道：『且住，待我將你這「好了歌」解註出來何如？』道人笑道：『你解，你解。』

士隱乃說道：

『陋室空堂，當年笏滿床。衰草枯楊，曾為歌舞場。蛛絲兒結滿雕梁，綠紗今又糊在蓬窗。說甚麼脂正濃，粉正香，如何兩鬢又成霜。昨日黃土隴頭送白骨，今宵紅燈帳底臥鴛套。金滿箱，銀滿箱，轉眼乞丐人皆謗。正歎他人命不長，那知自己歸來喪。訓有方，保不定日後作強梁。擇膏粱，誰承望流落在煙花巷。因嫌紗帽小，致使鎖枷扛。昨憐破襖寒，今嫌紫蟒長。亂烘烘，你方唱罷我登場，反認他鄉是故鄉。甚荒唐，到頭來，都是為他人作嫁衣裳。」

那瘋跛道人聽了拍掌笑道：『解得切，解得切！』士隱便說一聲：『走罷！』將道人肩上搭連搶了過來背著，竟不回家，同了瘋道人飄飄而去。當下烘動街坊眾人，當作一件新聞傳說。封氏聞得此信，哭個死去活來，只得與父親商議，遣人各處訪尋，那討音信。無奈何，少不得依靠着他父母度日。幸而身邊還有兩個舊日的丫鬟伏侍，主僕三人日夜作些針線發賣，幫著父親用度。那封肅雖然日日抱怨，也無可如何了。

這日到家大丫頭在門前買線，忽聽街上喝道之聲，眾人都說新太爺到任。丫鬟隱在門內看時，只見軍牢快手一對一對的過去，俄而大轎內擡着一個烏紗猩袍的官府過去。丫鬟倒發了個怔，自忖這官好面善，倒像在那裏見過的。於是進入房中，也就丟過不在心上。至晚間正待歇息之時，忽聽一片聲打的門響，許多人亂嚷，說本府太爺的差人來傳人問話。封肅聽了，嚇得目瞪口呆。不知有何禍事，且聽下回分解。

The Taoist smiled and said: "Comment! Comment!"[44] Chen realizes that his efforts to cling to the security and happiness of a simple domestic life result from secular ignorance and personal vanity. He proceeds to sing a song in a light folk-ballad style in which he elucidates the serious hao-liao "Sweeter-Over" theme that life is an illusory experience of painful mutability whose only good is to be found in annihilation. Closely paralleling the stanzaic structure of the "Sweeter-Over Song", Chen describes a superstructure of wealth and power, romantic love and familial affection, which crumbles about a scaffolding of time:

I ghetto hovels vacant halls
      spaces once filled with official calls
   seared grass withered poplar
      stages past of song and laughter
   spiders weave o'er carven beams
      homespun green enwraps window streams

II powder so fragrant
    cream so sleek
       how then did temples change to hoar-frost bleak?
    yesterday at an amber grave
       to her white bones adieu
    tonight beneath crimson canopies
       with a love-bird new

III boxes of gold and boxes of silver
        turn beggar bedamned before the eyes but quiver
     alas! the brevity of another's life we sigh
        too soon we discover our mortality is nigh

IV parental counsel's well made
       but what guarantee against a renegade?
    your daughter's well bred
       yet well may she be into Flower Lane led

----

[44]HLMPSHCP, chap. 1, p. 12, lines 10-13. For text, see p. 98. Alternate lines in the Taoist's song end with hao 好 "good" and liao 了 "finished", which we have translated as "sweeter" and "over" in an effort to capture both the rhyme and the Buddhist concept that the content of mortal life and the way mortals perceive it are illusory. Salvation and enlightenment, that which is "sweet" or "good", is reached when the individual realizes that suffering ends when illusory experience is finished, that is, when illusory life is gotten "over".

V you grudge your official cap too low of rank
   you end up in chains, fetter and cangue
   yesterday you bewailed the tattered coat's cold
   today too much in office you wish to be old

VI turmoil and torrid heat
   one sings
    then another climbs
     the stage mistaken for the true sublime
  what insanity!
    a lifetime of labor for another's marital vanity![45]
A literal translation, including footnotes, may amplify the meaning
of the above rhymed translation:
  Rustic rooms and empty halls--in former years officials'
  slates[46] covered the beds.
  Dead grass and withered poplars--once song and dance stages.
  Spider webs wrap around carved beams, and now green homespun silk[47] papers over the overgrown windows.

  Exclaim over cream's thickness and powder's fragrance--
  how did two temples then turn to hoarfrost?
  Yesterday at the yellow earthen grave, adieu[48] to white
  bones, this evening beneath the red lanterns of the
  canopy lie mandarin ducks.[49]

  Gold filled boxes, silver filled boxes, in the turn
  of an eye[50] you become a beggar whom others all scorn.
  You who are just bewailing the shortness of another's
  life, how could you know you would die on the way home?

----

[45]HLMPSHCP, chap. 1, p. 12, line 15 through p. 13, line 6.
For text, see pp. 98-99.
  [46]hu 笏, "officials' slates", the tablets the officials carried
into their superior's presence during court calls.
  [47]sha 紗, light spun silk in a plain weave. Here a sign of
poverty.
  [48]sung 送, "adieu". Alternative readings in the chia-hsu
manuscript and the Kao E 1792 printed text are mai 埋 and tui 堆,
"pile up", "heap up", "bury".
  [49]yuan-yang 鴛鴦, the male and female pair, a symbol of
romantic love.
  [50]chuan yen 轉眼, "to turn the eye", a metaphor for split
second change; the transition from wealth to poverty is here described.

The education is upright, but there is no guarantee
[the child] won't later become a robber.[51]
Who would expect that one who feeds on dainties
would fall in the lane of misty flowers?[52]

Complaint about the smallness of the Homespun Cap[53]
causes one to be placed in chain and cangue.
Yesterday regret over the coldness of the tattered
coat, today complaint about the length of the Purple
Python.[54]

Turmoil and parching heat. After you sing I'll climb
the stage and mistake another's country for the native
land.[55]
What absurdity! In the end, it's all been but the making
of wedding garments for another.[56]

After listening to Chen Shih-yin's song commentary on the "Sweeter-Over Song":

    . . . the crazy club footed Taoist clapped his hands, giggled,
    and said: "A definitive commentary! A definitive commentary!"

----

[51]hsun yu fang 訓有方 , "the education is upright", a reference to the instruction and moral guidance parents give children.
   [52]kao-liang 膏粱 , "feeds on dainties", a metaphor for someone who is careful about what he or she eats. This sort of person
would not be expected to fall into "the lane of misty flowers", 落
在烟花巷 lo tsai yen hua hsiang, i.e., to become a prostitute.
   [53]sha mao 紗帽 , "Homespun Cap", a hat worn by gentlemen
and nobility, i.e., a sign of rank.
   [54]tzu mang 紫蟒 ,"Purple Python", ceremonial robes, i.e.,
another metaphor for officialdom and the responsibilities of office.
   [55]This line represents the interplay between appearance and
reality in the novel. It is also a metaphorical expression for the
ups and downs of official life and the turns of fortune. Men mistake appearance for reality, thus they are involved in ceaseless
activity--here the metaphor of going off and coming on the stage.
   [56]wei ta-jen tso chia i-shang 為他人作嫁衣裳   from
a T'ang poem by Ch'in T'ao-yu 秦韜玉; "make wedding clothes
for someone else", a metaphorical expression describing the vanity
of human activity.

Shih-yin then uttered but two words: "Let's go!" . . . why
he did not even return home, but wafted off with the Taoist
in a whirlwind.[57]
One may wonder why the Taoist feels that Chen Shih-yin's verse
is a "definitive commentary", or, to translate literally, how it
reveals a "thorough understanding"[58] of the "Sweeter-Over" theme.
How is Chen's song part of the enlightenment paradigm?
Chen Shih-yin's song predicts some of the most important plot
developments of the novel, although the reader is not aware of this
fact--unless he reads the annotated manuscripts of Chih-yen Chai
--until he finishes Dream of the Red Chamber. A similar technique
is used throughout the novel. In chapter 5, for example, Pao-yu
has a dream in which he visits the Great Void Illusion Land and the
Beware Illusion Fairy presents him with dossiers containing riddle-
poems which pertain to the fates of various female characters as
well as the general plan of the novel.[59] The meaning of these riddle-poems can be understood only after the novel is completed.
Chih-yen Chai identifies certain lines from Chen Shih-yin's song
with various figures in Dream of the Red Chamber and thus clarifies
the plot of the novel. (For our detailed explication of the relevance of Chih-yen Chai's commentary to the plot of the novel, we
refer the reader to some scholarly arguments in Appendix D). The
real significance of his commentary has to do with the enlightenment motif. His commentary was probably only intended to be read
by a coterie of friends of his and Ts'ao Hsueh-ch'in during that
period when various copies of the manuscripts were circulating
among them. In other words, as the printed texts of the novel indicate (there is no commentary in the printed editions of the novel),
the general reader is not meant to decipher the allegorical meaning
of Chen Shih-yin's song until late in the novel. He is to be attracted by the announcement that this song is a symbol of enlightenment,
but his own awareness cannot develop until he reads Dream of the
Red Chamber, that is, until he discovers enlightenment as experi-

----

[57]HLMPSHCP, chap. 1, p. 13, lines 5-6. For text, see p. 99.
[58] 解 得 切.
[59]Professor Cyril Birch has kindly lent me a manuscript copy of
an unpublished article he has written in which he explains the
meaning of the riddle-poems of chapter 5. It is interesting that
Chen's "commentary" on the "Sweeter-Over Song" in chapter 1
prefigures much of the imagery of the riddle-poems of chapter 5.

ence. One other point about Chih-yen Chai's commentary, and
one which is altogether consonant with the structure of the novel,
is that the mimetic and allegoric modes are intertwined. The song
at one level appears to be an allegorical statement about enlightenment, the meaning of which is unclear. At the same time, the
allegorical mode leads to the mimetic--the song is allegorically
outlining the plot of some of the realistic stories of Dream of the
Red Chamber. Here we have another example of the union of
Ts'ao's technique with his theme.

Perhaps the simple song remains confusing to the reader despite
our efforts to offer him a literal and a free translation, plus explanatory footnotes and reference to the commentary of Chih-yen Chai.
We suggest that the mosaic structure, the seemingly unrelated stanzas, and the paradoxical couplets are part of Ts'ao's deliberate
enlightenment style. In this regard, Chih-yen Chai makes an important upper margin comment at the close of Chen Shih-yin's song:

> This type of song actually ought not to be too elegant, for
> then it probably cannot be popular. Therefore one like this
> is consumate in its excellence, for where it is acutely pene-
> trating, mere pedestrian language would not suffice.[60]

And on the final line of the song Chih-yen Chai remarks in an interlinear comment:

> Although this is a language of trite clichés, applied here
> it is perfect. Just right![61]

In the former comment, Chih-yen Chai is saying, in effect, that
the province of the song is folk idiom, but that such is ineffective
when "acutely penetrating"[62] language is needed. Chen Shih-
yin's verse is "consumate in its excellence" because its form, meter,
and rhyme identify it with the genre of the popular folk song, while
its more elegant language means that it does not belong exclusively
to the popular idiom. In other words, this song which Chih-yen
Chai applauds is composed in a light ballad style which hides a
profound statement about the human condition. On the other hand,
the style of the song is not so simple as it appears. The sing-song
rhythm and single rhyme of the original need no explication, yet,

----

    [60]CYCHLMCP, chap. 1, p. 20: 此等歌謠原不宜太雅,恐
其不能通俗,故只此便妙極.其説得痛切處,又非一味俗語可到.
    [61]CYCHLMCP, chap. 1, p. 22, chia-hsu chia-p'i: 語雖舊句,
用於此妥極,是極.
    [62] 痛切處.

other than a thematic unity, there seems to be little connection
between the stanzas and the subject of each is not apparent. The
reader of Dream of the Red Chamber is aware that such a montage
is deliberately created by Ts'ao Hsueh-ch'in to attract his audience.
It might be called the "riddling technique for enlightenment" in the
novel, a surface appearance of simplicity belies an underlying puz-
zling complexity. What is the relation between ghetto hovels and
women's cosmetics, boxes of gold and parental advice, hat sizes
and stage performances? We wonder what Chen Shih-yin is talking
about since he is obviously spelling out his enlightenment while we
remain uncertain of his meaning.[63]

In his second comment about the "trite clichés"[64] Chih-yen Chai
points to another example of the "riddling" enlightenment style.
An old Chinese expression about making marriage clothes, that is,
mechanically spending oneself for another,[65] deftly describes the
vanity of human action. The commentator adds:

If one can see all this, one can get "over".[66]

In short, Chih-yen Chai marvels at the enlightenment style: Ts'ao
adopts a popular song form and makes it elegant; at the same time,
when he uses stale clichés and tired idioms, he applies them in
such a way that they become fresh and vital.

In addition to content and style, Chen Shih-yin's song is thematically related to the enlightenment paradigm. In the "Sweeter-
Over Song", the Taoist sings of mutability. His examples are fame
and fortune (stanza one), wealth (stanza two), marital love (stanza
three), and children (stanza four). Shih-yin elaborates at length
on the same theme of mutability, and in the margin above each of
the song stanzas, Chih-yen Chai underscores and clarifies Chen
Shih-yin's meaning and notes how the latter is related to the novel:

On stanza I:

First is described the stage: now fresh, now withered,
now lovely, now decayed--an ebb and flow continuous

----

[63]We are curious despite the fact that neither the "Sweeter-
Over Song" nor Chen Shih-yin's song is outstanding as lyrical poetry.
Within the context of the enlightenment motif, whatever Chen
Shih-yin does or says may be fraught with significance.

[64] 舊句.

[65]See note 56, above.

[66]CYCHLMCP, chap. 1, p. 22, chia-hsu chia-p'i: 苟能如此,
便能了得.

without ever getting "over".[67]

On stanza II:

A section on wives and concubines: the new are welcomed, the old are bid farewell: sudden affection, sudden love, sudden pain, sudden tragedy--all inextricable and impossible to get "over".[68]

On stanza III:

A section on the shortness of life and the fluctuation of extremes: dew in the wind, frost on the grass, wealth, desire, avarice--impossible to get "over".[69]

On stanza IV:

A section on the unreliability of sons and daughters after one's death: during one's lifetime--vain figuring, endless planning, foolish doting--impossible to get "over".[70]

On stanza V:

A section on the fortuitousness of tenure and dismissal: struggles for wealth, bitter competition, joy and forboding --impossible to get "over".[71]

On stanza VI:

A summary of the innumerable perennial fools who together

---

[67] ch'ang mien 場面, "stage pit", "stage section". Here a metaphor for life. CYCHLMCP, chap. 1, p. 20, chia-hsu mei-p'i: 先說場面忽新忽敗忽麗忽朽, 已見得反覆不了.

[68] The chia-chen manuscript has ku 故 instead of szu 死 (as in chia-hsu ms.), probably because szu is so taboo that it's use in a poem is bad style. CYCHLMCP, chap. 1, p. 20, chia-hsu mei-p'i: 一段妻妾迎新送故, 倏恩倏愛, 倏痛倏悲, 纏綿不了.

[69] shih-huo 石火, "stone-fire", i.e., "flintstone". The spark that is struck is a metaphor for the shortness of time. kuang-yin 光陰 & pei-hsi 悲喜, metaphors for the theme of complementary opposites. Everything becomes its opposite and undergoes endless fluctuation. CYCHLMCP, chap. 1, p. 20, chia-hsu mei-p'i: 一段石火光陰, 悲喜不了. 風露草霜, 富貴嗜欲, 貪婪不了.

[70] CYCHLMCP, chap. 1, p. 20, chia-hsu mei-p'i: 一段兒女死後無憑, 生前空為籌劃, 計算癡心不了.

[71] CYCHLMCP, chap. 1, p. 20, chia-hsu mei-p'i: 一段功名陞黜無時, 強奪苦爭, 喜懼不了

go through a stage of illusion: illusory events, jostle and
jumble, day after day--impossible to get "over".[72]
We see clearly from Chih-yen Chai's observations that he would
readily agree with the Taoist that Chen Shih-yin's verse is a "definitive commentary" on the "Sweeter-Over Song", as well as a fore-
shadowing of plot developments in Dream of the Red Chamber.
Several motifs of the novel are outlined in Chih-yen Chai's comments: family decline (stanza one); the victimization of women
(stanza two); complementary opposites--especially the image of
the fire producing stone (stanza three); the lack of an heir, or the
orphaned heir (stanza four); the dominance of circumstance (stanza
five); reality is an illusion (stanza six). Some of these motifs
which are archetypal in the novel are discussed at length in "Persona".
Others, such as the theme that reality is an illusion and opposites
are complementary are discussed in detail below. What is repeatedly stressed in Chih-yen Chai's comments, as well as in Chen Shih-
yin's song and the Taoist's "Sweeter-Over Song", is mutability.
We note that even in his observations on the various manifestations
of mutability, such as the helplessness of human beings before change
and the unexpectedness of events, Chih-yen Chai borrows the word,
"over", liao,[73] from the Taoist and from Chen Shih-yin. Nearly
every comment ends with the phrase, pu liao,[74] which we have
translated as, "impossible to get over". The chief sense of liao is
"finish", hence, "cut off" or "put an end". To the Taoist, Chen
Shih-yin, and Chih-yen Chai, it suggests, therefore, transcendence.
For the Taoist and for Chen Shih-yin, the word signifies the ending
of samsāra, the endless ebb and flow of life, and of karma, the patterns of cause and effect, birth and rebirth. For Chih-yen Chai,
liao is a superlative which describes samsāra and karma themselves
as patterns of repetitious mutability which seem impossible to get
"over".[75]

----

[72]Another general thematic comment. CYCHLMCP, chap. 1,
p. 20, chia-hsu mei-p'i: 總收古今億兆癡人,共歷幻場此
幻事,擾擾紛紛,無日可了.
[73]了
[74]不了
[75]Chih-yen Chai's comment on the line, "turmoil and torrid
heat/one sings another climbs", is, "A summary". CYCHLMCP,
chap. 1, p. 22, chia-hsu chia-p'i: 總收 . He is well aware
of the endless cycle of mutability.

Chen Shih-yin's paradigmatic song of enlightenment thus works at
various levels: realistic (plot), allegoric (hidden meaning), and
thematic. Like the whole of Dream of the Red Chamber, the song
enjoys a polysemous structure. After the above review of the narrative, stylistic, and thematic significance of Chen's song, we may
realize that enlightenment in the novel is not a matter of personal
restructuring, as in the modern West, nor is it merited through individual effort or goodness. As we shall observe, Chia Yu-ts'un
and Chia Pao-yu are especially noteworthy for their intelligence
or sensitivity, but not for their virtue. Chen Shih-yin's freedom to
comment on the "Sweeter-Over Song" is a sign of his profound
understanding and indicates that he is recognized by otherworldly
spirits. His experience of both joy and suffering and his attendant
devotion to wisdom seeking allow him to be placed in a position
from which he might receive enlightenment. In other words, the
point of the Chen Shih-yin enlightenment paradigm is that salvation
is a gift which comes spontaneously, but only to one who happens
to meet these criteria: keen sensitivity, diverse experience, total
commitment, and proper circumstance.

Chen Shih-yin becomes aware of his foolishness as he endures
personal mutability. He experiences a salvation that is to be found
in "getting over" life, and he sings of his enlightenment in a light
ballad style and a comic mode. In contrast to Chen Shih-yin, Chia
Yu-ts'un represents a negative archetype in the enlightenment
paradigm. He is committed to earthly vanities, such as the Civil
Service Examinations,[76] and he tries to thwart life's natural rhythm
of change by seeking security and stability rather than self-awareness. He too, despite special gifts of intelligence, is a particular
kind of ignorant fool--contrary to Chen Shih-yin, he is fond of
indulging in somber philosophical commentary on the meaning of
human existence even before he has had any significant experience.

Chia Yu-ts'un is one who seeks change in an effort to find permanence. He experiences alternating success and failure and is vic-
timized by his desire for change and his ironical subjection to un-

----

[76]Here we have another example of "opposites". Chia Yu-ts'un's
desire, expressed early in the novel, to pass the Civil Service Examinations is paralleled by Chia Pao-yu's early and constant expression of contempt for the same. Yet, Pao-yu does successfully pass
these Examinations at the end of Dream of the Red Chamber. Thus,
Chia Yu-ts'un is an example of stylistic typology: he is a prediction
of what Chia Pao-yu is to become (his "opposite").

wanted mutability:

> This Chia Yu-ts'un was originally a man of Hu-chou, of a clan of learning and official service, but because he lived in a period of generation decline, the patrimony of parents and ancestors had already been exhuasted, the members of the clan had declined and passed away, and all that was left was his own lone self. Since there was no advantage in his remaining in his home country, he entered the Capital to seek a career and to restore the patrimony of his family. He had arrived here the previous year, and had fallen on evil days, so that he temporarily lodged in the temple and made his living by every day selling calligraphy and writing letters . . . .[77]

The instability of Yu-ts'un's existence causes him to yearn for the position of a literatus. Thus he befriends Chen Shih-yin and through the latter's financial assistance he sets forth on the road to literocracy: the Capital and the imperial Civil Service Examinations. Everything that subsequently happens to him reflects the whims of fortune. To his distant "relatives", the members of the Chia clan, he is an example of mutability. To Chia Cheng, Pao-yu's father, Chia Yu-ts'un is a disconcerting moral exemplum. During the course of a conversation with friends which appears late in the novel, Chia Cheng recapitulates the story of Yu-ts'un. He recalls the latter's humble beginnings, his friendship with Chen Shih-yin and his marriage to the latter's servant, his tutoring of Lin Tai-yu, and his remote blood ties with the Chia family. Chia Cheng notes that in only a few short years, Yu-ts'un has been promoted and demoted through a series of official posts. Noting the equally sad example of Chen Ying-chia,[78] the father of Chen Pao-yu, Chia Cheng asks: "When you see that things are this way, don't you think officials are afraid?"[79]

Chia Yu-ts'un does not perceive that he is an "enlightening" example to others. While he does become enlightened in the very last chapter of the novel, the type of sensitivity that he exhibits

----

[77]HLMPSHCP, chap. 1, p. 8, lines 3-5. For text, see p. 110. Yu-ts'un is one of the many examples in the novel of only sons who are the sole hope of their families. Chih-yen Chai remarks: "Again is described a son of generation decline". CYCHLMCP, chap. 1, p. 16, chia-hsu chai-p'i: 又 寫 一 末 世 男 子

[78] 甄 應 嘉．

[79]HLMPSHCP, chap. 92, p. 125, line 11: 看 了 這 樣，你 想 做 官 的 怕 不 怕．

第一回　甄士隱夢幻識通靈　賈雨村風塵懷閨秀

人一去，再不見個踪影了。士隱心中此時自忖，這兩個人必有來歷，該試一問，如今悔卻晚也。

這士隱正凝想，忽見隔壁葫蘆廟內，寄居一個窮儒，姓賈名化，表字時飛，別號雨村者，走了出來。這賈雨村係湖州人氏，也是詩書仕宦之族，因他生於末世，父母祖宗根基已盡，人口衰喪，只剩得他一身一口，在家鄉無益，因進京求取功名，再整基業。自前歲來此，又淹蹇住了，暫寄廟中安身，每日賣字作文為生，故士隱常與他交接。

當下雨村見了士隱，忙施禮陪笑道：『老先生倚門佇望，敢街市上有甚新聞否？』士隱笑道：『非也。適因小女啼哭，引他出來作耍，正是無聊之甚。兄來得正妙，請入小齋一談，彼此皆可消此永晝。』說着便令人送女兒進去，自攜了雨村來至書房中。小童獻茶，方談得三五句話，忽家人飛報嚴老爺來拜。士隱慌的忙起身謝罪道：『恕誑駕之罪，略坐，弟即來陪。』雨村忙起身亦讓道：『老先生請便。晚生乃常造之客，稍候何妨。』說着，士隱已出前廳去了。

這裏雨村且翻弄書籍解悶。忽聽得窗外有女子嗽聲，雨村遂起身往窗外一看，原來是一個丫鬟在那裏掐花，生得儀容不俗，眉目清明，雖無十分姿色，卻也有動人之處，雨村不覺看得呆了。那甄家丫鬟掐了花，方欲走時，猛抬頭見窗內有人，敞巾舊服雖是貧窘，然生得腰圓背厚，面闊口方，更兼劍眉星眼，直鼻權腮。這丫鬟忙轉身回避，心下乃想：『這人生得這樣雄壯，卻又這樣襤褸，想他定是我家主人常說的什麼賈雨村了，每有意幫助周濟，只是無甚機會。我家並無這樣貧窘親友，想定是此人無疑了。怪道又說他必非久困之人。』如此想，不免又回頭兩次。雨村見他回頭，便以為這女子心中有意於他，便狂喜不禁，自為此女子必是個巨眼英豪，風塵中之知己也。一時小童進來，雨村打

八

up until that point is intellectual rather than mystical. He is such a contradictory character that his own self-awareness can only be severely limited. A scholar who is capable of tutoring Lin Tai-yu, (she is the most brilliant character in the novel), he is fond of engaging in learned philosophical conversations with his social inferiors (like Leng Tzu-hsing in chapter 2), but he never perceives the deeper implications of what he says. The dimensions of his foolishness will be understood when we discuss his final encounter with the sanctified and enlightened Chen Shih-yin in chapters 103 and 120.

While Chen Shih-yin and Chia Yu-ts'un are, respectively, convincing representations of enlightenment and mutability, they are more than merely mimetic characters. The Chih-yen Chai commentary on their names reveals the thematic significance of these personalities. Remarking on the family name,[80] Chen,[81] and the courtesy or social name,[82] Shih-yin,[83] Chih-yen Chai notes that the former is a homophone for chen,[84] and the latter is a homophone for shih-yin.[85] Thus, Chen Shih-yin[86] stands for chen-shih yin,[87] "true affairs hidden".[88]

----

80 姓.
81 甄.
82 字.
83 士隱.
84 真.
85 事隱.
86 甄士隱.
87 真事隱.

[88]Chih-yen Chai points out that Chia Pao-yu's counterpart, Chen Pao-yu, 甄寶玉, also has the sound chen 真 in his surname. Chen Pao-yu is another example of the interplay between Chen 甄 and Chia 賈, chen 真 and chia 假, "real" and "unreal". The commentator further states that Chen Shih-yin's given name, Fei 費 means fei 廢, "waste", "expend", or "destroy", perhaps referring to the destruction of Chen's family property through a fire and the subsequent disappearance of Chen Shih-yin when he goes off with a Taoist at the end of chapter 1. Fei may also be an allusion to chapter 104 where a temple in which Chen Shih-yin is found by Chia Yu-ts'un burns to the ground leaving no trace of the former. For these and the above comments, see CYCHLMCP, chap. 1, p. 10. Chen Shih-yin is first described in HLMPSHCP, chap. 1, p. 5, line 7ff.

Chia Yu-ts'un is surnamed Chia,[89] his given name is Hua,[90] his styled name[91] is Shih-fei,[92] and his appellation[93] is Yu-ts'un.[94] Chih-yen Chai finds all of these names to be marvellously apt choices on the part of Ts'ao Hsueh-ch'in: Chia Hua[95] means chia-hua,[96] "fictive language"; Shih-fei[97] is the homonym of shih-fei,[98] "actually untrue"; Yu-ts'un[99] implies ts'un-yen tzu-yu,[100] "folk language and coarse vocabulary", or, "using coarse vocabulary in expressing fictive language".[101] Chia Yu-ts'un[102] is then a homophonic expression of chia-yu ts'un-yen,[103] "fictive language and vulgar words".[104]

Even the names ot the places and locations in which the two figures live have hidden meanings. Thus, Chen Shih-yin dwells in the area of Ku-su (Su-chou)[105] in the walled city of Ch'ang-men.[106]

---

89 賈.
90 化.
91 表字.
92 時飛.
93 別號.
94 雨村.
95 賈化.
96 假話.
97 時飛.
98 實非,
99 雨村.
100 村言粗語.
101 言以村粗之言演出一段假話也,
102 賈雨村.
103 假語村言.

[104]Chia Yu-ts'un is first described in HLMPSHCP, chap. 1, p. 8, line 2ff. For the corresponding Chih-yen Chai commentary, see CYCHLMCP, chap. 1, p. 15. Wu Shih-ch'ang suggests that a preferable homophone for Chia Yu-ts'un would be chia-yu ts'un 假語存, "fictitious stories recorded", since, says Mr. Wu, "ts'un is obviously an antonym for yin". (隱). On the Red Chamber Dream, p. 65, note 4.

Further puns: chia-chen manuscript has su-yu 俗語 for tsu-yu 粗語; Yu-cheng manuscript says that Yu-ts'un means "folk vocabulary, coarse vocabulary, coarse language", 村言粗言粗語也. See CYCHLMCP, chap. 1, p. 16.

[105]See note 8, above.

106 閶門.

Ch'ang may mean ch'ang,[107] a loud sound. Ch'ang-ho[108] can mean "gate of heaven". Possibly Ts'ao is playing with a combination of meanings: loudness and the bustle of city life, through which one such as Chen Shih-yin must pass on the way to salvation. The lane on which Chen Shih-yin lives, Jen-ch'ing Hsiang,[109] says Chih-yen Chai, also means "human heartedness", jen-ch'ing,[110] and refers to the story of Chen Shih-yin's goodness in returning to enlighten Chia Yu-ts'un after the former's disappearance in fire.[111] On the same lane is a temple, and because the lane is chai hsia,[112] "narrow" and "contracted", the temple is popularly known as "Bottle Gourd Temple".[113] Chih-yen Chai's observation that the number of broad quiet paths in the world is very few[114] indicates that Jen-ch'ing Hsiang in its narrowness and its noise is symbolic of the world. The popular name of the temple, Hu-lu, says Chih-yen Chai, means hu-tu,[115] "muddled", "stupid", "foolish", "bumble headed". Such a temple, he observes, is the sort of place in which "fictive language" (Chia Yu-ts'un) arises.[116] Chia Yu-ts'un is said to be of a clan originally from Hu-chou[117] which Chih-yen Chai informs us means hu-chou,[118] "wild incoherent talk". Here we have a reference to Chia Yu-ts'un's habitual abuse of language.[119]

----

107 倡.
108 閶闔.
109 仁清巷.
110 人情.
111 CYCHLMCP, chap. 1, p. 9: 又言人情, 總為士隱火後伏筆. huo-hou 火後 may be a pun: "his time is ripe".
112 窄狹.
113 葫蘆廟.
114 世路寬平者甚少.
115 糊塗.
116 CYCHLMCP, chap. 1, p. 10, chia-hsu chia-p'i: 故假語從具(興)焉.
117 湖州.
118 胡謅.
119 Throughout chapter 1 and the whole of the novel there are similar examples of symbolic characterization through names. Chao Kang points out that the homophone for Chen Ying-chia 甄應嘉, the father of Chen Pao-yu, is chen ying chia 真應假, "the true calls forth the false", or, chen ying chia 真影假, "the true reflects the false". See Chao Kang, "Lun chin-pen Hung-lou meng

A final example of Ts'ao Hsueh-ch'in's use of names is the place Chia Yu-ts'un wanders about in chapter 2. It is the city in which is located the mansions of the Ning-kuo and Jung-kuo branches of the Chia family. They are situated in Shih-t'ou ch'eng,[120] "Stone City". Thus the title of the novel might be, Story of Stone City, rather than just Stone Record.[121] The importance of Stone City has to do with the Stone myth. Even on earth there is a correlation with the Stone myth and the origins of Pao-yu in the names of real cities. He is a "precious stone" from Stone City on earth.

Clearly, the mimetic and mythic layers of the novel are inter-

----

te hou ssu-shih-hui" 論今本紅樓夢的後四十回, in Tzu-yu Chung-kuo 自由中國 , XXII: vi (March, 1960), 23.

The servant of Chen Shih-yin who loses Ying-lien (Chen's daughter) at the Lantern Festival is Huo-ch'i, 霍啟 , which is a homophone for huo ch'i 禍起 , "calamity starts". CYCHLMCP, chap. 1, p. 19, chia-hsu chia-p'i.

Chen's wife belongs to the Feng 封 clan, which Chih-yen Chai notes means feng 風 , "wind", and refers to the coming of feng su 風俗, "social customs", i.e., the way of the mean world. CYCHLMCP, chap. 1, pp. 10 & 19, chia-hsu chia-p'i.

Chen's daughter is named Ying-lien 英蓮 , referring to the fact that she "calls forth sorrow" 應憐 , ying lien, for her parents when she is kidnapped. CYCHLMCP, chap. 1, p. 11, chia-hsu chia-p'i.

When a guest arrives at Chen Shih-yin's home named Master Yen (Yen Lao-yeh 嚴老爺), Chih-yen Chai points out that this name foreshadows the fire which is soon to destroy the home of Chen Shih-yin. CYCHLMCP, chap. 1, p. 16, chia-hsu chia-p'i: 炎既來, 火將至矣.

Sometimes Ts'ao uses names in a humorous vein. For example, the styled name of Hsueh P'an is Wen-chi 文起 , "literature arising". Hsueh P'an is, of course, nearly an illiterate, and thus his name is ironical.

120 石頭城

121HLMPSHCP, chap. 2, p. 17, line 13. Shih-t'ou ch'eng is a district west of Chin-ling (i.e., Nanking) and is named after a mountain called Shih-t'ou. Thus the title, Shih-t'ou chi (Stone Record), also has autobiographical significance since it alludes to an area near where the Ts'ao family lived in Nanking.

woven. The mimetic story of Chen Shih-yin and Chia Yu-ts'un
serves to introduce the allegorical and thematic significance of
Dream of the Red Chamber. Chia Yu-ts'un is the reverse of Chen
Shin-yin, just as chia, meaning "false", "unreal", is the opposite
of chen, "true, "real". The rise and fall of Chia Yu-ts'un's fortunes consistently contrasts to the fortunes of the family of Pao-yu.
Taken together, these two figures, Chen Shih-yin and Chia Yu-ts'un,
set forth a basic theme of the novel: all living matter is constantly
in a state of flux, phenomena are continually moving from one pole
to another. That which is "false" or "unreal" is becoming that
which is "true" or "real".

In chapter 1, this concept is stated explicitly in Chen Shih-yin's
dream encounter with the two otherworldly figures at the border of
the Great Void Illusion Realm:

When the Unreal is conceived as the Real,
  the Real is simultaneously Unreal;
Where Non-Being is taken for Being,
  Being turns into Non-Being.[122]

Ts'ao is here expressing a non-dualistic concept of polarity: each
object is or is in the process of becoming its opposite, for each object contains the seed of its opposite. According to this concept,
to hold that matter falls into "either-or" categories of "true" or
"false", "real" or "unreal", is erroneous, for opposites are complementary. This is essentially the meaning of the relation between
Chen Shih-yin and Chia Yu-ts'un, a meaning which underlies Ts'ao
Hsueh-ch'in's narrative technique.

Chen Shih-yin seems to make this concept clear to Chia Yu-ts'un
late in Dream of the Red Chamber. There has been no sign of Chen
Shih-yin since his mysterious disappearance with the Taoist who
sang the "Sweeter-Over Song" (chapter 1). In chapter 103, we
learn that Chia Yu-ts'un has recently been elevated once again to
government service. He is now a Prefect in a district in which the
Capital is located, and he is in charge of the Revenue Office.[123]
One day he goes on a tour to inspect and to explore his territory
outside the Capital. It happens that the road passes through the
district of Understanding (Penumbra?) Mechanics,[124] and that he

----

122For text, see p. 52.
123HLMPSHCP, chap. 103, p. 239, line 10.
124This district title, "Understanding Mechanics" (知機縣)
chih-chi hsien, reminds the reader of the "Penumbra Mechanics"
Chen Shih-yin cannot understand in his dream-vision. See "Myth"
chapter, note 96.

has to wait for a ferry at Rapid Flow River.[125] Therefore he descends from his sedan chair and strolls leisurely about the area. Chia notices a small temple whose walls have crumbled and through which he can see several lovely old pine trees. Upon inspection, he discovers that the statues and images in the temple are crumbled, the roof of the shrine is awry, and the stone tablets at the side are broken so that the engraved words cannot be deciphered. Suddenly, he glimpses a reed hut beneath a cypress tree in which there is a Taoist[126] sitting in the posture of meditation:

Yu-ts'un walked closer to look--the face seemed very familiar--as though he had actually seen it somewhere before, but he couldn't place it in that instant. His aide was about to call out, when Yu-ts'un stopped him, then very deliberately pacing forward, he addressed the person saying: "Venerable Taoist?"

The Taoist's eyes opened a bit. Then he smiled very faintly and said: "What business, Honorable Official?"

"This Prefect left the Capital on a tour of inspection", said Yu-ts'un, "and the road passed this way. Having observed you in such quiet self-contained contemplation, I think that your cultivation of the tao must have been far reaching, and I therefore have the impertinence to seek your instructions".

"There is a place to come from, and a direction to go to", said the Taoist.

Yu-ts'un was certain there was something behind this phrase, so he made a profound obeisance and asked: "Where did you receive your ascetic training that you should build your retreat here? What is the name of this temple? Altogether how many people are there in it? If you desire true ascetic practice, how can such occur without a famous mountain? If you wish to win followers, why not be at the thoroughfare?"

The Taoist replied: "The bottle-gourd[127] can lodge the body,

---

125 急流津.

126 In the following passage tao-shih 道士 is translated as "Taoist" since, in chapter 1, Chen Shih-yin leaves the world to follow a Taoist (later in this same passage he calls himself a p'in tao 貧道 , a "Poor Follower of the Way", thus implying a Buddhist monk). The obscure lines of distinction between Taoism and Buddhism in the novel are a reflection of popular folk religion.

127 "bottle-gourd", i.e., the Bottle-Gourd Temple where Chia once lived.

what need for a famous mountain to build a retreat? The temple name has long been hidden, the broken tablets are yet
extant. Form and shadow follow one another, what need for
soliciting? How could I be like those who chant:
   'Jade in the chest seeks a good price;
   Hairpins in the dressing case await the time to fly'?"
  Yu-ts'un being the clever person that he was, no sooner heard
the two words, 'bottle-gourd', and then the couplet about 'jade'
and 'hairpins', than he suddenly remembered the Chen Shih-
yin affair, and taking another glance at the Taoist, he saw that
the face was identical. After dismissing his aide, he asked:
  "Is not the Gentleman the Honorable Mr. Chen?"
  The Taoist, with an easy relaxed smile, said: "What chen
('real')? What chia ('unreal')? One ought to know chen is but
chia, chia is but chen".
  When Yu-ts'un heard the word "Chia", he no longer had any
doubt. With another ceremonious flourish, he said: "Since I
as a student was a recipient of your generosity, I was presented
at the Capital.128 Indebted to your favor, I was able to be
appointed to official position in the Chair of State. Granted
an appointment in thy Worthy Homeland, I then learned that the
Honorable One had become illuminated and transcended the
Red Dust, and had been wafted off and elevated to Sylphdom.
Although this student has thought of you time and again, I felt
that as a vulgar bureaucrat fallen in wind and dust I would have
no opportunity to have again an audience before your Divine
Countenance. Today what luck to meet you fortuitously in this
location! Please Venerable Immortal Elder, expound on the
stupor of delusion. My Capital residence is very near, and
should I be accepted and not rejected, I will have an opportunity
to serve and to receive instruction morning and evening".
  The Taoist likewise stood up and returned the courtesy: "Beyond
the reed mat, I know not what yet exists between Heaven and
Earth. It just happens that this Poor Follower of the Way does
not understand one whit of what the Worthy Official has just
said". With that he sat down in his former position.
  Once again Yu-ts'un's heart began to have misgivings and he
thought: If this is not Shih-yin, how is it that in face and word

----

128 In this paragraph of rhetorical courtesy, Chia recalls Chen's
former financial assistance.

there is such similarity? Though it has been nineteen years
since our parting, his facial color is the same as ever. Surely
it's that his ascetic practice has become efficacious, and he is
unwilling to divulge information about his former self. But
since I've happened upon my benefactor, I cannot pass up this
face to face opportunity. It seems that I cannot use wealth to
move him, and it would be worse to bring up the private matter
of his wife and daughter.

Thinking thus he said again: "If the Immortal Master is after
all unwilling to divulge his karma of the past, how can the
disciple endure it in his heart?"

Just as he was about to bow in reverence, his aide entered
and announced: "It is nearly dark. Please quickly ferry across
the river".

As Yu-ts'un was trying to make up his mind, the Taoist said:
"Please Worthy Lord, speedily mount the opposite shore. There
will be time to meet face to face again. If you are slow, wind
and wave will suddenly arise. Should you really accept and not
reject me, this Poor Follower of the Way will wait at this ferry
crossing for your instruction on another day".

When he finished speaking, he closed his eyes and sat in the
position of meditation as before. There was nothing for Yu-ts'un
to do but to depart from the Taoist and to leave the temple.

Just as he was about to ferry across the river, a man came
dashing forward. [129]

It happens that the temple has suddenly caught fire and no one has
seen a sign of the Taoist. Chia Yu-ts'un is torn between the desire
to return to look for Chen Shih-yin and the need to cross the river.
Being a man selfishly concerned with fame and fortune, he decides
on the latter course, but leaves an aide to search the temple after
the fire cools. [130]   Later when the aide reports on his findings, Chia
Yu-ts'un learns that absolutely no "trace" or "shadow", ying, [131]
of Chen Shih-yin can be found. A prayer mat and begging bowl
are all that remain, but when Chia's servant tries to pick them up
to bring them to show Yu-ts'un, they immediately turn to ashes. [132]

----

[129]HLMPSHCP, chap. 103, p. 239, line 13, through p. 240,
line 14. For text, see pp. 119-120.

[130]HLMPSHCP, chap. 104, p. 241, lines 5-6.

[131]影.

[132]This episode ends in chapter 104, HLMPSHCP, pp. 244-245.

那香菱也不覺餓，兩個人都喝道兒，我正笑香菱沒嘴道兒，那裏知道這死鬼奶奶要樂香菱，必定趁我
不在將砒霜撒上了，也不知道我換碗，這可就是天理昭彰，自害自身了。」於是衆人往前後一想，眞正
一絲不錯，便將香菱也放了，扶着他仍舊睡在床上。不說香菱得放，且說金桂的母親心慮事質，遲想
辯賴。薛姨媽等你言我語，反要他兒子倘還金桂之命。正然吵嚷，賈璉在外嚷說：「不用多說了，快
收拾停當，刑部的老爺就到了。」此時惟有夏家母子着忙，想來總費吃虧的，不得已反求薛姨媽：
「一千不是萬不是終是我死的女孩兒不長進，這也是他自作自受。若是刑部相驗，到底府上臉面不好看。
求親家太太息了這件事罷。」賈鈇道：「那可使不得。已經報了，怎麽能歇呢。」周瑞家的等人大家做
好做歹的勸說：「若要息事，除非夏親家太太自己出去撒賴，我們不提長短罷了。」賈璉在外也將他兒
子嚇住，他情願迎到刑部具給撒賴。衆人依允。薛姨媽命人買棺成殮。不提。

　且說賈雨村陞了京兆府尹，兼管稅務。一日出都查勘開墾地畝，路過知機縣。到了急流津，正要渡過
彼岸，因待人夫，暫且停轎。只見村旁有一座小廟，牆壁坍頽，露出幾株古松，倒也蒼老。雨村下轎，
閒步進廟，但見廟內神像金身脫落，殿宇歪斜，旁有斷碣，字跡模糊，也看不明白。意欲行至後殿，
只見一株翠栢下隂着一間茅庵，盦中有一道士合眼打坐。雨村走近看時，面貌甚熟，想着倒像在那
裏見來的，一時再想不出來。從人便欲呼喝，雨村此住，徐步向前，叫一聲老道。那道士雙眼微啟，微
微的笑道：「貴官何事？」雨村便道：「本府出都查勘事件，路過此地，見老道靜修自得，想來道行
深通，意欲冒昧請教。」那道人說：「來自有地，去自有方。」雨村知是有些來歷的，便長揖請問：「老道

從何處修來在此結庵？此廟何名？廟中共有幾人？或欲真修，豈無名山？或欲結緣，何不通衢？」那道人道：「葫蘆尚可安身，何必名山結舍。廟名久隱，斷碣猶存。形影相隨，何須修葺，豈似那「玉在匵中求善價，釵於匣內待時飛」之謎耶！」雨村原是個頴悟人，初聞見葫蘆雨字，後聞玉釵一對，忽然想起甄士隱的事來，貢復將那道士端詳一回，見他容貌依然，便屏退從人，問道：「君家莫非甄老先生麼？」那道人從容笑道：「什麼真，什麼假！要知道真即是假，假即是真。」雨村聽說出買字來，益發無疑，便從新施禮道：「學生自蒙慨贈到都，託庇獲雋公車，受任貴鄉，始知老先生超悟塵凡，學生雖溷跡泥途，自念風塵俗吏，未由再親仙顏。今何幸於此覯相遇。求老仙翁指示愚蒙。」尚荷不棄，京寓甚近，學生當得供奉，得以朝夕聆教。」那道人也站起來回禮道：「我於蒲團之外不知天地間尚有何物。適纔尊官所言，貧道一概不解。」說畢，依舊坐下。雨村復又心疑，想去「若非士隱，何貌言相似若此，離別來十九載面色如舊，必是修煉有成，未肯將前身說破。但我既遇恩公，又不可當面錯過。若來不能以富貴動之，那妻女之私更不必說了。」想罷，又道：「仙師既不肯說破前因，弟子於心何忍！」正要下禮，只見從人進來稟說：「天色將晚，快請渡河。」雨村正無主意，那道人道：「請尊官速登彼岸，見面有期，遲則風浪頓起。果蒙不棄，貧道他日尚在渡頭候教。」說畢，仍合眼打坐。雨村無奈，只得辭了道人出廟。正要過渡，只見一人飛奔而來。未知何事，下回分解。

This encounter between Chen Shih-yin and Chia Yu-ts'un, occur-
ing some nineteen years and one hundred chapters after their initial
contact, is an archetypal scene combining the dominant theme and
symbols of Dream of the Red Chamber. If we take Chen's statement
literally, ". . . chen is but chia, chia is but chen", it is an expression of the theme of complementary opposites: the real and the
unreal are one. If we read it figuratively, that is, as referring to
Chen Shih-yin and Chia Yu-ts'un, then we realize that Chen is
saying, in effect, that he and Chia Yu-ts'un represent an archetypal
pattern. They have the same identity despite basic dissimilarities
in name, appearance, and life style. Yet, Chia Yu-ts'un cannot
understand Chen's language in either a symbolic or figurative sense.
He takes Chen only literally, ot course, for when he hears the word
chia, he is reminded of his friend Chen Shih-yin. But he does not
realize that in an extra-literal sense, inasmuch as "Chen (chen) is
Chia (chia)" or "true is false", Chen Shih-yin is identifying himself
with Chia Yu-ts'un.

We should note that Chen's statement occurs at what might be
called the "climax of opposites" in the novel. Chia Yu-ts'un is
at the high point of his official career while Chen Shih-yin is living
as an impoverished recluse in a ruined temple. At the end of chapter 103, Chen undergoes a religious death: he is consumed in the
flames of the temple fire--an event which symbolizes his final enlightenment and emancipation from the Red Dust. Chia Yu-ts'un,
on the other hand, after receiving religious instruction from the
holy man Chen as to the true meaning of human existence immediately proceeds to act in a decidedly irreligious and irreverent
fashion: he has a poor drunk severely beaten when the latter im-
pedes the forward progress of his sedan chair.[133] Enlightenment for
Chia has to wait until chapter 120 when his official career is ended
and Chen Shih-yin, now an Immortal, returns to the Rapid Flow
River to try to give Chia more complete spiritual understanding.

We should also observe that Chen here pretends he is not Chen,
that he does not understand Chia's words. This is another pattern
of both style and meaning in Dream of the Red Chamber. At the
moment of complete inability to communicate are uttered the most
profound truths. One need only recall the relationship of Tai-yu
and Pao-yu for a general example.

There are certain symbols in this passage which are typical of the

----

[133]HLMSPHCP, chap. 104, pp. 242-244.

enlightenment pattern. The two opposite figures, "Mr. True" and
"Mr. False", meet at a ferry crossing, significantly named the
Rapid Flow River, where the enlightened should know to reverse
his course and the unenlightened may keep on drifting in peril.
Chen bids Chia to cross this river to the other bank--a move towards
salvation. Chia is well representative of worldly manners and ambitions, what with his position as tax collector, his inspection tour,
and his sedan chair. Chen is otherworldly in his disregard for his
poverty and his ability to see through human affairs. Other symbols
are the pine trees which first attract Chia--they represent beauty
and longevity; the dilapidated temple with its fallen images, actually an illusory surface appearance which hids a truly enlightened
being; the river crossing at which the unenlightened Chia is forced
to wait and thus to come in contact with the enlightened Chen;
the thatched hut under a tree, a Buddhist sign of retirement from the
world and of wisdom; the "shadow", ying, prayer-mat and begging
bowl of Chen which disappear when Yu-ts'un's servant tries to re-
trieve them--a sure sign of Chen's transcendence--his belongings
cannot be touched by mortal hands.

Several motifs are repeated here which occur earlier in the novel,
or which will re-occur in chapter 120. Thus Ts'ao Hsueh-ch'in quite
deliberately maintains the continuity of his framework. As in chapter 1, Yu-ts'un seeks help from his "opposite", Chen Shih-yin.
There, of course, that aid is financial, not spiritual. Again, however, it is ironical. That is, it is ironical that it is Chen Shih-yin,
one who is ready to transcend the world, who is the source of financial support for Chia Yu-ts'un, an active seeker of worldly success
(in chapter 1). It is equally unexpected that Chen should be interested in enlightening one who is so deeply engrossed in worldly
success (in chapter 103). Again, as in our "Myth" chapter, we are
reminded of synchronicity, "meaningful chance", in the presence
of a brilliant coherence of fortuitous circumstances. As we have
seen, Yu-ts'un happens to have recently received an appointment
which requires that he travel outside the Capital. By chance he is
delayed at a river crossing so that accidentally he discovers a
temple near which, to his utter surprise, is his old friend, Chen
Shih-yin: "Today what luck to meet you fortuitously in this location!" Just as Chia is trying to discover the secrets of Chen's past,
a ferry happens to arrive. And just as Chia is on the ferry crossing
the river, the temple happens to catch fire and burn to the ground.
This whole episode is linked to the final meeting of Chen Shih-yin
and Chia Yu-ts'un in chapter 120. There, at the site of the Rapid

Flow River and the ruined temple, Chia receives final instructions.

The couplet which Chen Shih-yin recites, "Jade in the chest seeks a good price; Hairpins in the dressing case await the time to fly", is a poem first uttered by Chia Yu-ts'un in chapter 1 and overheard by Chen Shih-yin. We recall the context in which the couplet occurs in chapter 1. Yu-ts'un has glimpsed the sight of a pretty servant girl of Chen Shih-yin and he falls in love with her. In fact, after his successful completion of the examinations, he will return to marry her (chapter 2). At this point, however, he mournfully notes that he is an unlikely candidate for marriage, just as he is poor and unknown:

> . . . he thought of how he had yet to fulfill his life's ambitions, whereupon he scratched his head and made a long sigh towards Heaven and loudly chanted a couplet which said:
> 'Jade in the chest seeks a good price;
> Hairpins[134] in the dressing case await the time to fly'.
> Just then Shih-yin happened along and overheard him. He laughed and said: "Brother Yu-ts'un, you certainly are one of uncommon ambitions!"
> Yu-ts'un immediately smiled back: "How should I dare? 'twas just the casual intoning of a line composed by somebody earlier. How should I dare to expect your extravagant plaudits?"[135]

Both are in agreement that the reference to jade and hairpins implies worldly ambition for success. Thus, when Chen Shih-yin recites the same couplet in chapter 103, Chia "suddenly remembered the Chen Shih-yin affair". Chen hints towards his own identity and reminds Chia of the latter's original ambitions.

As the Chih-yen Chai commentary indicates, there is obviously an allegorical meaning to the jade and the hairpins, a meaning of which Chia Yu-ts'un is unaware. The jade may refer to Tai-yu, "Black Jade", and the hairpin to Pao-ch'ai, "Precious Hairpin", or the jade may indicate Pao-yu, "Precious Jade". Tai-yu struggles to surpass Pao-ch'ai in the eyes of Pao-yu, while Pao-yu and

----

[134]Hairpins 釵 usually have bird ornaments, thus the appropriateness of the image.

[135]HLMPSHCP, chap. 1, p. 9, lines 9-12. For text, see p. 124.

聽得前面有留飯，不可久待，遂從夾道中自便出門去了。士隱待客飯散，知雨村自便，也不去再邀。原來

雨村自那日見了甄家之婢，曾回顧他兩次，自爲是個知己，便時刻放在心上。今又正値中秋，不免對

月有懷，因而口占五言一律云：

　　未卜三生願，頻添一段愁。

　　悶來時歛額，行去幾回頭。

　　自顧風前影，誰堪月下儔。

　　蟾光如有意，先上玉人樓。

雨村吟罷，因又思及平生抱負苦未逢時，乃又搔首對天長歎，復高吟一聯云：

　　玉在匵中求善價，釵於奩內待時飛。

恰値士隱走來聽見，笑道：「雨村兄眞抱負不淺也！」雨村忙笑道：「豈敢。不過偶吟前人之句，何

敢狂誕至此。」因問「老先生何興而至此？」士隱笑道：「今夜中秋，俗謂團圓之節，想尊兄旅寄僧房，

不無寂寥之感，故特具小酌，邀兄到敝齋一飲，不知可納芹意否？」雨村聽了，並不推辭，便笑道：

「旣蒙謬愛，何敢拂此盛情。」說着，便同士隱過這邊書院中來。須臾茶畢，早已設下盃盤，那美酒

佳肴自不必說。二人歸坐，先是款斟慢飲，漸次談至興濃，不覺飛觥限斝起來。當時街坊上家家簫管，

戶戶弦歌，當頭一輪明月飛彩凝輝，二人愈添豪興，酒到杯乾。雨村此時已有七八分酒意，狂興不禁，

Pao-ch'ai are destined to marry.[136] It is a typical pattern in the
novel, and especially typical of Chia Yu-ts'un, that an individual
expresses a truth of which he himself is not conscious.[137]

The couplet has quite a different usage in chapter 103. The entire passage may be read as a paradigm of one kind of enlightenment: a search for awareness coupled with an inability to communicate. Chia Yu-ts'un alternates between doubt and certainty as to
the identity of the Taoist, but his only concern is with surface facial
appearances. He seems to sense the contrast between his activities
as a revenue official and the freedom of the Taoist, and he seeks
to be enlightened about tao and karma. But to him karma is simply
the story behind Chen's loss of family and wealth while tao represents practical problems which are solvable according to one's own
methods. Thus he allocates his early morning and late evening
hours when he is free from his official duties for religious instruction. He is so naive as to imagine that he may have both enlightenment and his job. He represents a further contrast to Chen in terms
of mood. Chia is nervous and tense, as his flurry of questions shows,
while Chen converses in a comfortable relaxed manner. Chia's
rhetoric, his supercilious courtesy, and his inane questions concerning the name of the temple and the number of people there, indicate his superficiality. How can tao be understood, he asks, unless
it is taught at a popular and accessible resort? The Taoist replies
to Chia's questions with the comment:

"The bottle-gourd can lodge the body, what need for a famous
mountain to build a retreat? . . . Form and shadow follow one
another, what need for soliciting? How could I be like those
who chant:

'Jade in the chest seeks a good price;
Hairpins in the dressing case await the time to fly'?"

----

[136]CYCHLMCP, chap. 1, p. 17, chia-hsu chia-p'i: 表過黛玉
則緊接寶釵,前用二玉合傳,今用二寶合傳,自是書中正眼
Wu Shih-ch'ang notes that tai 黛 does not mean "Black", but
"pencilled" or "eyebrow pencil" or "pretty eyebrows". See On
the Red Chamber Dream, pp. xxii-xxiii, footnote 2.

[137]Later in the novel Yu-ts'un becomes closely linked with
Tai-yu (as her tutor) and with Pao-ch'ai (as the magistrate who
frees her brother from a charge of homicide). However, at this
point in chapter 1 under discussion, Yu-ts'un has yet to meet either
Pao-ch'ai or Tai-yu.

When Chen Shih-yin says, "How could I?", he is correlating Chia's
questions and the couplet as expressions of ambition. Chia has not
changed. He is yet the victim of his desires. In the line, "Form
and shadow follow one another", Chen speaks of destiny. Causes,
forms, and questions naturally resolve themselves in results, shadows,
and answers.

But Chia Yu-ts'un, "being the clever person that he was", understands none of Chen's allusions to the vanity of desire, the meaning
of destiny, and the union of complementary opposites. Yet, as he
slowly grasps that this Taoist may be Chen Shih-yin, he adopts the
external signs of enlightenment, that is, polite formal language
which befits the Master-Disciple relationship. Chia first calls
Chen, "Venerable Taoist",[138] when he sees the latter contemplat-
ing. When he thinks the Taoist is Chen, he refers to him as a
"Gentleman",[139] the "Honorable Mr. Chen".[140] Realizing that
Chen has become a Taoist, he calls him, "Venerable Immortal Elder".[141] Finally, deeply impressed by the observation that Chen
has not aged since he was last seen, Chia addresses him as "Immortal
Master".[142] Chia may believe that at the base of Chen's practice
of asceticism, hsiu lien,[143] is alchemy--the ability to refine cinnabar into some potion of immortality.[144] Again, Chia reveres
what Chen can do, rather than what he is.

Chen Shih-yin refers to himself only as a "Poor Follower of the
Way"[145] and with consistently courteous deference calls Chia Yu-

----

138 老道.
139 君家.
140 甄老先生.
141 老仙翁.
142 仙師.
143 修煉.
[144]In HLMPSHCP, chap. 2, p. 18, line 7, Leng Tzu-hsing tells
Chia Yu-ts'un about Chia Ching 賈敬 , the oldest surviving male
of the Ning-kuo mansion, who is addicted to Taoist pursuits, such
as refining cinnabar to attain immortality: 燒丹煉汞   He
dies from imbibing his experimental potions late in the novel.
Chih-yen Chai sighs when Leng tells about Chia Cheng. He laments
that such deplorable practices as alchemaic searches for immortality are common signs of decline in spent generations. CYCHLMCP,
chap. 2, p. 33, chia-hsu chia-p'i:亦是大族末世常有之事,嘆嘆!
145 貧道.

ts'un, "Honorable Official"[146] and "Worthy Official".[147]   In
contrast to Chia, Chen does not indicate his awareness of his own
enlightened position by the use of titles which would elevate himself and deprecate Chia Yu-ts'un. Chia, however, hypocritically
attempts to demonstrate how aware he is of his spiritual inferiority
by gradually speaking of himself in the language of self-depreca-
tion. He first refers to himself as "this Prefect",[148] later as
"student",[149] and finally as "disciple".[150] His hypocrisy is
proven when he abandons Chen, despite some reluctance, to the
temple fire.

Initial insight into the character of Chia Yu-ts'un, the theme of
complementary opposites, and the unity of the novel is provided in
chapter 2 in Yu-ts'un's visit to a temple and his subsequent conversation with one Leng Tzu-hsing. These episodes illustrate why
Shih-yin's words, such as, "There is a place to come from, and a
direction to go to", remain enigmatic to Yu-ts'un until nearly the
end of Dream of the Red Chamber.

Chapter 2 is the source of the archetypal temple visit we have
just reviewed in chapter 103. In chapter 2, Chia Yu-ts'un becomes
the tutor of Lin Tai-yu, but because the latter's mother has died
recently, Yu-ts'un has the leisure to pursue his hobby--visiting
ancient ruins in the countryside. As in chapter 103, he happens
upon a dilapidated hermitage and a monk (this time a Buddhist rather
than a Taoist) with whom he is unable to communicate. Again he
finds several obscurely written characters:
    . . . before the gate on the overhang there was the heading in
    three words: 'Hermitage of Cognition of Knowledge'. And
    at the sides of the gate was an old cracked couplet which read:
    'After death there's abundance left over,
       you forgot to pull back your hand;
    When there's no more road before your eyes,
       you think of turning round your head'.
After he read this, Yu-ts'un thought: "Though these two lines
are of a shallow style, their meaning is deep. And while I
have toured several famous mountain monasteries, as a matter

----

146 貴官.
147 尊官.
148 本府.
149 學生.
150 弟子.

of fact I have never seen words written in this fashion. There
must be one here who has 'flipped head-over-heels'--though
there's no telling that--why not go in and give it a try?"

He was thinking along these lines as he entered to look, when
who should he find inside but a decrepit old Bonze boiling
rice-gruel. Seeing him, Yu-ts'un felt ill at ease, but when
he went ahead and asked him a couple of questions, why the
old Bonze turned out to be deaf and dumb, gap-toothed and
tongue-tied, so that whatever it was he replied was not what
he was asked.[151]

The brief episode translated above well represents the paradigm
of enlightenment and the theme of complementary opposites. On
the one hand, Yu-ts'un is perfectly correct: there is a monk in the
hermitage who has "flipped head-over-heels", that is, one who
has passed through the hurly-burly of the world and attained the
tao. On the other hand, he is completely mistaken: he fails to
recognize that, as Chih-yen Chai observes, the demented state of
the monk symbolizes his triumphant removal from the world. He
represents cognition and knowledge which are both true and
arcane.[152] Furthermore, the style of the couplet is quite commonplace in its exact word-for-word parallel structure, but the meaning
is not deep. A paraphrase might be:

When you have plenty to fall back on, you don't
think to retrench;
it's only when the future's hopeless that you begin
to look back.

In other words, the couplet is an appropriate statement in a Buddhist
retreat. As Wu Shih-ch'ang remarks, "to turn round the head" is

----

[152]CYCHLMCP, chap. 2, p. 30, chia-hsu chia-p'i. After the
description of the monk's deaf and dumb state as well as the poor
condition of his teeth and tongue, Chih-yen Chai writes: 是翻
過來的 "one who is transformed"; literally: "one who has
turned over", or, "this is [an instance] of turning over".

He further notes that for Chia Yu-ts'un, this possibly enlightening
experience is instead infuriating. When Chia sees the hermit
making rice-gruel, he feels angry and indignant. CYCHLMCP,
chap. 2, p. 30, chia-hsu chia-p'i: 是雨村火氣.

第二回　賈夫人仙逝揚州城　冷子興演說榮國府

女，乳名黛玉，年方五歲。夫妻無子，故愛女如珍；且又見他聰明清秀，便也欲使他讀書識幾個字，

不過假充養子之意，聊解膝下荒涼之歎。

雨村正值偶感風寒，病在旅店，將一月光景方漸愈。一因身體勞倦，二因盤費不繼，也正欲尋個

合式之處暫且歇下。幸有兩個舊友亦在此境作居，因聞得塩政欲聘一西賓，雨村便相託友力，謀了進

去，且作安身之計。妙在只一個女學生，并兩個伴讀丫鬟。這女學生年又小，身體又極怯弱，功課不

限多寡，故十分省力。看看又是一載的光景，誰知女學生之母賈氏夫人一疾而終，女學生侍湯奉藥，

守喪盡哀，遂又將辭館別圖。林如海意欲令女守制讀書，故又將他留下。近因女學生哀痛過傷，本

自怯弱多病的，觸犯舊症，遂連日不曾上學。雨村閒居無聊，每當風日晴和，飯後便出來閒步。

這日偶至郭外，意欲賞鑒那村野風光。忽信步至一山環水旋，茂林深竹之處，隱隱有座廟宇，門

巷傾頹，牆垣朽敗，門前有額題著『智通寺』三字。門旁又有一副舊破的對聯曰：

『身後有餘忘縮手，眼前無路想回頭。』

雨村看了，因想道：『這兩句話，文雖淺近，其意則深。也曾遊過些名山大剎，倒不曾見過這話

頭。其中想必有個翻過筋斗來的，也未可知，何不進去試試。』想着，走入看時，只有一個龍鍾老僧

在那裏煮粥。雨村見了，便不在意，及至問他兩句話，那老僧既聾且昏，齒落舌鈍，所答非所問。

雨村不耐煩，便仍出來，意欲到那村肆中沽飲三杯，以助野趣。於是款步行來，剛入肆門，只見

座上吃酒之客有一人起身大笑，接了出來，口內說：『奇遇，奇遇。』雨村忙看時，此人是都中在古

a Buddhist allusion meaning to return to enlightenment.[153] The couplet reminds its readers to live a pious life--do not put otf until tomorrow what you ought to do today, or, do not do today what you will regret tomorrow--which is a simple enough aphorism in English or Chinese.[154] The irony here, as in chapter 103, is that Chia Yu-ts'un is one who makes his living partly through his ability in calligraphy: he sells letters and tutors Tai-yu. He has the natural curiosity of the unenlightened--he seeks to investigate ruins (a hobby which is an important sign of his potential for enlighten-ment)--but he never deciphers or understands their meaning. As in chapter 103, he naively believes that religious enlightenment is simply a matter ot getting the right answers to the questions <u>he</u> thinks of and that it can only take place at the site of a "famous mountain shrine". He continually overlooks those out-of-the-way places ot light which he accidentally comes across. If we consider the Buddhist as a symbolic figure, the text which reads, "what-ever it was he replied was not what he was asked", implies that Chia's problem of misunderstanding is due to his questions. His perceptions are equally faulty. Chih-yen Chai observes that in Chia's thought, "Though these two lines are ot a shallow style, their meaning is deep", we have a general commentary on the novel.[155] In other words, even with the realization that the couplet is some-thing other than it appears to be, Chia, with his "vulgar eye",[156]

----

[153]"The whole proverb says, 'Boundless is the Sea of sufferings (in the mundane world), turn your head and there is land!'--name-ly, The Pure Land of the Buddhist Paradise". Wu, <u>On the Red Chamber Dream</u>, p. 91.

[154]Chih-yen Chai says the hermitage's name signifies a lament over the human condition: "Who is one of Cognition? And who is one of knowledge? Alas!" CYCHLMCP, chap. 2, p. 29, <u>chia-hsu chia-p'i</u>: 誰為智者, 又誰能通, 一嘆. Those who follow the advice of the couplet are few. Chia Yu-ts'un is a typical example of folly.

[155]CYCHLMCP, chap. 2, p. 20, <u>chia-hsu chia-p'i</u>: 一部書之總批. Chih-yen Chai feels that the couplet is a warning to the members of the Chia family. Wu Shih-ch'ang, <u>On the Red Chamber Dream</u>, p. 91, says that the second line of the couplet refers to Pao-yu's abandonment of his wife and family when he becomes a monk at the end of the novel.

[156] 俗眼.

fails to comprehend its simple truth, let alone its hidden one, and thus he remains deluded by the mask of his own intelligence.

Ts'ao Hsueh-ch'in directly follows this narrative of enlightenment overlooked and the Way unattained with a piece of tavern gossip. After leaving the Temple of Cognition of Knowledge in disgust, Chia Yu-ts'un goes to a tavern to refresh himself, and there he accidentally finds another kind of revelation: rumors about the Chia family as voiced by Leng Tzu-hsing, a curio dealer from the Capital.[157] While neither Leng Tzu-hsing nor Chia Yu-ts'un have had much contact with the Chia clan,[158] their gossip provides the reader with a kind of intimate introduction.[159] When Chia Yu-ts'un

----

[157] Leng Tzu-hsing and Chia Yu-ts'un had previously become acquainted when the latter was preparing for his Civil Service Examinations in the Capital.

[158] Leng politely pretends to think that Chia Yu-ts'un is related to the Chia clan. Since the surnames are the same, he tells Yu-ts'un, they must have the same ancestry and therefore the same clan. As Chih-yen Chai says, such a claim is ridiculous. CYCHLMCP, chap. 2, p. 31, chia-hsu mei-p'i: 同姓即同宗 出，可發一笑 In fact, Chia Yu-ts'un, as noted earlier, is the sole remaining member of his family and he himself tells Leng that he has no relative in the Capital. But when Chia realizes that Leng is trying to link him to the Jung-kuo branch of the Chia clan, he goes along with the pretense by claiming that indeed, the Chia family was established in the Eastern Han dynasty and it has branches in every province. The only reason for the little intercourse between his family and that of the Jung-kuo mansion, says Chia, is social rank. Chih-yen Chai believes that this claim exemplifies Chia Yu-ts'un's deceit. CYCHLMCP, chap. 2, p. 31, chia-hsu chia-p'i: 此話縱真，亦必謂是雨村欺人語.

[159] This episode exemplifies the interplay between the mimetic and allegoric modes. The name, Leng Tzu-hsing 冷子興 , may be interpreted allegorically to mean, "desolate child surviving". This name parallels another translation for "Chia Yu-ts'un", "lying tales remaining"--the author's wry comments on his own position as family historian.

As the commentary indicates, the Story of Leng Tzu-hsing allegorically represents the theme of complementary opposites. CYCHLMCP, chap. 2, p. 24, k'ai-shih tsung-p'i: 此回亦非正文 本旨，只在冷子興一人，即俗謂冷中出熱，無中生有也.

learns that the remarkable Chia Pao-yu was born miraculously with
a piece of jade in his mouth, he exclaims to Leng Tzu-hsing:

This is indeed fantastic! In all probability this person's
background is of no small moment.[160]

This strange occurrence marks the birth into the world of the heavenly jade stone which becomes Pao-yu's amulet.[161]   What is
significant about Yu-ts'un's exclamation is his concern with lai
li,[162] "background" or "provenance".[163]   In other words, Chia
Yu-ts'un is quite correct in recognizing that Pao-yu does have
quite a past, although he is unaware of Pao-yu's origins, as well
as quite a future--Pao-yu will fully experience the passions of the
Red Dust before being released from the world.   Yu-ts'un is typically concerned with hidden meanings. We recall that when, in
chapter 103, Chen Shih-yin, now the Taoist adept, replied to
Chia's request for instruction with the statement: "There is a place
to come from, and a direction to go to", Chia thought to himself
that, "there was something behind this phrase", that is, background,
provenance, or hidden meaning. In both chapters 2 and 103, Chia
is completely mistaken about what that lai li might be. In chapter
103, he takes Chen Shih-yin's statement as an invitation to inquire
about the origins and developments of the dilapidated hermitage,
whereas Chen is actually exuding revelations about predestination,
enlightenment, and the unity of opposites. In chapter 2, Yu-ts'un
is totally ignorant of Pao-yu's lai li, yet he uses the absence of
knowledge as an excuse to theorize about human personality. What
is surprising to the reader is that the application of Chia's fantastic
views to Pao-yu is remarkably apt.

Leng Tzu-hsing tells Chia Yu-ts'un the story about how Pao-yu's
father, according to custom, placed various objects before his son
on the first anniversary of the latter's birth, and that the baby was
only attracted to feminine objects such as rouge, powder, and
hairpins. When Pao-yu is seven years old, his feminism is indicated
by such childish prattle as:

----

[160]HLMPSHCP, chap. 2, p. 19, lines 1 - 2: 果然奇異. 只怕
這人來歷不小.
[161]CYCHLMCP, chap. 2, p. 35, chia-hsu chia-p'i: 青埂頑石
已得下落.
[162] 來歷.
[163]"Provenance" for lai li is the excellent translation of Mr.
Richard Kunst, "The Beginning and Ending of The Dream of the Red
Chamber".

Little girls are made of water, little boys are made of mud.
When I see girls, I'm refreshed, but when I see boys, I gag.[164]
Leng Tzu-hsing then asks Chia Yu-ts'un:

Wouldn't you say that's funny? No doubt he'll be a wanton
devil in the future![165]

As Chih-yen Chai observes, this last prediction from Leng Tzu-hsing
about Pao-yu's sexuality arouses Yu-ts'un, whose public image is
puritanical and Confucian, to make a firm rebuttal. Without Leng's
comment, Chia Yu-ts'un would not become so stern, nor would he
deliver his "odd-ball queer-beer" thesis in which he endeavors to
account for Pao-yu's character type.[166]

He proceeds to tell Leng Tzu-hsing that he is "all wrong"[167] and
that the problem is that people simply do not know about Pao-yu's
lai li. This is why persons such as Chia Cheng, Pao-yu's father,
mistakenly attribute his interest in women to lust.[168] In fact, says
Yu-ts'un, while the majority of human beings are pretty much the
same,[169] there are the Very Good[170] who are born at the right
auspicious time, and the Very Evil[171] who are born at the wrong
inauspicious time. Examples of the former are the ancient emperors
Yao, Shun, and Yu,[172] and sages such as Confucius, Mencius,
and the neo-Confucian Chu Hsi.[173] These bring order into the
world. The Very Evil are those who cause disorder such as Ch'in
Shih Huang-ti,[174] the first Emperor of the Ch'in dynasty, Wang
Mang,[175] the Han usurper, and power mad generals such as Ts'ao

----

[164]HLMPSHCP, chap. 2, p. 19, line 6: 女兒是水作的骨肉，
男人是泥作的骨肉，我見了女兒，我便清爽，見了男子，
便覺濁臭逼人.
   [165]ibid., line 7: 你道好笑不好笑，將來色鬼無疑了.
   [166]CYCHLMCP, chap. 2, p. 35, chia-hsu chia-p'i: 沒有這一句，
雨村如何突然屬色，並後奇奇怪怪之論.
   [167] 非也.
   [168]HLMPSHCP, chap. 2, p. 19, line 8: 大約政老前輩也
錯以淫魔色鬼看待了.
   [169] 餘者皆無大異.
   [170] 大仁.
   [171] 大惡.
   [172] 堯；舜；禹；
   [173] 孔；孟；朱熹；
   [174] 秦始皇帝.
   [175] 王莽.

Ts'ao[176] of the Eastern Han, and rebels such as An Lu-shan[177] of the T'ang. The Very Good are born into the world with the Upright Breath[178] of Heaven and Earth, while the Very Evil are born with the Perverse Breath[179] of Heaven and Earth. Occasionally in the universal scheme of things, the Two Breaths come in violent contact, and out of this contact there arises men and women who are not capable of being the Very Good or the Very Evil, but always something in between. If these individuals are born into aristocratic families, they become foolish romantics.[180] In families of modest means, they become hermits and escapists.[181] In poor families, they become actors and courtesans.[182] Among the many historical examples Chia cites in this category are officials and even emperors who abandoned their careers for poetry or love such as T'ao Ch'ien, Hsi K'ang, Liu Ling, and Ming Huang.[183]

Here we have an example of Ts'ao Hsueh-ch'in's vision of human understanding. Chia Yu-ts'un's discussion yields a kind of insight of which, however, he is not quite aware. His analysis of the Two Breaths is preposterous. It certainly tells us nothing of Pao-yu's actual lai li, that is, his mythic origins. The rigid catalogue of names, divided as they are into narrow "either-or" categories of good and evil, must mean nothing but the sheerest pedantry to Leng Tzu-hsing, who is a merchant of slight education. Yu-ts'un is also both dogmatic and prejudiced. He has no personal knowledge of the Chia family, but he insistently generalizes on the basis of rumors.

----

176 曹操.
177 安祿山.
178 正氣.
179 邪氣.
180 情癡情種.
181 逸士高人.
182 奇優名娼.
An example of Ts'ao's style. Chia here accidentally accounts for the types of characters found in the novel. Liu Lao-lao makes a similar statement about children born into rich families. There is a parallel between Chia's Upright Breath which, when there is a surplus, makes "sweet dew" 甘露 throughout the world, and the "sweet dew" with which the Divine Crystal Page waters the Crimson Pearl Sylph Herb.

183 陶潛; 嵇康; 劉伶; 唐明皇;
For the whole of Chia's lecture, see HLMPSHCP, chap. 2, pp. 19-20.

Ironically, Chia Yu-ts'un is right. While Pao-yu is not made up of a mixture of the Two Breaths, as a divine rejected stone he has both a transcendent and a human nature. He is born into a wealthy aristocratic family, and he does manifest a recklessly romantic spirit. He even fits well into the catalogue of names Yu-ts'un chooses for him. He is one of those who seeks to escape the world through poetry and religious mysticism, such as Hsi K'ang, T'ao Ch'ien, Liu Ling, and Ming Huang.[184]

Ts'ao seems to reinforce the meaning of this passage with some extra touches of irony. When Chia Yu-ts'un finishes his discussion, Leng Tzu-hsing expresses his warped understanding in the following words:

> According to what you have said, those who succeed (in being influenced by the Upright Breath) become lords, while those who fail become thieves.[185]

Leng's simple terse summary, which states, in effect, "nothing succeeds like success", renders Chia's verbose harangue both meaningless and ridiculous--the captive auditor, a man of low rank, cannot understand the language of his superior. Yu-ts'un, nevertheless, replies to Tzu-hsing in the following words: "You are exactly right".[186] In other words, Chia Yu-ts'un does not know himself what he has been talking about. The point is brought home when we compare his observations on the two Pao-yus, Chen Pao-yu, whom Yu-ts'un has tutored, and Chia Pao-yu, whom he has never met. There is no reason for Yu-ts'un to defend so eagerly Chia Pao-yu, since he does not know him. Yet he claims for him a great lai li. He then reports to Leng that his former pupil, Chen Pao-yu, is one who cannot study unless girls are near him. This Pao-yu insists that girls are pure and boys are corrupt. In short, he is identical in his feminism to Chia Pao-yu. Yet, Chia Yu-ts'un

----

[184]Yu-ts'un's claim in chapter 120 that he is very familiar with Pao-yu and the Chia family is actually untrue. Yet one may agree on the basis of our above remarks that the Very Good and Very Evil, Upright Breath and Perverse Breath similes are apt. Chih-yen Chai remarks on the line from the novel, 正不容邪,邪復妒正 (HLMPSHCP, chap. 2, pp. 19-20), that this is an excellent simile. CYCHLMCP, chap. 2, p. 35, chia-hsu chia-p'i: 譬得好

[185]HLMPSHCP, chap. 2, p. 20, line 8: 依你說,成則公侯,敗則賊了.

[186]ibid., line 8: 正是這意.

claims that a boy like Chen Pao-yu will not preserve the patrimony
of his grandfather or follow the admonitions of his teachers and
friends.[187]   Again, Yu-ts'un is completely mistaken--this time
about his own pupil.   Chen Pao-yu eventually symbolizes the filial
son in Dream of the Red Chamber.   He gives up his adolescent
fondness for girls in preference for Confucian studies, while Chia
Pao-yu cannot bear to do anything which will remove him from the
presence of his female cousins.[188]
   What is the meaning of Chia Yu-ts'un's visit to the Temple of
Cognition of Knowledge and his tavern conversation with Leng Tzu-
hsing?   In both episodes we find evidence of Ts'ao Hsueh-ch'in's
indirect narrative technique.   He first describes a man of enlightenment, the Buddhist monk, and his "opposite", Chia Yu-ts'un, before
telling of the "deluded ones", mi-jen,[189] of the Chia family,
who are actually the main characters of the novel.[190]   The monk
is one who only appears deaf and dumb, while Chia Yu-ts'un, his
"opposite", is one who only appears to be wise, but who is actually
ensnared in the world of the Red Dust.   But Yu-ts'un has an occasional glimmering sense of karma which puts him beyond the pale of
the rest of the "deluded ones" of the Chia clan.   His theoretical
lecture to Leng Tzu-hsing on the Two Breaths indirectly introduces
us to the central figure of Dream of the Red Chamber, Chia Pao-yu.
Yu-ts'un's declamation comes from one who asks the wrong questions
and who cannot understand a simple Buddhist poem, yet his lecture
is actually meaningful.   He is a person who is unable to communicate with anyone, whether it be mystic monk or pragmatic shop
merchant.   Of vulgar ambition and a shallow awareness, he is a
dilettante who exemplifies the futility of the life of the literocrat.

----

[187]HLMPSHCP, chap. 2, p. 21, line 7: 你看這等子弟，必不
能守祖父之根基，從師友之規諫的。
   [188]Yu-ts'un persists in his dogmatic views until his conversation
with Tzu-hsing ends.   When the latter tells the former about other
members of the Chia family, Yu-ts'un observes they all fit his
theory of the Upright and Perverse Breaths.   HLMPSHCP, chap. 2,
p. 22, lines 9-10: 可知我前言不謬．你我方纔所說這幾
個人，都只怕是那正邪兩賦而來一路之人，未可知也。
   [189] 迷人
   [190]CYCHLMCP, chap. 2, p. 30, chia-hsu mei-p'i: 未出寧榮
繁華盛處，却先寫一荒涼小境；未寫通部入世迷人，
却先寫一出世醒人；迴風舞雪，倒峽逆波，別小說中
所無之法。

Yet, he sees what others do not see. Pao-yu is a person of important lai li. Who else in Pao-yu's family knows of this escapist
temperament as does Chia Yu-ts'un, an outsider? Who else is at
least cognizant that there are hidden meanings in ordinary events,
places, and personalities? Still, Chia suffers from a stigmatism--
there are certain things he cannot see no matter how hard he looks.
In the framework chapters 1, 2, and 103, Ts'ao Hsueh-ch'in seems
to mock rational efforts at understanding, as though he were claiming the superiority of imagination and intuition. If we turn to the
last chapter of Dream of the Red Chamber and the final encounter
between Chen Shih-yin and Chia Yu-ts'un, we shall be able to
test our observations.

The enlightenment paradigm of "true" and "false" is completed in
the last chapter of Dream of the Red Chamber and in the final meeting of Chen Shih-yin and Chia Yu-ts'un. There we find the repetition of archetypes. Yu-ts'un is at the lowest point of his official
career. Though he is guilty of extortion, there is a general amnesty,
so that he only suffers being removed from office and being ordered
to return to his birthplace. Thus he ends up in that humble condition he has sought to escape ever since his first acquaintance with
Chen Shih-yin. Once again, as in chapter 103, the two figures
accidentally meet at Rapid Flow River. Significantly, there is the
addition of a new name. The ford where passengers cross Rapid
Flow River is called Awake Delusion Ford.[191] As in chapter 1,
when Chen invited Chia to eat and drink with him during the Mid-
Autumn festival, Chia now goes off with Chen to the latter's
thatched hut to have an intimate conversation--this time over a cup
of tea. One initial indication of a new understanding between the

---

191 覺迷渡口．This name is not entirely new, of course, for
in chapter 5, when Pao-yu makes his first dream visit to the Great
Void Illusion Land, and after he has his first sexual experience
there with a fairy, he nearly falls into Delusion River or Delusion
Ford 迷津 which is full of the demons of passion. In chapter 5,
then, this river crossing and the river itself are symbols of death.
In chapter 120, the same river becomes a symbol of salvation and
enlightenment with the addition of the two characters, chiao 覺
and tu 渡, "to awake" and "to ferry across" or "ferry". See
HLMPSHCP, chap. 5, p. 57, line 16: 警幻道：此即迷津也……

two characters is that they go off together hand in hand.[192] Chia
Yu-ts'un is aroused to some degree of awareness at the mere sight
of Chen Shih-yin, who, after all, he assumed to have died in the
burning of the Hermitage of Cognition of Knowledge. Chia is presumably made acutely conscious of his own misfortunes and of his
vain attempts to escape from mutability when he is greeted by Chen
in the following words: "Honorable Mr. Chia! No troubles since
we parted?"[193] This is not a simple "How are you?", as Chen
uses the word yang[194] (a worm within the vitals). The word is
commonly used in greetings, although it seldom appears in Dream
of the Red Chamber, but in the context of Chia's downfall, yang
has a greater significance.

Chen and Chia first attempt to explain their inability to communicate during their previous meeting:

"Worthy Immortal! Aren't you really the Honorable Mr.
Chen? How is it that when last we met, though it was face
to face, you showed no recognition? Later when this lowly
one realized that fire had consumed your grass kiosk, he was
deeply alarmed. Today, chance occasions this encounter,
and thus I sigh, revering the height and depth of the Holy
One's cultivation. Alas! This lowly deluded one has remained unchanged, and now here he is!"

Chen Shih-yin replied: "in the past Your Honor was
resplendent with rank and dignity--how could a Poor Follower
of the Way show recognition? Even so I dared to offer a bit
of conversation--due to our former acquaintance . . . ."[195]

To Chia Yu-ts'un, Chen Shih-yin's survival of the temple fire attests
to his divinity. His main concern is, as usual, with change, although in a sense which differs radically from mutability. Here he
becomes aware that his life poses a moral contrast to that of his
friend. Both have been subjected to mutability, but only Chen
attains a form of transcendence. For his part, Chen points to a
somewhat peculiar fact which separated them in the past: social
rank. His example reveals one of the repeated motifs in Dream of
the Red Chamber: the drive for salvation and self-awareness razes

----

192 兩人攜手而行. See discussion in "Myth", pp. 70-71.
193HLMPSHCP, chap. 120, p. 416, line 3:賈老先生別來無恙?
194 恙.
195HLMPSHCP, chap. 120, p. 416, lines 3-5. For text, see
p. 139.

第一百二十回　甄士隱詳說太虛情　賈雨村歸結紅樓夢

不言襲人從此又是一番天地。且說那賈雨村犯了婪索的案件，審明定罪，今遇大赦，遞籍為民。雨村因叫家眷先行，自己帶了一個小廝一車行李來到急流津覺迷渡口。只見一個道者從那渡頭草棚裏出來，執手相迎。雨村認得是甄士隱，也連忙打恭。士隱道：「賈老先生別來無恙？」雨村道：「老仙長到底是甄老先生！何前次相逢，覿面不認？後知火焚草亭，下鄙深為悵恨。今日幸得相逢，益歎老仙翁道德高深。奈鄙人下愚不移，致有今日！」甄士隱道：「前者老大人高官顯爵，貧道怎敢相認！原因故交，敢贈片言，不意老大人相棄之深。然而富貴窮通，亦非偶然。今日復得相逢，也是一樁奇事。這裏離草菴不遠，暫請膝談，未知可否？」雨村欣然領命。兩人攜手而行，小廝驅車隨後。到了一座茅菴，士隱讓進。雨村坐下，小童獻上茶來。雨村便請教仙長超塵的始末。士隱笑道：「一念之間，塵凡頓易。老先生從繁華境中來，豈不知溫柔富貴鄉中有一寶玉乎？」雨村道：「怎麼不知。近聞紛紛傳述，說他也逃入空門。下愚當時也曾與他往來過數次，再不想此人覺有如是之決絕。」士隱道：「非也。這一段奇緣我先知之。昔年我與先生在仁清巷舊宅門口敘話之前，我已會過他一面。」雨村驚訝道：「京城離貴鄉甚遠，何以能見？」士隱道：「神交久矣。」雨村道：「既然如此，現今寶玉的下落，仙長定能知之。」士隱道：「寶玉，即寶玉也。那年榮寧查抄之前，欽黛分離之日，此玉早已離世。一為避禍，二為撮合。從此夙緣一了，形質歸一，又復稍示神靈，高魁貴子，方顯得此玉那天奇地靈煉之寶，非凡間可比。前經茫茫大士渺渺真人攜帶下凡，如今塵緣已滿，仍是此二人攜歸本處。這便是寶玉的下落。」雨村聽了，雖不能全然明白，卻也十知四五，便點頭歎道：「原來如此。下愚不知。」

但那寶玉既有如此的來歷，又何以情迷至此，復又豁悟如此？還要請教。」士隱笑道：「此事說來，老先生未必盡解。太虛幻境即是真如福地，雨番因册原始要終之道，歷歷生平如何不悟！仙草歸真，焉有通靈不復原之理呢！」雨村聽着却不明自了，知仙機也不便更問，因又說道：「寶玉之事旣得聞命，

但是敝族閨秀如此之多，何元妃以下算來結局俱屬平常呢？」士隱歎息道：「老先生莫怪拙言。貴族之女俱從情天孽海而來。大凡古今女子，那淫字固不可犯，只這情字也是沾染不得的。所以崔鶯蘇小無非仙子隱心，宋玉相如大是文人口孽。凡是情思綢繆的，那結局就不可問了。」雨村聽到這裏，不覺拈鬚長歎。因又問道：「請教老仙翁，那榮寧兩府尙可如前否？」士隱道：「福善禍淫，古今定理。現

今榮寧兩府善者修緣，惡者悔禍，將來蘭桂齊芳，家道復初，也是自然的道理。」雨村低了半日頭，忽然笑道：「是了，是了。現在他府中有一個名蘭的已中鄉榜，恰好應着蘭字。適間老仙翁說「蘭桂齊芳」，又道寶玉「高魁貴子」，莫非他有遺腹之子可以飛黃騰達的麼？」士隱微微笑道：「此係後事，未便預說。」雨村還要再問，士隱不答，便命人設具盤飧，邀雨村共食。食畢，雨村還要問自己的終

身，不知尙有何俗緣？」士隱道：「也不過是兒女私情罷了。」雨村聽了，益發驚異：「請問仙長純修若此，不知何日有何緣？」士隱道：「老先生草菴暫歇，我還有一段俗緣未了，正當今日完結。」雨村驚訝道：「仙長純修，出此言？」士隱道：「老先生有所不知，小女英蓮幼遭塵劫，老先生初任之時曾經判斷。今歸薛姓，

產難完劫，遣一子於薛家以承宗祧。此時正是塵緣脫盡之時，只好接引接引。」士隱說着拂袖而起，雨村心中恍恍惚惚，就在這急流津覺迷渡口草庵中睡着了。這士隱自去度脫了香菱，送到太虛幻境交那

第一百二十四　甄士隱詳說太虛情　賈雨村歸結紅樓夢

四一七

social structures.

Chen Shih-yin proceeds to criticize Chia's recognition of the place of chance in human affairs:

> . . . wealth, poverty, and well being are not accidental. Likewise, our second encounter here today is a marvelous event.[196]

Later in the course of their conversation, Chen comments:

> Happiness and goodness, disaster and lust, have always had given patterns . . . .[197]

As we have noted several times, every event which takes place in the novel is prefaced by some word or phrase which indicates the fortuitous nature of that event. Yet the novelist claims that what is described is appearance rather than reality, and thus the thrust of Dream of the Red Chamber towards the revelation--occurring only in the final pages--that in fact all phenomena follow a strict pattern of predestination. Thus in the schema of salvation, Chia must receive final instructions from Chen, even though he is unworthy.

Before considering the propriety of Chia Yu-ts'un's enlightenment, we ought to note the kinds of questions he asks his holy teacher, as well as the latter's answers.

In Chia's first question, he comes straight to the point while Chen is equally evasive:

> Yu-ts'un then requested to be instructed about the beginnings and ends of how the Master had transcended the Red Dust.
>
> Shih-yin smiled and said: "In but the space of a thought, the Red Dust suddenly changes. But the Honorable One is from the Realm of Luxuries. Did you not know of a Pao-yu in that rich homeland of soft, warm affection?"[198]

Chia wants to glean the secrets of Chen's salvation, while the latter couches his reply in terms of mutability--the world changes, so I too have changed. Chen prefers to turn to an example of salvation other than himself, and with this example, to another lesson for Chia Yu-ts'un. Thus the author uses the framework as a commentary on the whole novel.

Chia replies to Chen's question by making the preposterous claim that he was on very friendly terms with Pao-yu and the Chia family.

----

[196]ibid., line 6. For text, see p. 139.
[197]ibid., p. 417. For text, see p. 140.
[198]ibid., p. 416, lines 8-9. For text, see p. 139.

He notes the current rumor that Pao-yu has "vanished into the Fate of Nothingness",[199] that is, he has abandoned the world to embrace Buddhism:

". . . I never imagined that such a person would finally come to an ultimate decision like that".

Shih-yin said: "Such an error! I knew beforehand about this strange destiny. Even before that time years ago when you and I discoursed before my home gate on Benevolent Love Lane, I had had contact with him".

Yu-ts'un said quizzically: "The Capital is very far from your venerable home country, how is it possible that you had seen him?"

"We've long been kindred spirits".[200]

Shih-yin's last remark, couched in a conventional phrase, hides from Yu-ts'un the fact that the former's foreknowledge of Pao-yu came through the spiritual medium of dreams. He first learned of the jade stone's imminent birth in the Red Dust as Pao-yu through a vision of the Buddhist and Taoist Immortals (chapter 1). Thus there is an ironical presence of deceit within the paradigm of salvation and, at the same time, a reaffirmation of the importance of dreams. Chen denies to Chia knowledge of the original source of understanding. At the same time, in his claim of intimacy with Pao-yu, Chia Yu-ts'un tells lies even while on his way towards enlightenment. Truly, the "lowly deluded one has remained unchanged".

Since Chen has cited the example of Pao-yu, Chia decides that his second question will have to do with the latter's "whereabouts".[201] Through Chen Shih-yin, the author provides a brief recapitulation of the novel and the Stone Record:

"'Pao-yu' is but pao-yu ('precious jade'). Before the year in which the Ning-kuo and Jung-kuo mansions were searched and appropriated, and before Pao-ch'ai's and Tai-yu's separation day, this jade had already parted from the world: firstly to flee disaster, and secondly, for reunion. Once its destined involvements were over, form and substance returned to their

---

199 道入空門.

200 神交久矣 is a common saying of people who have never met but who know of each other by reputation or similar interest. HLMPSHCP, chap. 120, p. 416, lines 10-12. For text, see p. 139.

201 下落.

unity. There has also occurred a slight show of its spiritual efficacy--a magna cum laude and a man-child of noble promise--thus manifesting that this jade is the treasure formed by the smelting together of Heaven's Mystery and Earth's Soul. Nothing among ordinary mortals can compare with it. Formerly it passed through the hands of the Buddhist of Infinite Space and the Taoist of Boundless Time[202] and descended into the mortal world. As of now its Red Dust Destiny is fulfilled, so that again the two Otherworldlings have taken it in their hands and returned it to its native place. These then are the whereabouts of Pao-yu".

Yu-ts'un could not understand everything he heard, but he did grasp four or five parts out of ten.[203]

In this passage, Ts'ao Hsueh-ch'in offers a parallel experience to Chia Yu-ts'un and to the reader of Dream of the Red Chamber. Shih-yin's supposed elucidations are sufficiently enigmatic to be confusing to both protagonist and audience. Dream of the Red Chamber is not a mystery novel in which plot and theme may be understood by starting at the end. Just as the framework is vital for perceiving the core, so too the latter clarifies the former. The reader of the preceding sections of Dream of the Red Chamber will be aware that magna cum laude[204] refers to Pao-yu's successful passing of the Civil Service Examinations, and that "man-child of noble promise"[205] specifies his son who is born after his departure. Chia Yu-ts'un does not identify these allusions until later in his discussion with Chen Shih-yin. Certainly the references to the mythic Stone are of no help to him. Yet, despite somewhat enigmatic language, the passage does elucidate the meaning of enlightenment. The Stone, now a metaphor for Pao-yu, is said to have achieved reunion of body and spirit[206] in parting from this world. Pao-yu's release from mutability is an act which symbolizes "reunification" with his "destiny" or the "fulfillment of affinity". Once su yuan (an involvement which has been pre-determined from a

----

202These titles are C. C. Wang's translations for 茫 茫 大 士, 渺 渺 真 人. See Dream of the Red Chamber, New York, 1958.
203HLMPSHCP, chap. 120, p. 416, lines 13-16. For text, see p. 139.
204 高 魁.
205 貴 子.
206 撮 合.

"previous existence"),[207] has been realized, then "form",[208] meaning the manifestation of the pure Stone spirit in the body of Pao-yu, and "substance",[209] meaning the manifestation of the original essence of Pao-yu in the spirit of the Stone, become one.

If we view Dream of the Red Chamber as a criticism of life, what is most important to notice in this passage is that the "unity of being"--the oneness of Stone and person, divine and human, form and substance--is predestined. The reader is well aware that Ts'ao Hsueh-ch'in continually undercuts popular conceptions of reality by juxtaposing them against Buddhist visions of mutability and changing desire. But the religious and mystical conceptions are equally liable and subject to Ts'ao's ironic scrutiny. What is unique about Dream of the Red Chamber is that it represents a fusion of dimensions rather than a balance of forces or even an emphasis on one as opposed to another. Things are continually becoming their opposites --the real is evolving towards the unreal--and Ts'ao creates this fusion through irony. Thus the Fool, Chia Yu-ts'un, and the Wise Man, Chen Shih-yin, are not completely straightforward with one another, even while confessing their former inadequacies, and even at the point of total enlightenment. But if the world is falsely perceived by ordinary beings such as Chia Yu-ts'un, in what sense are exceptional mortals such as Pao-yu and Shih-yin respectable paradigms of enlightenment and worthy of admiration and imitation? With this question we realize that in a certain sense, Chia Pao-yu, Chen Shih-yin, and Chia Yu-ts'un are identical beings. Each of the three examples demonstrates that enlightenment and self-awareness are not attained through good intentions, tried virtue, or mundane learning. As in the case of Chen Shih-yin discussed earlier, enlightenment for Chia Yu-ts'un and Chia Pao-yu is a gift. It is the only real example of fortuitousness which Chen Shih-yin, using his personal experience, might acknowledge. Transcendence happens upon the individual always following suffering, but never solely because of suffering.[210]

----

207 夙緣.

208 形.

209 質.

210The lone example of deserved reward occurs when Pao-yu, by imperial decree, is given the posthumous title of Wen-miao Chen-jen 文妙真人 , "True Saint of Literary Sublimity". Pao-yu has placed high in the Examination lists and has left the world for Buddhism. In a sense, this exception proves our point that

Because Chia Yu-ts'un is ignorant of the mystical energies of enlightenment mechanics, he is bound to be querulous when he learns that the passionate Pao-yu has "vanished into the Gate of Nothingness". Here too we have an ironic view of the enlightenment paradigm: the best efforts of the divine teacher fail to impress the worldly disciple. What Chia does appreciate is Chen's handy reference to Pao-yu's lai li. As in his discussion with Leng Tzu-hsing about Pao-yu, and in his previous encounter with Chen Shih-yin, Yu-ts'un is obsessed with facile accounts of human character through appeals to what he believes to be pre-birth histories:

> "So that's the way it really is. In my inferior intelligence
> I did not know. But if this Pao-yu's lai li is actually of that
> sort, how is it possible that he became lost in passion to such
> an extent? And furthermore—how could he spontaneously
> attain enlightenment like that?"
>
> Shih-yin smiled and said: "To speak of this affair will not
> necessarily result in Your Honor's thorough understanding.
> The Great Void Illusion Realm is in fact the Paradise of
> Truth.[211] There, on two occasions, Pao-yu read the Destiny
> Dossiers which contained the Way from origin to culmination.
> With everything made clear there, how could he not attain
> enlightenment? The Sylph Herb returned to the Truth, what
> reason could there be for this Stone which Penetrates the
> Numinous to not return again to its origin!"
>
> In listening to this, Yu-ts'un could hardly understand any-
> thing at all, but he knew it would be inopportune to ask
> about Divine Mechanics . . . .[212]

Yu-ts'un cannot know that the Great Void Illusion Realm is the place where the Beware Illusion Fairy has her palace and where the Buddhist and Taoist Immortals take the jade Stone before its descent to earth. Nor is he aware that by "on two occasions", Chen is referring to two of Pao-yu's dreams (chapters 5 and 116) in which he visits the Illusion Realm and reads of the fates of the girls he

----

enlightenment is not the possession of anything to be earned, but a state of "getting over" everything. He has won a title as a reward, but his absence renders it completely meaningless.

211 真如福地) "Paradise of Truth". The Auspicious Stage of Thusness (Tathatā—things as they really are).

212 HLMPSHCP, chap. 120, pp. 416-417. For text, see pp. 139-140.

loves. The Sylph Herb is Tai-yu and the one who "penetrates the
Numinous" is Pao-yu. And because all this is unclear to Chia, he
does something which is typical for him and, at the same time, very
reminiscent of Chen Shih-yin: instead of seeking further information, he attributes his inability to understand to the ineffable
"Divine Mechanics".[213] This reference echoes across the one hundred and twenty chapters of Dream of the Red Chamber to Chen
Shih-yin's original dream-vision of the Buddhist and Taoist Immortals in chapter 1. When Chen tries to learn about Cause and Effect,
he is told that Penumbra Mechanics[214] may not be explained until
after one experiences the Red Dust: "Shih-yin understood. It
would be inopportune to inquire further".[215] Chia, at the very
end of the novel, unconsciously begins his first step towards becoming Chen; the "false" is evolving towards the "true".

According to the foreordination of the myth in chapter 1, Pao-yu
attains salvation because of his heavenly origins. He is destined to
be saved following his experience of nearly every form of youthful
passion. Certainly the reader is troubled by this gift of nirvana to
one who exploits his emotions--how can passion lead to salvation?
Yet, predestination and mythic origins are not entirely satisfactory
causes for enlightenment either, until, perhaps, we realize that
their "unreality" gives meaning to the bare facts of life. Through
myth, Ts'ao Hsueh-ch'in indicates that enlightenment and awareness, if there be such final forms of salvation, are indeed spontaneous evolutions which befall unique characters under certain circumstances.

At the same time, the author modifies spontaneity with vital
touches of elapsed time. Dream of the Red Chamber offers the
reader a lesson in enlightenment, one which we shall discuss further
in "Persona", but one which bears repeating here. We note that
Pao-yu's enlightenment is partially due to his reading of recondite
documents. There is a paradigm of "repeated readings" which runs
through the entire novel. In chapter 1, the Reverend Taoist Kosmo
Kosmos reads the Stone Record once, and is unimpressed. He reads
it twice and changes his own name to "Bonze of Love".[216] In
chapter 120, he again happens upon the Stone in the course of his
travels, and this time he notices that more characters are incised on

----

213 仙機,
214 玄機.
215HLMPSHCP, chap. 1, pp. 6-7. For text, see pp. 51-52.
216情僧.

the back of the Stone telling of its final fate. When he reads the
Stone Record for the third time, and especially the ending, he
reaches the following conclusion:
> ". . . in its strangeness, it is not strange; common, and yet
> not common; real, and yet not real; unreal, and yet not
> unreal".217

Here even he reaches a new stage of awareness. Upon his first
reading, he feels the story is not fit for human consumption; upon
the second, he experiences a profound change in his person and
life-style; with the third, he finds that the story may be used to
enlighten mortals. He has learned to perceive that opposites are
identical.

Similarly, Chia Yu-ts'un must meet with Chen Shih-yin three
times (in chapters 1, 103, and 120) before he experiences a changing perspective. On the first occasion, he views Chen solely as a
political Maecenas--a person who will speed him towards officialdom. On the second, Chen is a symbol of withdrawal which serves
to challenge Chia's worldly success. In the final encounter, Chia
ceases to be the victim of mutability. Likewise, Pao-yu needs a
repeated reading of the Destiny Dossiers containing the fates of the
women he loves before he is convinced that he cannot make time
stand still. His father, Chia Cheng, also becomes aware of the
importance of the repeated pattern of threes in the life of his son.
He observes the three different occasions on which he saw monks
make use of the jade to teach Pao-yu or to save his life.218 Ts'ao's
technique here is not based on some simple numerologist's theory of
cyclic repetition, but on the experience of elapsed time. The novel
changes according to time and occasion, and thus demands of the
author repeated writings and of the reader successive readings.
There is a particularly unique reward, for in both the beginning and
the ending of the novel, the author claims, through the Reverend
Taoist Kosmo Kosmos and Chen Shih-yin, that Dream of the Red
Chamber offers its reader an embodiment and an experience of tao.

In the course of his conversation with Chen Shih-yin, Chia Yu-
ts'un has difficulty understanding Shih-yin's explanations about
salvation, Pao-yu's enlightenment, and Divine Machinery. He
therefore turns to more mundane questions, such as those having to

----

217HLMPSHCP, chap. 120, p. 418, line 9: 奇而不奇,俗而不
俗,真而不真,假而不假.
218HLMPSHCP, chap. 120, p. 410, lines 11-12.

do with the fates of the Grand View Garden maidens and the futures
of the Ning-kuo and Jung-kuo mansions. Of particular interest is
Chen Shih-yin's view of life patterns:

> "Wealth and goodness, disaster and lust, have always had
> given patterns. Right now in the mansions of the Ning-kuo
> and Jung-kuo, the good cultivate their <u>karmas</u>, and the bad
> regret their faults. In the future the <u>lan</u> (magnolia) and the
> <u>kuei</u> (cassia) will be of equal fragrance and the family fortune
> <u>will</u> be restored--this is natural law".

> Yu-ts'un bowed his head for a long while, then suddenly he
> laughed and said: "That's it! That's it! Right now in the
> Jung-kuo mansion there is one with the given name of "Lan"
> who is a Candidate on the Examination list--this fits the
> character, <u>lan</u>, exactly. Just this minute, Venerable Sage,
> you said, 'the <u>lan</u> and the <u>kuei</u> will be of equal fragrance',
> and you also said of Pao-yu, '<u>magna cum laude</u> and a man-
> child of noble promise'. Surely he has a child left in his
> wife's womb who will 'fly and soar' with good fortune?"[219]

Yu-ts'un here exhibits his mental slowness and his naiveté. It has
taken him a long period of intent listening to realize that <u>lan</u> and
<u>kuei</u>, '<u>magna cum laude</u> and a man-child', refer, respectively, to
<u>Chia</u> Lan, who completed the Examinations with Pao-yu, and to
the son begotten by Pao-yu. He completely ignores the real meaning of Chen's fundamental statement, "this is natural law". Chia
takes this statement as a sign of hope: the Chia clan will be restored, there will be posterity, and the good old days of the past
may return. Its view of the contrapuntal rhythms of the entire
novel and the opinions of Chen Shih-yin, "this is natural law",
can only be a reference to the meaningless of human life. The
family will rise again, just as it will decline again, for the human
cycle of growth and decay, desire and disappointment, is endless.

There are two concluding ironies in the exchange between Chen
and Chia. One is the former's refusal to answer the latter's more
important questions; the other is the presence of character flaws
and shortcomings of knowledge in the figures of enlightenment. We
have observed that Chen Shih-yin will not say how he himself
transcended the Red Dust. Since, according to the novel, enlightenment is a gift, one can hardly expect either the exemplar, Chen
Shih-yin, or the author, Ts'ao Hsueh-ch'in, to divulge such secrets

----

219<u>HLMPSHCP</u>, chap. 120, p. 417, lines 7-10. For text, see
p. 140.

of "Divine Mechanics". Chen also will tell Chia nothing about
the latter's fate, and when asked, he says:

"Honorable One. Rest for awhile in the reed hut. I still
have a slight bit of worldly involvement to conclude, and it
must be tidied up today".

Yu-ts'un exclaimed in surprise: "Master of utmost purity--
what worldly involvement could there be remaining for you?"

"Just a private affair having to do with children", said
Shih-yin.[220]

Shih-yin then informs Yu-ts'un about the fate of his daughter,
Ying-lien, who was sold by kidnappers to Hsueh P'an. She later
died in childbirth, leaving Hsueh P'an a posthumous son. Chen
uses this incident to remind Chia of his sins. Yu-ts'un was the
judge of the case in which Hsueh P'an killed a man in order to
procure Ying-lien, and Chia absolved Hsueh P'an of his crime. As
Chen Shih-yin leaves to liberate the soul of his daughter from the
Red Dust and to take her to the Great Void Illusion Land so that
the Beware Illusion Fairy will check off her name from the Register
of Lovers, the Chia Yu-ts'un enlightenment paradigm nears its
completion:

. . . Yu-ts'un felt numb and dazed. He fell asleep in the
grass hut at the ford of the Awake Delusion Ferry on Rapid
Flow River.[221]

Apparently, Chen Shih-yin is not entirely free of the Red Dust
and thus he is less than perfect. He has become a salvation figure
only to be required to act in that role to save his own daughter as
well as Chia Yu-ts'un. There is a certain irony too in his statement, "Just a private affair having to do with children", for this
line is a fair description of the whole of Dream of the Red Chamber,
Ts'ao Hsueh-ch'in's personal story of the sad destinies of children.
The limitations of the divine are further evidenced at the close of
the Chen Shih-yin paradigm when the Venerable Sage travels to
the Great Void Illusion Realm with his daughter:

Just as he passed the corridor gate, he vaguely perceived
a Buddhist and a Taoist coming along as in a mist. Shih-yin
met them and said: "Holy Lord! True Saint! Congratulations!

----

[220]HLMPSHCP, chap. 120, p. 417, lines 12-13. For text, see
p. 140.
[221]HLMPSHCP, chap. 120, p. 417, lines 15-16. For text, see
p. 140.

Felicitations! Lovers' destinies are all concluded, and have
not the Register Books all been clearly balanced?"
    The Buddhist said: "The Lovers' destinies are yet to be
concluded, but that Foolish Thing has already come back!
So now it must be escorted and returned to its place of origin,
and final events in its life must be clearly explained, else
its stint in the world will have been in vain".[222]

The contrast between Shih-yin's delight at the conclusion of his
own daughter's fate, and the casualness of the Buddhist and Taoist
Immortals about that Foolish Thing, the Stone (Pao-yu), which has
come back and will be perfunctorily restored to its place, presents
a humorous image of enlightenment and exemplifies Ts'ao's portrayal of playful divinity. This passage represents one of the scores
of examples in Dream of the Red Chamber in which the divine and
human dimensions are parodies of one another.

    By the end of Dream of the Red Chamber, Chia Yu-ts'un may be
said to have become his opposite, Chen Shih-yin. In chapter 1,
Chen helps Chia, a literatus who has fallen on evil days, to begin
his official career and to restore the patrimony of his vanished
family. The contrapuntal rhythm of the novel is thus established.
Even as Chen's fortunes begin to decline, Chia's improve. At the
end of chapter 1, Chen becomes destitute. He also achieves a
certain level of emancipation from the world due to a religious
vision which informs him that earthly desire is but vanity. Conversely, Chia becomes a successful candidate in the Civil Service
Examinations and immediately becomes corrupted by ambition. At
the end of the novel, Chen instructs Chia as to the meaning of
human existence. Chia may be said to become enlightened to an
extreme degree. At the end of his instruction from Chen, Chia
falls asleep. This does not mean that he is bored or misunderstands
his teacher. Rather, his posture of sleep may symbolize his final
salvation from constant mutability and his final withdrawal from
earthly interests. When the Reverend Taoist Kosmo Kosmos passes
by searching for some mundane figure who has the leisure time to
pass on the excellent Stone Record, an exemplum to warn the world
against desire, Yu-ts'un merely gives a sleepy yawn and refuses
the responsibility:

    The Reverend Taoist Kosmo Kosmos searched straight on and
    came upon a man sleeping in a reed hut at the ford of the

----

222ibid., p. 418, lines 1-3. For text, see p. 151.

第一百二十回　甄士隱詳說太虛情　賈雨村歸結紅樓夢

警幻仙子對冊。剛過牌坊，見那一僧一道縹緲而來，士隱接着說道：「大士真人，恭喜賀喜！情緣完結，都交割清楚了麼？」那僧說道：「情緣尚未全結，倒是那蠢物已經回來了。還得把他送還原所，將他的後事叙明，也不枉他下世一回。」士隱聽了，便拱手而別。那僧道仍攜了玉到青埂峯下，將寶玉安放在女媧煉石補天之處，各自雲遊而去。從此後，天外書傳天外事，兩番人作一番人。

這一日空空道人又從青埂峯前經過，見那補天未用之石仍在那裏，上面字跡依然如舊。又從頭的細細看了一遍，見後面偈文後又敘了多少收緣結果的話頭，便點頭歎道：「我從前見石兄這段奇文，原說可以聞世傳奇，所以曾經抄錄，但未見返本還原。不知何時復有此一佳話。方知石兄下凡一次，磨出光明，修成圓覺，也可謂無復遺憾了。只怕年深日久，字跡模糊，反有舛錯，不如我再抄錄一番，尋個世上清閒無事的人，託他傳遍。知道奇而不奇，俗而不俗，真而不真，假而不假。或者塵夢勞人，聊倩鳥呼歸去；山靈好客，更從石化飛來。」想畢，便又抄了，仍袖至那繁華昌盛的地方遍尋了一番，不是建功立業之人，即係糊口謀衣之輩，那有閒情更去和石頭饒舌。直尋到急流津覺迷渡口，草菴中睡着一個人，因想他必是閒人，便要將這抄錄的石頭記給他看看。那知那人再叫不醒。空空道人復又使勁拉他，纔慢慢的開眼坐起，便接來草草一看，仍舊擲下道：「這事我已親見盡知，你這抄錄的尚無舛錯。我只指與你一個人，託他傳去，便可歸結這一新鮮公案了。」空空道人忙問何人。那人道：「你須待某年某月某日到一個悼紅軒中，有個曹雪芹先生，只說賈雨村言託他如此如此。」說畢，仍舊睡下了。那空空道人牢牢記着此言，又不知過了幾世幾劫，果然有個悼紅軒，見那曹

四一八

雪芹先生正在那裏翻閱歷來的古史，空空道人便將賈雨村言了，方把這石頭記示看。那雪芹先生笑道：

「果然是賈雨村言了。」空空道人便問：「先生何以認得此人，便肯替他傳述？」雪芹先生笑道：

「說你空空，原來你肚裏果然空空。既是假語村言，但無魯魚亥豕以及背謬矛盾之處，樂得與二三同

志，酒餘飯飽，雨夕燈窗之下，同消寂寞，又不必大人先生品題傳世。似你這樣尋根究底，便是刻舟

求劍，膠柱鼓瑟了。」那空空道人聽了，仰天大笑，擲下抄本，飄然而去，一面走着，口中說道：「果

然是敷衍荒唐！不但作者不知，抄者不知，並閱者也不知。不過游戲筆墨，陶情適性而已！」後人見

了這本傳奇，亦曾題過四句為作者緣起之言更轉一竿云：

「說到辛酸處，荒唐愈可悲。

由來同一夢，休笑世人癡。」

第一百二十回　甄士隱詳說太虛情　賈雨村歸結紅樓夢

四一九

Awake Delusion Ferry on the Rapid Flow River. Thinking that he was surely an idler, he took out his transcribed copy of the Stone Record and handed it over to the man to have a look at. Who would have expected this man to keep on sleeping? Kosmo then applied a little force and tugged the fellow, whereupon he lethargically sat up and cracked open his eyes. But after taking the copy and giving it a careless once over, he threw it down:

"I've already seen this stuff myself", he said, "and I know all about it--there aren't any mistakes in your transcribed copy. I'll only point out another fellow--you can commission him to pass this on--he can round out the additional material".

The Reverend Taoist quickly asked who was the other fellow?

The man said: "You'll have to wait until a certain year, a certain month, a certain day, and a certain hour, then there'll be a certain Mr. Ts'ao Hsueh-ch'in in the Grieving for Red Pavilion. Just mention to him that Chia Yu-ts'un said to request that he do this and that". And with that, the man fell asleep as before.223

It seems that Chia Yu-ts'un has learned enough from Chen Shih-yin's final lecture on the Stone Record to be warned against vain pursuits. He is enlightened. Perhaps he has also realized that the Stone Record is in itself a tale of vanity and that finally, it is hopeless to try to warn the world against the ambition, vulgarity, and pride he himself was unable to refuse. Perhaps too, his lack of interest in spreading salvation is a sign that he has gone one step further than Chen Shih-yin down the road of enlightenment. What is fascinating about this passage, however, is not the signs of Chia's faith, but Ts'ao's satire of the enlightenment syndrome he has labored so long to create. To demonstrate the way he undercuts Chia's sudden and spontaneous enlightenment, we need to make two translations of the puns on Chia's name.

Chia Yu-ts'un says to Kosmo Kosmos, "Just mention to him that

----

223HLMPSHCP, chap. 120, p. 418, lines 11-16. For text, see p. 151. There is a pun here. In the Grand View Garden, Pao-yu lives in the I-hung yuan 怡紅院 , "Delighting in Red Compound"; Ts'ao lives in the Tao hung hsuan 悼紅軒 "Grieving for Red Pavilion".

Chia Yu-ts'un said . . . ." If we take the phrase, Chia Yu-ts'un yen,[224] and substitute the homophones, chia-yu ts'un-yen [225] for the name, Chia Yu-ts'un, we have the meaning: "Just mention fictive language and vulgar words . . . ." Yu-ts'un does not intend to pun on his own name, nor does the Reverend Taoist Kosmo Kosmos understand there to be any pun, but when he passes the Stone Record on to Ts'ao Hsueh-ch'in, together with "the words of Chia Yu-ts'un",[226] Ts'ao delights in the joke:

> The Reverend Taoist Kosmo Kosmos firmly remembered these words of Chia Yu-ts'un --but we don't know how many ages and kalpas passed by--there really was a Grieving for Red Pavilion and Kosmo actually saw there Mr. Ts'ao Hsueh-ch'in flipping through pages of ancient histories. The Reverend Taoist then told of Chia Yu-ts'un and asked Ts'ao to look at the Stone Record.
>
> "Wow!" laughed this Mr. Hsueh-ch'in, "It sure is Chia Yu-ts'un yen!"
>
> The Taoist then asked: "Since, Sir, you are familiar with this man, then you'd be willing to pass this on for him?"
>
> Mr. Hsueh-ch'in laughed and said: "You're called 'Kosmo Kosmos', and your head really is full of space! Oh well, though this is but 'fictive language and vulgar words', it isn't full of errors and contradictions . . . ."[227]

Yu-ts'un is supposedly enlightened about the meaning of the Stone Record and the story of Pao-yu. After all, as he says himself,"I've already seen this stuff myself and I know all about it". What is comical here is that he is unaware of the possible puns on his own name. He indicates to the Reverend Taoist that all the latter has to do to get the Stone Record passed on is to mention that "Chia Yu-ts'un said . . .",[228] and he fails to realize that he is also inadvertently saying that all Kosmo Kosmos need do is bring up "fictive language and vulgar words".[229] For an enlightened char-

----

224 賈雨村言.
225 假語村言.
226 賈雨村言.
227 HLMPSHCP, chap. 120, pp. 418-419. For text, see pp. 151-152. "And your head really is full of space!" is, of course, a change of the original Chinese metaphor, which has to do with the emptiness of the belly.
228 賈雨村言.
229 假語村言.

acter to be so unaware of the meaning of what he says seems to be
contradictory, yet Chia's character is consistent with our earlier
glimpses of him in chapters 1, 2, and 103. As always, he makes
profound statements of truth, but when he does so, he never realizes
what he is saying. When he attempts to be deliberately profound,
he ends up speaking nonsense.

After the foregoing review, we have arrived at a point where we
may summarize our findings as to the meaning of enlightenment in
Dream of the Red Chamber. Who partakes of this gift of sudden
and complete perception which we have called "spontaneous enlightenment"? What do Chen Shih-yin, Chia Yu-ts'un, Chia Pao-yu,
and, for that matter, the Reverend Taoist Kosmo Kosmos, have in
common that we should affirm they are in some sense identical?
We remind the reader of the Hao-liao Ko, the "Sweeter-Over
Song". Enlightenment is a spontaneous gift, but it is only given to
those uniquely sensitive individuals who "get over" experience and
thus realize that opposites are one. The particular kind of experience would appear inconsequential so long as it is intense and of
long duration. Chen Shih-yin is committed to a life of simplicity
and virtue, Pao-yu yearns to delay time through the prolongation
of passion, Yu-ts'un struggles to become part of the orthodox literocracy, while Kosmo Kosmos eternally wanders as a pilgrim spirit
in search of tao. We can only add that Ts'ao Hsueh-ch'in's art
insists the reader be another paradigm in the list of pilgrim spirits.
Over a long period of elapsed time and repeated perusals, of inadvertent misinterpretations and sudden and surprising insights, we
endeavor to partake of the author's vision of spontaneous enlighten-
ment--the gift which follows the experience of faithful reading.

There is another "realistic" story which contributes to our understanding of the relationship between the mimetic and allegoric
modes and which further qualifies the meaning of enlightenment in
Dream of the Red Chamber. We noted earlier in our discussion of
Chia Yu-ts'un's Two Breaths theory the comparisons he makes between Chia Pao-yu and Chen Pao-yu. Like Chen Shih-yin and
Chia Yu-ts'un, the two Pao-yus exemplify Ts'ao Hsueh-ch'in's character reflection technique[230] and the theme of complementary

----

230We refer the reader to our Introduction in which we discuss
an early group of critics, the Allegorists. Developers of the allegorical approach to Dream of the Red Chamber argue the novel is a
ying shu, "shadow-book", and that every character is a ying-tzu,
"image", "reflection", or "opposite" of another.

opposites.[231]

In chapter 2, Chia Yu-ts'un hears of Chia Pao-yu through the account of the merchant, Leng Tzu-hsing. Yu-ts'un then exclaims over the fact that he has a pupil whose given name and personality are identical with that of Chia Pao-yu, but whose surname is Chen.[232] At this point in the narrative, Chih-yen Chai makes a comment. For reasons which will become apparent, we use the translation of Wu Shih-ch'ang:

> The Pao-yu in the Chen family is not mentioned in the first
> half of the novel, therefore he is emphatically described
> here in order to reflect from a distance the Pao-yu in the
> Chia family. Henceforth wherever Chia Pao-yu is described,
> it is the very portrayal of Chen Pao-yu.[233]

Obviously, Chia Pao-yu and the Chia family are "opposites" or "reflections" of Chen Pao-yu and the Chen family.[234] However,

----

[231]The story of Chen Pao-yu and his family unfolds in chapters 2, 56, 57, 75, 92, 93, 114, 115, and 116. In most of these chapters, the Chens are only indirectly mentioned. The important chapters are chapters 2, 56, and 115, of which chapter 56 is Chia Pao-yu's dream of Chen Pao-yu.

Chia Cheng and Chen Ying-chia, the fathers of the two Pao-yus, grew up in the same area in similar circumstances. The families at one time enjoyed close relations, but there are no blood ties between them. See HLMPSHCP, chap. 2, p. 20, line 11; chap. 92, p. 125, line 9; chap. 115, p. 355, line 6.

[232] 甄.

[233]Wu, On the Red Chamber Dream, p. 193, note 2. CYCHLMCP, chap. 2, p. 36, chia-hsu chia-p'i: 甄家之寶玉乃上半部不寫者, 故此書極力表明以遙照賈家之寶玉. 凡寫賈寶玉之文, 則正為真寶玉傳影. Wu's mistranslation of Chen 甄, for chen 真, will be discussed below.

[234]The fortunes of the two families often parallel one another and are examples of the Allegorists' "reflection" theory. Untoward events in the Chen family call forth untoward events in the Chia family. The imperial confiscation of the Chen family properties in chapter 75 is parallelled by an imperial appropriation of the Chia properties in chapter 105. In chapter 92, Chia Cheng laments that his and Chen Ying-chia's families suffer the same kind of decline.

Yu P'ing-po lists other examples of character reflection such as if we review the appearances of Chen Pao-yu in the novel, in the light of Chih-yen Chai's commentary just quoted, it is not altogether clear that, as Wu Shih-ch'ang believes, Chen Pao-yu is the "hidden" or "real self" of Chia Pao-yu. In what sense is the latter, as Chih-yen Chai apparently states, "the very portrayal of Chen Pao-yu"?

Chen Pao-yu is very similar to Chia Pao-yu in his fondness for girls. Yu-ts'un tells Leng Tzu-hsing that when Chen Pao-yu studies, he must be attended by females in order to understand what he reads. Chen informs his male servants that there is no purer name than that which is found in the two syllables, nu-erh,[235] "girl", and that men are dirty. Whenever the male servants mention the name, "woman", they must first, out of reverence, gargle with spring water and jasmine tea. When Chen Pao-yu is spanked for being mischieveous, he calls out the names of his sisters for comfort. Finally, again like Chia Pao-yu, Chen Pao-yu is spoiled by the maternal members of his family.[236]

This early portrait of Chen Pao-yu undergoes drastic change. In chapter 93, a servant in the Chen household is sent to call on Chia Cheng, the father of Chia Pao-yu. When Chia Cheng asks about Chen Pao-yu, the servant talks about a nightmare the young master has had. When Chen Pao-yu was small, the servant reports, he only wanted to be with girls and his parents could not change him. One day, he became seriously ill. During his illness, he dreamed that a woman took him to a temple where he found some register books telling about the sad fates of the women he knew. He also saw many girl acquaintances who had become ghosts and skeletons. Chen Pao-yu was terrified by this dream but after it was over, he recovered from his illness. From that day forward, he only wanted to

----

Tai-yu and Pao-ch'ai. See "Hung-lou meng chung shih-erh ch'ai te miao-hsien", 紅樓夢中十二釵的描寫 , in Wen-hsueh p'ing-lun 文學評論, IV (April, 1960), 26.

Sister Mary Gregory Knoerle, The Dream of the Red Chamber: A Critical Analysis, pp. 73-78, and, "A Critical Analysis of The Dream of the Red Chamber", p. 143, points out the parallels between the Matriarch of the Jung-kuo mansion (the Chia-mu) and the peasant woman, Liu Lao-lao.

235 女兒.

236 HLMPSHCP, chap. 2, p. 20, line 13, through p. 21, line 8.

study and to help his father manage the family affairs.[237]

Chen Pao-yu's dream, reported in chapter 93, harks back to a similar dream Chia Pao-yu had in chapter 5 which was intended to warn him against romantic passion but which instead led to his first sexual experience. Chen's dream also foreshadows a dream Chia has in chapter 116. In the latter, Chia Pao-yu visits the Great Void Illusion Land in the company of the monk who returns to him his lost jade piece. C. T. Hsia's comment on this episode brings out how similar the experience and effect of Chia Pao-yu's dream is to that of Chen Pao-yu:

> Immediately upon the recovery of his stone, Pao-yu is trans-ported, for the second time, to the Land of Illusion . . . he sees again, now strangely indifferent if not actively hostile, the many lovely girls who have departed from the world, and he reponders their fate and the fate of those girls still alive in the light of the verses and emblems which he had found merely puzzling on his first visit to the region. Armed with foreknowledge and resigned to the remorseless operations of fate, he awakens from the dream a changed and cold person, determined to sever all human ties. The solicitude and dis-tress of Precious Clasp and Pervading Fragrance pain him greatly but cannot change his will. With desolate determina-tion he now pursues the path of holy indifference, even while perfunctorily discharging his worldly duties.[238]

In terms of the theme of the novel, everything is becoming its oppo-site, we see that Chia Pao-yu is becoming Chen Pao-yu. They are identical twins, except for the fact that Chen Pao-yu is always an advancing mirage on the horizon of Chia Pao-yu's experience. To understand the significance of the change in Chia Pao-yu, we need to examine what Chen Pao-yu means to him.

In chapter 56, some of the older members of the Chen family visit the Chia family. When Chia Pao-yu learns that the Chen family has a son whose name and appearance are the same as his, he discusses this odd situation with Shih Hsiang-yun,[239] a grand-niece

----

[237]For this account, see HLMPSHCP, chap. 93, p. 131, line 10ff.

[238]C. T. Hsia, The Classic Chinese Novel, pp. 287-288. "Precious Clasp" is Pao-ch'ai, "Pervading Fragrance" is Hsi-jen.

239 史湘雲.

of the Matriarch, and one of the twelve principal maidens of the
novel. Hsiang-yun tries to comfort him by saying that there have
been other examples in history of duplicated persons, but Pao-yu
says that never have there been two persons of the same name and
personality. He is deeply troubled by this incidence of identity,
and when he goes to sleep, he dreams of a meeting between himself
and Chen Pao-yu. The following is Arthur Waley's fine translation
of that famous dream episode as found in his introduction to C. C.
Wang's partial translation (1929 edition) of the novel (a few important reservations concerning Waley's translation may be found in
our footnotes):

    So before he knew what had happened Pao-yu's head
nodded, and he fell asleep. It seemed to him presently that
he was in a great flower-garden which was extraordinarily
like his own garden at home. "Is it possible", he said to
himself in his dream, "that there is really another garden so
exactly like mine?" While he was thus wondering to himself,
there suddenly appeared in front of him a number of girls who
seemed all to be waiting-maids in some great house. And
Pao-yu, more than ever surprised, said to himself again--"Can
it really be that someone else has waiting-maids so exactly
like Hsi-jen, P'ing-erh, and all my own maids at home?"
Presently one of the girls called out: "Look, there's Pao-yu!
How ever did he get out here?" Pao-yu naturally supposed
that she knew it was he, and coming forward, he said: "I
was just going for a walk, and got here quite by accident.
I suppose this garden belongs to some family that my people
visit. But in any case, dear Sisters, let me join you in your
walk". No sooner had he finished speaking than the girls
burst into peals of laughter. "What a silly mistake!" they
said: "We thought you were our younger master Pao-yu. But
of course you are not half so good-looking and do not talk
nearly so nicely".[240] So they were servants of another Pao-
yu! "Dear Sisters", he said to them, "tell me who then is
your master?" "He is Pao-yu", they said. "It was his grandmother and mother who wished him to use these two characters
Pao (precious) and Yu (jade), hoping that such a name would

----

[240]A more accurate translation would be: "Really, this is not
our Pao-yu. He looks neat enough, and talks cleverly too".
HLMPSHCP, chap. 56, p. 620, line 3ff. For text, see p. 163.

make him have a long and happy life; and though we are only servants, it pleases him very much that we too should call him by this name. But where do you come from, we should like to know, and whose seedy little drudge are you, that you should use the same characters in your name? You dare try that on again, and we'll beat your nasty little body into jelly!" Another of them said, laughing: "Come on! Let's get away as quick as we can. What would our Pao-yu think if he saw us talking to such a ragamuffin?" Another said: "If we stay near him much longer we shall all smell nasty!" And at one streak they were gone.

Pao-yu was very much downcast. "No one", he thought, "has ever before treated me so rudely.[241] Why should these particular girls have taken such a dislike to me? And is there really another Pao-yu? I must somehow discover". While these thoughts were passing through his mind he had been walking on without noticing where he was going, and he now found himself in a courtyard that seemed strangely familiar. "Can there then", he asked himself, "be another courtyard exactly like ours at home?" He went up some steps and walked straight into a room. Here the first thing he saw was a young man lying on a bed, round which sat a number of girls laughing and playing while they did their needlework. The boy on the bed kept on sighing heavily, till at last one of the girls said to him--"Pao-yu, why do you keep on sighing? Can't you get to sleep? No doubt you are worried over your cousin's illness. But it is silly to make such a fuss". When the real Pao-yu heard this he was more than ever astonished . . . . "I have been having such an odd dream", said the young man on the bed. "I thought I was in a great flower-garden, where I met some girls who called me nasty names and would not play with me. But I followed them back to the house, and there what should I find but another Pao-yu, lying senseless on his bed, for all the world like an empty bag. His thoughts and feelings seemed all to have flown somewhere far, far away". When the real Pao-yu heard this dream, he could not contain him-self and cried out to the boy on the bed: "I came to look for a Pao-yu; and now it seems that you are the one!" The

----

241 塗毒 "cruelly", rather than "rudely".

boy on the bed rose and coming quickly toward him, embraced him, saying: "So you are Pao-yu, and it was not a dream!" "A dream!" cried Pao-yu. "No indeed. It was more true than truth itself". But hardly had he finished speaking when someone came to the door, crying: "Mr. Pao-yu is to go to his father's room at once". At the sound of these words both Pao-yus trembled from head to foot. The dream Pao-yu rushed away, and as he left the room the real Pao-yu called after him: "Come back soon, Pao-yu! Come back". His maid Hsi-jen was by the bed, and hearing him calling out his own name in his dream she woke him, and said, laughing: "Where is this Pao-yu that you are calling to?" Though he was no longer asleep, his mind was dazed and confused. "There he is", he said, pointing sleepily at the door. "He has just gone out". "Why, you are still dreaming!" said Hsi-jen, much amused, "Do you know what it is you are staring at, screwing up your eyes and making such a funny face? It is your own reflection in the mirror!"[242]

Chia Pao-yu does not meet Chen Pao-yu until chapter 115. What is the significance of this dream encounter in chapter 56? There are certain archetypes Chia Pao-yu discovers which impress upon him the reality of his dream. He accidentally meets the girls he knows in the familiar garden. There is talk about purity. Initially disturbed by the knowledge that there is someone who exists who is his twin self, Pao-yu encounters in his dream a Pao-yu who is his intellectual and physical superior. He also finds that what the girls are really praising in their Pao-yu is purity. Chia Pao-yu has become in the dream that which he most abhors, a male whose presence among females is liable to corrupt them. The episode harks back to his childish prattle:

Little girls are made of water, little boys are made of mud. When I see girls, I'm refreshed, but when I see boys, I gag.[243]

----

[242]Dream of the Red Chamber, trans. C. C. Wang, London, 1929., pp. xi-xiii. Waley notes that Ts'ao "rises to his greatest heights" in "his accounts of dreams", but that Wang, "in accordance with his scheme of abridgment" omits the above example. The passage is from HLMPSHCP, chap. 56, pp. 619-621. For text, see pp. 162-164. (There are almost no differences between this Collated Edition and the 1792 Kao E text, which I believe Wang and Waley used in their translation).

[243]See note 164, above.

們寶玉淘氣古怪，有時見了人客，規矩禮數更比大人有趣，所以無人見了不愛，只說為什麼這打他？殊不知他在家裏，無法無天，大人想不到的話偏會說，想不到的事他偏要行，所以老爺太太恨的無法。就是弄性，也是小孩子的常情；胡亂花費，這也是公子哥兒的常情；怕上學，也是小孩子的常情：都還治的過來。第一，天生下來這一種刁鑽古怪的脾氣，如何使得。」一語未了，人回：「太太回來了。」王夫人進來問過安，他四人請了安，大概說了兩句。賈母便命歇歇去。王夫人親捧過茶，方退出。四人告辭了賈母，便往王夫人處來，說了一回家務，打發他們回去。不必細說。

這裏賈母喜的逢人便告訴，也有一個寶玉，也都一般行景。眾人都為天下之大，世宦之多，同名者也甚多；祖母溺愛孫若亦古今之常情，不是什麼罕事，故皆不介意。獨寶玉是個迂闊獃公子的性情，自為是那四人承悅賈母之詞。後至園中去看湘雲病去。史湘雲說他：「你放心鬧罷。先是『單絲不成線，獨樹不成林』；如今有了個對子，鬧急了，再打狠了，你逃走到南京找那一個去。」寶玉道：「那裏的說話你也信了，偏又有個寶玉了。」湘雲道：「怎麼列國有個藺相如，漢朝又有個司馬相如呢。」寶玉笑道：「這也罷了。偏又模樣兒也一樣，這是沒有的事。」湘雲道：「怎麼匡人看見孔子，只當是陽虎呢。」寶玉笑道：「孔子陽虎雖同貌，卻不同性；藺與司馬雖同名，而又不同貌。偏我和他就兩樣俱同不成？」湘雲沒了話答對，因笑道：「你只會胡搅，我也不和你分證。有也罷，沒也罷，與我無干。」說着，便睡下了。寶玉心中便又疑惑起來：若說必無，然亦似有；若說必有，又並無目睹。心中悶悶，回至房中榻上，默默盤算，不覺就忽忽的睡去。竟到了一座花園之內。寶玉詫異道：「除了我們大觀園，竟又

第五十六回　敏探春興利除宿弊　識寶釵小惠全大體

六一九

第五十六回　敏探春與利除宿弊　識寶釵小惠全大體

有這一個園子。』正疑惑間，從那邊來了幾個女兒，都是丫鬟。寶玉又詫異道：『除了鴛鴦、襲人、平兒之外，也竟有這一干人。』只見那些丫鬟笑道：『寶玉怎麼跑到這裏來了？』寶玉只當是說他自己，忙來陪笑說道：『因我偶步到此，不知是那位世交的花園。好姐姐們，帶我逛逛。』衆丫鬟都笑道：『原來不是咱家的寶玉。他生的倒也乾淨，嘴兒也倒乖覺。』寶玉聽了，忙道：『姐姐們這裏也竟有個寶玉？』丫鬟們忙道：『「寶玉」二字，我們是奉老太太太之命，爲保佑他延壽消災的。我們叫他，他聽見喜歡，你這遠方來的臭小廝，也亂叫起他來。仔細你的臭肉，打不煳你的。』又一個丫鬟笑道：『咱們快走罷，別叫寶玉看見，又說同這臭小廝說了話，把咱們薰臭了。』說着，一逕去了。寶玉納悶道：『從來沒有人如此塗毒我，他們如何竟這樣？真亦有我這樣一個人不成？』一面想，一面順步早到了一所院內。寶玉又詫異道：『除了怡紅院，也竟還有這麼一個院落。』忽上了臺階，進入屋內，只見楊上有一個人臥着，那邊有幾個女孩兒做針線，也有嘻笑頑耍的。只見楊上那個少年歎了一聲，一個丫鬟笑問道：『寶玉，你不睡，又歎什麼？想必爲你妹妹病了，你又胡愁亂恨呢。』寶玉聽說，心下也便吃驚。只見楊上少年說道：『我聽見老太太說，長安都中也有個寶玉，和我一樣的性情，我只不信。我纔作了一個夢，竟夢中到了都中一個花園子裏頭，遇見幾個姐姐，都叫我臭小廝，不理我。好容易找到他房裏，偏他睡覺，空有皮囊，真性不知那去了。』寶玉聽說，忙說道：『我因找寶玉來到這裏。原來你就是寶玉。』楊上的忙下來拉住：『原來你就是寶玉。這可不是夢裏了。』寶玉道：『這如何是夢，眞而又眞了。』一語未了，只見人來說：『老爺叫寶玉。』嚇得二人皆慌了，一個寶玉就走，一個寶玉便

六二〇

忙叫：『寶玉快回來，快回來。』襲人在旁，聽他夢中自喚，忙推醒他，笑問道：『寶玉在那裏？』此時寶玉雖醒，神意尚恍惚，因向門外指說：『纔出去了。』襲人笑道：『那是你夢迷了。你揉眼細瞧，是鏡子裏照的你的影兒。』寶玉向前瞧了一瞧，原是那嵌的大鏡對面相照，自己也笑了。早有人捧過漱盂茶漱來漱了口。麝月道：『怪道老太太常囑咐說小人屋裏不可多有鏡子。人小魂不全，有鏡子照多了，睡覺愛恐作胡夢。如今倒在大鏡子那裏安了一張牀。有時放下鏡套遠好，往前來天熱，人肯因那裏想的到放他。比如方纔就忘了。自然是先躺下照着影兒頑的，一時合上眼，自然是胡夢顛倒。不然，如何得看着自己，叫自己的名字。不如明兒挪進牀來是正經。』一語未了，只見王夫人遣人來叫寶玉。

不知有何話說，且聽下回分解。

As one maid says, "If we stay near him much longer we shall all
smell nasty!"

At this point in the dream, Chia Pao-yu has yet to meet the other
Pao-yu. When he does, he encounters the image of himself: a
young man is lying on his bed moaning about his beloved (Tai-yu)--
he is just awakening from a dream in which he has encountered
another Pao-yu. Entranced with this image of himself, Chia Pao-
yu calls to the other Pao-yu. He tells him that their similar experience proves they are not dreaming: "It was more true than truth
itself". For the first time in Dream of the Red Chamber, its theme
is expressed in terms other than by means of interplay between true
and false. The experience of the "unreal" dream is more "true"
and "real" than an event about which one is conscious. One may
say that this is also the first time Pao-yu comes in contact with an
idealized image of truth and reality that he is ever so vainly seeking. Yet, immediately upon the briefest of contacts, the image
vanishes and Pao-yu wakes up facing his own image in a mirror.

There are some easy explanations of this dream within a dream,
such as the many mirrors within Pao-yu's room in which the reflecting surfaces reverberate with images of the young master. When he
wakes up, one of his maids, She-yueh,[244] tells him there is no
wonder he dreams of himself since he is surrounded by mirrors. The
dream itself has another kind of significance. Pao-yu cannot accept
that there is anyone who is equal to himself. He can accept en-
countering a flattering superior image of himself in a dream world.
It is also important to remember that his greatest fear is of mutabil-
ity--this is why he rebels whenever a change takes place in his
garden world, as when one of his sisters marries. In the dream world,
he finds a world exactly like the one he knows. The duplication
of time, place, and persons is comforting and miraculous--it means
that his world remains immutable. It is not simply that Chia Pao-
yu is becoming Chen Pao-yu, that what is chia, "unreal", is becoming its opposite, chen, "real", but that when there is an encounter between the two, when Chia dreams of Chen and Chen
dreams of Chia, in other words, when the real and the unreal unfold
towards one another, then at that point there is an intense awareness of their unity.

Significantly, Chia Pao-yu's startling encounter with an idealized
image of himself in a dream is completely different from his meeting

----

244 麝月.

with Chen Pao-yu is chapter 115. The relationship between them proves to be only external--they merely look alike. Clearly, the content of Chia Pao-yu's dream-vision is not true or real in terms of what it is supposed to represent in conscious life. Yet, the dream-vision remains "more true than truth itself", for to Pao-yu, it constitutes a haunting nightmare which persistently reminds him that the reality he clings to around him in the form of the garden and its maidens is but a vanishing absurdity.

One day a servant announces that Chen Pao-yu and his mother have come to the Chia home to pay a call. Pao-yu's father, Chia Cheng, uses the occasion to compare closely his son with Chen Pao-yu. He is very favorably impressed by the latter who, contrary to Chia Pao-yu, is very much the young gentleman lord, cultivated in manners and deferential towards his superiors. Chia Cheng even bids Chen Pao-yu to instruct his son.[245] Madame Wang, Chia Pao-yu's mother, compares the two boys and feels that Chen is superior to her own son.[246] When Tzu-chuan,[247] Tai-yu's former maid, sees Chen Pao-yu, she laments the vain death of Tai-yu for she believes that her mistress would have preferred him rather than Chia Pao-yu:

> What a pity Mistress Lin has died. Were she yet alive, she probably would have been willing to be matched with that Chen Pao-yu.[248]

Chia Pao-yu is profoundly changed by his encounter with Chen Pao-yu. When he first meets the latter he is shocked to discover someone with whom he feels intimately familiar:

> . . . why he is like an old familiar acquaintance.[249]

Chen Pao-yu also feels as though he has seen Chia Pao-yu somewhere.[250] The ostensible reason why they both feel as though they know one another is that in facial appearance they are identical twins. However, as Chia Pao-yu is well aware, behind this first face to face meeting lies the previous dream encounter (chapter 56).

245HLMPSHCP, chap. 115, p. 355, line 6. For text, see p. 168.

246ibid., p. 357, line 3. For text, see p. 170.

247 紫鵑,

248HLMPSHCP, chap. 115, p. 357, line 7. For text, see p. 170.

249ibid., p. 355, line 2. For text, see p. 168.

250ibid., p. 355, line 3. For text, see p. 168.

第一百十五回　惑偏私惜春矢素志　證同類寶玉失相知

合在機上，也顯不得了頭們在這裏，便將尤氏待他怎樣，前兒吞家的事說了一遍，並將頭髮指給他瞧道：『你打諒我是什麼沒主意戀火坑的人麼！早有這樣的心，只是想不出道兒來。』那姑子聽了，假作驚愕道：『姑娘再別說這個話，珍大奶奶聽見還要罵殺我們，摞出菴去呢。姑娘這樣人品，這樣人家，將來配個好姑爺，享一輩子的榮華富貴。』惜春不等說完，便紅了臉說：『珍大奶奶攆得你，我就攆不得麼！』那姑子知是真心，便索性激他一激，說道：『姑娘別怪我們說錯了話，太太奶奶們那裏就依得姑娘的性子呢。那時鬧出沒意思來倒不好。我們倒是為姑娘的話。』惜春道：『這也瞧罷咧。』彩屏等聽這話頭不好，便使個眼色兒給姑子，叫他走。那姑子會意，本來心裏也害怕，不敢挑逗，便告辭出去。惜春也不留他，便冷笑道：『打諒天下就是你們一個地藏菴麼！』那姑子也不敢答言，去了。彩屏見事不妥，恐耽不是，悄悄的去告訴了尤氏說：『四姑娘鉸頭髮的念頭還有些呢。他這幾天不是病，竟是怨命。奶奶隄防些，別鬧出事來，那會子歸罪我們身上。』尤氏道：『他那裏是為要出家，他為的是大爺不在家，安心和我過不去，也只好由他罷了。』彩屏等沒法，也只好常常勸解。豈知惜春一天一天的不吃飯，只想鉸頭髮。

邢王二夫人正要告訴賈政，只聽外頭傳進來說：『甄少爺在外書房同老爺說話說的投了機了，打發人來請我們二爺三爺，還叫蘭哥兒，在外頭吃飯。吃了飯進來。』說畢，裏頭也便擺飯。不提。且說賈政見出，便在王夫人處坐下。眾人行禮，敘些寒溫，不必細述。只言王夫人提起甄寶玉與自己的寶玉無二，要甄寶玉相貌果與寶玉一樣，試探他的文才竟是應對如流，甚是心敬，故叫寶玉等三人出來酬勵他們。再者，到底叫寶玉來比一比。寶玉聽命，穿了素服，帶了兄弟姪兒出來，見了甄寶玉，竟是舊相識一般。那甄寶玉也像那裏見過的。兩人行了禮，然後賈環賈蘭相見。本來賈政席地而坐，要讓甄寶玉在椅子上坐，甄寶玉因是晚輩不敢上坐，就在地下鋪下了褥子坐于。如今寶玉等出來，又不能同賈政一處坐着，為甄寶玉又是晚一輩，又不好叫寶玉等站着。賈政知是不便，站着又說了幾句話，叫人擺飯，說：

「我失陪，叫小兒輩陪着，大家說說話兒，好叫他們領領大教。」甄寶玉遜謝道：「老伯大人請便。姪兒正欲領世兄們的教呢。」賈政回覆了幾句，便自往內書房去。那甄寶玉反要送出來，賈政攔住。寶玉等先搶了一步出了書房門檻站立着，看賈政進去，然後進來讓甄寶玉坐下，彼此套叙了一回，諸如久慕渴想的話，也不必細述。且說賈寶玉見了甄寶玉，想到夢中之景，並且素知甄寶玉為人，必是和他同心，以為得了知己。因初次見面不便造次，只有極力誇讚說：「久仰芳名，無由親炙，今日見面，真是謫仙一流的人物。」那甄寶玉素來也知賈寶玉的為人，今日一見果然不差，便道：「只是可與我共學，不可與你適道。你既和我同名同貌，也是三生石上的舊精魂了。既我略知了些道理，怎麼不和他講講。但是初見，尚不知他的心與我同不同，只好緩緩的來。」便道：「世兄的才名弟所素知的。在世兄是數萬人的裏頭選出來最清最雅的，在弟是庸庸碌碌一等愚人，忝附同名，殊覺玷辱了這兩個字。」賈寶玉聽了，心想：「這個人果然同我的心一樣的。但是你我都是男人，不比那女孩兒們清潔，怎麼他拿我當作女孩兒看待起來？」便道：「世兄謬讚，弟不敢當！弟是至愚至陋，只不過一

第一百十五回　惑偏私情矢素志　證同類寶玉失相知

塊頭石耳，何敢比世兄品望高清，實稱此兩字。」甄寶玉道：「弟少時不知分量，自謂尚可琢磨，豈知家遭消索，數年來更比瓦礫猶賤，雖不敢說歷盡甘苦，然世道人情略略的領悟了好些。世兄是錦衣玉食，無不遂心的，必是文章經濟高出人上。所以老伯鍾愛，將為席上之珍，弟所以總說尊名方稱。」賈寶玉聽這話頭又近了祿蠹的舊套，想話回答。賈環見未與他說話，心中早不自在。倒是賈蘭聽了這話甚覺合意，便說道：「世叔所言固是太謙，若論到文章經濟，實在從歷練中出來的方為真才實學。在小姪年幼，雖不知文章為何物，然將讀過的細味起來，那古聖賢文糊比着今閱廣學實是不啻百倍的了。」賈寶玉未及答言，賈寶玉聽了蘭兒的話心裏越發不合，想道：「這孩子從幾時也學了這一派酸論！」便說道：「弟聞得世兄也詆諆流俗，性情中另有一番見解，今日弟幸會芝範，想欲領教一番超凡入聖的道理，從此可以淨洗俗腸，重開眼界。不意視弟為蠢物，所以將世路的話來酬應。」甄寶玉聽說，心裏曉得「他知我少年的性情，所以疑我為假。我索性把話說明，或者與我作個知心朋友也是好的。」便說道：「世兄高論固是真切。但弟少時也曾深惡那些舊套陳言，只是一年長似一年，家君致仕在家，懶於酬應，委弟接待。後來見過那些大人先生，盡都是顯親揚名的人；便是著書立說，無非言忠言孝，自有一番立德立言的事業方不枉生在聖明之時，也不致負了父親師長養育教誨之恩，所以把少時那一派迂想癡情漸漸的淘汰了些。如今尚欲訪師覓友，教導愚蒙，幸會世兄，定當有以教我。適纔所言並非虛意。」賈寶玉愈聽愈不耐煩，又不好冷淡，只得將言語支吾。幸喜裏頭傳出話來，說：「若是外頭爺們吃了飯，請甄少爺裏頭去坐呢。」寶玉聽了，趁勢便邀甄寶玉進去。那甄寶玉依命前行，賈寶玉等

陪着來見王夫人。賈寶玉見是甄太太上坐，便先請過了安。賈環賈蘭也見了。甄寶玉也請了王夫人的

安。兩母兩子互相廝認。雖是賈寶玉是娶過親的，那甄夫人年紀已老，又是老親，因見賈寶玉的相貌

身材與他兒子一般，不禁親熱起來。王夫人更不用說，拉着甄寶玉問長問短，覺得比自己家的寶玉老

成些。回看賈蘭也是清秀超羣的，雖不能像兩個寶玉的形像，也還隨他身上，只有賈環粗夯，未免有偏

愛之色。衆人一見兩個寶玉在這裏，都來瞧看，說道：「眞眞奇事，名字同了也罷，怎麼相貌身材都

是一樣的！虧得是我們賈寶玉穿孝，若是一樣的衣服穿着，一時也認不出來。」內中紫鵑一時觸意發作，

便想起黛玉來，心裏說道：「可惜林姑娘死了，若不死時，就將那甄寶玉配了他，只怕也是願意的。」正

想着，只聽得甄夫人說：「前日聽得我們老爺回來說，我們賈寶玉年紀也大了，求這裏老爺留心一門親

事。」王夫人正愛甄寶玉，順口便說道：「我也想要與令郎作伐。我家有四個姑娘，那三個都不用說死

的死嫁的嫁了。還有我們珍大姪兒的妹子，只是年紀過小幾歲，恐怕難配。倒是我們大媳婦的兩個堂

妹子生得人才齊正。二姑娘呢，已經許了人家；三姑娘正好與令郎為配。過一天我給令郎做媒。但是

他家的家計如今差些。」甄夫人道：「太太這話又客套了。如今我們家還有什麼，只怕人家嫌我們窮

罷了。」王夫人道：「現今府上復又出了差，將來不但復舊，必是比先前更要鼎盛起來。」甄夫人笑着

道：「但願依着太太的話更好。這麼着，就求太太作個保山。」甄寶玉聽他們說起親事，便告辭出來，

賈寶玉等只得陪着來到書房。見賈政已在那裏，復又立談幾句。忽見甄家的人來回甄寶玉道：「太太

要走了。請爺回去罷。」於是甄寶玉告辭出來。賈政命寶玉環蘭相送。不提。

第一百十五回．惑偏私惜春矢素志　證同類寶玉失相知

第一百十五回　惑偏私惜春矢素志　證同類寶玉失相知

且說寶玉自那日見了甄寶玉之父，知道甄寶玉來京，朝夕盼望。今日見面原想得一知己。豈知說了半

夫，竟有些冰炭不投。悶悶的回到自己房中，也不言也不笑，只管發怔。寶釵便問：「那甄寶玉果然像你

麼？」寶玉道：「相貌倒還是一樣的，只是言談間看起來並不知道什麼，不過也是個祿蠹。」寶釵道：

「你又編派人家了。怎麼就見得也是個祿蠹呢？」寶玉道：「他說了半天，並沒個明心見性之談，不

過說些什麼文章經濟，又說什麼爲忠爲孝，這樣人可不是個祿蠹麼！只可惜他也生了這樣一個相貌。

我想來有了他，我竟要連我這個相貌都不要了。」寶釵見他又發獃話，便說道：「你真真說出句話來叫

人發笑。這相貌怎麼能不要呢！況且人家這話是正理，做了一個男人原該要立身揚名的。誰像你一味

的柔情私意，不說自己沒有剛烈，倒說人家是祿蠹。」寶玉本聽了甄寶玉的話甚不耐煩，又被寶釵搶白

了一場，心中更加不樂，悶悶昏昏，不覺將舊病又勾起來了，並不言語，只是傻笑。寶釵不知，只道

是我的話錯了，他所以冷笑。也不理他。豈知那日便有些發獃，襲人等惱他也不言語。過了一夜，次

日起來只是發獃，竟有前番病的樣子。

一日，王夫人因爲惜春定要鉸髮出家，尤氏不能攔阻，看着惜春的樣子是若不依他，必要自盡的。踟

然整夜着人看着，終非常事，便告訴了賈政。賈政嘆氣跺腳，只說：「東府裏不知幹了什麼，鬧到如

此地位！」叫了賈蓉來說了一頓，叫他去和他母親說，認眞勸解勸解。「若是必要這樣，就不是我們

家的姑娘了。」豈知尤氏不勸還好，一勸了更要尋死，說：「做了女孩兒終不能在家一輩子的，若像二姐

姐一樣，老爺太太們倒要煩心，況且死了。如今譬如我死了是的，放我出了家，乾乾淨淨的一輩子就

三五八

Chen Pao-yu's association with Chia Pao-yu is even more mystical than the dream-vision of Chia Pao-yu. The difference between their initial reactions to one another is instructive:

> . . . seeing Chen Pao-yu, Chia Pao-yu recalled the image in his dream--besides, having known the kind of person Chen was, he felt that surely they shared a oneness of mind and heart. Thus he presumed to have encountered a soul mate--one who knew his inmost being. But because this was their first meeting, it would not do to be forward. . . he could but expend himself in formal flattery: "Long revering thy fragrant name, but lacking cause for intimacy; today thy countenance is beheld--truly a creature belonging to the Banished Sylphs".

Chia Pao-yu's person was likewise long well known to Chen Pao-yu, and in fact, this first glimpse today proved Chia to be the fulfillment of his expectations. Though you can study with me, he thought, I cannot share with you in Following the Way.[251] But since you have the same name and face as I, you must be the old quintessent soul of the same Tri-Births Stone.[252] As I do have some understanding of this principle, why not discuss it with you? But this is our first meeting, I still do not know whether his mind and heart are one with mine. It would be better to go slowly.[253]

Chia Pao-yu is surprised to discover that this Chen Pao-yu he has waited so long to see appears to be a familiar acquaintance. Chen Pao-yu, on the other hand, finds the fulfillment of his expectations. Chia, because of his dream-vision, fully anticipates that he and Chen are identical in their inmost beings. Chen realizes that an external similarity in name and appearance argues for a relation-

----

[251]shih tao 適道 , "Following the Way", is from Lun-yu, IX:30, and is a phrase the use of which shows Chen Pao-yu's innermost conventional Confucian bias (which is eventually a disappointment for Chia Pao-yu to discover).

[252]Wu Shih-ch'ang, On the Red Chamber Dream, p. 134, says Chen considers Chia as his soul originally located in the Tri-Births Stone. The latter suggests a destined affinity between the two Pao-yus. Wu believes Chen's statement an unnecessary interpolation of Kao E. For "Tri-Births Stone", see "Myth" chapter, note 122.

[253]HLMPSHCP, chap. 115, p. 355, lines 9-13. For text, see p. 168.

ship in a previous existence, thus the reference to the Tri-Births
Stone, but similar mystical origins do not guarantee that he and
Chia actually share the same emotions and personalities. Out of a
common concern for propriety, neither boy dares to express his
thoughts. Instead, they both engage in formal honorific language.

Perhaps the reader shares the hesitancy of Chia and Chen Pao-yu.
Early in the novel, Ts'ao Hsueh-ch'in clearly establishes the underlying meaning of the plot, that is, the theme of complementary
opposites, and therefore we are correct to look for hidden relations
in contradictory materials. Ts'ao also makes the point, however,
over and over again, that that which seems is not that which is.
This is simple enough, yet he teases the reader by refusing to inform
him which is which. Surely we identify with Chia Pao-yu and view
Chen Pao-yu as an outsider, yet the presence of this identical twin
upsets the very sense of reality we have slowly come to acquire as
a result of reading Dream of the Red Chamber. The author seems to
disorientate deliberately his most faithful readers. It is easy for us
to accept the philosophical and even stylistic viewpoint that everything is becoming its opposite or that external appearances are
deceiving and ultimately false. It is disconcerting--and finally
enlightening--to discover that, despite critical awareness and acumen, we may be as much the victims of the ambiguity between the
true and the false, the real and the unreal, as the protagonists of
Dream of the Red Chamber.

In the meeting of the two Pao-yus, Ts'ao brings together several
of the major symbols of the novel: jade, the fool, female purity,
the stone, immortals, true and false. Chen apologizes because he
has the same given name as Chia. He is but a "fool"[254] he claims,
whose given name, "Precious Jade", "blemishes"[255] the "precious
jade" of Chia Pao-yu. The latter, says Chen, is the name of a
person who is "most pure and most polished".[256] This concern for
purity and refinement bothers Chia Pao-yu for he customarily only
associates such terminology with maidens:

> Truly this person and I have identical minds. But he and I
> are males--we are not comparable to the purity of females.
> How is it that he considers me as though I were a girl?[257]

----

254 愚人.
255 玷辱.
256 HLMPSHCP, chap. 115, p. 355, line 14. For text, see p.
168.
257 ibid., p. 355, lines 15-16. For text, see p. 168.

With this characteristic thought of the superiority of women in mind, Chia Pao-yu replies to Chen Pao-yu that he is unworthy of his counterpart's surname, and he insists that he is the one who is the impure fool:

> "Truly, I, your junior, am unworthy of flattery. I am sordid and foolish to such an extent that I am but a mere sliver of stone. How dare I compare to you my elder one's lofty morality and pure reputation and really be named with these two characters?"[258]

In this rhetorical effort to play with the meaning of "precious stone" and "precious jade", Chia Pao-yu claims that purity belongs to women alone, yet we note than Chen appears to him as a "banished sylph", a symbol of the quintessence of purity in the mortal world. Behind Chia Pao-yu's formal rhetoric lies the effort to probe Chen Pao-yu's mind.

The result is one of bitter disappointment, but leads to a further step towards self-enlightenment. Chen Pao-yu tries to insist that Pao-yu is a fitting given name for Chia because the latter is "a person of outstanding literary cultivation and administrative capability".[259] This is why, says Chen, Chia Pao-yu's father so dearly love him.

Chia Pao-yu is sickened by this talk--it reminds him of the traditional standards he detests and the statement about his father's affection for him is untrue. He attempts to shift the conversation. He tells Chen Pao-yu that he has heard that the latter is one who has much contempt for the vulgar mentalities which are the victims of bureaucratic ambitions, and therefore he has desired to use this opportune meeting:

> ". . . to receive instruction on the principle of transcending the mortal world and entering divinity; whence I, thy younger brother, may purge and cleanse my vulgar heart and open up my eyes to the world. Contrary to expectations, I am dealt with as a Foolish Thing and politely treated to a conversation about the way of the world".[260]

Presumably, Chen Pao-yu realizes that Chia Pao-yu has heard stories about the former's youth and how his adolescent passions were sud-

---

258ibid., pp. 355, line 16, through p. 356, line 1. For text, see pp. 168-169.

259ibid., p. 354, line 3. For text, see p. 167.

260ibid., p. 356, lines 8-9. For text, see p. 169.

denly changed by a strange dream visit to the Great Void Illusion
Land. But instead of speaking of this unusual method of advancing
to worldly success, Chen points to a conventional upbringing. In
his youth, Chen reports, he was an iconoclast, but because of his
father's direction, he happened to be in charge of greeting guests.
Thus, he met many famous for their official works or literary accom-
plishments--all of them were dedicated to glorifying the names of
their families and themselves, and they only talked of loyalty and
filial piety. Much influenced and impressed by this experience,
Chen Pao-yu says he has sought instruction from his teachers and
friends, and has tried not to be unworthy of the love of his parents.[261]

While many members and servants of Chia Pao-yu's family are
unable to tell apart the two Pao-yus,[262] Chia Pao-yu is overwhelmed to find that Chen Pao-yu is his <u>opposite</u> rather than his
twin. After Chen leaves, Chia returns to his quarters, disconsolate:

> . . . ever since Pao-yu met Chen Pao-yu's father and learned
> that Chen Pao-yu was to come to the Capital, night and day
> he longed to see him. And today upon seeing his countenance
> he actually imagined that he had encountered a soul mate.
> How was he to know that after conversing awhile, why it was
> as impossible to be friends as to cast together ice and ashes.[263]

When Hsueh Pao-ch'ai asks her husband about Chen Pao-yu, he
observes that he and the latter are of identical external appearance,
but that Chen Pao-yu's conversation reveals that he is nothing but
a <u>lu tu</u>,[264] "bureaucratic parasite":

> ". . . his conversation was devoid of sensitivity and intuition.
> All he could talk about was "literary cultivation and admin-
> istrative capability" and something in behalf of loyalty and
> filial piety--is this type of person not a <u>lu tu</u>? The only pity
> is that he was born with that kind of face. When I think of
> him--why I don't even want my own face".[265]

----

[261]ibid., p. 354, lines 11-15. For text, see p. 167. It is
interesting that Chen Pao-yu's virtues are the very ones Ts'ao Hsueh-
ch'in confesses he lacks in his Preface to the novel. The Preface
will be discussed in our "Persona" chapter.

[262]ibid., p. 357, line 5. For text, see p. 170.

[263]ibid., p. 358, lines 1-2. For text, see p. 171.

[264] 祿蠧。

[265]HLMPSHCP, chap. 115, p. 358, lines 4-6. For text, see
p. 171.

The play on true and false, real and unreal, culminates at the
end of chapter 115 and in the whole of chapter 116. A monk mys-
teriously arrives with Pao-yu's missing jade talisman and thus rescues
him from death. In keeping with the chen-chia theme, Pao-yu's
father and mother are faced with the ambiguity of the real and the
unreal. If this jade talisman is truly Pao-yu's they will be unable
to pay the monk the price he demands.[266] In chapter 116, when
Pao-yu floats off with the monk to the Great Void Illusion Realm
(which turns out to be named Paradise of Truth),[267] it is unclear
whether or not this is a dream experience. Pao-yu himself says
when he wakes up: "I am one who has returned from death".[268]
Whether he has dreamt or died, he prepares for the Examinations
and loses all interest in romance, including sexual love. In other
words, despite his fondest ideals, he acts like, although he does
not really become, a Chen Pao-yu, a "precious treasure" to his
family; that is, one who is "true" and "real" because he accords
with the standards of the mortal world.

The story of Chen and Chia Pao-yu exemplifies Ts'ao Hsueh-ch'in's
character reflection technique and the interplay between their conceptions of the "true", "real", "false", and "unreal" is representative of the theme and structure of Dream of the Red Chamber. With
the foregoing presentation in mind, we might comment further on the
significance of this encounter between "Real Precious Jade" and
"Unreal Precious Jade" which occurs so late in the novel. We
learn of the other Pao-yu as early as chapter 2, we meet his image
in Chia Pao-yu's dream vision of chapter 56, and we finally observe him in chapter 115. We should reconsider the meaning of
Chih-yen Chai's comment on Chen Pao-yu in chapter 2 and we
should scrutinize more carefully Wu Shih-ch'ang's translation:

> The Pao-yu in the Chen family is not mentioned in the first
> half of the novel, therefore he is emphatically described
> here in order to reflect from a distance the Pao-yu in the
> Chia family. Henceforth wherever Chia Pao-yu is described,
> it is the very portrayal of Chen Pao-yu.[269]

Wu believes that Chih-yen Chai's comment here indicates that Chen

---

266 ibid., p. 360, lines 7-8.
267 For "Paradise of Truth", see above, note 211.
268 HLMPSHCP, chap. 116, p. 368, line 4: 我是死去過來的 .
269 On the Red Chamber Dream, see above, note 233.

Pao-yu is the "hidden" Pao-yu or his "real self".[270] According
to the 1963 revised edition of Yu P'ing-po's Chih-yen Chai Hung-
lou meng chi-p'ing, the word Wu translates (correctly) as "reflect"
is chao.[271] Thus Chih-yen Chai also may be suggesting that Chen
Pao-yu "bodies forth"--in other words, he calls forth or points
towards Chia Pao-yu. This simply represents the typical narrative
technique of Ts'ao Hsueh-ch'in. A character of minor importance,
such as Chen Pao-yu, is the means by which the author introduces
a character of major importance, in this case, Chia Pao-yu. Chen
is not, then, the "hidden" Pao-yu or his "real self". This is an
important distinction and it is reinforced by what we believe to be
a translation error on the part of Wu Shih-ch'ang. Again according to the 1963 edition of the Chih-yen Chai collected commentary
(and according to the chia-hsu manuscript of the novel),[272] the
word which Wu translates as the surname, Chen,[273] is actually
chen[274] meaning "real" or "true". Thus we should translate as
follows:

> Henceforth wherever Chia Pao-yu is described, it is truly
> then the image of the real Pao-yu.[275]

What Chih-yen Chai seems to be saying is that Chen Pao-yu is used
by the author according to a typical stylistic pattern and that, more
importantly, Chia Pao-yu ought to be considered as the "real"
"true" Pao-yu, rather than Chen Pao-yu, who is only more "real"
and "true" than Chia Pao-yu in terms of a surname. We note with
interest that Chih-yen Chai uses the word ying,[276] "image",
"shadow", or "reflection" to describe Chia Pao-yu. Chih-yen
Chai's vocabulary underscores an important thematic conception in
the novel. To any reader of the whole of Dream of the Red Chamber,
Chia Pao-yu, its hero, is an image, shadow, or reflection of the
real Pao-yu he is trying to become. He experiences exquisite passion through his love for the Twelve Maidens of Chin-ling and he

----

[270]ibid., p. 193.

[271] 照.

[272]See the chia-hsu manuscript, chap. 2, p. 31a, interlinear
commentary, lines 3-4 (our pagination is according to the reprint
of the Hu Shih chia-hsu edition in which pages are numbered con-
secutively).

[273] 甄.

[274] 真.

[275]CYCHLMCP, chap. 2, p. 36, chia-hsu chia-p'i: 凡寫賈寶
玉之文，則正為真寶玉傳影.

[276]影.

suffers intensely when confronted with their passing. He becomes "true" and "real", one might almost say "whole", in his effort to solve the problem of their mutability, as well as his own. Chia Pao-yu is well aware of this even before he passes the Civil Service Examinations. This constitutes his final act of contempt for mundane conceptions before abandoning the world.

From a psychological point of view, one may consider the two Pao-yus as a single personality--a split representation of the conscious and subconscious self. Chen is an image or mask of Chia's self into which the latter at one point is transformed. While Chia rejects that "opposite" image of himself and even detests his own physical likeness to the image, he does become a "true" Pao-yu, a "real precious treasure" to his family, by passing the Examinations. One may argue, then, that despite Pao-yu's own convictions, he becomes his mask before becoming "whole". Such a transformation is consistent with the novel's theme, and is an important feature of Ts'ao's concept of enlightenment. Furthermore, character presentation through complementary opposites is still another example of the unity of style and theme. One may disagree with those critics, such as Wu Shih-ch'ang, who find that the Examinations episode is an unnecessary addendum of the editor, Kao E, by citing the demonstrable fact that such an event is psychologically, stylistically, and thematically consistent with the whole of the novel.

Structurally speaking, chapter 115 represents a central moment in Pao-yu's life. He seeks Chen Pao-yu, "True" Pao-yu, and becomes deathly ill from the encounter. In the chapters which directly follow, his jade talisman is restored to him,[277] and he visits the Great Void Illusion Land for his final enlightenment prior to his success in the Examinations and his release from the mortal world. From Chia Pao-yu's point of view, then, the meeting with Chen Pao-yu is of importance, for it marks a crucial step towards self-understanding. He learns that dreams are not necessarily the source of truth, for when he relies on his dream of the other Pao-yu to assume that they are kindred spirits, he is rudely surprised. Chen

----

[277] Wu Shih-ch'ang believes that the Chih-yen Chai commentary indicates Ts'ao originally intended that Chen Pao-yu return the missing jade to Chia Pao-yu. Wu, On the Red Chamber Dream, pp. 165, 192-193. If this is true, it underscores the structural importance of chapter 115.

Pao-yu is not a "soul mate",[278] but rather a "bureaucratic para-site".[279] In the devastating encounter with his twin, he discovers an identical appearance and an opposite character, both of which repel him. He grows in self-knowledge when he comes to reject his idealized image of himself and to recognize his own face. At the same time as he declines in his own estimation, his parents and the maid-servant of Tai-yu are deciding that Chen Pao-yu is superior. Chia Pao-yu is no longer considered as a person worthy of Tai-yu's love--she truly dies in vain. He further learns the possible mean-ings of renouncing youthful passion. Through Chen Pao-yu, he discovers that such a move towards maturity signifies the embrace of passionate ties can only have an opposite meaning.

Confronted by the image of his "true" self as presented in the "this life" figure of Chen Pao-yu, and reminded of the love-death of Tai-yu, Chia Pao-yu is driven to idiocy. This is hardly an entirely negative image in the novel, although in comparison to Chen Pao-yu, the fool is a diseased symbol of Chia Pao-yu's self. As we have noted elsewhere in our review of this universal archetype in the novel, the fool is a symbol of imagination, intuition, and sensi-tivity. Yet, the fool is also a temporal image, but flotsam upon a sea of change. Foolishness, Pao-yu discovers, is not a form of immutable saving grace. The meeting of the two Pao-yus links the mimetic and mythic layers of the framework. Chia Pao-yu has to return to the mythic world in order to dissolve the image of himself he has come to hate. Neither the world of dreams with its idealized images of himself nor the conscious world with its Chen Pao-yus remains as a viable alternative.[280]

----

278 知己.
279 祿蠹.
280C. T. Hsia writes, The Classic Chinese Novel, p. 287: "The tragic dilemma posed in the drama of Pao-yu's spiritual awak-ening is surely this: Is insensibility the price of one's liberation? Is it better to suffer and sympathize, knowing one's complete im-potence to redeem the human order, or is it better to seek personal salvation, knowing that, in achieving this, one becomes a mere stone, impervious to the cries of distress around one?" This is a fine characterization of Pao-yu's abandonment of love. The psy-chological meaning of release from the world, as well as its religious significance, has yet to be explored.

In the story of Chen Shih-yin and Chia Yu-ts'un, and the parallel narrative of Chen Pao-yu and Chia Pao-yu, we find that Ts'ao Hsueh-ch'in's narrative technique is a reflection of his theme of complementary opposites and his conception of enlightenment. The mimetic core of the novel and the realism of the Chen-Chia framework are overlaid and supported by a highly allegorical technique. Again this is an outgrowth of Ts'ao's vision of complementary opposites. Upon a mechanical scaffolding he erects the vibrant figures of the novel. Artifice and ornament produce the illusion of reality. Thus Dream of the Red Chamber may be termed completely successful, at least in so far as the reader realizes with Ts'ao Hsueh-ch'in that, after all, reality is an illusion.

Persona:
the Narrative Mode

We have found that through the mythic mode Ts'ao Hsueh-ch'in presents his essentially ironic vision of the divine and human milieus, while in the mimetic we discovered the concept of complementary opposites and the significance of the contrapuntal rhythm of "true" and "false". The "allegoric" and "realistic" styles serve to formulate the major aesthetic patterns of Dream of the Red Chamber. We now need to identify the author's use of persona, a major feature of the narrative mode, as persona is directly relevant to an understanding of Ts'ao Hsueh-ch'in's concept of fiction.

When we ask ourselves what is the author's idea of fiction, we find ourselves presented with the kind of problem we have noted previously. Just as there are several beginnings of Dream of the Red Chamber and more than one stylistic mode, so too there is no single theory of fiction in the novel. What the author does instead is to present his reader with a number of literary viewpoints, some of them contradictory, through several personae: the dogmatic authority (the divine Buddhist Monk), the naive pedant (the Reverend Taoist Kosmo Kosmos), the objective innovator (the Stone), the autobiographical confessor (Ts'ao Hsueh-ch'in), and the faithful scribe (the anonymous narrator). To understand the meaning of fiction in Dream of the Red Chamber and the concomitant attractiveness of the novel, we shall examine these personae, and we also shall consider the critical mask of another figure not created

by Ts'ao Hsueh-ch'in: the hovering annotator and efficient commentator, Chih-yen Chai.

We begin by returning to the inexhaustible creation myth and
Chen Shih-yin's dream-vision, for the mythic mode yields basic
information about the work of fiction it serves to introduce, the
Stone Record. As we noted in our "Myth" chapter, the creation
myth contains a strong claim for fiction and an awareness of the
needs of the reader:

> Dear Reader, do you ask where this book came from?
> Although the account of its origin borders on the fantastic,
> once you are familiar with the details you will find it utterly
> fascinating. Allow me humbly to elucidate the background,
> for then you will not have any misgivings.[1]

The anonymous narrator of this passage takes the interesting view
that his reader is suspicious about what he reads and is therefore in
need of special guidance. Like the reader, the Stone too has
"misgivings", huo.[2] It appears to fear the meaning of the narrative that is to be inscribed upon its surface:

> "I do not know what unique signs you are to engrave on
> me . . . . How about an explanation so that I may have no
> misgivings?"[3]

But the "misgivings" of the reader and the "misgivings" of the Stone
will not be removed until the former is intimately familiar with every
detail of the novel and the latter has experienced the Red Dust.
The work of fiction, Dream of the Red Chamber, promises enlightenment to its reader; indeed, as we shall observe later, there is
the suggestion in the text that it is a revelation of tao. As Chen
Shih-yin notes, if he could only be enlightened about the Stone
which the Buddhist Immortal carries and know the meaning of the
characters written upon it, he might perceive the way to salvation.[4]

While the written word may contain enlightenment, ironically it
is also a form of falsification. In so far as the view of language is
concerned, the creation myth is similar to the first chapter of the
Tao te ching. If there is a tao that can be named and described, it
is not the true tao. The very existence of a text having to do with
tao would appear to be contradictory, until we realize that the Tao

----

[1] HLMPSHCP, chap. 1, p. 2, lines 2-3. For text, see p. 47.
[2] 惑 .
[3] HLMPSHCP, chap. 1, p. 3, lines 5-6. For text, see p. 48.
[4] HLMPSHCP, chap. 1, p. 6, line 15. For text, see p. 51.

te ching, like other works of mystical literature, does not suggest
that its words are equivalents of tao, but only faint similes. Through
the paradoxical use of language the text offers readings through
which the reader may intuit an experience of tao.   One theme of
Dream of the Red Chamber is that man, and by implication, the
reader, is only capable of appreciating the written word, and yet
the written word is but a "false" though attractive cover for that
which is "true".   The Chih-yen Chai commentary repeatedly stresses
the precious divinity of the pre-inscription and pre-literate state of
the Stone which mortals are unable to recognize. Without the fictive language of the written character, the Stone appears to be but
a "stepping stone".[5] "Several characters must be incised upon
you", says the Buddhist Monk to the Stone, "so that as soon as
people see you they will know you are rare and marvelous".[6]
Knowledge of the "rare and marvelous" may be spontaneous, but
it is realized only indirectly through the experience of the "false",
that is, Ts'ao Hsueh-ch'in's work of fiction.

It is through the figure of the divine Buddhist Monk that we receive our first critical impressions of the novel. Initially, in his
discussion with the Taoist Immortal, the Monk comments on a story
which is introductory to Dream of the Red Chamber, the account of
the Divine Crystal Page and the Crimson Pearl Sylph Herb:

> "This affair is a laughable story to tell", smiled the Monk.
> "Why, it is one of those oddities you would not hear of in a
> thousand ages!"[7]

The Monk's narrative is obviously convincing, for when he is finished, the Taoist Immortal exclaims over the tale:

> "Odd indeed!", said the Taoist. "Why never before have I
> heard of 'Repaying with Tears'".[8]

The Taoist is alluding to the fact that the Crimson Pearl Sylph Herb
wishes to descend to the earth with the Divine Crystal Page and
repay the latter for the favor of watering by shedding a lifetime of
tears. The important point is the stress on "odd" or "rare", han.[9]
The emphasis of the creation myth is that Dream of the Red Chamber

----

[5]CYCHLMCP, chap. 1, p. 4, chia-hsu chia-p'i. For text,
see chapter 1, note 80.
[6]HLMPSHCP, chap. 1, p. 3, line 4. For text, see p. 48.
[7]ibid., p. 5, line 16. For text, see p. 50.
[8]ibid., p. 6, line 7. For text, see p. 51.
[9] 罕.

and the tales which precede it are unique. Chih-yen Chai uses
similar expressions to characterize the novel. Thus, for example,
he borrows the vocabulary of the Buddhist Monk to say that Dream
of the Red Chamber is a work of sublime fiction which knows no
precedents.[10]

Wherever we find the Buddhist Monk and the Taoist Immortal appearing together, whether it be in the mythic world, or before Chen
Shih-yin, or as visitants to the Chia family compounds, we always
perceive that it is the Buddhist Monk who is the real figure of authority. In the discussion here with the Taoist Immortal, it is the
Buddhist Monk who bears the Stone to the Red Dust, who answers
the Taoist's questions, and who explains the background story of
the Divine Crystal Page and the Crimson Pearl Sylph Herb which
accounts for the subsequent love affair between Chia Pao-yu and
Lin Tai-yu.

This persona of authority is important in the presentation of critical
views of fiction. Ts'ao Hsueh-ch'in stresses the uniqueness of his
work by using the divine Buddhist Monk as his first literary spokesman. We note that when a difference of opinion appears between
the Taoist and the Buddhist as to the meaning of "odd", han, the
latter is quick to resort to his position of authority. The Taoist has
never heard of the phrase, "repaying with tears", but when he does,
he finds that it reminds him of inferior types of sentimental love
stories:

"I imagine that this story, compared to all the 'Wind and
Moon' romances up to this date, is even more detailed and
refined".[11]

The Buddhist Monk began his description by referring to the story of
the Divine Crystal Page and the Crimson Pearl Sylph Herb as "one
of those oddities you would not hear of in a thousand ages!" But
now he seems dissatisfied that the Taoist should call the "oddities"
only "detailed and refined". The Monk immediately corrects what
is to him an obviously false impression:

"Of the past figures of romance", replied the Buddhist Monk,
"all that is related is a general outline together with poems,
lyrics, and essays, and that's that. Nothing is recorded about

---

10CYCHLMCP, chap. 1, p. 13, chia-hsu chia-p'i: . . . 千古
未聞之奇文.
11HLMPSHCP, chap. 1, p. 6, lines 7-8. For text, see p. 51.

how they wine and dine in the ladies'boudoir. Furthermore, in most of the 'Wind and Moon' romances, all you get is: 'Pilfering Perfume', 'Snatching Jade', 'Evening Tryst', and 'Secret Runaway'. Never is there leaked even a hint or two of the genuine emotions of the lovers. I believe that what is told of this group who are about to enter the world--the foolish lovers, the wanton devils, the wise and the naive as well as the degenerate--will be different from that which has been narrated before".12

The Monk initially uses "odd" to mean that the Divine Crystal Page and Crimson Pearl Sylph Herb myth is "laughable" and there-fore entertaining, but he qualifies his original remarks by turning from that myth to the story which the myth serves to introduce, Dream of the Red Chamber. He proceeds to distinguish the latter from past romances by means of a dogmatic style and a series of broad generalizations which are representative of the authoritarian figure. In a single phrase,13 he gathers together romantic person-ages of the past and condemns their tales for being mere "general outlines"14 "and that's that".15 "Nothing" is even said about the eating habits of ladies.16 Thus the Buddhist Monk indicts the 'Wind and Moon'17 genre and its romantic stereotypes ('Pilfering Perfume',18 'Snatching Jade',19 'Evening Tryst',20 'Secret Runaway'21) as literary clichés. What the story which is about to unfold offers to the reader is "genuine emotions"22 and variety in characterization ("foolish lovers",23 "wanton devils",24 "the

----

12ibid., lines 8-10. For text, see p. 51.
13 歷來幾個風流人物.
14 大概.
15 而已.
16 一飲一食總未述記.
17 風月.
18 偷香.
19 竊玉.
20 暗約.
21 私奔.
22 真情.
23 情癡.
24 色鬼, or "sex maniacs".

wise",[25] "the naive",[26] "the degenerate"[27]). Above all, it is
a story which is "different"[28] from any which has ever been told
before.

The Monk's views of fiction are important not merely because he
deems them so or because they are especially perspicacious. The
knowledge that a novel exhibits real feelings, interesting characterization, or is just plain "different" hardly amounts to a theory of
criticism. The significance of the Buddhist's position is owing to a
persona which is naive as well as authoritarian. Since he is a figure of divine vision, we expect him to score the foolish desires of
the Stone, the Divine Crystal Page, and the Crimson Pearl Sylph
Herb to be reborn in the Red Dust. Conversely, we do not expect
him to appear as literary theoretician and defender of an earthly
love tragedy. An unworldly monk ought not to be attracted by a
mundane romance. Thus the Buddhist's persona is contradictory and
inconsistent: his unselfconscious approval of a work of fiction is a
betrayal of that dogmatism by which he condemns earthly desire.
He may scorn the Red Dust, hung ch'en,[29] and Dream of the Red
Chamber, Hung-lou meng, but he may not disparage the former and
celebrate the latter. By creating a dogmatic authority who is
attracted to fiction without being aware of the meaning of that
attraction, Ts'ao Hsueh-ch'in gives proof of the Buddhist's claim
that the story is truly "odd", "unique", and "rare". At the same
time, and as we have noted repeatedly in "Myth" and "Mimesis",
the author's ironic vision provides a satire directed against the
divine realm. The kingdom of authorities is inhabited by insensitive
fools.

It is rather curious that the ubiquitous commentator, Chih-yen
Chai, makes no observations on the discussion of fiction between the
Buddhist Monk and the Taoist Immortal. However, prior to that
discussion we find that he too finds the Stone Record attractive, for
he expresses his desire to accompany the Stone on its earthly journey.[30] Elsewhere in his commentary on the creation myth and Chen

---

25 賢.
26 愚.
27 不肖者.
28 不同.
29 紅塵.
30 CYCHLMCP, chap. 1, p. 5, chia-hsu mei-p'i: 余亦恨不能
隨此石而去也 ....

Shih-yin's dream-vision, Chih-yen Chai is like the Buddhist Monk
in his emphasis on the uniqueness of Dream of the Red Chamber.
When the Monk observes to the Taoist that half of the Fated Lovers
have fallen into the Red Dust, but have yet to gather together,
Chih-yen Chai points out that this passage exemplifies Ts'ao Hsueh-
ch'in's indirect narrative technique. The author proceeds from the
general to the specific and from the world of the outsider to that
of the insider, and telescopes his descriptions where necessary.[31]
When Chen Shih-yin wakes up from his dream-vision, he only has
a vague memory of his experience.   In two separate comments,
Chih-yen Chai praises Ts'ao Hsueh-ch'in's refusal to follow the
traditional dream-vision stereotype in which the participant fully
recalls his dream and a story is structured upon a detailed elabora-
tion of that dream.[32]

The views of the Buddhist Monk and Chih-yen Chai which we have
thus far noted mainly have to do with a narrative which is about to
unfold. In contrast to the divine authority and efficient commentator, our third reader, the Reverend Taoist Kosmo Kosmos, criticizes
a narrative which is now nearly complete.[33]   The Stone has returned from its sojourn in the Red Dust and Kosmo discovers it lying
once again at the base of Blue-Channel Peak:

>Later on (and we do not know how many generations and
>cycles passed by), a Reverend Taoist Kosmo Kosmos was on
>a pilgrimage inquiring after tao and seeking Sylphdom, and
>he passed by the base of Blue-Channel Peak near Incredible

----

[31]ibid., chap. 1, p. 13, chia-hsu chia-p'i:若從頭逐個
寫去,成何文字 . In the Preface to chapter 2 of the novel,
there is again emphasis on Ts'ao's indirect and telescopic style.
The author, says the commentator, uses the story of Leng Tzu-hsing
as an introduction to the Chia household. If he were to include
everyone in his narrative, two chapters would not suffice to describe
all the members of the Chia clan. CYCHLMCP, chap. 2, tsung-
p'i (general commentary), p. 24: 此回亦非正文本旨,只在冷子
興一人,即俗謂冷中出熱,無中生有也.其演說榮府一篇者,
蓋因族大人多,若從作者筆下一一敘出,盡一二回不能得明,則成何文字.

[32]CYCHLMCP, chap. 1, p. 14, chia-hsu chia-p'i:醒得無
痕,不著舊套 . ibid., chia-hsu chia-p'i: 妙極,若記
得,便是俗筆了.

[33]As we shall note in our discussion of the view of fiction in
chapter 120, parts of the narrative puzzle are not found until the
final chapter of the novel.

Cliff at Mt. Fantasia. Suddenly he saw a large Stone with
a detailed narrative incised upon its surface. The Reverend
Taoist read the story from beginning to end: how the Stone,
being no material for repair of the Firmament, had entered
the world in a transitory form; and how it had been carried
into the Red Dust by the Buddhist of Infinite Space and the
Taoist of Boundless Time.[34] It was a story about experiencing
the Way of the World--parting and reunion, sorrow and joy,
affection both warm and cool. On the back side was also a
verse:
  Being no material to repair the blue Firmament,
    this Stone wasted several years in the Red Dust.
  This is the story of its before and after life,
    who can record and pass it on as a unique tale?
Following the poem there was a passage which explicated the
Stone's experiences, the realm into which it fell, and the
place of its rebirth. In it was a complete summary of domestic
details and boudoir vignettes, together with lyrics of pleasure
and leisure. These might be considered amusing and relaxing,
but the dynastic period, the dates, the area, and the country
were all unnamed and unverifiable.[35]
We should keep in mind that the above passage appears in chapter
1 and not in chapter 120. The Stone has returned to its place of
origin and the Stone Record (Shih-t'ou chi) is engraved upon it. In
other words, while the views of Kosmo Kosmos are a posteriori,
that is, based upon a reading of the text, they are similar to the
critical opinions of the Buddhist Monk in that they occur before the
general reader can become familiar with the narrative. Once
again Ts'ao Hsueh-ch'in deliberately allows certain pre-judgments
to be made about his novel by an outside party even before it begins.
We can better appreciate Ts'ao's approach when we understand the
persona of the Reverend Taoist Kosmo Kosmos. As a pilgrim in quest
of tao,[36] he finds it most upsetting that his important journey comes

----

[34]Two titles used by C. C. Wang, Dream of the Red Chamber,
New York, 1958.
[35]HLMPSHCP, chap. 1, p. 3, lines 7-14. For text, see p. 48.
This episode occurs immediately after the conversation between the
Stone and the two Immortals, and just prior to Chen Shih-yin's
dream-vision.
[36] 訪道求仙.

to a halt in the discovery of a rather shallow narrative written upon
a discarded Stone. The significance of the occasion eludes him,
although it is probably apparent to the general reader. The passage
does serve to provide us with an indirect, but necessary, review of
the plot of a rather complicated novel. What really matters is the
tone of these lines and what they tell us about the way in which
Kosmo reads. Instead of the enthusiastic authority of the Buddhist
Monk or the tragic apology of the author (discussed below), we
find an attitude which is both tired and flippant. Kosmo's immedi-
ate impression is that the story is just another series of Buddhist
clichés about the cyclic repetition of joy and sorrow. "In fact it
was just a story of . . . ."

Apparently, Kosmo's major criticism has to do with fact rather
than with fiction. Such features as "domestic details and boudoir
vignettes"[37] and "lyrics of pleasure and leisure"[38] "might be"[39]
entertaining, but without the factual evidence literature tradition-
ally presents, such as dynastic period, date, area, and country,[40]
the pleasures fiction offers are merely contemptible. The presence
of such criticism prior to the narrative proper is fascinating for, as
we noted repeatedly in "Myth" and "Mimesis", the author purposely
obscures such "facts" so that even his name and the proper name of
his novel are never properly identified. Facts, in Ts'ao Hsueh-
ch'in's conception, are not embodiments of reality but possible
misrepresentations, and thus they have no inherent right to a sacred
position in fiction.

Kosmo's pedantry is brought out in a comment of Chih-yen Chai's.
When the former uses the word huo, "might be", or, "perhaps", in
reference to the possible entertainment value of detailed descriptions and leisure poetry, Chih-yen Chai remarks that this usage is
a nice instance of modesty.[41] Probably the commentator is pointing
here, as he frequently does, to the author's humble view of his
work. But as a word used by the Reverend Taoist Kosmo Kosmos,
huo is an extremely supercilious expression. Since the basic content of the novel has to do with persons and events ("domestic details") in the Chia household, to merely suggest that this content

---

37 家庭閨閣瑣事.
38 閒情詩詞.
39 或.
40 朝代年紀,地輿邦國.
41CYCHLMCP, chap. 1, p. 6, chia-hsu chia-p'i:或字謙得好.

"might be considered amusing and relaxing" is to offer a rather devastating criticism of the novel. The words which we translate here as "relaxing", chieh men,[42] remind us that in the Preface to chapter 1 the author makes the modest claim that his words "can dispel a moment's blues".[43]   As we shall note in our discussion of the Preface, it is part of the persona of the author-as-narrator to make just such a humble claim for fiction. Conversely, it is part of the persona of Kosmo Kosmos to find such a claim, humble or not, rather unimportant.

The Reverend Taoist is so upset by the absence of certain facts in the Stone Record that he ceases to muse to himself about the meaning of the Stone. Instead of casting aside the Stone and continuing on in his search for the tao, Kosmo decides to argue:

"Brother Stone, according to your say-so, this story of yours has some interest and that's why it is written down here. Your desire is to tell the world your tale and to pass down what is unique. But in my opinion, first of all, there's neither dynasty nor dates that can be verified. Secondly, it lacks examples of Excellent Administrations in which High Character Statesmen and Great Loyal Ministers 'set in order the Court' and 'regulate customs'. In the main part of it there are only a few unusual females--some who loved and some who were foolish in love, plus some amateurish mediocre types. None of them are of the caliber of Lady Pan Chao or Madame Ts'ai Yen. Even if I were to copy it down, mortals probably wouldn't enjoy reading it".[44]

The Taoist begins his argument by questioning the authority of the Stone and the meaning of "unique", ch'i.[45] He tries to draw a distinction between himself and the Stone by identifying the latter as a dogmatist and himself as the cautious voice of personal opinion. The story is unique only because the Stone says so,[46] while Kosmo's views[47] are solidly based on the fact that certain critical materials are obviously missing. Without these materials and the verification

----

42 解悶.
43 可破一時之悶.
44HLMPSHCP, chap. 1, p. 3, line 14, through p. 4, line 1.
For text, see pp. 48-49.
45 奇.
46 據你自己說.
47 據我看來.

which accompanies them, the implication is that the story is not
true.

Chih-yen Chai's comments are germane to the present discussion.
The commentator is ever pointing to the unconventional in Dream
of the Red Chamber. When it is first mentioned that the dynastic
period, dates, area, and country are neither named nor verified in
the novel, Chih-yen Chai observes that the use of such stereotypes
would impede the imagination and the technique of the author.[48]
Furthermore, he notes (thus pointing to the autobiographical significance of Dream of the Red Chamber), so far as he is concerned,
the information which is supposedly missing is in fact readily ascer-
tainable.[49]   Given these stated views of Chih-yen Chai we are
somewhat surprised to find him compliment Kosmo's statement ". . .in
my opinion, first of all, there's neither dynasty nor dates that can be
verified", with the observation that this statement is an initially
successful refutation of the validity of the Stone Record.[50]   Chih-
yen Chai's point is that from a traditional point of view, the story
is not true because it leaves out some basic information--information
with which he is thoroughly familiar. But if we view the novel as
an unconventional literary work, the absence of conventions is
meaningless. As the Stone implies in its reply to Kosmo (and this is
the purport of its argument), facts corrupt, and absolute facts corrupt absolutely.

Before we turn to the Stone's refutation of Kosmo's criticisms, we
should observe two severe assertions made by the Reverend Taoist:
the Stone Record is neither didactic nor entertaining; indeed, because it fails to teach it fails to delight. The story is unique in
only a negative sense. It includes the love affairs of "a few unusual
females",[51] but leaves out models of exemplary behavior such as
Lady Pan Chao[52] and Madame Ts'ai Yen.[53]   Here again Chih-yen

----

[48]CYCHLMCP, chap. 1, p. 6, chia-hsu chia-p'i: 若用此套者
胸中必無好文字,手中斷無新筆墨.

[49]CYCHLMCP, chap. 1, p. 6, chia-hsu chia-p'i: 據余説,大
有考證.

[50]CYCHLMCP, chap. 1, p. 6, chia-hsu chia-p'i: 先駁得妙.

[51]幾個異樣的女子.

[52]Pan Chao 班昭 , who completed the Han shu 漢書   for
her father, Pan Piao 班彪 , and brother, Pan Ku 班固 , and
authoress of Nu-chieh 女誡 (Ladies'Guide), is a commonplace
example of female virtue.

[53]Ts'ai Yen 蔡琰 , also of the later Han period and also a

Chai is quick to insist on the achievement of Ts'ao Hsueh-ch'in. Phrases about "High Character Statesmen"[54] and "Great Loyal Ministers"[55] who "regulate customs"[56] in "Excellent Administrations"[57] are, says Chih-yen Chai, "bromides"[58] (literally, "rotten words"; that is, platitudes) which the mediocre will wish to offer to dispute the author's claims to excellence. By having a substitute mediocrity (Kosmo Kosmos) present these platitudes in advance, the author cleverly deals with them and allows the Stone to dispose of them.[59] To the commentator, the indirect satire of the passage is delightfully instructive.

Kosmo's subsequent complete capitulation is proof of the didactic content and entertainment value of Dream of the Red Chamber and also reveals the powerful persona of the Stone. Before analyzing the latter's comments on the Stone Record, let us complete our presentation of the persona of the Reverend Taoist by considering his reaction to the Stone's arguments:

> The Reverend Taoist Kosmo Kosmos listened to the way the Stone had spoken and he puzzled over what it had said for a long while. Then he took the Stone Record and once again

----

model of ideal feminine behavior like Pan Chao. Musician, talented and learned, she became a widow early in her life, was captured by and lived among the Hsiung-nu, and bore two sons. The citation of Ts'ai Yen suggests the tie between fiction and autobiography in Dream of the Red Chamber. Ts'ao Hsueh-ch'in's grandfather, Ts'ao Yin 曹寅 , is allegedly the author of a drama, Hou p'i-p'a 後 琵琶 (modeled after the Ming drama, P'i-p'a chi 琵琶記), which deals with the life of the Han scholar, Ts'ai Yung 蔡邕 and his daughter, Ts'ai Yen. Ts'ao Hsueh-ch'in's rejection of stereotypes of virtue, such as Ts'ai Yen, not only implies his criticism of traditional standards in literature, but may also suggest a reaction against his own family. See Eminent Chinese of the Ch'ing Period, ed. Arthur Hummel, Taipei, 1967, p. 741.

54 大賢.
55 大忠.
56 治風俗.
57 善政.
58 腐言.
59 CYCHLMCP, chap. 1, p. 6, chia-hsu chia-p'i: 將世人欲 駁之腐言,預先代人駁盡,妙.

read it through carefully.[60]
Chih-yen Chai declares that these lines indicate Kosmo's extreme
pedantry.[61] As we observed in "Mimesis", they also contain a
lesson in reading. Kosmo reads the Stone Record once and misunderstands its meaning. Attracted by the way in which the Stone
expresses itself (the attraction of style), the Reverend Taoist reads
the story a second time and changes his mind. What is fascinating
about his conversion is not his newly gained reverence for the text,
but that his misunderstanding has increased:

> While there were some biting words on the front side of the
> Stone about villainy and evil, the intent was not to sorrow
> over the world or to criticize the times. Whenever it touched
> upon natural moral obligations such as the humanity of the
> prince, the goodness of the minister, the compassion of the
> father, or the filial piety of the son, it always praised merits
> and eulogized virtue tirelessly and exhaustively. Indeed, no
> other book could compare with it! Although its main theme
> was love, the affairs were truthfully recorded. There were
> no false imitations or groundless talk. No work which was
> exclusively about "Licentious Engagements", "Private Discus-
> sions", or "Secret Oaths" was comparable. Because it did
> not even slightly touch upon the present day world, Kosmo
> copied it down from top to bottom so as to inform the world
> and pass on the unique.[62]

The Taoist's judgment that the Stone Record is an incomparable
story is just and his willingness to "pass on the unique" is commend-
able. To the reader of Dream of the Red Chamber, however, Kosmo's
other observations indicate that he has not listened to the Stone and
that his second reading of the story is as careless as his first.

It is true that one of the central themes of the novel is romantic
love and that, as the Stone asserts, what is recorded is based on
personal observations.[63] The Taoist is also correct in realizing that,

---

[60]HLMPSHCP, chap. 1, p. 4, line 15. For text, see p. 49.

[61]CYCHLMCP, chap. 1, p. 7, chia-hsu chia-p'i: 這空空道
人也太小心了, 想亦世之一腐儒耳.

[62]HLMPSHCP, chap. 1, p. 4, line 15, through p. 5, line 2.
For text, see pp. 49–50.

[63]Remarking on the line, "there were no false imitations or
groundless talk", Chih-yen Chai says,"an important sentence".
CYCHLMCP, chap. 1, p. 8, chia-hsu chia-p'i: 要緊句. He thus
underscores the point that this narrative is true.

while Dream of the Red Chamber has to do with human passions, it
is in no way a conventional love story. Where his claims become
absurd is in the area of political and moral relevance. As we note
in an observation on a phrase used by the Buddhist Monk,[64] "the
prosperity and tranquility of the present dynasty", certain formulaic
clichés appear in the novel which sound politically condescending.
We have yet to determine the political significance of Dream of
the Red Chamber but the conversation of the Buddhist Monk, the
disavowals of Kosmo Kosmos, and the denials in the General Editorial Principles[65] may suggest that the novel has a political content. In the passage presently under discussion, the Chih-yen Chai
commentary supports this view. Where the passage reads, "the
intent was not to sorrow over the world or to criticize the times",
the commentator remarks, "an important sentence".[66] And of the
closing sentence, "because it did not even slightly touch upon the
present day world", he again states, "an important clause".[67]

Kosmo is exceedingly naive to believe the novel does not "even
slightly touch upon the present day world", but we must remember
that his foolishness and pedantry are part of a persona created by
Ts'ao Hsueh-ch'in. A similar sort of silliness is found in the Reverend Taoist's moral reading of Dream of the Red Chamber. If there
is anything that is obvious about the novel, it is that neither the
narrator nor the hero, Pao-yu, is willing "to praise merits and
eulogize virtue tirelessly and exhaustively". The bane of Pao-yu's
existence is moral obligation.

We may view Kosmo's interpretation as a distasteful, yet informative, misreading of Dream of the Red Chamber. Apparently, he
does not hear the note of anti-traditionalism in the Stone's arguments.
But his reaction is not merely due to his not listening or to his hearing only what he wants to hear; rather, it is yet another ironic commentary on language in the novel. Kosmo is so seduced by the
Stone's persuasive rhetoric into believing in the Stone Record that
he imagines a kind of fiction that is not really there. He eagerly
copies the narrative because he is certain that it is safe, irrelevant,

----

[64]See "Myth" chapter, note 92.
[65]See the Fourth of the General Editorial Principles.
CYCHLMCP, chap. 1, p. 1, chia-hsu pen fan-li: 此書不敢于
涉朝廷.凡有不得不用朝政者,只略用一筆帶出,蓋實不敢
以寫兒女之筆墨唐突朝廷之上也.又不得謂其不備.
[66]CYCHLMCP, chap. 1, p. 8, chia-hsu chia-p'i: 要緊句.
[67]ibid.

and traditional. Like the Buddhist Monk, he is unaware of the
inconsistencies in his appreciation. Since the story does not touch
upon the present day world, it is good; since it is full of traditional
moral platitudes, no other work is comparable.

The very style of the above passage informs us about the persona
of the Reverend Taoist and his concept of fiction. His thoughts are
not only generalizations and abstractions, but they are presented
in balanced phrases. "While there were some . . . .",[68] "the intent
was not . . . ."[69] "Whenever it touched . . .",[70] "it always
praised . . . ."[71] "Although its main theme was love . . . ,"[72]
"the affairs were truthfully recorded".[73] "Because it did not
. . . ,"[74] "Kosmo copied it down".[75] Ts'ao thus creates the
image of an objective critic for the Reverend Taoist who is, in fact,
a dealer in platitudes and a completely disoriented seeker of sylphdom.

Perhaps the fiction that Kosmo hears and reads affects other readers
as it affects himself. The mask of objectivity and the concomitant
judgment that the novel is a work of orthodoxy may seduce the
cautiously orthodox reader into a perusal. But Kosmo's persona is
too varied and contradictory for Ts'ao Hsueh-ch'in to enlist it solely
in the service of seduction. He appears as the traditional critic
whose ossified opinions epitomize pedantry. It is because we are
conscious of the persona of orthodoxy that Kosmo's final conversion
seems so startling to us--a conversion which is yet another revelation of Ts'ao Hsueh-ch'in's concept of fiction. After the Taoist
copies the Stone Record, his subsequent sudden enlightenment is thus
described:

> In the Void was perceived Appearance, from Appearance was
> born love, love then entered into Appearance, and by Appear-
> ance the Void was illuminated. Consequently, the Reverend
> Taoist Kosmo Kosmos changed his name to "Bonze of Love"
> and changed Stone Record to Memoirs of the Bonze of Love.[76]

----

68 雖有些，
69 …亦非…之旨．
70 乃至．
71 皆是稱，
72 雖其中大旨談情，
73 亦不過實錄其事．
74 因毫不，
75 方…抄錄回來．
76HLMPSHCP, chap. 1, p. 5, lines 2-3. For text, see p. 50.

After a list of various alternate titles is given in the text, such as
Twelve Hairpins of Chin-ling, Precious Mirror of Wind and Moon,
and Red Chamber Dream,[77] there appears the following quatrain:
> Paper covered with absurd words
> A handful of hot bitter tears.
> All say the author is crazy
> But who understands the essence?[78]

Since the quatrain appears immediately after Kosmo's conversion,
the question it poses has to do with the conversion as well as with
the meaning of Dream of the Red Chamber. As we note in "Myth",
it is in the world of myth that Ts'ao Hsueh-ch'in develops his sense
of reality. The "essence" of the novel evolves out of absurdity.
This phenomenon implies that in the present case Kosmo's conversion
is not a process to be understood but an experience to be re-created
by the reader through a reading of a particular work of fiction.
Thus the description of enlightenment in terms of a circular movement from the Void to Appearance to love, and from love to Appearance and thence to the Void, is probably deliberately intended to
dazzle the reader rather than to be merely another restatement of
the theme of complementary opposites.

Surely the final irony of Kosmo's persona is that the pilgrim who
is "inquiring after tao and seeking Sylphdom" becomes a convert to
romantic love, the "Bonze of Love". In the light of his conversion,
his former name, the "Reverend Taoist Kosmo Kosmos", is ridiculous:
a Taoist who is in search of tao; a totally conditioned being of
illusory appearance rather than an "Unconditioned-Unconditional"
or a "Voided-Void" (k'ung-k'ung),[79] as his name implies.[80]
Indeed, the completeness of his conversion and the strength of his
newly found devotion argue that originally he was unconsciously a
seeker of se,[81] that is, conditioned existence in the form of love

----

[77]For discussion of titles, see "Myth", pp. 30-33.
[78]HLMPSHCP, chap. 1, p. 5, lines 5-6. For text, see p. 50.
[79] 空空.
[80]k'ung 空 is a "numinous" term in Chinese Buddhism. It is
sometimes used to translate the Sanskrit nirvana and sūnyatā.
English approximations are: "signless", "empty", "wishless",
"deathless", "at peace", "extinction of self", "blowing out". See
Edward Conze, Buddhist Thought in India, Ann Arbor, 1967, passim.
[81] 色 , Sanskrit rūpa.

and passion.[82] We have only to recall his earlier disdain for the story, "there's only a few unusual females--some who loved and some who were foolish in love", to realize the nature of his change.

In the place of tao Kosmo finds a Stone which tells a story of love. This seemingly coincidental link Ts'ao forges between tao, love, and the Stone Record, suggests the seriousness with which he views his work of fiction and at least partially indicates the meaning of Dream of the Red Chamber. The novel is his imaginative re-creation of metaphysical truth, or, to use Tillich's phrase, the Ground of Being. The entertaining persona of the Reverend Taoist Kosmo Kosmos contains, then, a lesson in reading. Here we recall Mr. Richard Kunst's very suggestive idea that the Taoist symbolizes the general reader and the Stone symbolizes the narrator.[83] He happens along consciously searching for tao, and when a kind of enlightenment ensues, he is unconscious of how it came about, that is, through a misreading of a text. He thinks he likes the book because it is orthodox, but it is not orthodoxy that could possess him with the passion to be a disciple of love. In fact, if Dream of the Red Chamber may be read as a moral exemplum, it is then a warning against the vanity of human desire. Kosmo's conversion is thus a stunning testament to the ambiguous and contradictory power of fiction, and his mask is a forbidding symbol of the reader: he becomes a follower of the Stone for all the wrong reasons.

Perhaps we may say that, despite the Stone's instructions as to the true content of its story, Kosmo wrongly relies on his own sensibilities and inadvertently converts himself from being a seeker of tao to becoming a "Bonze of Love". There is, of course, no direct indication from Ts'ao Hsueh-ch'in as to whether or not the Reverend Taoist perceives the Stone Record correctly. Clearly, however, he is what we might call a taonocrat, a religious idealist with political sensibilities--one who protects his idealism by an insistence upon the social and political irrelevance of tao. Moreover, at the very

----

[82] se 色 . The suggestion about Kosmo's unconscious desires is supported by reference to the familiar Buddhist saying, 色即是空, 空即是色 "passion (se) is but the Void (k'ung) and the Void is but Passion". K'ung-k'ung tao-jen's name, "Unconditioned-Unconditional" (or, "Voided-Void"), ironically suggests conditioned existence. "Voided-Void" is but another name for passionate attachment.

[83] Kunst, "The Beginning and Ending of The Dream of the Red Chamber", p. 36.

end of chapter 1 there is the contrasting example of a second reader
and convert, Chen Shih-yin. As soon as he begins to read the inscription upon the Stone, he is converted to a vision of life which
is the reverse of that of the "Bonze of Love". Chen longs to leave
the Red Dust of passion and love so as to embrace mystical faith.
Ironically, the Buddhist Monk only allows Chen to read the title
on the Stone, "Precious Jade for Penetrating the Numinous", t'ung-
ling pao-yu, lest he have too much insight into the meaning of
metaphysical reality. There is conversion which results from misreading, and an enlightenment which is based upon almost no
reading at all.

   We noted earlier that the critical opinions of the Buddhist Monk
are introductory to a narrative which is about to unfold, while the
views of the Reverend Taoist Kosmo Kosmos are a commentary on a
story which is nearly complete. In contrast to these two external
critics, the Stone's review of the Stone Record is a discussion of a
personal experience and a defense of a new form of fiction. When
Kosmo complains about missing facts and the absence of virtuous
personalities in the narrative, the Stone laughs in reply:

   "Master, why are you so pedantic? If you say that there
   are no verifiable dates, you may purloin the golden ones of
   Han, T'ang, or the like, and weave them into the Story.
   There's nothing hard about that. But I think the Provisional
   Historical Tales[84] of the past all fall into the same rut.
   Nothing compares to my Story, for as I do not borrow such
   camouflage,[85] I end up with freshness and originality. There
   is some selection of materials and motifs from other books, but
   that is all. Why must one be restricted by dynasty and date?

   Furthermore, ordinary persons who are fond of reading books
   about 'ordering' and 'regulating' are very few, while there
   are indeed many who enjoy reading light amusing literature.
   Now as for those Provisional Historical Tales of the past, either
   they lampoon literocrats and statesmen or rail at women--licen-
   tiousness and malevolence ad infinitum and ad nauseum.
   Worse are the erotic writings of the 'Wind and Moon' variety--
   their obscenity and filth contaminate literature and corrupt
   youngsters--this type is also numberless. When it comes to

----

   84 野史 . Yeh shih. Private records not included by official historicans in orthodox histories.
   85 套 t'ao. Clichés, but also "cover", and therefore, "camouflage".

the 'Bright Boy-Pretty Girl'[86] books, and their ilk, then you have the same cover on a thousand tomes. They can't seem to avoid touching on the licentious to the extent that the pages are filled with handsome and talented youths like P'an An, Ts'ao Tzu-chien, Hsi-shih, and Cho Wen-chun.[87]

It is just that when the author wishes to write a couple of personal Love Lyrics or elegant Exhibitory Essays, he therefore fabricates the family and given names of two lovers, and he insists on inserting "A Schemer Sows Intrigue Within"--a role just like the low comedy Spoiler in the theater. There too are those slave girls who no sooner open their mouths than out comes classical language particles like che, yeh, chih, and hu--thus claiming to be either literary or philosophical.

When these types of literature are reviewed one by one, it may be said that they are all full of self-contradictions and that they are not even approximations of reality.[88] The upshot is there is no one who has spent half a lifetime observing these women with his own eyes and ears as I have. And though I won't go so far as to claim that they are superior to the individuals found in the literature of pervious eras, still, tracing the origins and ends of their affairs soothes melancholy and dispels the blues. As for the several amateurish verses, they're

----

86 佳人才子 chia-jen ts'ai-tzu. Romantic literature about "handsome and talented youths".

87P'an An 潘安 , of the Tsin 晉 period. Famous for his handsomeness. Girls fell in love with him when they met him.

Ts'ao Tzu-chien 曹子建 (Ts'ao Chih 曹植), beloved third son of Ts'ao Ts'ao 曹操 . His elder brother, Ts'ao Pei 曹丕 , was jealous of his talent and good looks.

Hsi-shih 西施 of the Ch'un-ch'iu period. Girl of Yueh 越 . When Yueh was defeated by Wu 吳 , the king of Yueh, Kou Chien 句踐 , chose Hsi-shih to go to Fu Ch'ai 夫差 , the king of Wu, in order to distract him with her beauty.

Cho Wen-chun 卓文君 . Han 漢 beauty. When Ssu-ma Hsiang-ju was once visiting her family, he won her love by playing the ch'in 琴 . She ran away with him.

88ch'ing li 情理 . Abbreviation for jen-ch'ing tao-li 人情道理 , "human heartedness" (feeling) and "reason". In other words, such literature which does not include these basic human elements is unreal.

good for belly laughs[89] and 'bottoms up!'[90]

Here are met with the grief and joy of partings and reunions
and the drama of rises and declines. All accord with the clues
and comply with the evidence. I do not dare dress it up and
vainly beguile others lest that which is a transmission of truth
be lost. Of the people of the present time, the poor are
worried every day about food and clothing, while the rich
have in their hearts unfulfilled desires. Even if these persons
have a little free time, it is taken up with the pursuit of sex,
pleasure, material goods, or emotional inspiration. Where
is there the leisure to read those books about 'ordering' and
'regulating'? So far as my bit of a Story is concerned, I don't
care to have my contemporaries say it is unique or sublime,
and I don't necessarily want them to relish studying it. My
only wish is that they will have fun with it when they are
enraptured with wine, an amour, delicacies, or slumber, or
at a point where they are free of their affairs and their melancholy is relieved. Would not this ease their lives and preserve
their vigor and be superior to plotting after vanity and questing
for the absurd?

What is more, this would save them from dangers that come
from gossip and argument, and the pain which results from
running madly about. Furthermore, this book may also give
contemporaries a fresh way of viewing the world. It is not
comparable to those carelessly put together fictions about
'Sudden Parting' and 'Chance Encounter' in which whole texts
are filled with Talented Men and Lovely Ladies like Ts'ao Tzu-
chien, Cho Wen-chun, Hung-niang, and Huo Hsiao-yu[91] --

----

89 噴飯 p'en fan. Su T'ung-po is said to have heard something so funny that he couldn't avoid spitting out his food. A
common expression for that which is hilarious.

90 供酒 kung chiu. To serve wine, but here refers to literature which entertains while one is drinking.

91 Hung-niang 紅娘, maid in Hsi-hsiang chi who brings
together her mistress, Ying-ying, and the latter's lover, Chang.

Huo Hsiao-yu 霍小玉, famous T'ang prostitute, accomplished
in poetry and music. Her story, in which she was deserted by her
lover and died of a broken heart, is celebrated in T'ang ch'uan-
chi.

without exception that is the old style literature of well worn
cliches.

My Master, what is your thinking?"[92]

We are now familiar with Kosmo's "thinking" concerning the Stone
Record and the arguments of the Stone. As we read the preceding
quotation, we realize that the conversion of the Taoist results from
the sheer weight and persuasiveness of the Stone's presentation,
rather than from a profound understanding of its substance.

One of the most striking aspects of this passage is that it reveals
that the Stone has also undergone a "conversion". In order to
accurately interpret its comments on fiction, we need to keep in
mind the persona of the Stone prior to its sojourn in the Red Dust.
In the creation myth Ts'ao Hsueh-ch'in establishes an initial image
of the Stone which contrasts with the personality we meet in the
argument over the meaning of the Stone Record. In the earlier
passage, the Stone is described as being excessively depressed because the goddess Nu-kua finds it unworthy of selection. Despite
a divine spiritual nature, it longs for the splendor and riches of the
Red Dust; because of this desire, the Buddhist Monk calls the Stone
"a plain fool", and both he and the Taoist continually refer to it
as a "Foolish Thing". While the Immortals take a mocking view of
the "stepping stone", it is exceedingly polite towards them in order
to woo their support. The final characteristic of the Stone is curiosity. It wishes to know what words are to be engraved upon it
and where it is going.

In the discussion between the Stone and Kosmo Kosmos concerning
the meaning of the Stone Record, we find the former's persona
takes on entirely new dimensions. Obviously the experience of the
Red Dust has rendered a drastic change. The Stone is no longer
depressed. Despite a new knowledge of mutability--"the grief and
joy of partings and reunions and the drama of rises and declines"--
it is elated about its earthly sojourn and it exudes confidence and
satisfaction. Kosmo has now become the one who is the pedantic
"fool".[93] No longer is the Stone excessively polite in its conversation. If Kosmo does not like the Story, he may plagiarize materials[94] from the golden eras of the Han and T'ang dynasties,

----

[92]HLMPSHCP, chap. 1, p. 4, lines 1-15. For text, see p. 49.
[93] 我師何大癡也！
[94]Chih-yen Chai applauds what he considers to be an excellent
retort to the Reverend Taoist's objections. CYCHLMCP, chap. 1,
p. 6, chia-hsu chia-p'i: 所以答的好．

"there's nothing hard about that". Nor is the Stone so serious about itself as it originally was; its poems are merely "amateurish verses" which are "good for belly laughs and 'bottoms up!'" Lastly, the Stone annoys Kosmo by being completely uninterested in the location of its Story and, no longer curious about the Stone Record, it only wishes that the narrative be passed on as a vehicle of entertainment.

Once again through persona Ts'ao reveals the power of fiction. We have noted before the presence of contradictory elements within the same persona. The Buddhist Monk is both authoritarian and naive, Kosmo is both a Taoist and a romantic, while the Stone is both passionate and disinterested. Just as the variety of "beginnings", the number of styles, and the absence of date, title, and author's name, contribute to the vision of fiction, so too the polarity within a given persona is informative. The persona of authority, religious idealism, or passionate desire is only present when the protagonist has yet to encounter the Stone Record. When fictional art is experienced, the former mask dissolves, like melted wax dripping into a mold, and takes the new shape of the figure of naiveté, romance, or humble objectivity.

The Stone's defense of fiction is a criticism of the literary tradition and a celebration of a new form. It begins by attacking the Taoist's concept of acceptable literature--didactic tomes which contain verifiable dates. The types which the Stone singles out are Provisional Historical Tales, Wind and Moon Romances, Stories of Handsome and Talented Youths, Love Lyrics, Exhibitory Essays, and Musical Drama. The Stone is not being critical of each of these genres per se. Rather, it is suggesting that these types of literature are frequently the reverse of what they are supposed to be. They are unconvincing because, in trying to be satirical or entertaining, they have become libelous and scatological.[95] Love Lyrics and Exhibitory Essays ought to be personal expressions, but authors insist on inserting fictitious names for the lovers. Wind and Moon Romances should provide light enjoyable reading, but their real attraction is that they are obscene. The popular forms of Musical Drama and Stories of Handsome and Talented Youths are made unrealistic by the presence of slave girls who supposedly speak in the classical

----

[95]Chih-yen Chai observes that Ts'ao first attacks the major points of libelous and slanderous literature. CYCHLMCP, chap. 1, p. 6, chia-hsu chia-p'i: 先批其大端.

language (an attempt to give vernacular literature the veneer of culture). The Stone finds such literature to be full of contradictions. It remains unconvincing because it does not accord with emotion and reason (it is "unreal"). Thus the Stone refuses to adhere to the traditional need to fabricate in order to make fiction acceptable.

Several claims are made for the Stone Record which counter the views of Kosmo Kosmos. At first the Reverend Taoist decides that the narrative is not entertaining, but finally he comes to the opinion that it is unique because it is irrelevant. Furthermore, he is overwhelmed by what he takes to be an emphasis on romantic love. Such suggestions, however, do not come from the Stone. It hopes that people will find its Story entertaining and that they "will have fun with it". The Stone is not the least bit interested in having people consider the Stone Record "unique or sublime". This is a remarkable viewpoint in the light of the fact that the Buddhist Monk, Chih-yen Chai, and Kosmo Kosmos continually stress uniqueness.96 Finally, in repeatedly criticizing eroticism and licentiousness in works of romantic passion, the Stone de-emphasizes the subject of love.

The Stone's reading of the Stone Record is, then, quite different from the viewpoint of Kosmo Kosmos. The former satirizes the latter's naive celebration of the accepted literary canon which is ridden with clichés, meaningless particles, stereotyped personalities, and insipid classical allusions to bygone golden ages. By attacking obscene and slanderous literature, it proclaims that its Story is a moral one besides being entertaining. To the Stone, the Stone Record not only promises "to soothe melancholy and to dispel the blues", and to enable the reader not to waste time in "gossip and argument", it will also teach one to avoid "running madly about", and will give people "a fresh way of viewing the world". The Stone Record will, the Stone suggests, convert men from those lives of vanity and absurdity typically represented in conventional literature.

While the Stone is not interested in having its Story considered "unique", it does claim that the Stone Record is autobiographical,

----

96Chih-yen Chai finds the Stone's statement that it does not care if people consider its Story unique or if they enjoy studying it to be an excellent turn in the argument with the Reverend Taoist. CYCHLMCP, chap. 1, p. 7, chia-hsu chia-p'i: 轉得更好.

that is, original, personal, and true. Here the Stone divulges the
secret of its technique. Instead of using the "camouflage" of
clichés, the Stone writes an account based on the personal observations of half a lifetime:

> "All accord with the clues and comply with the evidence.
> I dare not dress it up and vainly beguile others lest that which
> is a transmission of truth be lost".[97]

Secondly, the Stone may be justified in saying, "nothing compares
to my Story", because of the unusual attention given to the interests
of the common reader. In contrast to Kosmo Kosmos, the Stone is
aware of the audience of the Stone Record:

> ". . . ordinary persons who are fond of reading books about
> 'ordering' and 'regulating' are very few, while there are
> indeed many who enjoy reading light amusing literature".[98]

The Stone goes on to say that not only ordinary persons, but the
rich as well as the poor simply do not have the time or inclination
to read the sort of irrelevant literature Kosmo considers good.
While the latter may like the Stone Record because he imagines
that it does not touch upon the contemporary scene, the Stone is
obviously willing to offer direct criticisms of the world. Thus it
reveals the view that if fiction is to be entertaining it must be
"relevant":

> "Of the people of the present time, the poor are worried
> every day about food and clothing, while the rich have in
> their hearts unfulfilled desires. Even if these persons have
> a little free time, it is taken up with the pursuit of sex,
> pleasure, material goods, or emotional inspiration. Where
> is there the leisure to read those books about 'ordering' and
> 'regulating'?"[99]

Literature about "ordering" and "regulating" is to be disregarded
because such does not concern itself with the actual human condition.

We should be careful to delineate what the Stone claims is unique
about its Story. When it states, earlier in the passage, "I won't
go so far as to claim that they [the women it has observed] are
superior to the individuals found in the literature of previous eras",[100]

----

[97]HLMPSHCP, chap. 1, p. 4, line 10. For text, see p. 49.
[98]HLMPSHCP, chap. 1, p. 4, lines 3-4. For text, see p. 49.
[99]HLMPSHCP, chap. 1, p. 4, lines 10-11. For text, see p. 49.
[100]ibid., lines 8-9. For text, see p. 49.

it is not implying that the form of its Story is superior to conventional fiction, but that the latter is incapable of expressing the meaning of the Stone Record. Thus the Stone's viewpoint reveals Ts'ao
Hsueh-ch'in's awareness that form is content, and that to write in
a conventional form would be to change the meaning of Dream of
the Red Chamber. We further observe that the Stone is perfectly
willing to make strong assertions about its Story, but not excessive
ones. It takes the ironic pose which the reader finds dominating the
novel, a pose which, as we shall note below, is basic to the
persona of the author-as-narrator. The Stone disavows slanderous
literature, yet, as we know from the mention of "amateurish verses",
it delights in lampooning itself. There is a certain humor in the
fact that the Stone has spent, as it says, "half a lifetime" observing
women, and yet is hesitant to say that they are superior to famous
figures of history. The Stone is not simply speaking out of deference
for the classical tradition. The passage surely is meant to contrast
with the author-as-narrator's own avowal in the Preface to the first
chapter that women are definitely more interesting than himself.

Beside talking about the needs of the common reader, the Stone
discusses the idea of when to read:

"My only wish is that they will have fun with it when they
are enraptured with wine, an amour, delicacies, or slumber,
or at a point where they are free of their affairs and their
melancholy is relieved".[101]

The common quality in each of these individual moments is ecstasy--
that state which lies somewhere between consciousness and uncon-
sciousness. This seems to be very peculiar advice until we correlate
it with the author's vision reviewed in our first two chapters that
truth encompasses mythic and mundane reality. It is at the moment
when we emerge from our dreams that we correctly perceive that
fact and fiction are one.

In the contrasting opinions of the Stone and the Reverend Taoist
Kosmo Kosmos concerning the same narrative, we have a play on
the theme of "opposites" described in "Mimesis". Even the seemingly contradictory expressions of the Stone may be understood in
terms of the polarity between the "true" and the "false". The light
amusing story which is neither unique, sublime, nor intended for
serious study may become an unusual presentation of personal observations which will render a serious and original vision of the world.

----

[101]HLMPSHCP, chap. 1, p. 4, lines 12-13. For text, see p. 49.

The literature which the Reverend Taoist favors becomes in this
light gradually unreal, while the unconventionality and anti-traditionalism of the Stone Record--its "unreality" according to Kosmo's
viewpoint--is precisely what makes it sublime.

We have next to consider the persona of the author, for it is our
opinion, based on a study of the Preface and various passages
throughout Dream of the Red Chamber, that Ts'ao Hsueh-ch'in
creates a mask for himself through which he can present still another
concept of fiction. Various students of manuscript and printed editions of the novel have questioned the authenticity of the Preface
and have expressed doubts about its inclusion in chapter 1. Ch'en
Yu-p'i says Dream of the Red Chamber really begins with the address
to the reader which introduces the mythic origins of the novel.
The preceding section which supposedly includes the author's state--
ment of why he wrote the novel is actually a Preface written by the
commentator, Chih-yen Chai.[102] Wu Shih-ch'ang believes the
Preface is by Ts'ao's younger brother, Ts'ao T'ang-ts'un. He suggests that the latter wrote prefaces to each chapter of an early draft
of the novel, Precious Mirror of Wind and Moon, and that some of
these were preserved in later manuscripts.[103] In the chia-hsu manuscript, the Preface to chapter 1 is actually the last of five General
Editorial Principles and, like them, is transcribed two spaces lower
than the rest of the text.[104] Thus, Wu argues, the Preface does
not belong to the novel proper, but earlier readers mistakenly believed it was the author's work because it erroneously appears as
part of chapter 1 in printed editions of the novel.[105]

Richard Kunst's thorough comparison of various manuscript and
printed editions of Dream of the Red Chamber reveals that there is
almost no evidence to show that the Preface is the work of Ts'ao
T'ang-ts'un.[106] He does doubt, however, that Ts'ao Hsueh-ch'in

----

[102]The latter and Ts'ao Hsueh-ch'in are very different in their
thinking, Ch'en asserts, and only Chih-yen Chai would emphasize
dreams as the theme of the novel and be so nostalgic about the
family's former glories. Ch'en Yu-p'i 陳毓羆, "Hung-lou
meng shih tsen-yang k'ai-t'ou te", 紅樓夢是怎樣開頭的,
Wen-shih 文史, 3 (Oct., 1963), 333-338.

[103]Wu, On the Red Chamber Dream, p. 71.

[104]Wu, ibid., p. 64.

[105]Wu, ibid., p. 71.

[106]Kunst, "The Beginning and Ending of The Dream of the Red
Chamber", p. 13.

could have written the Preface and he cites internal evidence in the
General Editorial Principles to support his suspicions. The writer
of the first of the General Editorial Principles, for example, cites
the various known titles of the novel and points to the locations
within the text where such names may have originated. The same
person is also struck by one curious title, "Twelve Hairpins of
Chin-ling, and wonders if this does not refer to the Twelve Maidens
of Chin-ling of the novel. He then notes that there are many more
women in the novel than twelve.[107] Such musings would be very unlikely to come from the author of Dream of the Red Chamber, suggests Mr. Kunst.[108]

Chao Kang and Ch'en Chung-i assert that the Preface belongs to
the General Editorial Principles written by Ts'ao Hsueh-ch'in's
father, Ts'ao Fu (the commentator, Chi-hu), rather than by Ts'ao
Hsueh-ch'in's cousin, Ts'ao T'ien-yu (Chih-yen Chai), or his
brother, Ts'ao T'ang-ts'un (K'ung Mei-hsi).[109] These critics theorize that Ts'ao Fu prepared copies of the novel for public distribution after Ts'ao Hsueh-ch'in died, and he composed the General
Editorial Principles. Since Ts'ao Hsueh-ch'in intended the novel
for his family, he had no need to write the present Preface which
explains that the subject of this work is neither politics nor the court.
But, Chao and Ch'en speculate, Ts'ao Fu had to make these assertions when he released copies of the novel to the public in order to
placate imperial authorities.[110]

The question of the authorship of the Preface is an important one
and an acceptable answer is vital to an understanding of Dream of
the Red Chamber. The enormous body of textual studies of the

107chia-hsu manuscript (Ch'ien-lung chia-hsu Chih-yen Chai
ch'ung-p'ing Shih-t'ou chi), vol. 1, p. 21, line 12, through p. 2b.,
line 6. For text, see pp. 212-213.

108Kunst, p. 12.

109Ts'ao Fu, 曹頫 (Chi-hu, 畸笏); Ts'ao T'ien-yu, 曹
天祐 (Chih-yen Chai, 脂硯齋); Ts'ao T'ang-ts'un, 曹
棠村 (K'ung Mei-hsi, 孔梅溪). See Hung-lou meng hsin-
t'an, pp. 153-164, 206-211.

110Chao Kang and Ch'en Chung-i believe, for example, that
Ts'ao Fu feared the Court's negative reaction to the story of the
imperial confiscation of the Chia clan properties. Hung-lou meng
hsin-t'an, pp. 135-136, 210-212, 376.

novel attests to the fact that, on the basis of textual evidence alone, it is extremely difficult to determine whether a certain line or passage is definitely by Ts'ao or by someone else. We shall not attempt to refute the plausible textual interpretations of competent critics, but we should like to invite the reader to take an alternative approach to the Preface, that is, to look upon the Preface as a problem of stylistics as well as of authorship.

Interestingly, the problem is unconsciously set in these terms by Wu Shih-ch'ang himself. In the course of his textual analysis of the Preface to chapter 1, he makes the following observation:

Now this arrangement of having two different and separate introductions in the first chapter is very odd; and odder still, nobody seems to have noticed its oddness.[111]

Even Yu P'ing-po includes the Preface as the introductory part of chapter 1 in his Collated Eighty Chapter Hung-lou meng (Hung-lou meng pa-shih-hui chiao-pen). Actually, if we consider the Preface as a presentation of the persona of the author, we shall understand that it is not at all odd that "nobody seems to have noticed its oddness". In other words, what is significant is not whether Ts'ao Hsueh-ch'in or someone else has created that image of the author, but that generations of readers have not questioned the presence of that persona in chapter 1 because it is stylistically appropriate. As we have already noted, the use of persona is a basic feature of the style of Dream of the Red Chamber. To have the author present his reasons for writing the novel is fitting, for that presentation belongs to the same literary mode as do the independent criticisms of the Stone Record by the authoritarian Buddhist Monk, the skeptical Reverend Taoist Kosmo Kosmos, and the defensive Stone. As we shall observe, another reason why the Preface has not been questioned is that the persona established there is a complementary part of the persona of the author-as-narrator which periodically reveals itself throughout Dream of the Red Chamber.

The following translation of the Preface is from the chia-hsu manuscript of the novel. Important elaborations of this Preface in Kao E's 1792 printed edition of Dream of the Red Chamber will be noted below and discussed. We remind the reader that in the chia-hsu manuscript the Preface appears to be the last of the General Editorial Principles, and we ask him to consider it as an example of persona technique:

----

[111]Wu, On the Red Chamber Dream, p. 64.

This is the first chapter as you open the volume of this book.
The author relates that he once passed through a dream-vision,
and afterwards he hid the real affairs therein and composed
this book, the Stone Record. Therefore he says: 'In a Dream-
Vision Chen Shih-yin has cognition of the Precious Jade for
Penetrating the Numinous'.[112] But what affairs does the
author record, and how did he come to compose this book?
He goes on to say:[113]

> "Through the wind and dust of time I have plodded along,
> and I have brought nothing to fruition. When I think back
> to those maidens of former days and recall them one by one,
> I realize that they surpassed me in both their actions and
> their perceptions. How is it that I, dignified by beard and
> brow, am hardly equal to the wearers of skirts and hairpins!
> Truly I am overwhelmed with shame--such a day of useless
> regret and helplessness!
> On this day I wish to compile a Record so as to proclaim to
> all the world that in my youth, when I wore silk upper

----

[112]An obvious homophonic pun in Chinese on the previous sentence. The line here quoted by the author is the first half of the
chapter title of chapter 1: 甄士隱夢幻識通靈, Chen
Shih-yin meng huan shih t'ung ling (italics added for emphasis on
the pun). Substituting the homophone, chen shih yin 真事隱,
the sentence would read: "In a Dream-Vision of True Affairs Hidden
(chen shih yin), There is Cognition of the Precious Jade for Penetrating the Numinous".

[113]We translate the immediately following section of the passage
as a direct statement in English because an indirect statement would
not agree with the content and context of the Preface. We also
place these remarks of the author in quotation marks as a means of
disputing the opinion of Wu Shih-ch'ang that the Preface should not
be considered as a part of the novel. Wu, On the Red Chamber
Dream, pp. 65-66, suggests that the passage should be placed in
quotation marks to show the passage is not written by Ts'ao Hsueh-
ch'in. We agree with the suggestion, but not with Wu's conclusion.
In fact, a direct quotation reveals the passage should be considered
as a brilliant example of persona technique.

garments and trousers and surfeited myself with rich foods
and delicacies, I benefited from the grace of Heaven above
and the worth of my Ancestors below, but was ungrateful
for the education my parents gave me and did not appreciate
the good counsel of my teachers and elder brothers. That
is why up to the present moment I have brought nothing to
fruition, and have but the guilt of half a lifetime of failure.
Although I cannot assuage my guilt, there were indeed
people of marked distinction once in the women's apartments, and on no account may I cause their complete oblivion just because I was degenerate.
Though today my dwelling consists of reed covered rafters
and overgrown windows, a rope bed and clay tile oven, in
such an environment there are the morning breeze and
evening moon, the willow beside the stairs and the courtyard blossoms. There is no lack of inspiration for my
writing. Why not use fictive language and vulgar words
to expatiate upon a story so as to please the eye and ear
of others?"

Thus the author says that, 'In the Wind and Dust, Longing for
a Boudoir Beauty', is the principal idea of chapter 1.[114] When
you open the text and read, 'In the Wind and Dust, Longing
for a Boudoir Beauty', you know the author's original intention
is to describe friends and their sentiments in the ladies'apartments. Hence, his is not a book which complains about the
times. Although once in a while it touches upon the Way of

----

[114]As in note 112, here we have again an obvious homophonic
pun in Chinese on the previous sentence. The line quoted, "In
the Wind and Dust, Longing for a Boudoir Beauty", is the second
half of the chapter title of chapter 1. For it to be exactly parallel
to the first half, and to agree with the actual chapter heading of
chapter 1, we need to insert the name of "Chia Yu-ts'un". We
then have the line: "In the Wind and Dust, Chia Yu-ts'un longs
for a Boudoir Beauty" (賈雨村風塵懷閨秀   ). "Chia Yu-
ts'un 賈雨村 is a homophone for chia-yü ts'un-yen 假語村
言, "fictive language and vulgar words". Thus the pun: "In the
Wind and Dust of Fictive Language and Vulgar Words, there is
Longing for a Boudoir Beauty".

the World, this cannot be entirely avoided in a narrative, and emphatically is not its fundamental intent. Reader firmly remember this.[115]

The moving personal nature of this passage may enable us to understand why this fifth of the five General Editorial Principles has been considered to be the opening section of chapter 1 and the Preface to Dream of the Red Chamber. Indeed, it is difficult to imagine how or why anyone other than Ts'ao Hsueh-ch'in could be the spokesman behind the autobiographical apology evidenced in the direct statement of the author's words which is quoted in the preceding excerpt. What possible motive could the writer of the present passage have, whether he be Ts'ao Hsueh-ch'in's cousin, brother, father, or anyone else, to pretend to such an image of the author unless that image is Ts'ao Hsueh-ch'in's own conception?

We wish to go beyond the question of whether or not the quoted words are autobiographical or biographical to try to determine what function they have in the novel. The fifth of the General Editorial Principles is distinct from the other four, not only because it is by far the longest, but because it is the only Principle which is about the author. Our suggestion, that the touching autobiographical or biographical statement quoted above is a marked example of a highly sophisticated persona technique, may seem callous until the reader realizes that various concepts of the novel are deliberately presented through a variety of personae, and that it is the persona of the author which makes the passage in question dramatically effective.

What then is the persona of the author in the Preface and what does it tell us about Ts'ao Hsueh-ch'in's conception of Dream of the Red Chamber? The first point the writer of the Preface makes is that the author of Dream of the Red Chamber is a dreamer who is fond of allegory. Thus the Preface, with its stress on the origins of the novel in a dream-vision,[116] and the hidden meaning of its affairs,[117] points to the theme of illusion, huan, and the theme of complementary opposites, chen-chia, which dominate Dream of the Red Chamber and which we have discussed at length in our "Myth" and "Mimesis" chapters. Because of his awareness of the possible allegorical meaning of the story, the writer is careful to explain

---

[115]chia-hsu manuscript, p. 3a, line 5, through p. 4a, line 3. For text, see pp. 214-216.

[116] 夢幻.

[117] 真事隱去.

脂硯齋重評石頭記
凡例

紅樓夢旨義

是書題名極

夢是總其全部之名也又曰風月寶鑑是

戒妄動風月之情又曰石頭記是自譬石

頭所記之事也此三名皆書中曾已點睛

矣如寶玉作夢夢中有曲名曰紅樓夢十

二支此則紅樓夢之點睛又如賈瑞病跛

道人持一鏡來上面即鏨風月寶鑑四字

此則風月寶鑑之點睛又如道人親眼見

石上大書一篇故事則係石頭所記之往

來此則石頭記之點睛處然此書又名曰

金陵十二釵審其名則必係金陵十二女
子也然通部細搜檢去上中下女子豈止
十二人哉若云其中自有十二個則又未
嘗指明白係某某極至紅樓夢一回中亦
曾翻出金陵十二釵之簿籍又有十二支
曲可考
書中凡寫長安在文人筆墨之間則從古
之稱凡愚夫婦兒女子家常口角則曰中
京是不欲着跡于方向也蓋天子之邦亦
當以中為尊特避其東南西北四字樣也
此書只是着意于閨中故敘閨中之事切
略涉於外事者則簡不得謂其不均也

此書不敢干涉朝廷凡有不得不用朝政著只畧用一筆帶出盖實不敢以寫兒女之筆墨唐突朝廷之上也又不得謂其不備

此書開卷第一回也作者自云因會歷過一畨夢幻之後故將真事隱去而撰此石頭記一書也故曰甄士隱夢幻識通靈但書中所記何事又因何而撰是書哉自云今風塵碌碌一事無成忽念及當日所有之女子一一細推了去覺其行止見識皆出于我之上何堂堂之鬚眉誠不若彼一干裙釵實愧則有餘悔則無益之大無可

綱正義也開卷即云風塵懷閨秀則知作

耳目哉故曰風塵懷閨秀乃是第一回題

假語村言敷演出一段故事來以悅人之

亦未有傷于我之襟懷筆墨者何爲不用

椽蓬牖瓦竈繩床其風晨月夕堦柳庭花

我不肖則一併使其泯滅也雖今日之茅

能免然閨閣中本自歷歷有人萬不可因

編述一記以告普天下人雖我之罪固不

之德已致今日一事無成半生潦倒之罪

饜美之日背父母教育之恩負師兄規訓

上賴天恩下承祖德錦衣紈袴之時飫甘

奈何之日也當此時則自欲將已往所賴

者本意原爲記述當日閨友閨情並非怨

世罵時之書矣雖一時有涉于世態然亦

不得不叙者但非其本旨耳閱者切記之

詩曰

浮生着甚苦奔忙　盛席華筵終散場

悲喜千般同幻渺　古今一夢盡荒唐

謾言紅袖啼痕重　更有情癡抱恨長

字字看來皆是血　十年辛苦不尋常

the chapter titles of chapter 1. Thus, for example, he notes that in the title, "In a Dream-Vision Chen Shih-yin has Cognition of the Precious Jade for Penetrating the Numinous", "Chen Shih-yin"[118] is a pun on "chen-shih yin",[119] "real affairs hidden". Likewise, he indicates that Ts'ao's mention of "chia-yu ts'un-yen",[120] "fictive language and vulgar words", is a homophone for the second half of the chapter title and points to the story in chapter 1 of "Chia Yu-ts'un".[121]

The final paragraph of the Preface reminds us of Kosmo's findings upon his second reading of the Stone Record. He approves because he believes "the intent was not to sorrow over the world or to criticize the times", and the Story does not "even slightly touch upon the present day world". Similar denials are found in the General Editorial Principles. The third notes that the novel focuses on life within the ladies' apartment rather than on outside affairs.[122] The fourth states that the book would not dare to speak of court or government affairs, although it is admitted that sometimes such subject matter inadvertently enters the narrative.[123] Similarly, in the fifth Principle, the writer insists that the "original intention" of Ts'ao Hsueh-ch'in is to describe life within the "ladies' apartments" and he scrupulously points out that touching upon the "Way of the World...cannot be entirely avoided...and emphatically is not its fundamental intent". His description of Dream of the Red Chamber reminds us of Kosmo Kosmos--it is "not a book which complains about the times".

We are told, finally, to "firmly remember this"; presumably we are to keep in mind the guidelines of the General Editorial Principles as we read in order that no false conceptions of the novel may arise. But of course we cannot be but also mindful of the conversation between the Stone and the Reverend Taoist and of the context in which such warnings are made. The former claims that its Story is based upon a long period of personal observation and experience and it speaks of the reading needs of contemporary man, but Kosmo's inter-

----

118 甄士隱.
119 真事隱.
120 假語村言.
121 賈雨村.
122 chia-hsu manuscript, p. 2b, lines 11-12. For text, see p. 213.
123 ibid., p. 3a, lines 1-4. For text, see p. 214.

pretation is altogether different. Similarly, the writer of the last
paragraph of the General Editorial Principles seems to over react
to the stated views of Ts'ao Hsueh-ch'in, who again, as in the
example of the Stone, emphasizes personal experience and expresses
a specific opinion of that experience. To assert that the theme of
the novel is only life in the ladies' apartments is to contradict the
author's own poignant complaint and painful lamentation.

According to the Preface, as we have noted, the author is char-
acterized as a dreamer. There is a wonderful play on the <u>chen-
chia</u> theme in the seemingly straightforward line the Preface writer
uses to describe the origin of <u>Dream of the Red Chamber</u>:

> The author relates that he once passed through a dream-vision,
> and afterwards he hid the real affairs therein and composed
> this book, the <u>Stone Record</u>.[124]

The passage points to a continual question in the novel, what is
ultimately real? This line suggests that Ts'ao takes what is "real"
in a dream-vision and hides that reality to create his work of fiction,
or, conversely, that he uses a dream-vision to disguise the facts of
"real", that is, conscious, life. Whichever reading we adhere to,
a neat ambiguity has been built which signifies the unity of dreams
and reality, the unconscious and conscious experience, and of
"true" and "false". The reality of dreams has to be hidden in a real
life story, and real life is disguised in a story of dreams.

Ts'ao Hsueh-ch'in presents himself as a miserable failure, besides
being an incorrigible dreamer. His acclaimed feminism appears in
the Preface in his nostalgic memory of "the wearers of skirts and
hairpins", those lovely maidens who were so superior to himself,
"dignified by beard and brow". He sees the day on which he decides to begin his novel as a terrible moment in his life--the very
respect he has for the women he has known which causes him to
write overwhelms him with a sense of his shortcomings as a man--
and even that sense of shame is of no avail. He also imagines himself as a guilt ridden figure: a profligate in his youth and an in-
grate towards his parents, teachers, and elders. "That is why",
he says, "up to the present moment I have brought nothing to fruition,
and have but the guilt of half a lifetime of failure". It is this
guilt, the author suggests, which moves him to write a confession--
not to pay for his sins, to be sure, for there is no payment that can
be made--but to tell the world of his youth and to bequeath a name

---

124 因曾歷過一番夢幻之後，故將真事隱去而
撰此石頭記一書也.

to deserving women. Lastly, he characterizes himself as a destitute
artist (an image supported by what we know of his later life) who
is inspired by the simple beauties of nature to create a harmless
story of "fictive language and vulgar words" for the sake of a little
entertainment.

Further clarification of the persona of the author is found in the
elaborations of the chia-hsu Preface in the Ch'eng Wei-yuan Kao E
edition of Dream of the Red Chamber printed in 1792:

> The author relates that he once passed through a dream-vision,
> and afterwards he hid the real affairs therein and, availing
> himself of what is called 'Penetrating the Numinous', he
> composed the Stone Record.
> "Moreover, I am even more aware that the morning breeze and
> the evening moon, the willow beside the stairs and the court-
> yard blossoms add lustre and smoothness to one's writing.
> Though I am without literary talent, what is the harm of using
> fictive language and vulgar words to expatiate upon them?
> Thus, I can make the women's apartment renown and dispel
> a moment's blues and present some pleasing sights before my
> compeers. Isn't this also a nice thing to do?"
> . . . in the text are used "dream", "illusion", and other such
> words. Actually these are the main themes of this book and
> hidden in them is the idea of awakening those who read.[125]

Most of this material is simply an emphasis upon what is said in the
chia-hsu Preface. The author notes that the observation of nature
improves his writing. He admits that he has little ability and does
not believe he can do any harm. Where Kao E is especially successful is in capturing the apparently flippant, but actually very sophisticated, self-denigrating tone of the original Preface. The novel
promises to make certain women famous and to entertain contemporaries, and, reminding us of the Stone's speech, it will "dispel
the blues"; but such promises are lightly dismissed with the comment,
"isn't this also a nice thing to do?"

An interesting addition is the line "availing himself of what is
called 'Penetrating the Numinous'". The reference to Pao-yu's
t'ung-ling pao-yu, "Precious Jade for Penetrating the Numinous",
as a writing technique points to Ts'ao Hsueh-ch'in's use of the myth

----

[125]Hung-lou meng, Shih-chieh shu-chu reprint (120 chapter
edition), chap. 1, p. 1, lines 1-2, 7-8, and 8-9. Taipei, 1960.
For text, see p. 220.

第一回　甄士隱夢幻識通靈　賈雨村風塵懷閨秀

此開卷第一回也。作者自云曾歷過一番夢幻之後，故將真事隱去，而借「通靈」說此石頭記一書

也，故曰「甄士隱」云云。但書中所記何事何人？自己又云：今風塵碌碌，一事無成，忽念及當日所有

之女子，一一細考較去，覺其行止見識皆出我之上，我堂堂鬚眉，誠不若彼裙釵。我實愧則有餘，悔又

無益，大無可如何之日也！當此日，欲將已往所賴天恩祖德錦衣紈袴之時，飫甘饜肥之日，背父兄教育

之恩，負師友規訓之德，以致今日一技無成，半生潦倒之罪，編述一集，以告天下。知我之負罪固多，

然閨閣中歷歷有人，萬不可因我之不肖自護己短，一併使其泯滅也。所以蓬牖茅椽，繩床瓦竈，並不足

妨我襟懷。況那晨風夕月，階柳庭花，更覺潤人筆墨。我雖不學無文，又何妨用假語村言敷衍出來，

亦可使閨閣昭傳。復可破一時之悶，醒同人之目，不亦宜乎？故曰「賈雨村」云云。更於篇中間用「夢」

「幻」等字，卻是此書本旨，兼寓提醒閱者之意。

看官！你道此書從何而起？說來雖近荒唐，細玩頗有趣味。

却說那女媧氏煉石補天之時，於大荒山無稽崖煉成高十二丈、見方二十四丈大的頑石三萬六千五百

零一塊。那媧皇只用了三萬六千五百塊，單單剩下一塊未用，棄在青埂峰下。誰知此石自經鍛煉之後，

靈性已通，自去自來，可大可小。因見眾石俱得補天，獨自己無才，不得入選，遂自怨自愧，日夜悲

of the discarded divine stone with which he begins his novel. Two other elaborations in the above passages seem to us to be accurate additions based on a reading of the novel. There is little doubt that Ts'ao wishes to "awaken" the reader rather than simply to entertain him by removing from him the cloud of melancholy. As the Stone suggests, the Stone Record "may also give contemporaries a fresh way of viewing the world". It is also true that the "main themes" ("fundamental intent", pen chih)[126] of Dream of the Red Chamber have to do with dreams. Kao E's clarifications indicate that he too is conscious of an attempt to create the persona of Ts'ao Hsueh-ch'in in the Preface.

Superficially, there exists a parallel between the Preface and the view of the Reverend Taoist Kosmo Kosmos that the novel is not a complaint about life, but merely a book about women. The more intriguing parallels are those which we may draw between the Preface and the speech of the Stone. While Ts'ao Hsueh-ch'in appears to be much more pensive than the Stone, much of his language indicates that he shares with the Stone certain qualities of mind and a similar concept of fiction. Just as he carefully considers the attributes of the women of his youth "one by one",[127] the Stone diligently reviews the clichés in traditional literary genres "one by one".[128] Both figures say that their stories are an outflow of past personal experience and are oriented towards the contemporary world. Ts'ao speaks in terms of the guilt of "half a lifetime"[129] for which the only saving grace is his knowledge of women, while the Stone proclaims the accuracy of its Story for only it has spent "half a lifetime"[130] observing females. Ts'ao and the Stone similarly present their fictional works as simple entertainments designed to keep the reader free from boredom. It is true that there is a much greater tendency on Ts'ao's part to debunk himself and his novel. He presents himself as a dilettante and fiction as but the waste product of his dilettantism. But the introductory image of the novel presented by both Ts'ao Hsueh-ch'in and the Stone is comical in view of the simple fact that this "entertainment" consists of over four hundred persons, seven hundred thousand charac-

----

126 本旨.
127 一一.
128 逐一看去.
129 半生.
130 半世.

ters, one hundred and twenty chapters, and nearly thirteen hundred pages.[131] We have only to recall the description in chapter 1 of the figure of the "editor", one Ts'ao Hsueh-ch'in, who is said to have labored on the novel for ten years and to have emended it five times, for with this description we realize that the rubric, "entertainment", is used to protect a quite different conception of fiction. As we read at the end of the Preface:

All the words read are blood
Ten years of uncommon suffering.[132]

We are also mindful of the quatrain which follows the conversion of the Reverend Taoist Kosmo Kosmos:

Paper covered with absurd words
A handful of hot bitter tears.
All say the author is crazy
But who understands the essence?[133]

There is little doubt that there are close similarities between Ts'ao Hsueh-ch'in and the Stone. In the preface, Ts'ao notes that he wishes to compile a chi, "Record";[134] likewise, the Stone desires to tell the world its tale which is named the Shih-t'ou chi, "Stone Record". As we shall soon observe, in the body of Dream of the Red Chamber the Stone may be said to appear periodically as the ostensible narrator, and we might at times identify its persona as the "author-as-narrator". We find direct commentary being made about events in the novel, and the image of the commentator agrees with the image of the Stone first encountered in chapter 1. Then there is the author, Ts'ao Hsueh-ch'in, behind the text who periodically shows his control and direction by means of indirect narrative techniques and by freely moving back and forth between his own persona and that of the Stone.

What is the significance of the persona of Ts'ao Hsueh-ch'in and what is the effect of having someone else convey the information that the author is a nostalgic dreamer, a penitent confessor, and a

----

[131]C. C. Wang, Dream of the Red Chamber, London, 1929, p. xxiv, names these figures. Here we are talking about the 120 chapter novel, of course; the 80 chapter manuscript would total two-thirds of the above given figures.

[132]chia-hsu manuscript, p. 4a, last line. For text, see p. 216.
[133]HLMPSHCP, chap. 1, p. 5, lines 5-6. For text, see p. 50.
[134]記.

guilt-ridden failure? In his esteem for women, the author, like the Stone, stands against the literary tradition. At the same time, and this is an admirable instance of Ts'ao's use of irony, he pretends to cater to traditional masculine ideals by saying, in effect, it is really shameful to care about women so much as I do! There is another irony in the Preface which has probably perplexed many readers of Dream of the Red Chamber who have noted it. In the light of Pao-yu's resistance to conventional values, Ts'ao Hsueh-ch'in's stated reasons as to why he has "brought nothing to fruition" may seem strange. He accounts for his failures in terms of his youthful disregard for "Heaven's grace", "ancestral worth", "paren-tal instruction", and "counsel of teachers and elder brothers". But these represent the orthodoxy Pao-yu spends "half a lifetime" flee-ing, for orthodoxy offers no solution to the problem of mutability. One cannot say that Pao-yu triumphs over this problem merely because he abhors orthodoxy, nor can we believe that Ts'ao con-siders himself a victim of mutability due to his failure to honor orthodoxy.

The irony is brilliant. Dream of the Red Chamber is a testament to the view that there is no rationale for suffering and seldom can one assuage it. Yet, even Ts'ao Hsueh-ch'in, the arch-enemy of clichés, self-consciously turns to formulaic platitudes in a feigned attempt to account for the vicissitudes of his life. We use the word, "feigned", because the author is obviously aware of the inadequa-cies of formulae. His failure to render an account is an ultimate triumph, of course, for it is the story of Dream of the Red Chamber. The reason why this mask of failure is so compelling is because it is passed along by someone other than the author and in the form of a long direct quotation of the author. Therefore, as the Stone would say, the autobiographical information is important and, above all, personal and true. All of the personae we have discussed are, like the Preface, introductions to the novel which woo the reader with their contradictory appeal. The various concepts of fiction which are presented to the reader before he has the oppor-tunity to read very far have the cumulative effect of prevailing upon him to seek his own conception of the reality of Dream of the Red Chamber.

We have pointed out the similarities between the persona of Ts'ao Hsueh-ch'in and that of the Stone. As we suggested, if the Stone is to be considered as the narrator of the novel, it may be viewed as the persona of the author-as-narrator, that humble figure in the Preface who speaks his halting lines out of penitence for a guilty

past. As a matter of fact, with the exception of one important
instance discussed below, the narrator of Dream of the Red Chamber
is never clearly identified in the main body of the novel. The
information we have reviewed about the Stone and Ts'ao Hsueh-
ch'in is all to be found within chapter 1. There it is certain that
both figures discuss their own "Record", but, at least in the case
of the Stone, it is not clear that the latter is the author of its Story.
The Stone desires that the Stone Record be copied down by Kosmo
Kosmos and passed on to the world, but no statement is made as to
who originally inscribed the Story onto the surface of the Stone.

In "Myth" and "Mimesis" we have frequently observed that Chih-
yen Chai identifies both the Stone and Pao-yu with Ts'ao Hsueh-
ch'in, yet it must be added that these identifications come, as it
were, "outside" the text. In Dream of the Red Chamber itself,
Ts'ao Hsueh-ch'in is described only as being one of the late and
somewhat pedantic editors of the novel and he is never mentioned
as its actual author. In short, Ts'ao Hsueh-ch'in uses the cloak of
persona "to take real affairs and hide them", that is, he disguises
himself and thus delicately excuses himself from the responsibility
of authorship. This is not a matter of cowardly evasion, obviously,
but a deliberate literary conceit which is consonant with a concept
of fiction that insists the Stone Record "dropped from heaven" as a
work without identifiable time, place, beginning, or author.

Whatever the anonymity of the narrator, one is constantly reminded
of his presence in Dream of the Red Chamber. Here we must qualify
the view of Wu Shih-ch'ang that Ts'ao Hsueh-ch'in "never wrote
any comment or annotation even in the text" of Dream of the Red
Chamber (Wu's italics).[135] As proof, he cites the following commentary by Chih-yen Chai:

> In commenting on this book, I have learned a secret, and I
> wish to tell you gentlemen . . . . The nice thing about this
> book is that the author himself would never put down any
> comment or annotation, saying, 'So-and-so is such-and-such
> a person'. He only borrows one or two words of occasional
> remarks from the characters in the book, therefore there are
> no unclosed seams that could be discovered by the reader.

----

[135]Wu, On the Red Chamber Dream, p. 59.

His pen is really tricky.[136]
But Chih-yen Chai is merely talking about a particular type of
comment, for through the persona of the Stone and the anonymous
author-as-narrator Ts'ao frequently inserts both direct and indirect
comments in the text. Indeed, somewhat contradictorily, Wu himself cites a few examples elsewhere in his study of the novel.[137]

The observations of the anonymous narrator reveal a varied persona
which in turn reflects an attitude towards fiction we have not fully
encountered previously. At times the narrator demonstrates complete control over his materials, at others he pretends that he is the
bewildered scribe who can give no direction to the myriad events
he is trying to record. When Lin Tai-yu first enters the Jung-kuo
mansion of the Chia family following the death of her mother, the
narrator causes us to follow her about as she wanders through the
household and admires her lavish surroundings. After an exhaustive
description of innumerable items, no matter how minor (of several
pages duration), the narrator casually remarks: "no need for details
about the remainder".[138] The phrase itself is typical storyteller
language which a narrator uses when he wishes to shift subjects,
but because of the context in which the phrase occurs, it is a deliberate overstatement on the part of the narrator--further details
are practically impossible at this point--and it exemplifies his humorous awareness of the limitations of his own narrative technique.

Another instance of his humor is his application of colloquial
sayings to undercut tension in a dramatic scene. Following one of
the innumerable arguments between Wang Shi-feng and her husband,
Chia Lien, over a love affair, the Matriarch attempts to reconcile

----

[136]Wu's translation, ibid., p. 60. CYCHLMCP, chap. 49,
keng-ch'en commentary: 我批此書竟得一秘訣以告諸公:⋯⋯
妙在此書從不肯自下評注,云此人係何等人,只借書中人
閒評一二語,故不得有未密之縫被看書者指出,真狡猾之筆
耳.
[137]Wu, On the Red Chamber Dream, p. 203, notes that the
author directly addresses the reader in chapter 6 when Liu Lao-lao's
son-in-law is introduced; he observes, pp. 203-204, that the Stone
directly comments on the beauties of the Grand View Garden in
chapter 18; on pp. 258-259 and p. 204, Wu refers to the author's
long commentary within the text (my italics) on Pao-yu's fu written
in honor of the deceased Ch'ing-wen in chapter 78.
[138]HLMPSHCP, chap. 3, p. 29, lines 11-12: 其餘陳設自不
必細說.

the two by getting them to apologize to one another. It happens
that Hsi-feng has beaten her maid, P'ing-erh, because she believed
that the latter had had illicit relations with Chia Lien. When the
Matriarch has P'ing-erh brought forward in order that Chia Lien and
Hsi-feng might apologize to the maid for abusing her, Chia Lien
becomes so spellbound by the sight of P'ing-erh that he immediately
forgets that he has just begged both the Matriarch and his wife for
forgiveness for his profligacy. The narrator undermines the dramatic
seriousness of the occasion by an aside to the reader. Citing a
popular adage, he observes that this is a case of the so-called: "a
consort is preferable to a wife, seduction is preferable to a consort".139

From time to time the anonymous storyteller reveals his delicate
narrative touch. In chapter 5 a tea party is held in the garden of
the Ning-kuo mansion in honor of the plum blossoms which are just
beginning to open. Our narrator tells us that this occasion is merely
one of many and that there is really nothing of particular interest
which he cares to record.140 This playing down of the moment is
a narrative technique which nearly always is a sign that a significant
event is about to occur. In this instance, it is the very tediousness
of the party which leads the adolescent Pao-yu to his first sexual
experience.141 Realizing that he is bored, his maids lead him to
the bed chamber of his niece, Ch'in K'o-ch'ing, for a noon time
nap. In a dream-vision he has his famous sexual encounter with a
girl who appears to be a combination of Lin Tai-yu and Hsueh Pao-
ch'ai. Upon awakening, he practices what he has learned with his
maid, Hsi-jen.

Sometimes the narrator wears Ts'ao Hsueh-ch'in's mask of diffidence
which originates in the Preface. This persona serves to underscore
the fundamental attractiveness of the persons and events in the narrative and it marks the extent to which the storyteller is personally
touched by the tale he unravels. Thus, for example, Pao-yu and
Tai-yu are at one time arguing bitterly about whether they actually
will have a future together. The former throws down his precious
jade talisman and the latter cuts into pieces the tassel she once
made for him. The narrator at first explains for his readers that this

----

139HLMPSHCP, chap. 44, p. 473, lines 2-3: 所謂妻不如妾,
妾不如偷....
140ibid., chap. 5, p. 46, line 4.
141ibid., line 4.

argument is typical of the personal style of Pao-yu and Tai-yu. They use the false to arrive at the true. Tai-yu feigns that she is hurt in order to win Pao-yu's affections; he in turn hides his real emotions to see first if Tai-yu cares for him. Suddenly, after this rather pat analysis, the narrator is at a loss for words. He confesses that he cannot describe, really, the inner feelings of the lovers; he can only present their actions and outward appearances.[142] Again we find that the stance of the storyteller is an effective stylistic pose. Just prior to this confession of inadequacy, there is a passage in which the silent inner thoughts of both Pao-yu and Tai-yu are in evidence.[143] The narrator's discreet withdrawal serves to heighten the passion of the lovers and his perception of the indescribable reminds us that the Stone Record has a life of its own which cannot be controlled or understood.[144]

The pretense that the Stone Record spontaneously unfolds before the very eyes of the narrator is evidenced when Liu Lao-lao, a comical peasant woman, first visits the Chia clan to which she is vaguely "related". The narrator facetiously remarks that while the population of the Jung-kuo and Ning-kuo mansions is small, there are three or four hundred individuals in the family, and that while little goes on in the Chia household, ten to twenty major events take place every day. He is thoroughly confused by what he calls a "tangled hemp", luan ma,[145] of materials and he does not have a "thread", t'ou-hsu ("clue"),[146] by which he can unravel it.[147] Suddenly there appears on the horizon Liu Lao-lao:

----

[142]HLMPSHCP, chap. 29, p. 310, lines 10-11.

[143]ibid., lines 2 and 4: 寶玉心內想的是‥‥那林黛玉心裡想著.

[144]Another example where the narrator withdraws before the indescribable is found in chapters 17-18, p. 178, line 11 (HLMPSHCP). The Stone states that the Grand View Garden is too beautiful for words and it expresses its preference for earth over heaven. This passage will be discussed below.

[145]亂麻,

[146]頭緒.

[147]HLMPSHCP, chap. 6, p. 60, lines 2-3: 按榮府中一宅中合算起來,人口雖不多,從上至下也有三四百丁;事雖不多,一天也有一二十件,竟如亂麻一般,並無個頭緒可作綱領.

Just as I am trying to figure out what individual and what
event I should start by describing, behold! On this very
day, from over a thousand li away, a little person of the
size of a mustard seed suddenly arrives at the Jung-kuo
mansion who is somewhat related to the family. Though a
minor figure, she does provide a thread.[148]

The narrator is not always such a helpless scribe. The most recur-
rent sign of his control is the continuous reticence he displays in
matters of sex--a narrative mask that he uses to indulge in suggestive innuendo. On the night after the funeral of Ch'in K'o-
ch'ing,[149] Pao-yu and the brother of Ch'in K'o-ch'ing, Ch'in
Chung,[150] stay with Wang Hsi-feng at a nunnery before travelling
back home. It happens that Pao-yu catches Ch'in Chung making
love with a nun, Chih-neng.[151] Ch'in Chung prevails upon Pao-
yu to tell no one by promising to accord with whatever Pao-yu
wishes. The text is not clear about what this is--Pao-yu himself
merely tells Ch'in Chung that he will wait until they go to bed for
a "detailed reckoning of accounts".[152] Of course the reader of
Dream of the Red Chamber is mindful that the two Ch'ins are noto-
rious for their sexual promiscuity. In chapter 7, an old family
servant of the Chia household, Chiao-ta,[153] berates the younger
generation of the Chia family for its corruption and he seems to
suggest that Ch'in K'o-ch'ing is having incestuous relations with
her father-in-law, Chia Chen.[154] We further recall that it is

----

148ibid., lines 3-5: 正尋思從那一件事, 自那一個人寫起
方妙, 恰好忽從千里之外, 芥豆之微, 小小一個人家, 向
與榮府略有些瓜葛, 這日正往榮府中來, 因此便就
這一家說來, 倒還是個頭緒.
Still another example of the "I'm just passing along a story" approach
occurs in chapter 8, pp. 83-86, where Pao-yu and Pao-ch'ai compare their matching amulets. The narrator quotes the poem of
another person about the amulets and he reminds us that Pao-yu's
amulet is the Stone of divine origins. We discuss this passage below.
149 秦可卿.
150 秦鐘.
151 智能.
152HLMPSHCP, chap. 15, p. 148, line 11: 寶玉笑道; 這會子
也不用說, 等一會睡下, 再細細的算帳.
153 焦大.
154 賈珍, HLMPSHCP, chap. 7, pp. 79-80.

Ch'in K'o-ch'ing who leads Pao-yu to her bedroom for a noontime nap. It is here that he has a dream-vision of his first sexual experience. The fact that Ch'in Chung has an affair with a nun on the night after the funeral is indicative of the sexual significance of both himself and his sister.

Actually, Ch'in Chung himself is more frequently identified with homosexual activity in Dream of the Red Chamber. The main section of chapter 9, for example, revolves around male homosexual activity in the Chia family school, with Pao-yu and Ch'ing Chung being attracted to Hsiang-lien and Yu-ai, two male intimates of Hsueh P'an (the "prodigal son" of the novel).[155] Ch'in Chung's background serves to elucidate Pao-yu's request for a "detailed reckoning of accounts". This passage is important in so far as our study of the narrator is concerned, for it is a delightful example of the latter's ability to combine apparent objectivity and blatant absenteeism for the purpose of creating suggestive innuendo. Thus, immediately after Pao-yu's request, the narrator claims ignorance by pretending that he cannot say anything more about how Ch'in Chung paid back Pao-yu for keeping quiet. There is no record, he insists; it is a disputed case and evidence is missing so that one should not dare to speculate.[156] In summary, the mask of sexual reticence stimulates the sensibilities of the reader and leads him to take charge of the facts of the story. We unconsciously challenge the storyteller with our superior knowledge--and our criticism, of course, is intentionally aroused by the persona of the narrator.[157]

----

[155]Hsiang-lien 香憐 and Yu-ai 玉愛 are nicknames given by the school boys to two especially feminine looking members of the class. The narrator says that he does not know the real family and given names of the two boys. ibid., chap. 9, p. 96, lines 4-5.

[156]HLMPSHCP, chap. 15, p. 148, line 13.

[157]For other examples of Ts'ao's development of innuendo under the guise of reticence about sexual matters, see the following episodes: Pao-yu's relation with the actress, Fang-kuan, HLMPSHCP, chap. 63, p. 702; the clandestine union of Chia Lien, the husband of Wang Hsi-feng, with his consort, Yu Erh-chieh, HLMPSHCP, chap. 65, p. 726; the discovery of a purse with a licentious design by Big Sister Simple (Sha Ta-chieh), HLMPSHCP, chap. 73, p. 819; Pao-yu's sexual relations with his maid, Hsi-jen, HLMPSHCP, chap. 82, p. 13; the consumation of the marriage of Pao-yu and Pao-ch'ai, HLMPSHCP, chap. 109, p. 295; the abduction of the Buddhist nun, Miao-yu, HLMPSHCP, chap. 112, p. 327.

Various characteristic features of the persona of the anonymous narrator that we have reviewed remind us both of Ts'ao Hsueh-ch'in and the Stone. We recall the author's self-image in the Preface when the narrator confesses that he is incapable of presenting certain materials, such as the interior feelings of Pao-yu and Tai-yu. An exhibition of tight control over the text, a careful selection of examples, a confident guidance of the narrative, a sure ability to emphasize and to deemphasize where needed, a certain wry humor directed towards the chosen form and content of the story--all of these qualities bring to mind the persona of the Stone evidenced in chapter 1. Lastly, in the narrator's sexual reticence we find a delightful answer to the Stone's caustic criticisms of "Wind and Moon" literature and "Bright Boy--Pretty Girl" books.[158]

In other respects the persona of the storyteller is a fulfillment of the confessional autobiographical tone of the Preface. Throughout Dream of the Red Chamber, the narrator reveals a deep personal involvement with the lives of major characters, especially Pao-yu. In chapter 78, for example, he alternately defends and criticizes Pao-yu. Chia Cheng, Pao-yu's father, summons his son to write an elegiac verse commemorating the deeds of a romantic heroine, Lin Ssu-niang,[159] whose story he has recently heard. Ssu-niang is the concubine of a prince, Heng Wang,[160] who trains her to be a warrior. According to the tale, after her master is killed by a band of robbers, she goes to their camp and kills many of the enemy before she herself is caught and put to death. Apparently the narrator senses the reader's misgivings concerning Pao-yu's ability to write a stock commemorative piece and he also realizes that we

----

[158]The narrator of Chaucer's Troilus and Criseyde is likewise delightfully reticent about sexual details. When the two lovers are finally united in bed, he discreetly withdraws: "Of hire delit, or joies oon the leestes / Were impossible to my wit to seye; / But juggeth ye that han ben at the feste / Of swich gladnesse, if that hem liste pleye! / I kan namore, but thus thise ilke tweye, / That nyght, bitwixen dreade and sikernesse, / Felten in love the grete worthynesse . . . lat hem in this hevene blisse dwelle, / That is so heigh that al ne kan I telle!" III, 1310-1323. The Works of Geofrey Chaucer, second edition, Boston, 1957, ed. F.N. Robinson.

[159] 林四娘.

[160] 恒王.

are mindful of the tension between father and son. How can Pao-
yu carry out his father's assignment? The narrator admits with Chia
Cheng that Pao-yu cannot be called a scholar, but defends him by
saying that he is brilliant and reads a great deal of miscellaneous
literature. Therefore, asserts the narrator, Pao-yu easily writes on
given themes and is in no need of inspiration.[161] And indeed,
the friends of Chia Cheng who read Pao-yu's piece all marvel at
his talent.

Subsequently, when Pao-yu is dismissed by his father, he goes out
into the garden and begins to think of Ch'ing-wen, one of his
favorite maids who has recently died of consumption.[162] Pao-yu
decides that he will write an elegy in memory of Ch'ing-wen and
a long passage follows in which he debates with himself the form
and style he should use to appropriately commemorate Ch'ing-wen.
Here the narrator hastens to insert a comment in which he criticizes
Pao-yu:

> Now Pao-yu was one who never read books.[163] Moreover,
> as he now entertained such perverse ideas, how could he
> produce any good verse or prose? Yet he just wilfully in-
> dulged in whatever he wanted to write and did not want his
> work to be appreciated or admired by others. Thus having
> his fling of these absurd notions, he actually fabricated a
> longish essay . . . . When you gentlemen come to this place,
> just take it as a joke, and it will keep you from getting
> drowsy.[164]

----

[161]HLMPSHCP, chap. 78, pp. 892-894. For another example
of the narrator's personal commentary on Pao-yu, see HLMPSHCP,
chap. 36, pp. 378-381.

[162]女兒癆.

[163]Wu's translation here is too literal. The phrase, 不讀書之人,
should be translated as, "was not a learned man".

[164]HLMPSHCP, chap. 78, p. 899, lines 6-8: 寶玉本是個不讀
書之人, 再心中有了這篇歪意怎得有好詩好文作出來. 他自己卻
任意纂著並不為人知慕, 所以大肆妄誕, 竟杜撰成一篇長文 ‥‥
Wu Shih-ch'ang's translation here includes a sentence, beginning
with, "When you gentlemen . . .", which is not found in the editions
of the novel we have used. This sentence, Wu reports, is in the
Chih-yen Chai Ch'ung-p'ing Shih-t'ou chi (the so-called 80 chapter
keng-ch'en pen), Classical Literature Press, Peking, 1955, pp.
1924-1925. We do not have a copy of this edition but we do not

Wu Shih-ch'ang observes (thus contradicting his view noted earlier
that Ts'ao "never wrote any comment or annotation even in the
text"):

> This is an extraordinary technique which Ts'ao Chan uses
> more than once. He praises the hero by denouncing him from
> his opponent's point of view. The denunciation ostensibly
> counter-balances his thinly disguised sarcasm, which is in
> fact raised to an even higher relief by the very contrast. The
> apology offered by the author in his suggestion that the reader
> should treat Pao-yu's essay as a joke makes it clear that in the
> end he identifies himself with the hero.[165]

Actually, what is really "extraordinary" about the narrator's comment is that it points to the theme of the novel that Pao-yu is an
incurable romantic. The irony inherent in Pao-yu's elegy for Ch'ing-
wen is that it is really about himself--it reveals that he is absorbed
with the problem of writing and with fears about his personal mutability even more than he is concerned with Ch'ing-wen's death.[166]

In the last forty chapters of the one hundred and twenty chapter
editions of the novel, while the narrator makes fewer appearances,
he still reveals his presence. From time to time he tries to explain
various events to his readers or call important affairs to their attention.[167] When Pao-yu returns to the Great Void Illusion Land, for
example, the narrator directly addresses the reader and wonders with
him whether Pao-yu has actually died--in other words, he under-

----

find that the sentence does more than complete the thought of the
narrator as it stands in the HLMPSHCP. See Wu, On the Red Chamber Dream, p. 259.

165Wu, ibid., p. 259.

166Pao-yu's experience is analogous to that of John Milton who,
in commemorating the deaths of Edward King and Charles Diodati
in, respectively, Lycidas and Epitaphium Damonis, became overwhelmed by the reminder of his own helplessness before the advance
of time. The subject of these poems is actually Milton and mutability.

167Poems, colloquialisms, or Buddhist aphorisms are used to
point a moral or to comment on an event. These seem to us to be
atypical of Ts'ao Hsueh-ch'in and we suspect they are the work of
an editor. Examples: chapter 87, p. 73, line 5; chap. 89, p. 96,
line 15; chap. 89, p. 97, line 7; chap. 90, p. 100, lines 14-15.

scores the questions constantly asked in the novel about the real-
ness of mutability and death.[168] He is moved to comment on the
fate of Hsi-jen[169] and he cries out at the death of Tai-yu, the
tragic moment which coincides with the marriage of Pao-yu and
Pao-ch'ai.[170]

The persona of the narrator is most intriguing when Ts'ao Hsueh-
ch'in uses it to play on what we might call the "Stone conceit"--
the view that the Stone Record is a narrative both experienced and
compiled by the Stone. In chapter 4, Chia Yu-ts'un becomes a
prefect. It happens that one of his first duties in his new office is
to take charge of a case in which Hsueh P'an, the brother of Hsueh
Pao-ch'ai, is accused of homicide. Just as he is about to execute
his responsibilities, a clerk presents him with a "mandarin's
charm",[171] a talisman which has written on it popular epithets
and proverbs of the common people about the leading local families.
Beneath these enigmatic sayings there are explanatory footnotes
which name the families of the area, to whom the sayings allude.
Thus, Chia Yu-ts'un discovers that Hsueh P'an belongs to an important clan and that, in order to protect his position, he must absolve
Hsueh P'an from any guilt. From the viewpoint of persona technique, the episode is important in that it is a reminder of the Stone
conceit:

> The Stone had also copied a section and on the Stone was
> copied the following . . . .[172]

Ts'ao is having fun with the Stone motif and he is preparing his
readers to learn to decipher the kind of riddles they will continu-
ously encounter in the novel. Dream of the Red Chamber is a
"Story of a Stone" copied on a stone, and the narrator is, in this
example, the Stone who compiles its story by copying what is
written on a stone, in this case, the "mandarin charm". The implications of the passage are both comical and enlightening in so far
as Ts'ao's concept of fiction is concerned, for since what is copied

----

[168]HLMPSHCP, chap. 116, p. 362, line 6.
[169]ibid., chap. 120, p. 415, lines 14-16.
[170]ibid., chap. 98, p. 189, lines 11-12. See chapter 108,
p. 285, lines 12-13 (Pao-yu's return to the Grand View Garden
following Tai-yu's death) for another example of the narrator's
guidance.
[171] 護官符.C.C. Wang's translation, Dream of the Red Chamber, London, 1929, p. 42.
[172]HLMPSHCP, chap. 4, p. 38, lines 3-4: 石頭亦曾抄寫了一
張, 今據石上所抄云:

must be footnoted to be understood, and since the remainder of the
novel is without footnotes, it is suggested that Dream of the Red
Chamber is to remain somewhat of an enigma.

One of the most brilliant passages in Dream of the Red Chamber
occurs in chapter 8 when the narrator suddenly turns aside from the
narrative to enfold a realistic scene in a layer of the Stone myth.
One day when Pao-yu pays a visit to Pao-ch'ai, she asks him to
show her his jade talisman about which she has heard so much. As
she takes it in her hand, the narrator describes it in the following
terms:

> When Pao-ch'ai took the jade, she saw that is was as large
> as a sparrow's egg. It glittered like sky-fairing morning
> clouds, it was translucent and smooth like congealed cream,
> and it was surrounded and protected by variegated designs.
> This was indeed the transformed shape of that piece of stone
> from the base of Blue-Channel Peak near Mt. Fantasia. [173]

After quoting a sarcastic poem about the Stone and its origins by an
anonymous individual (another pointed refusal to identify the
author?), the narrator goes on to say:

> The Stone had also recorded the seal characters which the
> scabby-headed Monk had carved and these were now drawn
> on the back. But the actual form of the characters was as
> small as it could be so that an unborn baby could hold the
> jade in its mouth. If now I should imitate that form, I am
> afraid that the written characters would be too small. This
> would be injurious to the reader's eyesight and by no means
> be a pleasing matter. So now I'll just accord with the shape
> of the characters but enlarge them somewhat so that one can
> read them by lantern light or even when one is drunk. Now
> the notes which clarify this Story do not consider the kind
> of criticism raised by the following question and its ilk: 'An
> unborn baby's mouth is but so big, how could it hold such an
> awkward foolish thing?' [174]

The narrator thus directly intervenes in the story and reminds his
reader of the importance of the mythic mode. In playing on the
illusion-reality theme of Dream of the Red Chamber, he castigates

----

[173]HLMPSHCP, chap. 8, p. 83, lines 8-9. For text, see p.
235.

[174]ibid., p. 83, line 15, through p. 84, line 1. For text,
see p. 235-236.

炕上做針線。頭上挽着漆黑油光的鬐兒，窰合色棉襖，玫瑰紫二色金銀鼠比肩掛，葱黄綾綿裙，一色半新不舊，看去不覺奢華。唇不點而紅，眉不畫而翠，臉若銀盆，眼如水杏。罕言寡語，人謂藏愚；安分隨時，自云守拙。寶玉一面看，一面口內問：『姐姐可大愈了？』寶釵擡頭，只見寶玉進來，連忙起身，含笑答道：『已經大好了，倒多謝記掛着。』說着，讓他在炕沿上坐了，即命鶯兒斟茶來。一面又問老太太姨娘安，別的姊妹們都好。一面看寶玉頭上戴着纍絲嵌寶紫金冠，額上勒着二龍搶珠金抹額，身上穿着秋香色立蟒白狐腋箭袖，繫着五色蝴蝶鸞縧，項上掛着長命鎖，記名符，另外有那一塊落草時啣下來的寶玉。寶釵因笑說道：『成日家說你的這玉，究竟未曾細細的賞鑒，我今兒要瞧瞧。』說着，便挪近前來。寶玉亦湊了上去，從項上摘了下來，遞在寶釵手內。寶釵托於掌上，只見大如雀卵，燦若明霞，瑩潤如酥，五色花紋纏護。這就是大荒山中青埂峯下的那塊頑石的幻相。後人曾有詩嘲云：

『女媧煉石已荒唐，又向荒唐演大荒。

失去幽靈眞境界，幻來親就臭皮囊。

好知運敗金無彩，堪歎時乖玉不光。

白骨如山忘姓氏，無非公子與紅妝。』

那頑石亦曾記下他這幻相並癩僧所鐫的篆文，今亦按圖畫於後。但其眞體最小，方能從胎中小兒口中啣下。今若按其體畫，恐字跡過於微細，使觀者大費眼光，亦非暢事。故今只按其形式，無非略展放些規

第八回　比通靈金鶯微露意　探寶釵黛玉半含酸

矩，使觀者便於燈下醉中可閱。今註明此故，方無氣胎中之兒口有多大，怎得啣此狠犺蠢物等語之謗。

通靈寶玉正面圖式

通

靈　莫失莫忘

寶　仙壽恒昌

玉

通靈寶玉反面圖式

一除邪祟

二療冤疾

三知禍福

the "realistic" critic who cannot understand the story because his insistence on a literal interpretation hides from him mystic truth. Yet, even as he laughs at those readers who delude themselves with mundane questions about whether an infant in the womb could carry a piece of jade in its mouth, he delights in catering to their needs and expectations. To make the myth "realistic", he scrupulously brings in details, comical in their tediousness, about the size of the jade piece and of the characters engraved upon it, and he shows the utmost concern for the reader whose vision might be harmed by the perusal of the original, mythic stone. Even the explanatory commentary is sarcastic, for it is precisely in informing the literal-minded individual that he satirizes him. While the narrator carries on the guise that he just happens to be passing on a story which he has read, hidden in his commentary are certain keys to wisdom which will be pleasantly obvious to the astute reader alone. As we repeatedly noted in both "Myth" and "Mimesis", the "Foolish Thing", ch'un wu, is the major symbol of enlightened understanding in Dream of the Red Chamber, and, as the Stone insists in chapter 1, the time for enlightening reading is when one is enraptured with wine. Here in the present passage, the narrator hints to the mundane reader that one will benefit from the enlarged text of the original "even when drunk".

The reader will observe that in the above passage the identity of the individual who enlarges characters inscribed on the charm is unknown. On the basis of our reading of Dream of the Red Chamber, we should not be able to prove that the anonymous narrator may be identified with the Reverend Taoist Kosmo Kosmos, but an interesting parallel exists between the narrator of the passage under discussion and the Kosmo Kosmos of chapter 1. Like the latter, the narrator is merely the copier, and not the innovator, of a story which he finds interesting enough to pass along. He hopes the tale will be considered entertaining and he wishes to forestall any of his reader's objections.

Our final example of narrative persona occurs when Yuan-ch'un, Pao-yu's elder sister who is chosen to be an imperial concubine, returns home to visit her parents. As we began our survey we noted that there is only one instance in Dream of the Red Chamber where the storyteller appears to be clearly identified as the Stone. In our review we have tried to point out those passages which exemplify the styles and personalities of Ts'ao Hsueh-ch'in and the Stone that are presented in the Preface and chapter 1, and we have suggested that the anonymous narrator also might be linked to Kosmo Kosmos.

We turn now to the moment when Yuan-ch'un wanders about the
Grand View Garden that has been built to honor her home visit,
and to the Stone's ecstatic comment:

> And now I think back to that time of grieved solitude at Mt.
> Fantasia beneath Blue-Channel Peak. If the scabby-headed
> Buddhist Monk and the lame-footed Taoist had not carried
> me here, how could I have attained this kind of world! I
> did intend to write an Exhibitory Essay on 'Lanterns and
> Moonlight' or an Ode on 'Visiting Parents' to commemorate
> the events of this day, but I was afraid of getting into the
> clichés of other writings. Now as for the present scenery,
> even if I were to write an Exhibitory Essay or a Eulogy, I
> could not adequately describe its sublimity, and if I do not
> write either one the Reader can know its luxuriance and
> exquisiteness by using his imagination. So I'll save time and
> writing materials and tell instead the main story line of the
> narrative.[175]

Chih-yen Chai quotes this entire passage and makes much of the
fact that it represents the speech of the Stone which is recalling its
mythic origins.[176] He cites the uniqueness of Ts'ao's technique--
the sudden and dramatic use of the Stone's words which vividly
contrast to the preceding long passage of ornate description of the
garden. There is no other novel which has such a style.[177]

The Stone's intervention in the narrative underscores vital themes
of Dream of the Red Chamber. Not that heaven isn't beautiful, it
seems to say, but the earth is beautiful too! Indeed, the criticism
of the divine realm we observed in "Myth" is perceivable in the
words of the Stone--it is so exhilarated by the surprising beauty of
this world that the other world is only a painful memory. This
comment, of course, exemplifies a technique which in itself makes
the narrative terribly attractive. The Stone is so transfixed by the
indescribable beauty that unfolds before it in the narrative that it
cannot help insert itself in the text to confess its inadequacy. It
reminds the reader of its abhorrence for literary stereotypes and
traditional forms which it first mentions in chapter 1. What enhances

----

[175]HLMPSHCP, chap. 17-18, p. 176, lines 11-14. For text,
see p. 239.
[176]CYCHLMCP, chap. 17-18, p. 236, chia-chen. For text,
see pp. 240-241.
[177]ibid., p. 237, chia-chen mei-p'i. For text, see p. 241.

第十七、十八回　大觀園試才題對額　榮國府歸省慶元宵

完時，忽聽外邊馬跑之聲。一時，又十來個太監都喘吁吁跑來拍手兒。這些太監會意，都知道是來了，各按方向站住。賈赦領合族子姪在西街門外，賈母領合族女眷在大門外迎接。半日靜悄悄的。忽見一對紅衣太監騎馬緩緩的走來，至西街門下了馬，將馬趕出圍幕之外，便垂手面西站住。半日，又是一對，亦是如此。少時便來了十來對，方聞得隱隱細樂之聲。一對對龍旌鳳翣，雉羽夔頭，又有銷金提爐，焚着御香；然後一把曲柄七鳳黃金傘過來，便是冠袍帶履。又有值事太監捧着香珠、繡帕、漱盂、拂塵等類。一隊隊過完，後面方是八個太監擡着一頂金頂金黃繡鳳版輿，緩緩行來。賈母等連忙路旁跪下。早飛跑過幾個太監跪請下與更衣，於是擡輿入門，太監等散去，只有昭容彩嬪等引領元春下輿。只見院內各色花燈爛灼，皆係紗綾扎成，精緻非常。上面有一匾燈，寫着「體仁沐德」四字。元春入室更衣畢，復出上輿進園。只見園中香烟繚繞，花彩繽紛，處處燈光相映，時時細樂聲喧，說不盡這太平氣象，富貴風流。——此時自己回想當初在大荒山中，青埂峯下，那等淒涼寂寞，若不虧癩僧跛道二人攜來到此，又安得能這般世面。本欲作一篇燈月賦，省親頌，以誌今日之事，但又恐入了別書的俗套。按此時之景，即作一賦一讚也不能形容得盡其妙，即不作賦讚，其豪華富麗，觀者諸公亦可想而知矣。所以倒是省了這工夫紙墨，且說正經為是。

且說賈妃在轎內看此園內外如此豪華，因默默歎息「奢華過費」。忽又見執拂太監跪請登舟，賈妃乃下輿。只見清流一帶，勢如遊龍，兩邊石欄上皆係水晶玻璃各色風燈，點的如銀光雪浪，上面柳杏諸

一七六

（庚辰）淨（脂）極故聞之，細惡。（己卯同。有正『淨』作『靜』，餘同）

又十來個太監都喘吁吁跑來拍手兒。

（庚辰）蚕出內家風範，石頭記叚難之處，別眷中換不着。（己卯同。有正開頭多『神異』二字，餘同）

這些太監會意，都知道是來了。

（庚辰夾批）雖得他（寫）的出，是經過之人也。

忽見一對紅衣太監騎馬緩緩的走來。

（庚辰）形容畢肖。（己卯、有正同）

便垂手面西站住。

（庚辰）形容畢肖。（己卯、有正同）

賈母等連忙路傍跪下。

（庚辰夾批）一絲不亂。

只見院內各色花燈炯灼。

（庚辰夾批）元春月（目）中。

說不盡這太平氣象，富貴風流。

（甲辰）此石頭記自敍：想當初在大荒山中青埂峰下那等淒涼寂寞，若非癩僧跛道二人攜來到此，又安能見這世面，本欲作一篇燈賦省親頌以誌今日之盛，但恐入了小說家俗套。按此時之景，即一賦一贊也不能形容得盡其妙，即不作賦頌，而其豪華富麗，觀者諸公亦可想而知也。所以倒是省了些筆墨。（庚辰、己卯、有正俱作正文，

〔文字略異〕

『此時自己回想當初在大荒山中』一段。

〔庚辰眉批〕如此繁華盛極花團錦簇之文，忽用石兄自語收住，是何筆力，令人安得不拍案叫絕。是閱歷來諸小

說中有如此章法乎。

〔庚辰墨筆眉批〕此時句以下一段似應作注。其作親賦之注或以謊作訛不可知。綺園。

且說正經為是。（以上一七六頁）

〔庚辰〕自此時以下皆石頭之語，真是千奇百怪之文。（己卯、有正同）

真係玻璃世界，珠寶乾坤。

〔庚辰墨筆眉批〕玻璃世界，珠寶乾坤，恰是新妙。鎧堂。

明現著『蓼汀花漵』四字。

〔甲辰〕按此四字並『有鳳來儀』等匾，皆係上回賈政偶一試寶玉之才情耳，今日認真用之。況賈府世代詩書，來

往文墨之士正自不乏，豈無一二名手題詠，竟用一小兒語唐塞，直似暴發之家所為，豈石頭記所表之寧榮府哉。

。按此是自相矛盾了。 須將作者原委說明方為了了。（庚辰、己卯、有正俱作正文，文字略異）

何今日認真用此匾聯。

〔庚辰眉批〕駁得好。

竟用小兒一戲之辭苟且唐塞。

〔庚辰眉批〕石頭記貸（償）用特犯不犯之筆，真令人齰心駭目鬒之。

this passage and makes it doubly delightful is the context in which
it appears. As the reader is blissfully aware, whole pages are spent
on describing the Grand View Garden before there appears the
Stone's confession of inadequacy. The garden is set forth in elaborate detail through the eyes of Chia Cheng, his friends, Pao-yu,
and finally Yuan-ch'un. We interpret this apparent contradiction
to be another instance of Ts'ao's technique. It is precisely at the
moment when the Stone enters the text, identifies itself as narrator,
confesses its inadequacies, and pleads for the reader's use of his
imagination, that it reveals its ignorance of what has thus far tran-
spired in the Stone Record--someone else has already described the
indescribable, Ts'ao Hsueh-ch'in!

The many examples we have cited in our review of the persona of
the narrator perhaps convey the impression that the latter is of key
importance in every episode of Dream of the Red Chamber. We
should qualify this notion by pointing out that the narrator generally
seems to be content to play a more conventional role that is typical
of the storyteller in traditional Chinese fiction. He is given to
using formulaic language in telling his story, he asks questions of
his audience, and he tries to answer the questions which he pretends
his listeners ask him. Only rarely does he make such a stunning
personal appearance as he does in the examples of the Stone conceit
we have just cited. Nevertheless, it is obvious that he does control the narrative and that his is the most varied persona of the
several we have studied. Besides being an embodiment of Ts'ao
Hsueh-ch'in, the Stone, and even the Reverend Taoist Kosmo Kosmos,
he has his own mask of ambiguity. His control is exhibited by his
pretending, from time to time, that he is but a helpless scribe who
has much difficulty simply copying down what he sees before him.
He is alternately shying away from sexual matters and triumphantly
delighting in innuendo. He demonstrates an acute awareness of the
philosophical significance of the creation myth about the Stone and,
at the same time, he is intimately involved with and profoundly
moved by the triumphs and tragedies of his protagonists. As he
laughs and cries with Pao-yu and Tai-yu and asks his readers questions about the lives which are unfolding before him, he creates the
impression that Dream of the Red Chamber is an event, rather than
just another story.

Thus, through the persona of the narrator, Ts'ao gives his fiction
still another significance. He dramatizes the narrative by corrob-
orating the persona of himself and the persona of the Stone in the
persona of the narrator, and he creates the impression that the novel

is an event happening before us and one with which we are personally concerned. Like the narrator in Chaucer's Troilus and
Criseyde, the narrator plays a pivotal role in which he is alternately
independent of his narrative and dependent upon it, at times naive
and at others authoritarian. Prone to sympathize with the love
between Pao-yu and Tai-yu and yet willing to exploit it, he makes
their relationship appear both attractive and absurd. But however
cosmic his vision is in contrast to the limited vision of the characters he presents, the variety and ambiguity in his persona cause us
to continually evaluate his meaning.[178]

We have observed the personae presented in the General Editorial
Principles and in chapter 1 of Dream of the Red Chamber and we
have traced the persona of the narrator through the body of the
novel. In the last pages of Dream of the Red Chamber, Ts'ao Hsueh-
ch'in brings together several individuals, including himself, for a
final view of the fiction he has created.

The first interpretation comes from Chen Shih-yin in the course of
his conversation with Chia Yu-ts'un. As we noted in "Mimesis",
Chia Yu-ts'un does not understand everything Chen Shih-yin tries
to explain to him and, indeed, at the outset of their conversation,
Chen tells Chia that the latter will never understand completely
the story of Chia Pao-yu's enlightenment.[179] When Yu-ts'un asks
about the fates of the women of the Chia clan, Shih-yin replies
that they all belonged to the "Heaven of Love" and the "Sea of
Retribution" and that there is no use in asking about the final destinies of those whose lives were involved with passion. He notes
too that while women may not commit transgressions of bodily lust,
yin,[180] it is equally important that they do not become infected
with romantic love, ch'ing.[181] The implication of his remarks is
that the women of the Chia clan have suffered because of romantic

----

[178]Sister Ann Barbara Gill's discussion of the role of the narrator
in Troilus and Criseyde has helped us to evaluate Ts'ao's achievement. See Paradoxical Patterns in Chaucer's Troilus: An Explanation of the Palinode. Washington, D.C. 1960, introduction, pp.
ix-xxii.

[179]HLMPSHCP, chap. 120, p. 417, lines 1-2. For text, see
p. 246.

[180] 淫 .

[181] 情 HLMPSHCP, chap. 120, p. 417, lines 4-6. For text,
see p. 246.

passion. By criticizing them, Chen Shih-yin in effect rejects one of the most attractive features of Dream of the Red Chamber.

We turn to where we left Chia Yu-ts'un in "Mimesis"--asleep in a grass hut at the ford of the Awake Delusion Ferry on the Rapid Flow River. At this point in the narrative, we also learn that the two celestials, the Buddhist Monk and the Taoist, have just taken the Stone back to its original location beneath Blue-Channel Peak and that an explanation of the final events in the life of the Stone has been added to its reverse side:[182]

On this very day the Reverend Taoist Kosmo Kosmos once again passed by Blue-Channel Peak, and he saw that the Stone which had not been used to repair the firmament was once again located at the base of the Peak, and that the words written on it were the same as before. Once again he read the narrative carefully from top to bottom, and then he noticed that after the closing poem on the reverse side of the Stone there were some further words about the conclusion of the narrative. Kosmo nodded his head and sighed:

"Formerly I saw this marvelous tale of the Stone and I said then that I could tell it to the world and pass down what was unique. So I copied it down--but I didn't see the conclusion about returning to origins and I don't know when this elegant writing [183] was added. Now I am aware that Brother Stone descended into the Red Dust, was scoured bright and transformed into enlightenment, and it can be said that it has no more regrets. But I am afraid of letting too much time go by, for the lettering will get blurred and mistakes will appear. I'd better copy it down again and seek some worldly idler to pass down the whole narrative. Then it will be known that in its strangeness, it is not strange; common, and yet not common; real, and yet not real; unreal, and yet not unreal. Perhaps some suffering soul in the dream world of the Red Dust, as though depending on the call of a bird of good omen, will return

----

182HLMPSHCP, chap. 120, p. 418, lines 2-4. For text, see p. 247.

183佳話. Read chia hua there is possibly the intended pun, chia hua 假話. That is, the final episode of the novel is another play on the "true-false", "real-unreal" (chen-chia) theme; the "elegant writing" is but more "fictive language".

home to his source; perhaps the good spirit (genus loci) of
the mountain will be metamorphosized out of the stone
state. But this too I cannot know".

Having thought it out he again copied down the Story, and,
as before, with the Record in his sleeve pocket, he took it to
the place of luxuriance and splendor. He searched everywhere,
but either the person was one of those ambitious empire building types, or else he was of the pedestrian variety who was
solely interested in making a living. Where was there an idler
who could yet waggle his tongue with the Stone? 184

Kosmo subsequently discovers the sleeping Chia Yu-ts'un and he
mistakenly believes that he has at last found the "idle type" who
will pass on his transcribed copy of the Stone Record. As we explained in "Mimesis", Chia Yu-ts'un's sleepiness symbolizes his
release from mutability and his withdrawal from earthly interests.
Irritated by being forcefully awakened by Kosmo, Yu-ts'un professes
no interest in the Stone Record. What is important about his indif-
ference towards the novel is that he begrudgingly admits that the
fiction is true:

> . . . after taking the copy and giving it a careless once over,
> he threw it down:
>> "I've already seen this stuff myself", he said, "and I know
>> all about it--there aren't any mistakes in your transcribed
>> copy. I'll only point out another fellow--you can commis-
>> sion him to pass this on--he can round out the additional
>> material".185

"Another fellow" is, of course, Ts'ao Hsueh-ch'in. Before we
observe his reaction to the Stone Record, several comments ought
to be made about Kosmos's re-discovery of the Stone. His persona
is basically the same. As he enters the narrative, he returns us to
the mythic world of chapter 1 and he reminds us of the archetypes
we first encountered there. He is still travelling--apparently his
early conversion to love has not satisfied his yearning. Once again
the Stone Record is the answer to his search and this time the addition of new materials promises a higher form of enlightenment. In
the past he only knew the Story as a romantic tale of love and

----

184HLMPSHCP, chap. 120, p. 418, lines 5-11. For text, see
p. 247.

185HLMPSHCP, chap. 120, p. 418, lines 13-14. For text,
see p. 247.

但那寶玉旣有如此的來歷，又何以情迷至此，復又豁悟如此？還要請教。」士隱笑道：「此事說來，老先生未必盡解。太虛幻境卽是眞如福地，兩番閱冊原始要終之道，歷歷生平如何不悟！仙草歸眞，焉有遺靈不復原之理呢！」雨村聽著却不明白了，知仙機也不便更問，因又說道：「寶玉之事旣得聞命。但是敝族閨秀如此之多，何元妃以下算來結局俱屬平常呢？」士隱歎息道：「老先生莫怪拙言。貴族之女俱屬從情天孽海而來。大凡古今女子，那淫字固不可犯，只這情字也是沾染不得的。所以崔鶯蘇小無非仙子塵心，宋玉相如大是文人口孽。凡是情思繾綣的，那結局就不可問了。」雨村聽到這裏，忽擰長歎。因又問道：「請致老仙翁，那榮寧兩府尙可如前否？」士隱道：「福善禍淫，古今定理。現今榮寧兩府善者修緣，惡者悔禍，將來蘭桂齊芳，家道復初，也是自然的道理。」雨村低了半日頭，忽然笑道：「是了，是了——現在他府中有一個名蘭的已中鄉榜，恰好應着蘭字。適間老仙翁說「蘭桂齊芳」，又道寶玉「高魁貴子」，莫非他有遺腹之子可以飛黃騰達的麼？」士隱微微笑道：「此係後事，未便預說。」雨村還要再問，士隱不答，便命人設具盛饌，邀雨村共食。食畢，雨村還要問自己的終身，士隱便道：「老先生草菴暫歇，我還有一段俗緣未了，正當今日完結。」雨村驚訝道：「請問仙長純修若此，不知尙有何俗緣？」士隱道：「也不過是兒女私情罷了。」雨村驚異道：「請問仙長何出此言？」士隱道：「老先生有所不知，小女英蓮幼遭塵劫，老先生初任之時曾經判斷。今歸薛姓，產難完劫，遣一子於薛家以承宗祧。此時正是塵緣脫盡之時，只好接引接引。」士隱說著拂袖而起，雨村心中恍恍惚惚，就在這急流津覺迷渡口草菴中睡着了。這士隱自去度脫了香菱，送到太虛幻境交那

第一百二十回　甄士隱詳說太虛情　賈雨村歸結紅樓夢

四一七

第一百二十回　甄士隱詳說太虛情　賈雨村歸結紅樓夢

四一八

警幻仙子對冊。剛過牌坊，見那一僧一道縹緲而來，士隱接着說道：「大士真人，恭喜賀喜！情緣完結，都交割清楚了麼？」那僧說道：「情緣尚未全結，倒是那蠢物已經回來了。還得把他送還原所，將他的後事叙明，也不枉他下世一回。」士隱聽了，便拱手而別。那僧道仍攜了玉到青埂峰下，將寶玉安放在女媧煉石補天之處，各自雲遊而去。從此後：天外書傳天外事，兩番人作一番人。

這一日空空道人又從青埂峰前經過，見那補天未用之石仍在那裏，上面字跡依然如舊。又從頭的細細看了一遍，見後面偈文後又歷叙了多少收緣結果的話頭，便點頭歎道：「我從前見石兄這段奇文，原說可以聞世傳奇，所以曾經抄錄，但未見返本還原。不知何時復有此一佳話。方知石兄下凡一次，磨出光明，修成圓覺，也可謂無復遺憾了。只怕年深日久，字跡模糊，反有舛錯。不如我再抄錄一番，尋個世上清閒無事的人，託他傳遍。知道奇而不奇，俗而不俗，眞而不眞，假而不假。或者塵夢勞人，聊倩鳥呼歸去；山靈好客，更從石化飛來。亦未可知。」想罷，便又抄了，仍袖至那繁華昌盛的地方，遍尋了一番，不是建功立業之人，即係糊口謀衣之輩，那有閒情更去和石頭饒舌。直尋到急流津覺迷渡口，草菴中睡着一個人，因想他必是閒人，便要將這抄錄的石頭記給他看看。那知那人再叫不醒。空空道人復又使勁拉他，方慢慢的開眼坐起，便接來草草一看，仍舊擲下道：「這事我已親見盡知，你這抄錄的尚無舛錯。我只指與你一個人，託他傳去，便可歸結這一新鮮公案了。」空空道人忙問何人。那人道：「你須待某年某月某日某時，到一個悼紅軒中，有個曹雪芹先生，只說賈雨村言託他如此如此。」說畢，仍舊睡下了。那空空道人牢牢記着此言，又不知過了幾世幾劫，果然有個悼紅軒，見那曹雪芹先生正在那裏翻閱歷來的古史，空空道人便將賈雨村言了，方把這石頭記示看。那雪芹先生笑道：

「果然是賈雨村言了。」空空道人便問：「先生何以認得此人，便肯替他傳述？」雪芹先生笑道：

「說你空空，原來你肚裏果然空空。既是假語村言，但無魯魚亥豕以及背謬矛盾之處，樂得與二三同

志，酒餘飯飽，雨夕燈窗之下，同消寂寞，又不必大人先生品題傳世。似你這樣尋根究底，便是刻舟

求劍，膠柱鼓瑟了。」那空空道人聽了，仰天大笑，擲下抄本，飄然而去，一面走着，口中說道：「果

然是敷衍荒唐！不但作者不知，抄者不知，並閱者也不知。不過游戲筆墨，陶情適性而已！」後人見

了這本傳奇，亦曾題過四句為作者緣起之言更轉一竿云：

「說到辛酸處，荒唐愈可悲。

由來同一夢，休笑世人癡。」

第一百二十回　甄士隱詳說太虛情　賈雨村歸結紅樓夢

passion. Now he discovers the perfect completion of that tale in
which passion is resolved in the divine dimension. He finds tragic
suffering, but also emancipation and transcendence. Above all,
there are "no later regrets". This is an important observation, for
we recall the Buddhist Monk's warning to the Stone to avoid the
Red Dust and the Stone's subsequent promise that if it is carried to
the earth it will have "no later regrets". But the phrase takes on
a different meaning in the context of the ending of the novel. The
Stone has no regrets because, contrary to the expectation of the
two celestial Immortals, its life in the Red Dust has been a completely fulfilling experience.

What Kosmo believes he finds in the novel is the promise of an
enlightenment--so long as the new ending is kept intact--that goes
beyond the warnings of the mythic world and which surpasses the
attractions of the mimetic. We remind the reader of the theme of
triple repetition we discussed in "Mimesis". This represents Kosmo's
third reading of the Stone Record. The first time he makes several
conventional criticisms; the second leads to his conversion to "Bonze
of Love"; upon this third reading he becomes really worried about
the actual text of the novel. Ironically, this concern is a sign of
his yet limited spiritual advancement. He perceives the unity of
the strange and the not strange, of the common and the not common,
of the real and the unreal, yet he is fearful about the passage of
time and the eventual corruption of the text. He has got to find
someone who has the leisure to show the world his copy of the novel.

In spite of Kosmo's enchantment with the Stone Record, his
persona serves to debunk the novel. In his ignorance about the
source of the ending he safeguards the conceit that Dream of the Red
Chamber has no author of known reputation. Everyone is much too
busy to care about such a novel. Kosmo cannot even prevail upon
an idler who has nothing to do, like Chia Yu-ts'un, to advertise it.
Thus Kosmo's view of the novel and his narrow conception of its
audience in chapter 120 are much different from the opinions of the
Stone in chapter 1. The Stone champions the Stone Record because
it is light amusing literature for the ordinary reader, to use Kosmo's
vocabulary, the "pedestrian variety", who is indeed too harried to
read stuffy moral tomes, but who will read the Stone Record when
he is "enraptured with wine, an amour, delicacies, or slumber".
Only the common reader can become "stoned" on enlightenment.

Ts'ao Hsueh-ch'in's opinion of the novel is perhaps the most important if only by virtue of the fact that it is through his persona of
the author-as-commentator that final criticisms are voiced. Upon

the advice of Chia Yu-ts'un, Kosmo delivers the Stone Record to
the right man, Ts'ao Hsueh-ch'in, one who likes to browse through
ancient histories in the Grieving for Red Pavilion. The latter immediately laughs at both the story and at Kosmo Kosmos. He criticizes the narrative by punning on its chia-yu ts'un-yen,[186] "fictive
language and vulgar words", but Kosmo fails to get the pun. Ts'ao
then somewhat reluctantly says that he won't mind editing the novel
to dispel melancholy on rainy evenings when he is eating and drinking with friends. He adds that there is no need for anyone important
to edit the materials.[187]   Lastly, he satirizes Kosmo's pedantry and
thereby indirectly attests to the consistency of Kosmo's persona:

   "Your searching after roots and fundamentals is the same as
   'marking the boat to locate the sword that's gone over-
   board,[188] gluing the frets to play the zither'".[189]

Kosmo, consonant with his image in chapter 1 where he "was on a
pilgrimage inquiring after tao and seeking Sylphdom", is still the
wisdom seeker who misses the whole point, according to an editor,
Ts'ao Hsueh-ch'in.

   The intended irony here, of course, is that in debunking the
Reverend Taoist Kosmo Kosmos, Ts'ao Hsueh-ch'in debunks both
Dream of the Red Chamber and himself. There is no reason for any
worthy individual to take charge of the text, so the work is left for
a true "idler" who whiles away his time "flipping through pages of
ancient histories", namely, Ts'ao Hsueh-ch'in. This contemptuous
view of the novel brilliantly contrasts to the persona of the author
in the Preface who writes out of a dire need to save the women of
his youth from oblivion. On the other hand, Ts'ao's attitude at the
end of Dream of the Red Chamber also implies he has taken on the
persona of the Stone and that he is the kind of reader the Stone has
in mind when it says, "My only wish is that they [readers] will have

---

186假語村言.
187HLMPSHCP, chap. 120, p. 418, line 16, through p. 419,
line 4. For text, see pp. 246-248.
   188A story from the Lu-shih ch'un-ch'iu 呂氏春秋 , about
a man who dropped his sword over the side of a boat and who thought
he could find the sword later by making a mark on the boat.
   189HLMPSHCP, chap. 120, p. 419, lines 4-5. For text, see
p. 248. Our translation and understanding of this aphorism is based
on Richard Kunst's fine rendering and explication. Kunst, "The
Beginning and Ending of The Dream of the Red Chamber", p. 54.

fun with it . . . ." Ts'ao's opinion is that the novel is light amusing literature, the kind he and his drinking companions can enjoy over a glass of wine.

In the final pages of Dream of the Red Chamber the various personae become one. Each is silenced by its successor and each in turn takes on an attitude of disinterested joy. Chen Shih-yin derides Chia Yu-ts'un's limited understanding, but the former must seek a final explanation of the fate of Pao-yu from the two celestial Immortals. Chia Yu-ts'un subsequently ridicules Kosmo's sincere attempt to foster the acceptance of the Stone Record. Ts'ao Hsueh-ch'in then speaks derisively of the "fictive language and vulgar words" of Chia Yu-ts'un and he lampoons the pedantry of the earnest Kosmo Kosmos. The last laugh belongs, and this is both appropriate and charming, to the Reverend Taoist. As in the case of each of the other personae, once the critical mask is displayed it is gleefully cast aside, and behind it we discover the figure of joyous enlightenment who has passed all caring about the fates of persons such as Pao-yu and books such as the Stone Record. Criticism is the preface to joyful enlightenment, and once that is realized further concern is meaningless.

Like Ts'ao Hsueh-ch'in, the Reverend Taoist Kosmo Kosmos may be said to become "Stone-like". In answer to Ts'ao Hsueh-ch'in's criticisms of his pedantry, he throws down the transcribed copy of the novel (as does Chia Yu-ts'un before him) and laughs ecstatically even as he floats away an enlightened being:

> "Truly it is an explication of absurdity! Not only do the
> author and copyist not get it, neither does the reader. It is
> but jolly jabberwocky and indulgent self-amusement--and
> that's that!"[190]

Kosmo's comment reminds us that Dream of the Red Chamber is a novel which originates in the absurd and that it is a tale of the absurd. His last laugh also stresses the key word, chih,[191] "awareness", or "understanding", which we have rendered colloquially as, "get it". We recall in this context Chia Yu-ts'un's unsuccessful visit to the "Hermitage of Cognition of Knowledge".[192] There is a constant play in the novel on the homonyms chih,[193] "awareness",

----

[190]HLMPSHCP, chap. 120, p. 419, lines 5-6. For text, see p. 248.
[191] 知.
[192] 智通寺.
[193] 知.

and chih,[194] "cognition". Kosmo is "not aware", pu chih,[195] of who has added the ending to the Stone Record. He will copy it down so that others may "know the strange but not regard it as strange", chih-tao ch'i erh pu-ch'i.[196] "I cannot know", wei k'o chih,[197] he says, whether the Stone Record will exert an en-lightening influence upon others. "How can one know?", na chih ("expect"),[198] that Chia Yu-ts'un would keep sleeping when asked to transmit the narrative. Chia Yu-ts'un is uninterested because he is already aware--as he says, "I know all about it", wo i ch'in chien chin chih.[199] Finally, it is mentioned in the course of the narrative that it is "not known", pu chih,[200] how many eons of time go by before Kosmo delivers the Stone Record to Ts'ao Hsueh-ch'in. Thus, there is a steady line of development which leads to Kosmo's stunning statement that nobody "gets it". His statement may be interpreted as a brilliant final touch of ambiguity, that "prevailing wind" in Dream of the Red Chamber. His joyful reply to Ts'ao Hsueh-ch'in says, paradoxically, I "get it"; that is, Kosmo suddenly realizes that he has been pedantic, and now he becomes aware of "opposites": the long pilgrimage towards salva-tion and the concomitant devotion to the written word end with the spontaneous perception that in jabberwocky, self-amusement, and absurdity lies the "root and fundamental" of enlightenment. At the same time, his language implies that neither the unknown author, nor the copyist, nor the reader "gets it"--every reading and every resultant encounter with enlightenment is a unique and private experience--therefore everyone has his own view of Dream of the Red Chamber and every opinion is contradictory.

  Before the Stone Record is really underway, the celestial Buddhist Monk insists that the Story will be unique, and Chih-yen Chai agrees. The Reverend Taoist Kosmo Kosmos decries the absence of conventional didacticism, while the Stone promises amusement and originality. In the main body of the novel, the anonymous narrator, displaying a variety of personae, does his best to keep up with a

----

194 智.
195 不知.
196 知道奇而不奇
197 未可知.
198 那知.
199 我已親見盡知
200 不知.

Story which continues to leave him breathless. At the end of the Stone Record, Chen Shih-yin tells Chia Yu-ts'un that the latter will never understand this tale of enlightenment, and then, in his rejection of all love, Shih-yin proceeds to reject this tale of love. Chia Yu-ts'un throws down the transcribed copy when he is asked to transmit it. Kosmo re-copies the narrative with its new ending but later comes to discard the novel too. Ts'ao Hsueh-ch'in is slow to admit that the narrative may be suitable for a rainy night's entertainment.

Do the various opinions we have reviewed constitute a total theory of fiction? Does the author, through a variety of personae, present a unified vision? We think not, for that theory of fiction and that unified vision lie elsewhere in Dream of the Red Chamber--in the innumerable discussions of art, poetry, drama, and painting which take place among the characters of the novel. What we can say, and what we hope is now clear to the reader, is that it is through persona that Ts'ao Hsueh-ch'in shapes the attitude of his reader and charms him, with his ineffable grace, into wearing a mask which belongs to the reader alone, the mask of ecstatic receptivity.

Conclusion

At the beginning of our study we said that we wished to elucidate the aesthetic appeal of Dream of the Red Chamber and to correct the predilection of critics for "realism"--a bias which unfortunately has obscured Ts'ao Hsueh-ch'in's achievement. We have endeavored to analyze the relation between the novel's framework and its core, and we hope that we have faithfully depicted the interplay between various stylistic modes.

Our effort has been to expose before the reader the particular form and content of a unique literary work. Dream of the Red Chamber, as Chih-yen Chai repeatedly reminds us, is unique--it does not accord with many technical precepts of Western fiction and it clearly undermines the conventions of traditional Chinese fiction. The author quite deliberately hides true affairs in a dream-vision, excises facts of authorship and dates, and obscures the novel's structure with a series of beginnings and a constant and unannounced shift among literary modes. Because by the very nature of his fiction he cannot inform his reader that Dream of the Red Chamber is composed of polysemous layers and varied styles, he suffers the criticism that his work is disorganized and unwieldy. Indeed, the structural aspects of his style have been misunderstood, ignored, or missed entirely.

As we have discovered, the form of Ts'ao's novel has to be faithful to its content. The author perceives reality in terms of a tension between the divine and the human and he enfolds that reality in the

254

movement of complementary opposites--thus a Chia Pao-yu moves towards a Chen Pao-yu, a casual tea party becomes the initiation rite for an adolescent's first sexual experience, a "by chance" encounter with a scabby headed monk is a predestined meeting with enlightenment, and a discarded mythic Stone evolves into the "precious treasure" of everyday reality. All of these transitions are made to appear haphazard by Ts'ao Hsueh-ch'in, but critical study reveals there is rarely a passage in the novel which does not exemplify the author's conscious choice and which does not adhere to specific stylistic patterns and a coherent world view.

Through the allegory of the Stone Ts'ao Hsueh-ch'in presents the basic philosophical problems of the novel. The mythic mode does not resolve these problems; instead, it provides a radically ironic view of the imperfect refining processes of divinity which can only be made perfect by the addition of earthly developments. If a human being is pervaded by divine nature, he must be born into the world to attain psychological wholeness and divine salvation. In myth we find a blend of didacticism and irony, of allegory and mundane reality, which is the source of the novel's unity and exemplifies the synthesizing power of Ts'ao's imagination. Through this mode, the author builds the divine machinery of karma and yin-kuo which supposedly explains the action of the novel. In fact, this machinery reveals that perfection and divinity are not synonymous and that a supernatural deus ex machina issues forth from a moral void. Archetypes and synchronic time encompass an "illusion realm" which includes the supernatural world as well as the world of everyday experience and which insists upon idiocy as the key to divine or human glory.

Ts'ao Hsueh-ch'in envisions the mimetic mode as a witty verbal play on the mythic. Life-like characters whose stories are imitations of everyday reality, such as Chia Yu-ts'un, Chen Shih-yin, Chia Pao-yu, and Chen Pao-yu, are symbols of the archetypal polarity which exists between reality and appearance. These mimetic paradigms are obvious allegories which represent the harmony operative among literary modes. The unstable victim of mutability, Chia Yu-ts'un, is metamorphosized into his opposite, the secure image of permanence and transcendence, Chen Shih-yin. Chia Pao-Yu's drive to preserve love and beauty by stopping time ends in idiocy, that mutable image of imagination and intuition, when he discovers the shattering knowledge that the ideal image of his self, Chen Pao-yu, is the negative mask of his own reality.

In the narrative mode, Ts'ao uses a variety of personae. Figures

of authority and naiveté, objective and subjective voices, critics
both defensive and offensive, guilty dreamers and nonchalant
hobbyists, all of these serve to attract the uncommitted reader by
a barrage of contradictory opinions both before and during the course
of the narrative. These insist that the reader interpret what passes
before him even if that interpretation brings him perilously close to
error.

What is the "message" of Dream of the Red Chamber, that particular quality of didacticism which flows from the interplay of form
and content? The reader's perennial delight lies in his disorienta-
tion. The author dazzles the reader by loosely locating him between
dream and waking reality, and thus causes him to wonder about the
nature of that reality as well as about the nature of fiction. What
is really unique about Dream of the Red Chamber is that it is a novel
the reading of which renders an experience of enlightenment, although realists and literalists will miss this meaning. In entertaining us it leads us astray so that we do not remember the question of
origins until long after we have found that wisdom and delight result from our own critical experience. The meaning of the written
word, the "fictive language and vulgar words", is that one must
have a pilgrim spirit as do Kosmo Kosmos and Pao-yu to discover
enlightenment. The latter is a fortuitous and not consciously sought
event, a moment which follows suffering, when we are able to experience both joy and sorrow with equanimity.

To become a convert to Ts'ao's fiction, as does Kosmo Kosmos, is
to subject oneself to the possibility of self-satire which can be delightfully instructive and enormously painful. To know the truth,
we have to discover that the written word is a form of falsification
which paradoxically promises enlightenment and a revelation of tao.
The ironic power of Ts'ao's language may seduce us into a reading,
but it may also cause us to read what is not really there, or worse,
to find with Chia Yu-ts'un and Kosmo Kosmos that we will never
"get it". At least our careful criticism, that prelude to literary enlightenment, will inform us that Ts'ao's "entertainment" is really
the product of enormous suffering, and that while this personal tome
about the ever-contemporary world by a crazy author whom no one
understands will not offer an acceptable reason for suffering, it may
convert some men from their lives of vanity and absurdity, and certainly it will "dispel blues" and provide a fresh way of viewing the
world.

Appendix A: THE HUNG-LOU MENG TEXT AND TEXTUAL CRITICS

The large number of manuscripts and printed versions of <u>Dream of the Red Chamber</u> have made the establishment of a definitive <u>Dream of the Red Chamber</u> text exceedingly difficult.[1] Partly because of the complexity of this problem, and partly due to a general preference in China for textual rather than literary criticism, the majority of native Chinese discussions of the novel are textual studies.[2] For

----

[1] See our Introduction, p. 4, for reference to the number of manuscripts and printed versions.

[2] The main bibliographies of studies of the novel are the following:
C.T. Hsia, <u>The Classic Chinese Novel</u>, New York and London, 1968, pp. 396–399;
I-Su 一粟 (Ch'ien Hsing-ts'un 錢杏村), <u>Hung-lou meng shu-lu</u> 紅樓夢書錄 , Shanghai, Ku-tien wen-hsueh ch'u-pan she, 1958. Tien-yi Li, <u>Chinese Fiction: A Bibliography of Books and Articles in Chinese and English</u>, New Haven, 1968, pp. 175–212.
P'an Ch'ung-kuei 潘重規 ,"Chin-erh hung-hsueh" 今日紅學 , in <u>Hung-lou meng yen-chiu chuan-k'an</u> 紅樓夢研究專刊 , No. 7 (Jan., 1970), 111–117.
Research Group on the <u>Hung-lou meng</u>, ed. (Chinese Department, New Asia College, Hong Kong Chinese University), "<u>Hung-lou</u>

well over one hundred years, Chinese readers believed that the one
hundred and twenty chapter edition of Dream of the Red Chamber,
edited by Kao E and printed by Ch'eng Wei-yuan in 1791 and
emended in 1792, was the complete version of the novel written by
Ts'ao Hsueh-ch'in. It was not until Dr. Hu Shih published his
Hung-lou meng k'ao-cheng[3] that the existence of manuscripts of
the novel, with commentaries by one Chih-yen Chai, "Master of
the Red Ink-slab Studio", became generally known. Hu Shih noted
that since there were no manuscripts of more than eighty chapters,
Ts'ao Hsueh-ch'in must have died before completing his novel, and
the last forty chapters of the one hundred and twenty chapter edition must represent the additions written by Kao E.

Hu Shih's assertions began a scholarly controversy which has yet
to be resolved satisfactorily. In On the Red Chamber Dream, a
monument of Chinese textual criticism,[4] Wu Shih-ch'ang attempts
to solve many problems having to do with questions of authorship
and text by making exhaustive use of the Chih-yen Chai annotated
manuscripts of the novel. The subtitle of On the Red Chamber
Dream is: A Critical Study of Two Annotated Manuscripts of the
18th Century. Wu bases most of his investigations on two manuscripts which he calls V1, the so-called chia-hsu pen,[5] and V3,
the so-called keng-ch'en pen.[6] However, he did not have access
to V1 when carrying out his research as this manuscript was in the

----

meng shu-mu pu-i" 紅樓夢書目補遺   , in Hung-lou
meng yen-chiu chuan-k'an, No. 4 (Sept., 1968), 73-78; "Hsiang-
kang Hung-lou meng yen-chiu tzu-liao so-yin ch'u-kao" 香洪紅
樓夢研究資料索引初稿   , in Hung-lou meng
yen-chiu chuan-k'an, No. 8 (Sept., 1970), 53-63.
   Wu Shih-ch'ang, On the Red Chamber Dream. Oxford, 1961,
pp. 359-367.
   [3]Hu Shih 胡適   , "Hung-lou meng k'ao-cheng (kai-ting kao)"
紅樓夢考證(改定稿),in Hu Shih wen-ts'un 胡適文存 ,
Taipei, Yuan-tung t'u-shu kung-ssu, 1953, vol. 1, pp. 575-620.
   [4]Chen Wen-hua likens Wu Shih-ch'ang's accomplishment in On
the Red Chamber Dream to the study of the Shu Ching (Book of
History) by the celebrated Ch'ing scholar, Yen Jo-chu 閻若璩 .
See Chen's review of On the Red Chamber Dream in Tung-hai
hsueh-pao, VII: i (June, 1965), 141.
   [5] 甲戌本.
   [6] 庚辰.

private possession of Hu Shih from 1927 until it was reproduced in
Taipei in 1961, the year of the publication of On the Red Chamber
Dream. For his study of the commentary of V1, Wu Shih-ch'ang
only could use Yu P'ing-po's Chih-yen Chai Hung-lou meng chi-
p'ing, a collection of Chih-yen Chai commentaries on the novel
from various manuscripts.[7] When Yu P'ing-po made his collection
(CYCHLMCP), Hu Shih's copy of V1 had yet to be published, and
so Mr. Yu relied on V2 (the so-called chi-mao pen)[8] onto which
most of the V1 commentary had been transcribed.[9] However, since
there are differences between the V1 commentary in Yu's CYCHLMCP
and the commentary as it originally appears in Hu Shih's chia-hsu
manuscript copy, Wu Shih-ch'ang's views expressed in On the Red
Chamber Dream are not wholly reliable.[10]

When we say that we do not have an established text of Dream of
the Red Chamber, we are pointing to the question of the authorship
of the last forty chapters of the novel and to the problem of the relation between these chapters and the first eighty chapters. Yu
P'ing-po has collated the principal Chih-yen Chai annotated manuscripts in an effort to establish a text for the first eighty chapters of
the novel. While the result of Yu's collation, the Dream of the
Red Chamber text entitled Hung-lou meng pa-shih-hui chiao-pen,[11]
is not definitive, since it is the best available edition, we have
used it as the basis for our study of the novel.

A number of Chinese and Western scholars agree with Hu Shih's
view that the last forty chapters of Dream of the Red Chamber are
written by Kao E. Wang Huang argues that the vernacular language
in the last forty chapters is decidedly inferior to that found in the

----

[7]Yu P'ing-po 俞平伯 , Chih-yen Chai Hung-lou meng chi-
p'ing 脂硯齋紅樓夢輯評 . First published 1955. Revised
edition, Chung-hua shu-chu, Shanghai, 1963.

[8] 己卯本.

[9]See Yu's explanation, CYCHLMCP, p. 3.

[10]Lin Yu-t'ang 林語堂 finds the V1 commentary in Hu Shih's
chia-hsu pen and in Yu's HLMPSHCP sometimes differs in content
as well as in location in the novel. See Lin's "P'ing-hsin lun Kao
E" 平心論高鶚 , in Chung-yang yen-chiu-yuan li-shih yu-yen
yen-chiu-so chi-k'an, XXIX: ii (Nov., 1958), p. 332. Also see
Chen Wen-hua's review of On the Red Chamber Dream, Tung-hai
hsueh-pao, VII: 1 (1965), 141.

[11] 紅樓夢八十回校本,Jen-min wen-hsueh ch'u-pan
she, Peking, 1958.

first eighty chapters and therefore the former could not possibly be by Ts'ao Hsueh-ch'in.[12] In his initial investigations of the novel, Yu P'ing-po also supported the theory of the authorship of Kao E, but in more recent publications he revises his views. While no longer agreeing that Kao E wrote the last forty chapters, Yu still does not believe that they are the work of Ts'ao Hsueh-ch'in.[13]

In the Foreword to Wu Shih-ch'ang's On the Red Chamber Dream, Arthur Waley strongly disagrees with Bernhard Karlgren's conclusions, based on a study of thirty-eight grammatical constructions, that the first eighty and last forty chapters are written by the same hand (Karlgren refers to the former as "Hung-lou A" and the latter as "Hung-lou B"), that of Ts'ao Hsueh-ch'in. In agreement with Wu Shih-ch'ang that the final forty chapters were the work of Kao E, Waley makes the following statement about Kao and Ts'ao:

> But surely what gave them on the whole a common form of speech was the fact that they were both upper-class Chinese naturalized as Manchus. The language of the social milieu to which they belonged was a refined form of Pekinese. It was no evidence of "unheard of acumen" (Karlgren) that either of them should use this type of colloquial; it would, in fact, have been a tour de force for either of them to write in any other way.[14]

Waley is responding to Karlgren's view that:

----

[12]Wang Huang 王瑛 , "Lun Hung-lou meng li te wen-hsueh yung-yu" 論紅樓夢裡的文學用語 , Tung-fang tsa-chih 東方雜誌 , XL: xiii (July, 1944), 56–60.

[13]For Yu's early views see: "Kao-tso hou ssu-shih-hui te p'i-p'ing" 高作後四十回底批評, Hsiao-shuo yueh-pao 小説月報 , XIII:viii (August, 1922), 1–16; "Hou san-shih-hui te Hung-lou meng" 後三十回的紅樓夢 , Jen-min wen-hsueh 人民文學, No. 20 (June, 1951), 84–90. For his revised opinions see: Hung-lou meng yen-chiu 紅樓夢研究, Shanghai: T'ang-ti ch'u-pan she, 1952; "T'an hsin-k'an Ch'ien-lung ch'ao-pen pai-nien-hui Hung-lou meng kao" 談新刊乾隆抄本百廿回紅樓夢稿, Chung-hua wen-shih lun-ts'ung 中華文史論叢, V (June, 1964), 395–445.

[14]On the Red Chamber Dream, p. viii.

If Hung-lou B was the creation of Kao E, it would require, either that he was a compatriot (almost from the same district) of Ts'ao Sue-k'in's and spoke exactly the same dialect, in all the particulars studied above; or that he was a linguistic genius with an imitative ability of almost unheard-of acumen. Both surmises are so improbable that they can be safely rejected. The absolute fidelity in the grammatical agreement between Hung-lou A and Hung-lou B conclusively shows that the latter was written by the same author as the former. Possible discrepancies between the two in regard to the content are probably due to corruption and interpolations in the course of the text transmission.[15]

In a critique of Karlgren's views, Wu Shih-ch'ang raises several important questions and reaches the following conclusion:

But . . . is it really true that there is "absolute fidelity in the grammatical agreement between Hung-lou A and Hung-lou B", a criterion that enables Professor Karlgren to pass his final verdict that "the latter was written by the same author as the former"? Can two dozen examples of colloquial expressions. . . in a novel of 1,240 pages of close print . . . offer any absolute solution of all the complicated linguistic problems involved? As a matter of fact, the colloquial expressions in the two parts of the novel are not "exactly the same" even in "all the particulars studied" by Professor Karlgren.[16]

Elsewhere in On the Red Chamber Dream, Wu states:

It is apparent that at the time when the author died in 1764 (sic),[17] although he had in the main finished the first

---

[15]Bernhard Karlgren, "New Excursions in Chinese Grammar", Bulletin of the Museum of Far Eastern Antiquities, No. 24 (1952), p. 7.

[16]Wu, On the Red Chamber Dream, p. 347.

[17]Scholarly evidence reveals that Ts'ao died in 1763. See: Chao Kang 趙岡 and Ch'en Chung-i 陳鍾毅, Hung-lou meng hsin-t'an 紅樓夢新探, Hong Kong, 1970, p. 28. Ch'en Yu-p'i 陳毓罷, "Yu-kuan Ts'ao Hsueh-ch'in tsu-nien wen-ti te shang-ch'ueh" 有關曹雪芹卒年問題的商榷, Kuang-ming jih-pao 光明日報 (April 8, 1962). Ch'en Yu-p'i, "Ts'ao Hsueh-ch'in tsu-nien wen-t'i te tsai shang-ch'ueh" 曹雪芹卒年問題的再商榷, Kuang-ming jih-pao (June 10, 1962).

Chou Ju-ch'ang 周汝昌 , "Ts'ao Hsueh-ch'in tsu-nien pien" 曹雪芹卒年辨 , Wen-hui-pao 文滙報 (May 4-5, 1962).

Chou Ju-ch'ang, "Tsai-shang Ts'ao Hsueh-ch'in tsu-nien" 再商曹 雪芹卒年 , Kuang-ming jih-pao (July 8, 1962).

Teng Yun-chien 鄧允建 , "Ts'ao Hsueh-ch'in tsu-nien wen-t'i shang-tui" 曹雪芹卒年問題商兌, Wen-hui-pao (Apr. 17, 1962). Teng Yun-chien, "Tsai-t'an Ts'ao Hsueh-ch'in te tsu-nien wen-t'i" 再談曹雪芹卒年問題, Kuang-ming jih-pao (June 10, 1962).

Tseng Tz'u-liang 曾次亮, "Ts'ao Hsueh-ch'in tsu-nien wen-t'i te shang-t'ao" 曹雪芹卒年問題的商討 Kuang-ming jih-pao (Apr. 26, 1954).

Wang Li-ch'i 王利器 , "Ch'ung-hsin k'ao-lu Ts'ao Hsueh-ch'in te sheng-p'ing" 重新考慮曹雪芹的生平, Wen-hsueh i-ch'an hsuan-chi 文學遺產選集, 2 (Apr., 1957), 238-246.

Wang P'ei-chang 王佩璋, "Ts'ao Hsueh-ch'in te sheng-tsu nien chi ch'i-t'a" 曹雪芹的生卒年及其他, Wen-hsueh yen-chiu chi-k'an 文學研究集刊, 5 (May, 1957), 217-257. See especially p. 227.

Wu En-yu 吳恩裕 , "Ts'ao Hsueh-ch'in te tsu-nien wen-t'i" 曹雪芹的卒年問題, Kuang-ming jih-pao (Mar. 10, 1952). Wu En-yu, "Ts'ao Hsueh-ch'in tsu-nien jen-wu shuo chih-i" 曹雪芹卒年壬午說質疑, Kuang-ming jih-pao (May 6, 1962). Wu En-yu, "'Tu Chih-p'i Shih-t'ou chi sui-cha' tu-hou" 讀脂批石頭記隨札讀後, Kuang-ming jih-pao (June 23, 1962). Wu En-yu, "K'ao-cheng Ts'ao Hsueh-ch'in tsu-nien wo-chien" 考證曹雪芹卒年我見 Kuang-ming jih-pao (July 8, 1962).

Wu Hsiao-ju 吳小如 , "Tu Chih-p'i Shih-t'ou chi sui-cha erh-tse" 讀脂批石頭記隨札二則, Kuang-ming jih-pao (June 5, 1962).

Wu Shih-ch'ang's opinion that Ts'ao Hsueh-ch'in died on February 1, 1764, is based on his interpretation of a poem by Tun Min 敦敏. See: Wu Shih-ch'ang, "Ts'ao Hsueh-ch'in te sheng-tsu nien" 曹雪芹的生卒年 , Kuang-ming jih-pao (Apr. 21, 1962). Wu Shih-ch'ang, "Tun Ch'eng wan Ts'ao Hsueh-ch'in shih chien-shih" 敦誠輓曹雪芹詩箋釋, Kuang-ming jih-pao (June 17, 1962).

Wu's view is proven erroneous in the above listed articles. See too Yu P'ing-po's "Ts'ao Hsueh-ch'in te tsu-nien" 曹雪芹 的卒年, Kuang-ming jih-pao (March 1, 1954).

eighty, and nearly completed the last thirty or so chapters,
there were still a few final touches to be made.[18]
He also notes that the Chih-yen Chai commentary indicates that
Ts'ao Hsueh-ch'in had a complete plan for the novel and had
written several chapters including the last one, before he died.[19]
Wu Shih-ch'ang, then, admits the former existence of a "nearly"
complete Dream of the Red Chamber but believes it is no longer
extant. He categorically states that the present complete version
of Dream of the Red Chamber (the Kao E--Ch'eng Wei-yuan one
hundred and twenty chapter edition):

. . . was excised, supplemented, and redacted by another
writer Kao E under the political pressure of Emperor Ch'ien-
lung's "Literary Inquisition".[20]

There is indeed good evidence that the Ch'ien-lung Emperor did
read the novel [21]--although in an abridged version. In one of his
first articles on the novel, Chao Kang suggests the last part of
Dream of the Red Chamber was changed by an unknown Manchu before the novel was presented to the Emperor. A benevolent imperial
restoration of the Chia family properties was inserted in order to
avoid offending the Emperor with the original story of ruthless imperial confiscation.[22] Wu Shih-ch'ang observes that the earliest
hint we have that Dream of the Red Chamber might contain political
criticism of the Manchu regime is found in the comments of Hung-
wu,[23] a grandson of the K'ang-hsi Emperor and a cousin to the

----

[18]Wu, On the Red Chamber Dream, p. 195. For further criticism of Karlgren's view that the first 80 and last 40 chapters were
by the same author, see Chao Kang and Ch'en Chung-i, Hung-lou
meng hsin-t'an, ibid., pp. 356-370.
[19]Wu, On the Red Chamber Dream, ibid., p. 148.
[20]ibid., Introduction, p. xviii.
[21]Wu, ibid., p. 6, cites Chiang Jui-ts'ao's 蔣瑞藻 Hsiao-
shuo k'ao-cheng, Changhai, 1957, p. 556. Chiang notes that the
Ch'ien-lung Emperor received a copy from his minister, Ho Shen,
and that he enjoyed it.
[22]Chao Kang, "Lun chin-pen Hung-lou meng te hou ssu-shih-
hui" 論今本紅樓夢的後四十回, Tzu-yu Chung-kuo
自由中國, XXII:vii (April, 1960), 21-23.
[23]弘旿.

Ch'ien-lung Emperor, after he read the novel in 1768.[24]

Ch'ien Hsing-ts'un points out that while the official Indexes ban-
ning books in the Ch'ien-lung period did not include novels (Indexes
made up during the compilation of the Ssu-k'u ch'uan-shu), there
were definitely proscriptions against works of fiction from early
through late Ch'ing. However, it was not until the nineteenth
century[25] that Dream of the Red Chamber appears in lists of proscribed novels.[26]

----

[24]Wu, On the Red Chamber Dream, pp. 264-265, records two
sources on Hung-wu's reading of the novel:
Hou E 侯塏 , "Chueh lo shih-jen yung-chung nien-p'u"
覺羅詩人永忠年譜, in Yen-ching hsueh-pao 燕京學報,
No. 12 (Dec., 1932), 2632-2633.

Wu En-yu 吳恩裕 , "Yung-chung tiao Ts'ao Hsueh-ch'in
te san-shou shih" 永忠弔曹雪芹的三首詩, Kuang-ming
jih-pao (Sept. 7, 1954).

[25]Ch'ien Hsing-ts'un 錢杏邨 (pseudonym, A Ying 阿英),
Hsiao-shuo erh-t'an 小説二談, Shanghai, Ku-tien wen-
hsueh ch'u-pan she, 1958, p. 135. In 1844 and 1868, Hung-lou
meng is included in official proscription lists. ibid., pp. 136-142.
Wu, On the Red Chamber Dream, p. 322, notes that the last index
including Hung-lou meng was published May 6, 1868. See K'ung
Ling-ching 孔另境 , Chung-kuo hsiao-shuo-liao 中國小
説史料, Shanghai, Ku-tien wen-hsueh ch'u-pan she, 1957,
pp. 263-265.

[26]We find no mention of Dream of the Red Chamber in the Ch'ing
lists of proscribed books compiled by the Ch'ing scholar, Yao Chin-
yuan, nor in the record of forbidden Ch'ing books completed by
the contemporary scholar, Sun Tien-chi. See: Yao Chin-yuan
姚觀元 , Ch'ing-tai chin-hui shu-mu ssu-chung so-yin 清代
禁毀書目四種索引 , Shanghai: Wan-yu wen-k'u edition,
1937; Yao Chin-yuan, Ch'ing-tai chin-hui shu-mu (pu-i) 清代
禁毀書目(補遺) , which is published together with Sun Tien-
chi's 孫殿起,Ch'ing-tai chin-shu chih-chien lu 清代禁書
知見錄 , Shanghai: Shang-wu yin-shu-kuan, 1957.
There is also no mention of Hung-lou meng in Arthur Hummel's
The Literary Inquisition of Ch'ien-lung, Baltimore, 1935.

In Alexander Wylie's Preface to his Notes on Chinese Literature,
Shanghai, 1922, p. xxii, he records seven "continuations" of
Dream of the Red Chamber which were included in a list of prohibited

Whether or not <u>Dream of the Red Chamber</u> was altered because of political pressure, Wu Shih-ch'ang's main proof that Kao E's work is a forgery is the fact that there are plot changes in the last forty chapters which do not accord with riddle poems and Chih-yen Chai commentary in the first eighty chapters. Wu does not raise the possibility that Ts'ao himself may have made alterations in the orig-inal plot. It is obvious from text and commentary in the Chih-yen Chai annotated manuscripts that Ts'ao was constantly revising the first eighty chapters of the novel. The other evidence Wu cites is even less satisfactory than the fact of plot changes. He finds the presence of supernatural motifs in the last forty chapters to be too dominant to be the work of Ts'ao Hsueh-ch'in:

> These stories are obviously too superstitious to be convincing. They are hardly relevant to the central theme of the novel or to other stories. Even if they are well written, so many of them must be boring to any reader; and the great space they occupy in the last forty chapters does little justice to the novel or to its reader. They look like grotesque buildings artifically scattered in one-third of a well-designed garden, neither serving any useful purpose nor adding any pleasant sight for the visitor.[27]

Wu then contrasts these "superstitious" stories to seemingly similar stories in the first eighty chapters which he finds to be more authen-tic:

> These stories are in fact relevant to the theme of the novel or to other significant stories. The first mythological, pre-natal account of the hero and heroine is really an Introduction (or <u>hsi-tzu</u>) to the novel, it is not part of the mundane drama; so is Chen Shih-yin's dream in the first chapter.[28]

He concludes that even if Kao had obtained fragmented manuscripts of the last forty chapters of the novel:

> . . . since they had been rewritten and reshuffled in the different context of Kao's own stories, they can hardly be regarded as Ts'ao's work any more than Lamb's <u>Tales from</u>

----

books which was being circulated among the bookstores in China around 1867: 前紅樓夢；後紅樓夢；續紅樓夢；補紅樓夢；復紅樓夢；綺樓重夢；紅樓幻夢.

[27]Wu, <u>On the Red Chamber Dream</u>, p. 309.
[28]Wu, <u>ibid.</u>, p. 309.

Shakespeare can be regarded as Shakespeare's work.[29]

Our study of persona and of the mythic and mimetic modes of Dream of the Red Chamber reveals that, contrary to Wu's opinion, the creation myth and Chen Shih-yin's dream are vital parts of the "mundane drama" of the novel's core. We also find that many of the "superstitious" stories of the last forty chapters are just as convincing and relevant to the major themes of the novel as are the creation myth and dream-visions of chapter 1. It is difficult to understand how Wu can find these "superstitious" stories both "well written" and at the same time "boring".

Aside from the Swedish sinologist, Bernhard Karlgren, Chinese critics such as Lin Yu-t'ang, P'ei-chih, Wang P'ei-chang, and Yuan Sheng-shih find that the first eighty and final forty chapters form a unified whole. Lin Yu-t'ang argues on the basis of probability. He notes that manuscript dates and biographical data indicate Ts'ao Hsueh-ch'in had eight to nine years to write the last part of Dream of the Red Chamber after he completed the first eighty chapters. Kao E, on the other hand, simply did not have sufficient time during his pursuit of an official career to create forty new chapters and it would have been impossible for him to imitate so closely another man's style. Lin further reminds us of the fact that several individuals report having seen completed versions of the novel before Ts'ao died.[30]

In a critical attack upon Lin Yu-t'ang's alleged faulty logic, Yen Ming observes that even if Ts'ao Hsueh-ch'in did finish his novel, we do not know if the last forty chapters are really his, since what we have was joined to the first eighty chapters long after the author's death. Furthermore, whether the style of the last forty chapters is good or bad, this does not in itself prove that they were written by either Ts'ao Hsueh-ch'in or by Kao E.[31]

29Wu, ibid., p. 344. For a brief resume of Wu's view of Kao's work, see Wu Shih-ch'ang, "History of The Red Chamber Dream", in Chinese Literature, No. 1 (1963), 87-100.

30Lin Yu-t'ang, "P'ing-hsin lun Kao E", 322-387.

31Yen Ming 嚴明 , "Hung-lou meng hou ssu-shih-hui te k'ao-cheng wen-t'i--Tui Lin Yu-t'ang hsien-sheng te fan-an t'i-ch'u shang-ch'ueh", 紅樓夢後四十回的考證問題 — 對林語堂先生的翻案提出商榷, Tzu-yu Chung-kuo, 自由中國 , XIX:xii (Dec., 1958), 24-28; XX:i (Jan., 1959), 33-37.

One of the first textual critics to hold that the two authors theory cannot be correct is P'ei-chih. However, his argument that the plot of the one hundred and twenty chapter edition is a generally tightly structured unit is a shallow one, for certainly plot consistency is relatively easy for anyone to produce.[32]   In a more recent article, Yuan Sheng-shih contributes to the view that Dream of the Red Chamber is by one hand since structure and style are the same in both the eighty chapters and the final forty chapters. Contrary to Wu Shih-ch'ang and mainland communist critics, Yuan finds that the ending of the novel, in which Pao-yu returns to the mythic world of chapter 1 as an enlightened Stone, is very appropriate-- and inevitable.[33] Wang P'ei-chang, Yu P'ing-po's former Research Assistant at the Research Institute of Literature, Peking University, holds that Kao E is innocent of deliberate changes in the last forty chapters, since he merely tries to follow earlier manuscripts in his possession in the course of editing the text of Dream of the Red Chamber.[34]

The tradition of k'ao-cheng (textual) criticism reached a pitiful level during the "Great Debate" over the meaning of Dream of the Red Chamber which began in mainland China in 1954. In his study of the "Great Debate", Jerome B. Grieder points out that the aim of the Chinese Communist Party was to destroy the reputation of those scholars who, beginning in the 1920's, first applied the techniques of textual and literary criticism to the study of Dream of the Red Chamber. This group includes members of the so-called "Hu Shih" clique, such as Yu P'ing-po and Ku Chieh-kang.[35]   The attack was initiated, Grieder notes, by Li Shih-fan and Lan Ling,[36] two former students of Yu P'ing-po's, and was carried on by Mao Tun, Kuo Mo-jo, Ai Ssu-ch'i, Cheng Chen-to, and Chou Yang.[37] The objective was to destroy the reputation of those scholars

----

[32]P'ei-chih 佩之 , "Hung-lou meng hsin-p'ing", 紅樓夢新評, Hsiao-shuo yueh-pao, 小説月報, XI:vi (June, 1920), 6-12; XI:vii (July, 1920), 5-12.

[33]Yuan Sheng-shih 袁聖時 , "Hung-lou meng yen chiu", 紅樓夢研究, Tung-fang tsa-chih, XLIV:xi (Nov., 1948), 47-48.

[34]Wang P'ei-chang, "Ts'ao Hsueh-ch'in te sheng-tsu nien chi ch'i-ta", 245-246.

35 顧頡剛.

36 李希凡, 藍翎.

37 茅盾, 郭沫若, 艾思奇, 鄭振鐸, 周揚.

belonging to the "Hu Shih" clique, mainly because their views of Dream of the Red Chamber were influenced by Hu Shih's "autobiography" theory of the novel. The second purpose of the attack was to bring about a new reading of the novel in terms of Marxist criticism.[38]

On October 24, 1954, a forum on Dream of the Red Chamber was held by the Department of Classical Literature of the Chinese Writers Union, presided over by Cheng Chen-to, in which there were forty-nine participants and nineteen speakers. Many of the most widely known names in Chinese literature were present at this all-China conference, including Lao She, Wu En-yu, Fan Ning, Ho Ch'i-fang, and Chou Yang.[39] It is interesting to note that at this forum, as well as in newspaper articles, critics previously considered orthodox Marxists such as Wu En-yu and Chou Ju-ch'ang were ostracized, along with Yu Ping-po. Yu made a pathetic public confession in which he came close to repudiating his thirty years of research on Dream of the Red Chamber.[40] He declared that while carrying out his work, his "political ideological level was too low". Speaking of his research, he said:

> I start from the viewpoint of interest, and have failed to grasp fully the political nature and ideological nature of the Dream of the Red Chamber . . . .[41]

----

[38]See Jerome B. Grieder, "The Communist Critique of Hung Lou Meng", Papers on China, X (Oct., 1956), 142-168.

[39]老舍, 吳恩裕, 范寧, 何其方, 周揚.

[40]For a general review of the forum, see "The Dream of the Red Chamber Case", Current Background, No. 315 (March 4, 1955), United States Department of State, American Consulate General, Hong Kong.

For other articles on the "Great Debate", see: Cheng Hsueh-chia 鄭學稼, "Hung-lou meng shih-chien te yin-kuo", 紅樓夢事件的因果, Min-chu p'ing-lun 民主評論, VI:vii (April, 1955), 12-15.

"San-ko yueh lai kuan-yu Hung-lou meng yen-chiu te p'i-p'an ho t'ao-lun", 三個月來關於紅樓夢研究的批判和討論, Hsin-hua yueh-pao 新華月報, No. 64 (Feb., 1955), 278-280.

Mao Tun, "What We Know of Ts'ao Hsueh-ch'in", Chinese Literature, No. 5 (1964), 85-104.

[41]Current Background, No. 315, pp. 40-41.

He then announced:

I am prepared through this meeting to study new things. I am
listening humbly to the views of all.[42]

In 1959 a copy of an early one hundred and twenty chapter draft
of Dream of the Red Chamber was discovered. This draft is entitled
Ch'ien-lung ch'ao-pen pai-nien-hui Hung-lou meng kao. It was
reprinted by the Chung-hua shu-chu (China Book Company) in
Peking in 1963.[43] In his colophon to the reprint, Fan Ning asserts
this one hundred and twenty chapter draft of Dream of the Red
Chamber is one of the copies used by Kao E and Ch'eng Wei-yuan
in the preparation of their printed editions of 1791 and 1792. It is
an editor's copy, full of corrections and appears at times very messy.
Until the discovery of this manuscript, the only evidence of any
pre-Kao E one hundred and twenty chapter Dream of the Red Chamber is the report of contemporaries of Ts'ao Hsueh-ch'in that they
had seen complete versions of the novel. Fan Ning's research leads
him to suggest that the date of this draft is between 1760 and 1784.
He concludes that the discovery of this manuscript proves that a
rough draft of a one hundred and twenty chapter Dream of the Red
Chamber was in existence before Kao E and Ch'eng Wei-yuan published their editions of 1791 and 1792. Kao E is not the author of
the last forty chapters of the novel, but merely the editor.

One should think that with the discovery of this manuscript, controversy over the text of Dream of the Red Chamber would have
abated, but such is not the case. In addition to Fan Ning, scholars
such as Chao Kang, C.T. Hsia, P'an Ch'ung-kuei, Wu Shih-ch'ang,
and Yu P'ing-po have written extensively about the significance of
this one hundred and twenty chapter manuscript. Nearly all commentators, with the sole exception of Wu Shih-ch'ang, agree that
Kao E was not deceiving his readers when he stated in the Preface
to the 1792 printed edition of the novel that he had obtained manuscripts of the last forty chapters which enabled him to put together

----

[42]ibid., pp. 40-41. Among other "revisionist" faults, Yu
admits:"My calling upon Wang P'ei-chang to write articles on my
behalf, which is the feudal work style exploiting the master-disciple
relationship, was very bad". ibid.

[43] 乾隆抄本百廿回紅樓夢稿.
Fan Ning's 范寧 colophon is dated November 1962. A copy of
this reprint is available in the East Asian Library, University of
California, Berkeley.

a complete edition of the novel. Yet, the question remains, is the author of these chapters Ts'ao Hsueh-ch'in or someone else?

C.T. Hsia notes that mainland scholars are currently engaged in looking for another author because they cannot admit that Ts'ao Hsueh-ch'in could have written so many chapters of non "realistic" fiction:

> . . . during the May Fourth period many scholars . . . could not stomach the last third of the novel because of its supposed compromises with feudal morality and its pronounced note of Taoist-Buddhist escapism; the Communists have continued to denounce it for the same reasons.[44]

Wu Shih-ch'ang maintains his opinion that Kao E is the creator of the last third of the novel by arbitrarily deciding that Kao E began to work on the novel as early as 1784. He believes that "Meng-chueh chu-jen" ("Master Awakened from Dream"),[45] the author of the Preface to the chia-chen ("1784") version of the novel, is Kao E. In other words, while Wu agrees that the Ch'ien-lung draft is of a date earlier than the 1791-1792 printed editions, he insists that it is written by Kao E.[46] In order to maintain his position on the Kao E authorship, Wu Shih-ch'ang has pushed his argument to the point of absurdity. In a biographical study of the life and works of Kao E, Wu clings to his theory of the Kao E authorship and as evidence, he cites a poem by Kao E.[47] In the poem, Kao E regrets his passionate youth and says that he corrected his mistakes in his middle age. Wu interprets the poem as an allegory in which Kao E is really saying that he wrote the last chapters of Dream of the

----

[44]Hsia, The Classic Chinese Novel, p. 252.

[45] 夢覺主人.

[46]Wu Shih-ch'ang, "Hung-lou meng kao te ch'eng-fen chi ch'i nien-tai", 紅樓夢稿的成分及其年代, T'u-shu kuan 圖書館, IV (Dec., 1963), p. 46. This essay is somewhat of an expansion of Wu's earlier views of the Ch'ien-lung draft as found in On the Red Chamber Dream, Appendix III, pp. 319-321. In this Appendix, Wu states that his views have been modified since he read a paper on the Ch'ien-lung draft at the XIIth International Sinological Conference, Cambridge University, September 9, 1959, entitled, "The Draft of The Red Chamber Dream". I have not been able to obtain a copy of that paper.

[47]The poem is entitled: 月小山房遺稿. Its "heading" (t'i 題) is: 重訂紅樓夢小說既竣題.

Red Chamber.[48]   The inanity of Wu's analysis is revealed in a
witty and devastating critique by P'an Ch'ung-kuei. He successfully demonstrates through examples of Kao E's editing of the Ch'ien-
lung manuscript that emendations occur only for the sake of clarity.
P'an thus supports Kao E's claim that he was merely the editor of
newly discovered manuscripts of the novel.[49]

   In another study of the Ch'ien-lung draft copy of Dream of the
Red Chamber, P'an Ch'ung-kuei finds that the text of the first
eighty chapters agrees with the text of the Chih-yen Chai annotated
Shih-t'ou chi, but the Ch'ien-lung draft has been emended so that
it agrees with the 1792 printed version.[50]   The text of the last forty
chapters, if we include interlinear and marginal emendations, also
agrees with the 1792 printed version. Furthermore, the corrections
and emendations in the first eighty and last forty chapters are made
by the same hand.   P'an Ch'ung-kuei interprets the evidence to
suggest that the Ch'ien-lung draft is one of the copies of the one
hundred and twenty chapter novel Kao E used in the course of editing the complete Dream of the Red Chamber.[51]   The fact that there
are minor differences between the Ch'ien-lung draft copy and the
printed version of 1792 indicates that the former was not made simply for the purpose of according with the latter.   It is difficult to
imagine that anyone would waste time making revisions in this copy
to accord with the 1792 edition when he could easily buy the
latter.[52]   However, as excellent a textual critic as Yu P'ing-po

----

[48]Wu Shih-ch'ang, "Ts'ung Kao E sheng-p'ing lun ch'i tso-p'in
ssu-hsiang", 從高鶚生平論其作品思想, Wen-shih 文史,
IV (June, 1965), 127-144. With the exception of the analysis of
Kao E's poem, this is a good study of Kao's works and his biography.
   [49]P'an Ch'ung-kuei 潘重規 , "Kao E pu tso Hung-lou meng
hou ssu-shih-hui te shang-ch'ueh", 高鶚補作紅樓夢紅四
十回的商榷, Hsin-ya hsueh-pao 新亞學報, VIII:i (Feb.,
1967), 367-382.
   [50]P'an Ch'ung-kuei, "Tu Ch'ien-lung ch'ao-pen pai-nien-hui
Hung-lou meng kao", 讀乾隆抄本百廿回紅樓夢稿,
Ta-lu tsa-chih, 大陸雜誌 , XXX:ii (Jan. 1965), pp. 1-2.
   [51]P'an Ch'ung-kuei, ibid., pp. 1-2, 5, 7.
   [52]An excellent point made by P'an Ch'ung-kuei. ibid., pp.
2, 5. One problem in identifying the Ch'ien-lung manuscript as
the editing job of Kao E is the absence of Kao E's signature. Only
at the end of chapter 78 do we find his courtesy name (Lan-shu) and
the phrase, "inspected by Lan-shu". P'an Ch'ung-kuei suggests

thinks the emendations found in the margins of the Ch'ien-lung draft were transcribed from the 1792 edition.[53]

Certainly the most brilliant textual critic of Dream of the Red Chamber to appear in recent years is Chao Kang, Professor of Economics at the University of Michigan. In his first article on Dream of the Red Chamber, he lists several facts which indicate that Kao E could not be the author of the last forty chapters of the novel. Chao establishes that Kao E took the chu-jen examinations in 1788 and then began to prepare for the chin-shih degree. This left him approximately nine months to work on Dream of the Red Chamber. While he had sufficient time to edit a given text, it would have been impossible for him to create forty chapters in such a brief period. Chao Kang also refers to the different backgrounds of Ts'ao Hsueh-ch'in and Kao E. Since Kao had no intimate knowledge of Ts'ao's experience of growing up in the Ts'ao family household--an experience which is the basis of a novel that some have typed "autobiography"--it is doubtful that Kao E could even approximate the life of Ts'ao Hsueh-ch'in in fiction.

However, Chao Kang himself does not raise the question of whether or not the last third of the novel is fictive autobiography. Furthermore, since Kao E did have the first eight chapters, he did possess a kind of intimate aquaintance with the life of the author in so far

----

that the pen name, ch'i-hsia jen, 旗下人 , which we frequently encounter in the margins of the manuscript is Kao E. This would prove that Kao E went over the text. See P'an, ibid., p. 3.

53Yu P'ing-po's study of the Ch'ien-lung manuscript is entitled, "T'an hsin-k'an Ch'ien-lung ch'ao-pen pai-nien-hui Hung-lou meng kao", 談新刊乾隆抄本百廿回紅樓夢稿, Chung-hua wen-shih lun-ts'ung, 中華文史論叢, V (June, 1964), 395-445.

Yu only examines the first eighty chapters of the manuscript. For a succinct summary of his views, see C.T. Hsia, The Classic Chinese Novel, p. 251. Yu's failure to examine the last forty chapters of the manuscript as well as his study of the first eighty chapters have been strongly criticized by P'an Ch'ung-kuei. See the latter's "Hsu-t'an hsin-k'an Ch'ien-lung ch'ao-pen pai-nien-hui Hung-lou meng kao", 續談新刊乾隆抄本百廿回紅樓夢稿, Ta-lu tsa-chih, 大陸雜誌, XXXI: iv (August, 1965), 1-6.

as it was represented in the novel. Chao Kang goes on to cite the
important recent discoveries of the Chih-yen Chai chia-chen manuscript ("1784") and a one hundred and twenty chapter edition of
1789 prefaced by Shu Yuan-wei.[54] These discoveries offer textual
evidence of the existence of a complete Dream of the Red Chamber
before Kao E began editing the novel. Finally, Chao Kang points
out that in the 1791 edition, the reader is confronted with the confusing phenomenon of a character, Chiao-chieh, the daughter of
Wang Hsi-feng, who periodically grows younger and older (Chao
Kang suggests that Ts'ao originally intended Wang Hsi-feng to have
two daughters). In the 1792 edition, Kao fails to correct this confusion. If he were the author of the last forty chapters, rather than
a sometime careless editor and reviser, he could not have committed
such mistakes.[55]   Chao Kang surmises that Kao E is not the author
of the last forty chapters of Dream of the Red Chamber, but merely
the compiler and collator of various manuscripts.
    On the other hand, he argues just as cogently that neither is Ts'ao
Hsueh-ch'in the author of the last forty chapters. He does not mean
that Ts'ao never wrote the last section of the novel, but that the
last forty chapters in the Ch'eng-Kao received text differs in plot
in several respects from the novel as originally envisioned by Ts'ao
Hsueh-ch'in. The basis for Chao's viewpoint is his study of the
Chih-yen Chai commentary. Several stories and episodes which the
commentary indicates are to occur in the last section of the novel
are, in fact, non-existent. Furthermore, other stories are found in
the Kao E editions which are never indicated in the Chih-yen Chai
commentary.[56] Despite this evidence, or the lack of it, it seems

----

54 舒元煒.

55Our summary of Chao Kang's argument is based on his article,
"Lun Hung-lou meng hou ssu-shih-hui te chu-che", 論紅樓
夢後四十回的著者 , Wen-hsueh tsa-chih 文學雜誌,
VII:iv (Dec., 1959), 4-7.

56Chao Kang, ibid., pp 7-9. Subsequent research by Chao
Kang and Ch'en Chung-i published in 1970 provides further support
for the above argument that Kao E edited the last forty chapters of
Dream of the Red Chamber and that they were not written in their
present form by Ts'ao Hsueh-ch'in. See: Hung-lou meng hsin-t'an,
pp. 263-301 (on the last forty chapters of the 120 chapter printed
editions); 330-368 (on the continuations of the novel and the contents of the last forty chapters); 369-379 (on the possible identity
of the writer of the last forty chapters).

possible Ts'ao Hsueh-ch'in could have revised his original plot.
As C.T. Hsia notes in commenting on the plot and character differences in the eighty and forty chapters, inconsistencies are not
necessarily proof that Ts'ao did not write the last third of the novel:

> To blunt the force of this argument . . . one can say that
> the first 80 chapters are by no means a coherent narrative
> of seamless unity.[57]

Hsia observes the presence of many discrepancies in the first eighty
chapters due to Ts'ao's constant revisions.

In a more recent publication, Chao Kang and Ch'en Chung-i
develop the interesting hypothesis that the author of the sequel to
the first eighty chapters of Dream of the Red Chamber is the commentator, Chi-hu, whom they identify as Ts'ao Hsueh-ch'in's
father, Ts'ao Fu.[58] The reason why there are no annotated manuscripts of the novel of more than eighty chapters is that subsequent
chapters contained material about the relations between the Ts'ao
family and the court which the latter would have considered offensive (for example, the story of the imperial confiscation of Chia
clan properties). The family therefore elected to withhold the last
portion of the novel from distribution. Chao and Ch'en speculate
that as the father of the deceased Ts'ao Hsueh-ch'in, Ts'ao Fu decided to continue and complete the work of his son. They point
out that Ts'ao Fu lived long enough to do this work, he did write
commentary on the novel (as "Chi-hu"), and that he revised and
issued the chia-hsu manuscript. Chao Kang and Ch'en Chung-i
suggest that probably Ts'ao Fu had at his disposal Ts'ao Hsueh-ch'in's
early drafts of the last chapters of the novel. Ts'ao Fu wrote the
General Editorial Principles to forestall the criticism of imperial
censors. Chao and Ch'en conclude that the last forty chapters became available sometime between 1786 and 1787.[59]

Chao Kang and Ch'en Chung-i further suggest the interesting
theory that the first eighty chapters of Dream of the Red Chamber
are the work of four collaborators: Ts'ao Hsueh-ch'in is the main
author, but his cousin, Ts'ao T'ien-yu (Chih-yen Chai), brother,
Ts'ao T'ang-ts'un (K'ung Mei-hsi), and father, Ts'ao Fu (Chi-hu),
helped him to remember past family history, and told him through
commentaries on the manuscripts when his story was accurate as well

----

[57]The Classic Chinese Novel, p. 253.
[58]Chi-hu 畸笏   ; Ts'ao Fu 曹頫   .
[59]Hung-lou meng hsin-t'an, pp. 370-378.

as when he should amend his text.[60] These critics hypothesize that after Ts'ao Hsueh-ch'in died, Ts'ao T'ien-yu completed unfinished sections. Ts'ao T'ang-ts'un's work was minimal because, as the youngest of the four, he was unable to remember much about the early history of the family. After Ts'ao T'ien-yu died,[61] Ts'ao Fu took over his work. It is Ts'ao Fu, Chao and Ch'en suggest, who edited early manuscript copies, entitled the novel "Dream of the Red Chamber" (rather than Shih-t'ou chi), wrote the General Editorial Principles, finished the novel "in tears", and distributed the novel outside the family.

In their conclusions to the study of the Ch'ien-lung copy of Dream of the Red Chamber, Chao Kang and Ch'en Chung-i differ considerably from the views of P'an Ch'ung-kuei, Wu Shih-ch'ang, Yu P'ing-po, and C.T. Hsia. Chao and Ch'en find that the first eighty chapters in this copy, the Chih-yen Chai annotated manuscripts, and the printed editions are all quite different from one another. They suggest that the first eighty chapters of the Ch'ien-lung copy originate in a Chih-yen Chai manuscript which is not the same as any we now have. Only nineteen chapters of the last forty chapters are the same as those in the Ch'eng-Kao printed editions. In short, these critics conclude, the first eighty and the last forty chapters are from different sources and the Ch'ien-lung copy of Dream of the Red Chamber is not one single text.

Chao Kang and Ch'en Chung-i state that their study of the Ch'ien-

----

[60]Ts'ao T'ien-yu 曹天祐 , (Chih-yen Chai,脂硯齋); Ts'ao T'ang-ts'un曹棠村 , (K'ung Mei-hsi,孔梅溪). See p. 209 of this study for further references to these persons. For the theory of joint authorship, see Hung-lou meng hsin-t'an, ibid., pp. 206-225. For the identities of the commentators, see ibid., pp. 153-164, 206-211. See too Chao Kang's "Lun Hung-lou meng hou ssu-shih-hui te chu-che", pp. 10-12; "Chih-yen Chai yu Hung-lou meng" 脂硯 齋與紅樓夢 , Ta-lu tsa-chih 大陸雜誌 , XX:ii (Jan., 1960), 8-12; XX:iii (Feb., 1960), 23-26; XX:iv (Feb., 1960), 22-30.

[61]The reasons for the identification of Chih-yen Chai as Ts'ao T'ien-yu are as follows: Chao Kang and Ch'en Chung-i suggest that Ts'ao T'ien-yu is the posthumous son of Ts'ao Yung (曹 顒). The name, T'ien-yu (天祐), was given in honor of a family heirloom (硯) which Ts'ao T'ien-yu inherited through his grandfather, Ts'ao Yin (曹寅). Chao and Ch'en speculate that the heirloom was red in color, therefore the pen name, "Chih-yen" (脂硯), "red ink-slab". See Hung-lou meng hsin-t'an, ibid., p. 164.

lung copy proves revisions were made to make this copy accord with
the second edition of the Ch'eng-Kao text printed in 1792. In
their reconstruction of the development of the Ch'ien-lung copy of
Dream of the Red Chamber, Chao and Ch'en suggest that someone
who owned an eighty chapter Chih-yen Chai manuscript heard that
Ch'eng Wei-yuan and Kao E had obtained the last forty chapters
of the novel, and this person then copied the latter and added these
chapters to the manuscript he had. Kao E, in turn, borrowed this
individual's eighty chapter Chih-yen Chai manuscript and read it
in the process of preparing the second printed edition of the novel.
Chao Kang and Ch'en Chung-i conclude that this one hundred and
twenty chapter manuscript was not the draft copy Kao E used to put
together a complete edition of Dream of the Red Chamber.[62]

We end our survey of Dream of the Red Chamber textual criticism
by noting a recently current mainland hypothesis, or rather, folk
theory (cited by Chao Kang), concerning the authorship of the last
forty chapters of Dream of the Red Chamber. In 1963, an old man
named Chang Yung-hai was discovered in Peking. He claimed that
his relatives and ancestors knew Ts'ao Hsueh-ch'in and that a true
story was handed down in his family concerning the authorship of
the final third of the novel. Apparently, since Ts'ao was impoverished when he died, there was no money to pay for his funeral
and to make offerings to his departed spirit. An old woman found
the manuscript of Dream of the Red Chamber on Ts'ao's desk, and
used the manuscript sheets to wrap up funeral offerings. On the way
to the funeral, she dropped the manuscript. One of Ts'ao friends,
E-pi, found it. He wanted to finish it for his dead friend, but could
not, so he gave it to his adopted son, Kao E,who completed it.
According to this folk tale, in the one hundred and twenty chapter
novel we have today, the last forty chapters were written by E-pi
and the revisions were by Kao E![63]

The preceding survey gives us some indication, entertaining folk
stories not withstanding, of the complexity of the textual problem.
It seems clear that Kao E is the editor rather than the author of the

----

[62]See Hung-lou meng hsin-t'an, ibid., pp. 302-314, 318-328.
See too Chao Kang's "Lun Ch'ien-lung ch'ao-pen pai-nien-hui
Hung-lou meng kao", 論乾隆抄本百廿回紅樓夢稿，　，
Ta-lu tsa-chih 大陸雜誌　, XXVIII:vi (March, 1964), 9-11.
   [63]Chao Kang, "Lun Ch'ien-lung ch'ao-pen", ibid., p. 13.

last forty chapters of <u>Dream of the Red Chamber</u>, and it appears that he revised and emended a rough draft of the final one third of the novel which Ts'ao Hsueh-ch'in had completed before he died. Obviously there is a need for a more thorough textual study of the Ch'ien-lung manuscript copy, since scholars such as C.T. Hsia, P'an Ch'ung-kuei, Wu Shih-ch'ang, Yu P'ing-po, and Chao Kang have such divergent opinions on the relationships between this manuscript, the Chih-yen Chai annotated manuscripts of <u>Shih-t'ou chi</u>, and the one hundred and twenty chapter printed editions of Ch'eng Wei-yuan and Kao E. Whether or not a solution to the most pressing textual problems is forthcoming,[64] we may certainly concur with the following statement by C.T. Hsia:

> But any fair-minded reader who reads the novel without preconceptions about its authorship will find no reason to disparage the last 40 chapters, for they give the most impressive proof of the work's tragic and philosophic depth, not plumbed by any other Chinese novel.[65]

----

[64]For examples of exploratory research, see the series of textual studies in <u>Hung-lou meng yen-chiu chuan-k'an</u>, Nos. 1-8 (April, 1967 - Sept., 1970), Research Group on the <u>Hung-lou meng</u>, ed. (Chinese Department, New Asia College, Hong Kong Chinese University).

[65]<u>The Classic Chinese Novel</u>, pp. 256-257.

Appendix B: FORMULAIC NARRATIVE PATTERNS AND NARRATIVE TECHNIQUES

Formulaic Narrative Patterns:
  The following survey consists of a few of the patterns and motifs which are established in the framework and which reappear in the main body of Dream of the Red Chamber. Some of these formulae represent general cultural or social patterns of Chinese society. The author uses them to reflect and embody the mythic mode.

Male children spoiled through maternal love:
  The chief examples of this pattern are Pao-yu and Hsueh P'an. Ts'ao Hsueh-ch'in uses the same vocabulary to describe the Matriarch's love for her grandson, Pao-yu, as he does to present Hsueh I-ma's love for her son, Hsueh P'an. In chapter 2, Leng Tzu-hsing notes that the Matriarch "dotes" on Pao-yu.[1] Because Hsueh P'an's father died when he was little, and he was the sole remaining male progeny of the family, "his widowed mother could not avoid spoiling him and indulging him--with the consequence that he grew up without ever maturing".[2]

Inherited patrimony versus success in the Civil Service Examinations:
  The consequences from spoiling a child may prove severe. Both

----

[1]HLMPSHCP, chap. 2, p. 19, line 2.
[2]ibid., chap. 4, p. 41, line 13.

Hsueh P'an and Pao-yu must pass the Civil Service Examinations in
order to restore the names and titles of their families. Both are from
illustrious literary families which are on the decline--Hsueh P'an is
from "a family in which there was the aroma of books for several
generations".3 Because he is spoiled by his mother, he does not
study, and remains an illiterate. Chia Cheng, Pao-yu's father,
constantly expresses his fear that his son will be a failure due to the
doting affection of the Matriarch. Chia Cheng's fears are of special
interest when we contrast him with Lin Ju-hai, the father of Lin
Tai-yu. Chia Cheng's family has held an inherited title for several
generations, but the title cannot be passed on legally to more than
four generations. Upon the death of Chia Cheng's father, the title
is lost. Consequently, Chia Cheng prepares diligently for the Civil
Service Examinations in order to maintain the rank and name of his
family. However, by special Imperial decree, the family title is
passed on to Chia Cheng without his having to take the Examinations.
There is no hint that a like dispensation may be extended to Chia
Cheng's son, Pao-yu, and therefore Chia Cheng takes a keen interest
in the scholarly preparations of his son.4
    Another example of this archetype is Chia Yu-ts'un. Chia is born
into a family of letters and official rank, but the patrimony of his
family has been exhausted, he is the sole remaining member, and it
is up to him to restore his family's name through the Civil Service
Examination.5
    Like Chia Cheng, Lin Ju-hai belongs to an aristocratic family
whose title is passed through four generations up to and excluding
Lin himself. In contrast to Chia Cheng, Lin Ju-hai re-establishes
his family's name and rank by placing high in the Examinations.6
One suspects that one of Chia Cheng's personal problems is that,
while his position is honorable, he did not earn it through his own
merit.

The ill-fated orphan:
    The three examples of this pattern found in the framework are Lin
Tai-yu, Ying-lien, and Feng Yuan. Both Tai-yu and Ying-lien
(the daughter of Chen Shih-yin) are born into families which have

----

3ibid., line 12.
4ibid., chap. 2, p. 18, lines 12-14.
5ibid., chap. 1, p. 8, lines 3-4.
6ibid., chap. 2, p. 15, lines 12-15.

no sons, and thus they are the focus of their fathers' hopes and affections. The fathers of both girls are warned by Buddhist monks that their daughters are ill-fated.[7] Lin's parents die when she is young while Ying-lien is kidnapped. Throughout the novel, Tai-yu laments her loneliness. She has no one, she insists, to look out for her interests, especially in the area of marriage. Feng Yuan is the orphan boy who is killed by Hsueh P'an in an argument about purchasing the kidnapped Ying-lien. His example simply reinforces the theme of the plight of the orphan in the novel. It also points to the contrast between the wealthy and the poor. Due to the wealth and influence of the Hsueh family, Hsueh P'an is exonerated from the charges of murder.[8]

Male inferiority, female superiority, and family decline:
   As early as chapter 2, the author establishes the fact that the Chia family is on the decline. Members of the family seem unaware or unconcerned, while outsiders such as Leng Tzu-hsing find the demise to be obvious. He refers to a popular saying to express the point to Chia Yu-ts'un, "a centipede may die , and yet remain standing".[9] The motif of decline and the related disregard of the family is connected to the inferiority of men and the superiority of women. Leng Tzu-hsing exclaims over the fact that each succeeding generation of males in the Chia family is worse than the last.[10] Family titles are inherited rather than earned. The most promising males die in their childhood and those who survive, such as Chia Ching, Chia Chen, and Chia Jung of the Ning-kuo mansion, and Chia She and Chia Lien of the Jung-kuo mansion, prove to be unfit managers of the family.[11] On the other hand, the capable members are women, such as the Matriarch and Wang Hsi-feng.[12] One of the most important motifs is Pao-yu's preference for women over men. Women are made of water and men of mud. At an early age his feminism shows in his fondness for cosmetics, such as rouge and powder, both

----

[7]ibid., chap. 1, p. 7, line 10, and chap. 3, p. 26, lines 7-9.
[8]ibid., chap. 4, pp. 38-42.
[9]ibid., chap. 2, p. 17, line 16.
[10]ibid., chap. 2, p. 18, line 3.
[11]ibid., chap. 2, p. 18, lines 1-16.
[12]ibid., p. 22, line 8. Hsi-feng eclipses her husband, Chia Lien.

of which he relishes eating.[13]

"Precious Treasure":

"Precious Treasure" is an archetype which receives endless play in the novel. Pao-yu, the given name of the hero, means "precious jade". He is so loved by the Matriarch that she considers him to be her "Precious Treasure".[14] He is born with a jade talisman in his mouth which he wears around his neck. It is his "root of life" or "life force".[15] To his grandmother, he is her "root of life".[16] Analogous "treasures" in the novel are gold, jade, and hairpins.

The figure of enlightenment:

Chen Shih-yin, discussed at length in "Mimesis", is an archetypal figure of enlightenment. He establishes a pattern which is repeated and imitated by Pao-yu.

Narrative Techniques:

In his commentary, Chih-yen Chai often points to passages in the novel in which a seemingly innocuous remark will develop into a major scene in a later chapter. This is the technique known as fu hsien,[17] meaning, the "laying down of threads". Wu Shih-ch'ang translates an example of such commentary from chapter 1:

This [story] at the same time adumbrates how Shih-yin was a real scholar, a true man-of-letters, not a miser. It anticipates (literally, 'it pours right down to') the chapter entitled 'mu-ya nu ya chi k'u yin shih' (the girl yearning for culture in a cultural gathering took pains to compose poetry).[18]

The "girl" referred to is Ying-lien (also called Hsiang-ling), Chen Shih-yin's daughter, who is lost in chapter 1 and later becomes the concubine of Hsueh P'an. Chih-yen Chai is pointing out the fact that the story of Ying-lien, faintly alluded to in chapter 1, will receive further development in chapter 48. There Ying-lien lives with Pao-ch'ai in the Grand View Garden, and studies poetry with Pao-ch'ai and Tai-yu.[19] This example of fu hsien is also an example of parallelism in character

----

[13]ibid., p. 19, lines 2-7.

[14]ibid., p. 19, line 2.

[15]ming ken 命根. chap. 3, p. 33, line 11.

[16]ming ken 命根. chap. 2, p. 19, line 5.

[17]伏線

[18]Wu, On the Red Chamber Dream, p. 23. CYCHLMCP, chap. 1, p. 16, chia-hsu chia-p'i.

[19]See Wu's explanatory footnote, ibid., p. 23.

construction. As the poor scholar, Chia Yu-ts'un, is given financial support by his patron, Chen Shih-yin, so too the ignorant but
avid poetress, Ying-lien, is taught by the cultivated ladies, Pao-
ch'ai and Tai-yu.

In chapter 1, the creation myth exemplifies fu hsien. It is a
"major strand" of Dream of the Red Chamber which unravels into a
large number of "minor threads", or stories. Also in chapter 1, the
story of Chen Shih-yin and Chia Yu-ts'un appears. These characters
are of minor importance in the body of the novel, but they do serve
to set forth basic themes. At the end of Dream of the Red Chamber,
they come together to "tie up" various narrative threads into a neat
package.

In chapter 2, Chia Yu-ts'un mentions that he has tutored one Chen
Pao-yu. Periodically in the novel, this individual appears as the
image of Chia Pao-yu in physical appearance, and his opposite in
personality. Also in chapter 2, Leng Tzu-hsing suggests that Yuan-
ch'un, the eldest sister of Pao-yu, will be appointed Imperial
Concubine. This story develops fully in chapters 16, 17, and 18.

When Tai-yu goes to live with her mother's relatives (chapter 3),
she tells her grandmother, the Matriarch, that once a monk warned
her not to ever go to her grandmother's residence as she would become very ill. Tai-yu's life there in fact becomes one long tale
of sickness. This type of warning, followed by the realization of
that which is warned against, is a common form of fu hsien in the
novel. Another important thread in this chapter is the jade motif.
Pao-yu discovers that Tai-yu does not have a sacred talisman like
his jade, so he attempts to throw his away. The jade, and the
doomed love it symbolizes, receive constant attention in Dream of
the Red Chamber.

In chapter 4, Tai-yu walks about the Ning-kuo and Jung-kuo
mansions attempting to pay her respects to her relatives, but they
are occupied with other matters. This "thread of loneliness" in
chapter 4 leads to chapter 82. There Tai-yu dreams that her grandmother and Madame Wang, the mother of Pao-yu, arrive to tell
her that her father has re-married (actually, he dies early in the
novel). They also congratulate Tai-yu, for they tell her that she
is to marry a relative of her new step-mother, a man who is a wid-
ower. Tai-yu dreams that she begs help from her grandmother and
her mother's relatives, but everyone refuses to help. The other
thread in this chapter is the story of Hsueh P'an. Here we are introduced to his sensuality. He is also guilty of murder. The story of
his various crimes is a minor plot line in Dream of the Red Chamber.

Wave technique:

Another narrative technique, which we might identify as the "wave" or "ring" method, is also descriptive of the composition of the novel. Li Ch'en-tung is, I believe, the first person to describe this wave-like structure:

> Lorsque nous lisons le Songe du Pavillon Rouge, sa composition complexe et ses plans multiples nous jettent en pleine mer; à gauche et à droite, devant et derrière nous, partous nous entourent des grandes vagues montantes et descendantes; les grandes vagues avalant les petites et les petites devenant des grandes, nous nous étonnons parfois d'où finissent toutes ces vagues. Quand nous prendrons le bain de la mer montantes, chaque vague nous porte caresses et plaisirs et cette vague à peine finissant et l'autre continuant, nous voudrions que le bain fût sans fin, même aux dépens de notre fatigue.[20]

Professor Knoerle finds that this wave structure represents the basic rhythm of Dream of the Red Chamber, "thesis–arsis–thesis". Individuals and families rise and fall according to a wave pattern.[21]

The "outsider" approach:

A corollary of the fu hsien and wave techniques is the "outsider" or indirect approach. Kuo Lin-ko observes that Dream of the Red Chamber is written according to a plan which imitates the natural order.[22] That is, Kuo is referring to Ts'ao's presentation of the Chia family first indirectly through the comments and views of out-

----

[20]Li Ch'en-tung 李辰冬 (French romanization, Lee Ghen-Tong), "Etude sur Le Songe du Pavillon Rouge", Doctoral thesis, University of Paris, 1934, p. 113. Li's thesis is the earliest attempt to make a comparative study of the novel, Dream of the Red Chamber. He compares it to various works of Balzac, Cervantes, Shakespeare, Goethe, Dante, Tolstoy, and Dostoevsky. His examples from Western authors are uninformative and the comparisons are shallow. His thesis is, I believe, the basis for his well known study of Dream of the Red Chamber in Chinese, Hung-lou meng yen-chiu, 紅樓夢研究, Nanking, Cheng-chung shu-chu, 1946; Taipei, Hsin-hsing shu-chu, 1951, 1962.

The comparative studies of Sister Mary Gregory Knoerle and Professor Chuang Hsing-cheng have been cited earlier (see bibliography).

[21]Knoerle,"A Critical Analysis", pp. 135 and 143.

[22]Kuo Lin-ko, "Essai dur le Hong Leou Mong", p. 145.

siders. The framework of the novel introduces the central subjects. In chapter 2, for example, the conversation between Chia Yu-ts'un and Leng Tzu-hsing in which Leng tells Chia all he knows about the latter's "relatives" serves to introduce the reader to the various members of the Ning-kuo and Jung-kuo mansions. At the beginning of chapter 2 there is a comment in manuscripts of the novel which underscores the "outsider" approach:

> This chapter is also not the fundamental meaning of the main text. The reason why it introduces Leng Tsu-shing's speech on Lord Jung's House (i.e., the Chia Clan) is because the Chia Clan is so big and its population so great that if all the characters were to emerge directly from the author's pen, even one or two full chapters would not be sufficient to present the situation clearly. Therefore he 'borrows' this Leng Tsu-shing to give a brief preliminary hint of what is going to happen and thus prepare the reader's mind for that Mansion, so that later on Tai-yu and Pao-yu can be gradually portrayed . . . . This is the painter's 'three touches' technique.[23]

The "outsider" approach also represents a variation upon the theme of "true" chen and "false" chia. The information about the Chia household is more true when imparted by an outsider such as Leng Tzu-hsing than when it is given by one of the family members. Ts'ao repeatedly indicates that that which is intuitive, indirect, and rumored, is more viable than that which is objective, direct, and declared.

The same technique is applied in chapter 6 when another outsider, Liu Lao-lao, an adopted relative of Madame Wang,   decides to make use of her tenuous ties to the Chia family to see if she can wheedle some financial support from them. Ts'ao skillfully uses this country bumpkin to allow his readers to gain a more intimate knowledge of the personalities of the important female members of the Chia household, such as the Matriarch and Wang Hsi-feng. The same technique is applied in miniature in chapter 7. Madame Wang sends one of her servants, Chou Jui's wife, to deliver some imitation

---

[23]Wu Shih-ch'ang's translation and romanization, On the Red Chamber Dream, p. 66. CYCHLMCP, chap. 2, p. 24, from chia-hsu, chi-mao, keng-ch'en, and yu-cheng manuscripts. Wu does not believe this comment belongs to Chih-yen Chai, but to Ts'ao T'ang-ts'un. His view remains unproven.

flowers to Ying-ch'un, T'an-ch'un, Hsi-ch'un, Lin Tai-yu, and
Wang Hsi-feng. As the servant tours the Chia family compounds
carrying out her errand, the reader learns of various events in the
Chia household. Pao-ch'ai, for example, has an unusual disease,
the symptoms of which are shortness of breath and the remedy for
which is a marvelous elixir prescribed by an old Buddhist monk--
only mystic medicine can cure diseases inherited from a previous
life. We also learn that Ying-lien, Chen Shih-yin's kidnapped
daughter, is now a servant in the Hsueh household where she is the
concubine of Hsueh P'an. Chou Jui's wife's travels also allow the
author to describe a rare scene: Wang Hsi-feng is found tittering
in sexual play with her husband, Chia Lien, while their baby sleeps.
We also discover that Leng Tzu-hsing is in trouble with the law.
Finally, when the flowers are delivered to Lin Tai-yu, we receive
our first glimpse of the latter's perverse personality. She scorns
the flowers since others have received the same present and Tai-yu
resents that she is also the last person to get them.

Character presentation in the form of parallelism, opposites, and
typology:
  When we turn to character presentation, we find that there are
three basic narrative techniques: characters are parallel to one
another, or they are opposites, or they are typological; that is,
one character may represent an early example or pattern of a character type which is encountered subsequently in the novel. In the
"Mimesis" chapter, we note that Chen Shih-yin and Chia Yu-ts'un,
as well as Chen Pao-yu and Chia Pao-yu, exemplify typological
and pairing techniques. Yu P'ing-po notes that Chen Shih-yin of
chapter 1 is an early image or type of what Chia Pao-yu is to become in the closing chapters of Dream of the Red Chamber. Pao-yu
suffers, learns the meaninglessness of desire, and abandons the
world to become an otherworldly saint.[24]

----

[24]Yu P'ing-po, Hung-lou meng yen-chiu, p. 8. Yu notes that
in a letter to him from Ku Chieh-kang, the latter stated that the
ending of the novel, which both Yu and Ku feel is by Kao E, is
appropriate. Ku believes that Pao-yu is probably a parallel to
Chen Shih-yin, and therefore it is appropriate that he proceeds
from a high position to a low one and goes off with the Taoist and
Buddhist otherworldly figures at the end of the novel. Enlightenment means unconcern for worldly affairs. Yu, ibid., p. 148.

Chen Shih-yin's daughter, Ying-lien, is a prototype of Lin Tai-yu. We have noted already that the fathers of the two girls are visited by monks who declare that their daughters are ill-fated. The Ying-lien episode in chapter 1 is a forecast of the story of Lin Tai-yu.

Appendix C: SYNCHRONICITY

The following is an outline of key examples of synchronicity, "meaningful chance", in <u>Dream of the Red Chamber</u>. It is intended to document our assertion that the concept of time in the novel involves the union of chance and predestination and that the aesthetic pattern of the work may be understood in part in terms of synchronicity.

<u>HLMPSHCP</u>, chap. 2, p. 15:
The promotion and demotion of Chia Yu-ts'un in official circles is presented as a matter of chance. His ill luck then forces him into contact with the Chia clan, thus allowing the reader an intimate view of the inside of the Chia household.

<u>HLMPSHCP</u>, chap. 2, pp. 14-16:
These pages are dominated by "by chance" vocabulary. Chen Shih-yin's maid, Chiao-hsing, happens to look at Chia Yu-ts'un when he is visiting Chen and this glance leads to her later marriage with Chia. Chia unexpectedly passes the Civil Service Examinations and is appointed to office: just as unexpectedly, he is dismissed from office. He happens to travel to the province of Lin Ju-hai, the father of Tai-yu. By chance he falls ill and resides in that province. Thus he happens to meet friends who tell him that Lin Ju-hai is looking for a tutor for his daughter. After Chia becomes

Tai-yu's tutor, her mother happens to die. Thus Tai-yu cannot
study, and Chia has free time to stroll about on excursions in the
country. Whereupon he happens to meet Leng Tzu-hsing and learns
of life in the Chia family. Because of the unexpected death of
Tai-yu's mother, Chia Yu-ts'un is unexpectedly asked to take Tai-
yu to her mother's relatives, and thus Chia Yu-ts'un gains entrance
into the coveted Chia household and is enabled to secure a job
from Chia Cheng, the father of Pao-yu.

HLMPSHCP, chap. 2, p. 13:
  Here we find an example of the author's strange sense of good
fortune. Chiao-hsing, Chen Shih-yin's maid, becomes "lucky".
She is chosen by Chia Yu-ts'un to be his concubine. But soon after
he takes her, his first wife "luckily" dies, thus allowing Chiao-
hsing to become the number one wife.

HLMPSHCP, chap. 4, pp. 38ff:
  The entire episode in which occurs the mortal conflict between
Hsueh P'an and Feng Yuan is described in the vocabulary of chance.
But of course the episode harks back to chapter 1, in which Chen
Shih-yin is warned that his daughter, Ying-lien, is "ill-fated".
In chapter 4, she turns out to be the source for the fight between
Hsueh and Feng. Various characters, such as Chia Yu-ts'un, com-
ment that the whole episode appears to be a matter of chance, but
is in fact one of predestination and retribution.

HLMPSHCP, chap. 5, p. 48:
  When Pao-yu falls asleep in his niece's (Ch'in K'o-ch'ing) bedroom and dreams that he is visiting the Great Void Illusion Realm,
the fairy who leads him there informs him that the whole experience
is hardly a matter of chance. The dream is predestined.

HLMPSHCP, chap. 6, p. 68:
  Wang Hsi-feng learns from Madame Wang that she is not really
related to Liu Lao-lao. Their grandfathers happened to have worked
together, and since the two had the same surname, Liu's grandfather
had himself "adopted" into the family. But the "by chance" relationship between Liu Lao-lao and the Matriarch of the Chia clan
turns out to be of extreme importance to the happiness of its members.

HLMPSHCP, chap. 7, p. 72ff:
  A typical example of the view of medicine in the novel. A pre-
scription is made up by luck and chance. Like social codes, medi-
cal formulae are set in motion "by chance".

HLMPSHCP, chap. 8, p. 85:
  Pao-yu observes that, miraculously, his amulet and that of Pao-
ch'ai are pairs and they have the same inscriptions on them. In
fact the words on both amulets have been inscribed by a scabby
headed Buddhist monk. In other words, the amulets are an obvious
symbol of mutual destinies.

HLMPSHCP, chap. 9, p. 96:
  Here occurs the incident of homosexual love among the boys of the
Chia family school. One of the points of the episode is that it
would not have occurred except for the "by chance" need of the
head of the school, Chia Tai-ju, to leave temporarily on an errand.

HLMPSHCP, chap. 11, pp. 115 and 117:
  Chia Jui, who is madly in love with Wang Hsi-feng, insists that
their chance meeting is really a matter of destiny. The latter re-
sponds by using the "destined" meeting to make a complete fool of
Chia Jui.
  In another incident in the same chapter, Ch'in K'o-ch'ing sees
her coming death as a matter of the inevitable. Other women pretend everything will be all right, but actually they feel helpless
before an impending disaster. Death is nearly always viewed in
Dream of the Red Chamber as a matter of "meaningful chance".

HLMPSHCP, chap. 12, p. 122:
  The climax of the Chia Jui affair with Wang Hsi-feng is an episode
of "by chance". A bucket of human excrement is dumped over a
wall and "amazingly" it happens to fall on the head of Chia Jui
while he is waiting for his "love", Wang Hsi-feng. The whole incident exemplifies Ts'ao's play on the synchronicity archetype, for
Chia Jui's bad luck is, of course, a matter of destiny; that is, the
whole thing has been quite deliberately planned by Wang Hsi-feng.

HLMPSHCP, chap. 15, p. 148:
  Here occurs the love affair between Ch'in Chung, Ch'in K'o-
ch'ing's brother, and a Buddhist nun. Ts'ao makes great use of the
phrase, "who would expect?", for every reader expects the affair
to take place since the author has skillfully set it up.

HLMPSHCP, chap. 16, pp. 151 and 154:
  The "by chance" love of Ch'in Chung for a nun becomes an affair
of retribution. He brings the nun home and is discovered by his
father. The latter then dies after beating Ch'in Chung and after becoming distraught over his fortune. Ch'in Chung subsequently becomes ill and dies. The episode is prefaced by the phrase, "who

would expect?". The point is that disastrous results are expected
in a case of debauchery; indeed, they are destined to occur.

Synchronicity dominates the lives of Wang Hsi-feng and her husband, Chia Lien. A series of "by chance" comments coming from
Wang Hsi-feng's maid, P'ing-erh, allow Wang Hsi-feng to protect
her secret sources of income, but also force her to allow her husband to take on a new concubine.

HLMPSHCP, chap. 21, p. 213:
  Tai-yu's accidental discovery of the fact that Pao-yu has been
reading Chuang-tzu allows her to gain useful insight into his character.

HLMPSHCP, chap. 22, pp. 217 and 222:
  "Who would expect?" the Matriarch to show favor to Pao-ch'ai,
as she does? In fact, Pao-ch'ai is favored to marry Pao-yu. In
another episode, Tai-yu discovers a poem by Pao-yu which she
shows to Hsiang-yun and Pao-ch'ai. Again chance leads to an encounter with destiny.

HLMPSHCP, chap. 23, p. 233:
  Pao-yu is here temporarily very happy, but his happiness unexpectedly leads to unhappiness. This, of course, belongs to the
pattern of opposites. Everything is destined to turn into its opposite,
and there is seldom an apparent cause.

HLMPSHCP, chap. 25, p. 250:
  Pao-yu falls in love with Hsiao-hung. Another "who would expect?" episode which, given the character of Pao-yu, is completely
expectable.

HLMPSHCP, chap. 28, p. 285ff:
  The "Flower Burial Song" episode. Pao-yu happens to overhear
Tai-yu singing a song about burying fallen flowers. This fortuitous
event causes him to speculate on the destined passing of both the
garden world and his own family.

HLMPSHCP, chap. 29, p. 309:
  Pao-yu is unexpectedly (read "expectedly") upset when he happens
to meet a Taoist, Chang Tao-shih, who speaks to him of his destined
marriage with Pao-ch'ai.

HLMPSHCP, chap. 30, p. 322:
  Pao-yu accidentally destroys those he loves. Here he inadvertently
kicks his maid, Hsi-jen, and causes her to spit blood. He is a "by
chance" agent of the mutability he abhors.

HLMPSHCP, chap. 32, p. 339:
The supposedly unexpected death of Chin Ch'uan is completely expected.

HLMPSHCP, chap. 36, pp. 373 and 378:
People know the future, but refuse to believe in it. In a dream, Pao-yu says he refuses to believe in the destiny of jade and gold (that is, his fated marriage with Pao-ch'ai).

HLMPSHCP, chap. 42, p. 443ff:
The belief in the importance of chance is underscored in an episode in which Wang Hsi-feng is engaged in fortune telling to cure illness.

HLMPSHCP, chap. 45, p. 481:
Tai-yu tells Pao-ch'ai that health, life and death, wealth and poverty are all matters of fate. Human effort is useless (yet, she fights against fate to win the love of Pao-yu).

HLMPSHCP, chap. 57, pp. 634-635:
Madame Hsueh explains to Pao-ch'ai and Tai-yu that marriage is fated.

HLMPSHCP, chap. 63, p. 704:
Pao-yu's accidental encounter with a friend of the nun, Miao-yu, leads to special knowledge of her.

HLMPSHCP, chap. 67, p. 744:
A typical emphasis on destiny. Pao-ch'ai explains the sad fate of San-chieh and Liu Hsiang-lien by blaming it on a previous life.

HLMPSHCP, chap. 68, p. 761:
The unexpected cruelty of Wang Hsi-feng's maids towards San-chieh is, of course, entirely expected.

HLMPSHCP, chap. 76, p. 856:
A repeated motif is that one cannot prepare for or do anything about the future. Here, the Matriarch remarks on the drastic changes which have taken place in her household. Everything is unexpected and unaccountable. To the Matriarch, change is the great fact of life.

HLMPSHCP, chap. 83:
An unhappy experience of Pao-yu's parallels Tai-yu's nightmare. The chance parallel is actually a destined sharing of fate.

HLMPSHCP, chap. 86:
It is rumored that Yuan-ch'un has died. But her horoscope says she will not die until a certain date, and that date has not yet arrived. The rumor then turns out to be false.

HLMPSHCP, chap. 93:
The sudden unexpected story of Chen Pao-yu which has been "destined" to be told since the beginning of the novel.

HLMPSHCP, chap. 94:
The loss of Pao-yu's jade and the difficulty in finding it is said to be unexpected. The event is in fact destined.

HLMPSHCP, chap. 106:
Even Chia Cheng believes that the confiscation of his property takes place because the faults of himself and his family must be answered with retribution.

HLMPSHCP, chap. 114:
The prediction of fate is no guarantee that one is right. Hsi-jen tries to insist that her correct prediction (via fortune telling) of the fate of Wang Hsi-feng is purely a matter of chance. She does not know her own fate, how can she know that of someone else?

HLMPSHCP, chap. 115:
Chai Pao-yu meets Chen Pao-yu and becomes deathly ill from the encounter. It is said that no one would expect that from that day on Pao-yu would become more of a fool.

HLMPSHCP, chap. 116:
Once again Pao-yu visits the Great Void Illusion Realm. All the events are described in terms of chance.

HLMPSHCP, chap. 120:
The truth is revealed. Chen Shih-yin informs Chia Yu-ts'un that good fortune in life is not a matter of chance, but of destiny. Having gained this kind of enlightenment, Chia unexpectedly (again read, "expectedly") falls asleep and remains uninterested in the desires of the world.

Appendix D: ALLUSIONS IN CHEN SHIH-YIN'S SONG COMMENTARY TO THE HAO-LIAO KO

According to Chih-yen Chai's interlinear comments, stanza one in Chen Shih-yin's song refers to the decline of the Ning-kuo and Jung-kuo mansions and to the ultimate vacancy of the living quarters of such persons as Tai-yu.[1] The covered over windows describe families such as that of Chia Yu-ts'un.[2] The fragrant powder and thick cream of stanza two refer to Hsueh Pao-ch'ai and Shih Hsiang-yun, while the temples which became grey like hoar-frost describe Lin Tai-yu and the maid-servant of Pao-yu, Ch'ing-wen.[3] Apparently, Ts'ao's point here is that while all four of these women were beautiful, even the use of rare cosmetics could not save Tai-yu and Ch'ing-wen from premature deaths, metaphorically represented by the image of greying temples.

Wu Shih-ch'ang strenuously objects to this interpretation, perhaps because of his sometime literal mindedness. Wu translates the lines from stanza two as follows: "While rouge was still thick and powder still fragrant, / How was it that the hairs on the temples turned hoary".[4] Since Tai-yu and Ch'ing-wen died prematurely,

----

[1]CYCHLMCP, chap. 1, p. 21.
[2]CYCHLMCP, chap. 1, p. 21.
[3]CYCHLMCP, chap. 1, p. 21.
[4]On the Red Chamber Dream, pp. 169-170, 187.

they could not have had grey hair, says Wu, and therefore the line about temples turning to hoarfrost could not refer to them. He believes that this line and the one immediately preceding it describe Pao-ch'ai and Hsiang-yun. Wu asserts that the mistake originates with Yu P'ing-po who did not have a copy of the chia-hsu pen when he compiled his CYCHLMCP. Since the Chih-yen Chai commentary from the chia-hsu pen was transcribed onto another manuscript, the chi-mao pen, Yu used the latter. But, says Wu, the Chih-yen Chai commentary in the latter does not appear in the places where it is found in the chia-hsu pen. Therefore, Mr. Yu's CYCHLMCP places Chih-yen Chai's commentary in the wrong places in, for example, Chen Shih-yin's song.

The problem is Mr. Wu's. As he himself admits,[5] he did not have access to a copy of the chia-hsu pen either when he was writing On the Red Chamber Dream, as the chia-hsu pen was then still in the private possession of Dr. Hu Shih. In my copy of the chia-hsu pen (Hu Shih allowed the chia-hsu pen to be reproduced soon after On the Red Chamber Dream was published), Chih-yen Chai's commentary appears in exactly the same places as it does in Mr. Yu's CYCHLMCP. The final source of the problem probably lies with the scribes who copied Chih-yen Chai's commentaries. Since none of the extant copies of the manuscripts and commentaries on the novel are originals, but merely copies of the originals, the scribes themselves may have placed Chih-yen Chai's commentary in the wrong places.

The line about the love-birds under the crimson lanterned canopy refers to Wang Hsi-feng, according to Chih-yen Chai.[6] There are moments in the novel which indicate, as Wu Shih-ch'ang notes, that P'ing-erh, Hsi-feng's maid, is considered to be superior to her mistress. Perhaps Ts'ao intended that after Hsi-feng's death, P'ing-erh was to become Chia Lien's wife. The two lines about "white bones" and "love-birds" could refer to the fact that Hsi-feng often caused the death of others, especially female rivals, but that no sooner did she get rid of one ("white bones"), than there was another beloved of her husband ("love-birds").

Wu Shih-ch'ang[7] says that this line about "love-birds" refers to the wedding of Pao-ch'ai while the preceding line about the burial

---

[5]On the Red Chamber Dream, pp. xv, 12.
[6]CYCHLMCP, chap. 1, p. 21.
[7]On the Red Chamber Dream, p. 169.

of "white bones" refers to the death of Tai-yu. We translates these
lines as follows: "Yesterday white bones were sent to the yellow-
earth mountains, / Today the love-birds sleep under red lanterns
inside the curtains". Wu notes the close connection in the novel
between the death of Tai-yu and the marriage of Pao-ch'ai. He
feels this is a matter of Mr. Yu's misplacing the Chih-yen Chai
commentary. Again, Yu did not, in fact, make a mistake.[8]

According to Chih-yen Chai, the "boxes of gold" and "boxes of
silver" in stanza three represent individuals such as Chia Pao-yu
and Chen Pao-yu.[9] The meaning of this stanza seems to be that
those who are in the possession of enormous wealth may suddenly
one day become beggars scorned by the world. Chih-yen Chai apparently is suggesting in identifying this stanza with Chen and Chia
Pao-yu that these two sons of illustrious families will one day be
destitute. Both the Chen and the Chia families have their properties confiscated by imperial order.[10] When Chen Pao-yu first meets
Chia Pao-yu, he tells the latter of his experience of poverty.[11]

Wu translates the latter part of stanza three as: "While deploring
another's short-lived life, / How could she have known that / She
would have to lose her own life on returning home?"[12] While
there is no indication in the Chinese original of the "she" Wu uses,
his suggestion that these lines refer to Wang Hsi-feng is interesting.
The "short-lived life", says Wu, refers to Ch'in K'o-ch'ing, Pao-yu's
niece, who dies prematurely in chapter 13. On the basis of his
study of the Chih-yen Chai commentary, Wu believes these lines
suggest that Wang Hsi-feng was divorced by her husband, Chia Lien,
and that she died on her return to her parents' home in Chin-ling.

Chih-yen Chai says stanza four refers to children's fates after the
deaths of their parents. He cites as an example Liu Hsiang-lien,
the actor friend of Hsueh P'an and Pao-yu who, while being born
into a family of the nobility, was orphaned at an early age. He

----

[8]In On the Red Chamber Dream, p. 177, Wu records those places
in Dream of the Red Chamber where P'ing-erh appears superior; on
pp. 173-174, he records the individuals Hsi-feng causes to die.
[9]CYCHLMCP, chap. 1, p. 21.
[10]Report of Chen family decline is mentioned in chapter 92;
Chia family property is confiscated in chapter 105.
[11]Chapter 115, p. 356, line 2ff.
[12]On the Red Chamber Dream, p. 178.

became fond of amateur acting and liked to play female roles.[13]
    Wu Shih-ch'ang says that the stanza describes Chia Huan and that
the reference to Liu Hsiang-lien is a mistake.[14] Wu translates the
stanza as follows: "Even though his family discipline was strict, /
There is no guarantee that / In later life [his son] would not degenerate into banditry". Wu gives the following reasons why he believes the song commentary could not be referring to Liu Hsiang-
lien: the other verses all refer to Chia clan members and Liu was
not related; he was an amateur actor and therefore was unlikely to
have had strict family discipline or to have received a Confucian
education; no parents are mentioned in the novel; he joins a
Buddhist monastery in the end,[15] i.e., he does not become a bandit. Wu also says that the phrase translated as "discipline" surely
refers to Chia Cheng's Confucian education. In other words, Chia
Cheng was strict towards his son Chia Huan, but the latter nevertheless became a bandit when he robbed the Chia family.
    Actually stanza four may well refer to Liu Hsiang-lien. In chap-
ter 47 of the Yu P'ing-po collated edition of the novel,[16] we are
told that Liu was born of an aristocratic family, but because he did
not study hard, and because his parents died when he was very
young, he became a person who liked to be an amateur actor who
played female roles. In other words, Liu is an example of a child
who turns out badly despite his parents' desires--there is no recourse
when parents die prematurely. Furthermore, "banditry" may fit
Liu. In chapter 66, Liu rescues Hsueh P'an from bandits, and Hsueh
P'an says: "Unexpectedly Second Brother Liu arrived from over
there and chased away the bandits".[17] That is, there is a very
faint suggestion in these words, perhaps, "unexpectedly" and "over
there" that Liu is associated with the bandits. How else is it possible for him to singlehandedly drive away a band of robbers and
to rescue Hsueh P'an? If we translate ch'iang liang,[18] "banditry",
as "dominating" or "overbearing", stanza four still may apply to
Liu. In chapter 66, Liu promises Chia Lien that he will marry one
Yu San-chieh, whom he has learned is in love with him. However,

---

13CYCHLMCP, chap. 1, p. 22.
14On the Red Chamber Dream, p. 294, footnotes 6 and 7.
15Chapter 66.
16HLMPSHCP, chap. 47, p. 504.
17HLMPSHCP, chap. 66, p. 739.
18 強梁.

he reneges on his promise for he cannot understand why he should
be pursued by a girl he does not know. He suspects she is not a
virgin and he tells Pao-yu that everyone, including the cats and
dogs, is impure and defiled in the Chia household. Liu insists on
believing the worst about Yu San-chieh. Thus, Liu's actions prove
him to be "overbearing".

Chih-yen Chai makes no comment about the lines: "daughter
well-bred / well may she be into Flower Lane led", but Wu Shih-
ch'ang suggests they refer to Ch'iao-chieh, who was pampered as
a child since she was the only daughter of Wang Hsi-feng. She
was very delicate and particular about what she ate. Wu believes
Wang Hsi-feng's brother and Chia Jung sold Ch'iao-chieh to a
brothel after the death of Wang Hsi-feng. From there she was rescued by Liu Lao-lao who was grateful to Hsi-feng for giving her
money early in the novel.[19] Ch'iao-chieh was to go to Liu's village and marry Liu's grandson Pao-erh according to Wu's restoration
of Ts'ao's original plan. As the novel now stands in the Kao E
printed editions, Ch'iao-chieh marries a wealthy man's son who has
passed the First Degree. Wu translates the corresponding lines from
stanza four as follows: "How could one expect that she who was
once fastidious even with / delicacies / Would sink into the 'land
of misty flowers' (i.e., brothel)?"[20]

The first two lines of stanza five Chih-yen Chai identifies with
such persons as Chia She and Chia Yu-ts'un, while the second half
he identifies with such persons as Chia Lan and Chia Chun.[21] I am
not sure why these lines are appropriate to Chia Lan and Chia Chun.
Wu says that the first lines of the stanza refer to chapter 48 of the
novel where there is the story of Chia She who coveted the picture-
fans of a poor student known as Shih the Idiot. Chia Yu-ts'un had
Shih arrested and the fans were given to Chia She. On the basis
of his study of the Chih-yin Chai commentary, Wu says that Ts'ao
planned that Chia She and Chia Yu-ts'un would be arrested for
their actions and that Chou Ju-ch'ang rightly says that these actions
were one cause of the downfall of the Chia clan.[22] Wu translates
these lines as follows: "Some resented that their official caps were
too small, / Consequently they had to wear locks and cangues".

----

[19]HLMPSHCP, chap. 6.
[20]On the Red Chamber Dream, pp. 183-185.
[21]CYCHLMCP, chap. 1, p. 23, chia-hsu mei-p'i.
[22]On the Red Chamber Dream, pp. 163-164.

BIBLIOGRAPHY OUTLINE

Bibliography

This bibliography contains the Chinese and western language sources consulted in the course of the present study. It reflects both an interest in determining how Dream of the Red Chamber has been read within the Chinese critical and scholarly tradition, and an effort to approach the novel from the point of view of western literary criticism. There is a good deal of Japanese writing on Dream of the Red Chamber, but having gone through some of it, I have found little that is directly relevant to this study. Due to my own limitations in reading Japanese, it is impractical at present to offer a comprehensive survey of Japanese scholarship on Dream of the Red Chamber. Students of Japanese will find that the Itō bibliography, cited below, is a useful introduction to available material in that language. It is with them in mind that I have included this item in the bibliography.

1. Bibliographies

Bibliography of Asian Studies 1971. Association for Asian Studies, Inc., 1973.

Chang, Ch'un 章群 , ed. Min-kuo hsueh-shu lun-wen so-yin 民國學術論文索引 . Taipei: Chung-hua wen-hua ch'u-pan shih-yen wei-yuan-hui, 1954.

Ch'en, T'ieh-fan 陳鐵凡 . "Hung-lou meng wai-wen i-i shu-lueh" 紅樓夢外文迻譯述略 , Ta-lu tsa-chih 大陸雜誌 , XXXI:vii (Oct., 1965), 1-6.

Ch'ien, Hsing-ts'un 錢杏邨 (I-su 一粟). Hung-lou meng shu-lu 紅樓夢書錄 . Shanghai: Ku-tien wen hsueh ch'u-pan she, 1958.

Cordier, Henri, ed. Bibliotheca Sinica. rev. ed., 4 vols. Paris, 1904-08.

—————Supplementary vol., Paris, 1924.

—————Supplement: Author Index. New York: Columbia University East Asiatic Library, 1953.

Cumulative Bibliography of Asian Studies 1941-1965. Boston: Association for Asian Studies, 1969.

—————1966-1970. Boston: Association for Asian Studies, 1973.

Davidson, Martha, ed. A List of Published Translations from Chinese into English, French, and German. 2 vols. Ann Arbor, 1952.

de Bary, William Theodore and Ainslie T. Embree, eds. A Guide to Oriental Classics. New York & London, 1964.

Franke, Herbert. Sinologie. Bern, 1953.

Hsia, C.T. The Classic Chinese Novel. New York & London, 1968. pp. 387-399.

Hucker, Charles O. China: A Critical Bibliography. Tucson, 1962.

Itō, Sōhei 伊藤漱平 , ed. "Kōrōmū Kenkyū Nihongo Bunken-Shiryō Mokuroku" 紅樓夢研究日本語文獻資料目錄 , Min-shin bungaku gengo kenkyūkai kaihō 明清文學言語研究會會報 , No. 6 (December, 1964).

Li, Tien-yi, ed. Chinese Fiction: A Bibliography of Books and Articles in Chinese and English. New Haven, 1968.

—————The History of Chinese Literature: A Selected Bibliography. (Sinological Series, No. 15). New Haven, 1968.

Liu, Ts'un-yan. Chinese Popular Fiction in Two London Libraries. Hong Kong, 1967.

Lust, John, ed. Index Sinicus. Cambridge, England, 1964.

Research Group on the Hung-lou meng, ed., (Chinese Department, New Asia College, Hong Kong Chinese University), Hung-lou meng yen-chiu chuan-k'an 紅樓夢研究專刊 , "Hung-lou meng shu-mu pu-i" 紅樓夢書目補遺 , No. 4 (Sept., 1968), 73-78.

—————P'an, Ch'ung-kuei 潘重規 . "Chin-erh hung-hsueh" 今日紅學 . No. 7 (Jan., 1970), 111-117.

_____ "Hsiang-kang Hung-lou meng yen-chiu tzu-liao so-yin ch'u-kao" 香港紅樓夢研究資料索引初稿, No. 8 (Sept., 1970), 53-63.

Revue Bibliographique de Sinologie. Paris, 1955--.

Sun, Tien-ch'i 孫殿起 . Ch'ing-tai chin-shu chih-chien lu, 清代禁書知見錄. Shanghai: Shang-wu yin-shu-kuan, 1957.

Teng, Ssu-yu and Knight Biggerstaff, eds. An Annotated Bibliography of Selected Chinese Reference Works. 3rd ed. Cambridge, Mass., 1971.

Wu, Shih-ch'ang 吳世昌 . "Hung-lou meng te hsi-wen i-wen ho lun-wen" 紅樓夢的西文譯文和論文, Wen-hsueh i-ch'an tseng-k'an 文學遺產增刊, 9 (June, 1962), 137-150.

_____ On the Red Chamber Dream: A Critical Study of Two Annotated Manuscripts of the 18th Century. "Bibliography A: Translation of and Works on The Red Chamber Dream in Western Languages," pp. 359-362. Oxford, 1961.

Wylie, A. Notes on Chinese Literature. Shanghai, 1922.

Yang, Winston L., ed. A Bibliography of the Chinese Language. New York, 1966.

Yao, Chin-yuan 姚覲元. Ch'ing-tai chin-hui shu-mu ssu-chung so-yin 清代禁燬書目四種索引. Shanghai: Wan-yu wen-k'u, 1937.

_____ Ch'ing-tai chin-hui shu-mu pu-i 清代禁燬書目補遺 . Shanghai: Shang-wu yin-shu-kuan, 1957.

Yuan, Tung-li, ed. China in Western Literature. New Haven, 1958.

II. Dream of the Red Chamber Editions & Commentaries Used in this Study

Ch'ien-lung ch'ao pen pai-nien-hui Hung-lou meng kao 乾隆抄本百廿回紅樓夢稿 . Fan Ning 范寧 , ed. Peking: Chung-hua shu-chu, 1963.

Ch'ien-lung chia-hsu Chih-yen Chai ch'ung-p'ing Shih-t'ou chi 乾隆甲戌脂硯齋重評石頭記. Hu Shih 胡適 , ed. 2 vols. Taipei: Shang-wu yin-shu-kuan, 1961.

Chih-yen Chai ch'ung-p'ing Shih-t'ou chi 脂硯齋重評石頭記 . Yu P'ing-po 俞平伯 , ed. 2 vols. Peking: Wen-hsueh ku-chi k'an-hsing she, 1955.

Chih-yen Chai Hung-lou meng chi-p'ing 脂硯齋紅樓夢輯評 . Yu P'ing-po 俞平伯 , ed. Revised ed. Shanghai: Chung-hua shu-chu, 1963.

Hung-lou meng 紅樓夢 . (reprint: Kao E 高鶚 & Ch'eng
   Wei-yuan 程偉元 120 chapter 1792 edition). Hong Kong:
   Shih-chieh shu-chu, 1960.
Hung-lou meng pa-shih hui chiao-pen 紅樓夢八十回校本 .
   Yu P'ing-po 俞平伯 , ed. Peking: Jen-min wen-hsueh
   ch'u-pan she, 1958.

III. Chinese Scholarship on Dream of the Red Chamber Used in
    this Study

Chang, Ai-ling 張愛玲 . "Hung-lou meng wei wan" 紅樓
夢未完 , Huang-kuan 皇冠 , XXX:iv (Dec., 1968),
   86-115.
Chang, Tai 張戴 . "Lun Hung-lou meng te shih-tai pei-ching
   ho Ts'ao Hsueh-ch'in te ch'uang-tso ssu-hsiang" 論紅樓夢
的時代背景和曹雪芹的創作思想 , Hsin
chien-she 新建設 , 3 (March, 1955), 32-37.
Chao, I-sheng 趙儷生 . "Lun Ch'ing chung-yeh Yang-chou
   hua-p'ai chung te i-tuan t'e-chih" 論清中葉揚州畫派
中的異端特質 , Wen-shih-che 文史哲 , 2 (Feb.,
   1956), 57-61.
Chao, Kang 趙岡 . "Ch'iao-chien te nien-ling wen-ti" 巧
姐的年齡問題 , Tzu-yu Chung-kuo 自由中國 ,
   XXII:iv (Feb., 1960), 20.
      "Chih-yen Chai yu Hung-lou meng" 脂硯齋與紅樓夢 ,
   Ta-lu tsa-chih 大陸雜誌 , XX:ii (Jan., 1960), 8-12;
   XX:iii (Feb., 1960), 23-26; XX:iv (Feb., 1960), 22-30.
      & Ch'en Chung-i 陳鍾毅 . Hung-lou meng hsin-t'an 紅
樓夢新探 . Hong Kong, 1970.
      Hung-lou meng k'ao-cheng shih-i 紅樓夢考證拾遺 .
   Hong Kong: Kao-yuan ch'u-pan she, 1963.
      "Kao E cheng-li Hung-lou meng hou ssu-shih-hui te ch'ing-
   hsing" 高鶚整理紅樓夢後四十回的情形 , Min-chu
p'ing-lun 民主評論 , XI:vi (March, 1960), 19-22.
      "Lun Ch'ien-lung ch'ao-pen pai-nien-hui Hung-lou meng
   kao" 論乾隆抄本百廿回紅樓夢稿 , Ta-lu tsa-chih
大陸雜誌 , XXVIII:vi (March, 1964), 8-14.
      "Lun chin-pen Hung-lou meng te hou ssu-shih-hui" 論今
本紅樓夢的後四十回 , Tzu-yu Chung-kuo 自由
中國 , XXII:vi (March, 1960), 23-26; XXII:vii (Apr.,
   1960), 21-24.

"Lun Hung-lou meng hou ssu-shih-hui te chu-che" 論紅樓夢後四十回的著者 , Wen-hsueh tsa-chih 文學雜誌 , VII:iv (Dec., 1959), 4-19.

"Lun Hung-lou meng ku-shih te ti-tien shih-chien yu jen-wu" 論紅樓夢故事的地點與時間人物 Yu-shih hsueh-pao 幼獅學報 , II:ii (Apr., 1960), 1-15.

"Yu-kuan Ts'ao Hsueh-ch'in te liang-chien-shih" 有關曹雪芹的兩件事 , Ta-lu tsa-chih 大陸雜誌 , XIX:vi (Sept., 1959), 16-21.

Ch'en, Chan-jo 陳湛若 . "Lueh-lun Hung-lou meng she-hui pei-ching" 略論紅樓夢社會背景 , Wen-shih-che 文史哲 , 4 (Apr., 1956), 32-44.

Ch'en, Ch'ing-hao 陳慶浩 . "Hung-lou meng Chih-p'ing chih yen-chiu" 紅樓夢脂評之研究, Hung-lou meng yen-chiu chuan-k'an 紅樓夢研究專刊 , Research Group on the Hung-lou meng, ed., Chinese Department, New Asia College, Hong Kong Chinese University, Nos. 5 & 6 (Jan., July, 1969).

Ch'en Chung-ch'ih 陳仲箎 . "Chih-yen Chai ch'ung-p'ing Shih-tou chi chih-t'an" 脂硯齋重評石頭記撫談 , T'u-shu-kuan 圖書館 , 3 (Sept., 1963), 31-35, 47.

"T'an chi-mao-pen Chih-yen Chai ch'ung-p'ing Shih-tou chi" 談己卯本脂硯齋重評石頭記, Wen-wu 文物 , 6 (June, 1963), 10-20.

Chen-Fu 振甫 . "T'ung-kuo tui Hung-lou meng yen-chiu te p'i-p'an lai jen-shih yueh-tu ku-tien tso-p'in" 通過對紅樓夢研究的批判來認識閱讀古典作品 , Yu-wen hsueh-hsi 語文學習 , No. 40 (Jan., 1955), 7-13.

Ch'en, Nai 陳鼐 & Ho, Ch'i-fang 何其芳 . "Kuan-yu Ts'ao Hsueh-ch'in te min-chu ssu-hsiang wen-t'i" 關於曹雪芹的民主思想問題 , Wen-hsueh p'ing-lun 文學評論 . 2 (Apr., 1964), 72-75.

Ch'en, Ting-hung 陳定閎 . "Kuan-yu Hung-lou meng chung chih chung chi ch'i-t'a" 關於紅樓夢中之鐘及其他 , Tung-fang tsa-chih 東方雜誌 , XL:xxi (Nov., 1944), 42-43.

Ch'en, Wei-mo 陳煒謨 . "Kuan-yu Hung-lou meng p'ing-chia te chi-ko wen-t'i" 關於紅樓夢評價的幾個問題 , Ssu-ch'uan ta-hsueh-pao (she-hui k'o-hsueh) 四川大學報 (社會科學), 2 (June, 1955), 91-116.

Ch'en, Yu-p'i 陳毓羆 . "Hung-lou meng shih tsen-yang k'ai-t'ou te" 紅樓夢是怎樣開頭的 Wen-shih 文史 , 3 (Oct., 1963), 333-338.

"Ts'ao Hsueh-ch'in tsu-nien wen-t'i te tsai shang-ch'ueh" 曹雪芹卒年問題的再商榷 , Kuang-ming jih-pao 光明日報 , (June 10, 1962).

———— "Yu-kuan Ts'ao Hsueh-ch'in tsu-nien wen-t'i te shang-ch'ueh" 有關曹雪芹卒年問題的商榷 , Kuang-ming jih-pao 光明日報 , (Apr. 8, 1962).

Cheng, Chen-to 鄭振鐸 . Wen-hsueh ta-kang 文學大綱 . Shanghai, 1927.

Cheng, Hsueh-chia 鄭學稼 . "Hung-lou meng shih-chien te yin-kuo" 紅樓夢事件的因果 , Min-chu p'ing-lun 民主評論 , VI:vii (Apr., 1955), 12-15.

Chia, I-chih 賈宜之 . "Ts'ao Hsueh-ch'in te chi-kuan pu shih Feng-jun" 曹雪芹的籍貫不是豐潤 , Wen-hsueh i-ch'an tseng-k'an 文學遺產增刊 , 5 (Dec., 1957), 318-328.

Chiang, Ho-sen 蔣和森 . "Chia Pao-yu lun" 賈寶玉論 , Jen-min wen-hsueh 人民文學 , No. 80 (June, 1956), 42-58.

———— "Hsueh Pao-ch'ai lun" 薛寶釵論 , Jen-min wen-hsueh 人民文學 , No. 68 (June, 1955), 118-124.

———— "Hung-lou meng ai-ch'ing miao-hsieh shih-tai i-i chi ch'i chu-hsien" 紅樓夢愛情描寫時代意義及其局限 , Wen-hsueh p'ing-lun 文學評論 , 6 (Dec., 1963), 20-44.

———— Hung-lou meng lun kao 紅樓夢論稿 . Peking: Jen-min wen-hsueh ch'u-pan-she, 1959.

———— "Ts'ao Hsueh-ch'in te Hung-lou meng" 曹雪芹的紅樓夢 , Wen-hsueh yen-chiu 文學研究 , No. 103 (June, 1958), 97-125.

Chiang, Jui-tsao 蔣瑞藻 . Hsiao-shuo k'ao-cheng 小說考證 . Shanghai, 1923.

Ch'ien, Ching-fang 錢靜方 . Hsiao-shuo ts'ung-k'ao 小說叢考 . Shanghai: Ku-tien wen-hsueh ch'u-pan she, 1957.

Ch'ien, Hsing-ts'un 錢杏邨 (A-Ying 阿英). Hsiao-shuo erh-t'an 小說二談 . Shanghai: Ku-tien wen-hsueh ch'u-pan she, 1958.

———— "Man-t'an Hung-lou meng te ch'a-t'u ho hua-ts'e" 漫談紅樓夢的插圖和畫冊 , Wen-wu 文物 , 6 (June, 1963), 1-9.

Ch'ien, Po-ts'an 翦伯贊 . "Lun shih-pa shih-chi shang pan-ch'i Chung-kuo she-hui ching-chi te hsing-chih chien lun Hung-lou meng chung so fan-ying te she-hui ching-chi ch'ing-k'uang" 論十八世紀上半期中國社會經濟的性質兼論紅樓夢中所反映的社會經濟情況 , Pei-ching ta-hsueh hsueh-pao (jen-wen k'o-hsueh) 北京大學學報 (人文科學),

No. 2 (1955), 79-124.

Chou, Ch'i 周琪 . "P'ing Hung-lou meng chung kuan-yu shih-erh ch'ai te miao-hsieh" 評紅樓中關於十二釵的描寫 , Wen-hsueh p'ing-lun 文學評論, 4 (Aug., 1964), 80-90.

Chou, Ch'un 周春 . Yueh Hung-lou meng sui-pi 閱紅樓夢隨筆, Peking: Chung-hua shu-chu, 1958.

Chou, Ju-ch'ang 周汝昌 . Hung-lou meng hsin-cheng 紅樓夢新證 . Shanghai: T'ang-ti ch'u-pan she, 1953.
_____ "Tsai-shang Ts'ao Hsueh-ch'in tsu-nien" 再商曹雪芹卒年 , Kuang-ming jih-pao 光明日報 , (July 8, 1962).
_____ "Ts'ao Hsueh-ch'in tsu-nien pien" 曹雪芹卒年辨 , Wen-hui-pao 文滙報 , (May 4-5, 1962).

Chou, Li-po 周立波 . "Tu Hung so-chi" 讀紅瑣記, Jen-min wen-hsueh 人民文學 , No. 168 (Nov., 1963), 58-61.

Chou, Yang 周揚 . "Tsai Chung-kuo tso-chia hsieh-hui chao-k'ai te Hung-lou meng yen-chiu tso-t'an hui shang te fa-yen" 在中國作家協會召開的紅樓研究座談會上的發言, Wen-hsueh i-ch'an hsuan-chi 文學遺產選集 , 1 (Jan., 1956), 4-7.

Chu, Nan-hsien 朱南銑 . "Kuan-yu Chih-yen Chai te chen hsing-ming" 關於脂硯齋的真姓名, Kuang-ming jih-pao 光明日報 , (May 10, 1962).

Fang, Hao 方豪 . "Hung-lou meng hsin-k'ao"紅樓夢新考 , Shuo-wen 說文 , 4 (June, 1944), 921-938.
_____ "Hung-lou meng k'ao-cheng chih hsin shih-liao" 紅樓夢考證之新史料 , Tung-fang tsa-chih 東方雜誌 XXXIX:ii (Mar., 1943), 53-54.

Fu, I 傅義 . "Hung-lou meng li te su-fei-fu" 紅樓夢裡的訴肺腑, Yu-wen hsueh-hsi 語文學習 , No. 73 (Oct., 1957), 16-18.

Ho, Ch'i-fang 何其芳 . "Lun Hung-lou meng" 論紅樓夢, Wen-hsueh yen-chiu chi-k'an 文學研究集刊 , 5 (May, 1957), 28-148.
_____ "Ts'ao Hsueh-ch'in te kung-hsien"曹雪芹的貢獻 , Wen-hsueh p'ing-lun 文學評論, 6 (Dec., 1963), 1-19.

Hou, E 侯堮 . "Chueh lo shih-jen Yung-chung nien-p'u"覺羅詩人永忠年譜 , Yen-ching hsueh-pao 燕京學報 , No. 12 (Dec., 1932), 2632-2633.

Hsieh, Wan-ying 謝婉瑩 (Ping-Hsin 冰心). "Hung-lou meng hsieh-tso chi-ch'iao te i-pan"紅樓夢寫作技巧的一斑, Jen-min wen-hsueh 人民文學 , No. 168 (Nov., 1963), 53-57.

Hsin-hua yueh-pao she 新華月報社 , ed. "San-ko yueh-lai kuan-yu Hung-lou meng yen-chiu te p'i-p'an ho t'ao-lun" 三個月來關於紅樓夢研究的批判和討論 , Hsin-hua yueh-pao 新華月報 , No. 64 (Feb., 1955), 278-280.

Hsu, Hsu 徐訏 . "Hung-lou meng te i-shu chia-chih ho hsiao-shuo li te tui-pai" 紅樓夢的藝術價值和小説裡的對白, Tzu-yu Chung-kuo 自由中國 , XVIII:iv (Feb., 1958), 24-28; XVIII:v (Mar., 1958), 23-27; XVIII:vi (Apr., 1958), 25-30.

Hu, Jen-lung 胡人龍 & Lei, Shih-yu 雷石榆 . "Kuan-yu Chia Pao-yu te tien-hsing hsing-ko" 關於賈寶玉的典型性格, Wen-hsueh i-ch'an tseng-k'an 文學遺產增刊 , 5 (Dec., 1957), 329-339.

Hu, Nien-i 胡念貽 . "P'ing chin-nien-lai kuan-yu Hung-lou meng yen-chiu chung te ts'uo-wu kuan-tien" 評今年來關於紅樓夢中的錯誤觀點 Jen-min wen-hsueh 人民文學 , No. 62 (Dec., 1954), 14-21.

Hu, Shih 胡適 . Hung-lou meng k'ao-cheng 紅樓夢考證 . Taipei: Yuan-tung t'u-shu kung-ssu, 1961.

_____ Hu Shih lun-hsueh chin-chu 胡適論學近著 . Shanghai: Shang-wu yin-shu kuan, 1934.

_____ Hu Shih wen-ts'un 胡適文存 . Yuan-tung t'u-shu kung-ssu, 1953.

_____ "Pa Ch'ien-lung keng-ch'en-pen Chih-yen Chai ch'ung-p'ing Shih-t'ou chi ch'ao-pen" 跋乾隆庚辰本脂硯齋重評石頭記鈔本 Kuo-hsueh chi-k'an 國學季刊 , III:iv (Dec., 1932), 721-731.

_____ "So-wei Ts'ao Hsueh-ch'in hsiao-hsiang te mi" 所謂曹雪芹小象的謎 , Hsin shih-tai 新時代 , I:iv (1961).

Jen-min wen-hsueh ch'u-pan she 人民文學出版社 , ed. Hung-lou meng yen-chiu lun-wen chi 紅樓夢研究論文集 , Peking: Jen-min wen-hsueh ch'u-pan she, 1959.

Kao, Tan-yun 高淡雲 . "P'ing Hung-lou meng chung kuan-yu shih-erh ch'ai te miao-hsieh" 評紅樓夢中關於十二釵的描寫, Wen-i-pao 文藝報 , No. 316 (Mar., 1964), 32-37.

Kao, Yu-han 高語罕 . "Hung-lou meng te wen-hsueh kuan" 紅樓夢的文學觀 , Tung-fang tsa-chih 東方雜誌 , XXXIX:xi (Aug., 1943), 57-59.

K'ung, Ling-ching 孔另境 . Chung-kuo hsiao-shuo shih-liao 中國小説史料 . Shanghai: Ku-tien wen-hsueh ch'u-pan she, 1957.

Kuo, Mo-jo 郭沫若 . "Hung-lou meng ti erh-wu-hui te i-chung chieh-shih" 紅樓夢第二五回的一種解釋 , Wen-i yueh-pao 文藝月報 , No. 51 (Mar., 1957), 7-9.

Li, Ch'en-tung 李辰冬 . Hung-lou meng yen-chiu 紅樓夢研究. Taipei: Hsin-hsing shu-chu, 1962.

Li, Ch'i 李祁 . "Lin Tai-yu shen-hua te pei-ching" 林黛玉神話的背景 , Ta-lu tsa-chih 大陸雜誌, XXX:x (May, 1965), 1-4.

Li, Hsi-fan 李希凡 & Lan, Ling 藍翎 . "Cheng-ch'ueh ku-chia Hung-lou meng chung Chih-yen Chai p'ing te i-ssu" 正確估價紅樓夢中脂硯齋評的意思 , Hsin-hua yueh-pao 新華月報 , No. 75 (Jan., 1956), 118-120.

_____ "Hung-lou meng hou ssu-shih-hui wei shen-ma neng ts'un-tsai hsia-lai?" 紅樓夢後四十回為甚麼能存在下來 , Wen-i yueh-pao 文藝月報 , No. 42 (June, 1956), 69-73.

_____ Hung-lou meng p'ing-lun chi 紅樓夢評論集 . Peking: Tso-chia ch'u-pan she, 1957.

_____ "Kuan-yu Hung-lou meng chien-lun chi ch'i-t'a" 關於紅樓夢簡論及其他, Wen-shih-che 文史哲 , 9 (Sept., 1954), 20-25.

_____ "Kuan-yu Hung-lou meng te ssu-hsiang ch'ing-hsiang-hsing wen-t'i" 關於紅樓夢的思想傾向性問題, Hsin-chien-she 新建設 , 4 (Apr., 1955), 44-52.

_____ "Lun Hung-lou meng te i-shu hsing-hsiang te ch'uang-tsao" 論紅樓夢的藝術形象的創造 , Jen-min wen-hsueh 人民文學 , No. 78 (Apr., 1956), 45-57.

_____ "P'ing Hung-lou meng hsin-cheng" 評紅樓夢新證 , Hsin-hua yueh-pao 新華月報 , No. 64 (Feb., 1955), 274-278.

_____ "P'ing Hung-lou meng yen-chiu" 評紅樓夢研究 , Wen-hsueh i-ch'an hsuan-chi 文學遺產選集 , 1 (Jan., 1956), 25-38.

Li-Hsin 立信 . "Ta-kuan-yuan t'u chi" 大觀園圖記 , Wen-wu 文物 , No. 152 (June, 1963), 21-22.

Li, Wei-ch'iu 李未秋 . "Hung-lou meng yu T'ai-wan" 紅樓夢與臺灣, T'ai-wan feng-wu 臺灣風物 , X:iv (Apr., 1960), 13-17.

Lin, Keng 林庚 . "Hung-lou meng chung so fan-ying te hsin-te i-shih hsiang-tai te meng-ya" 紅樓夢中所反映的新的意識形態的萌芽 , Wen-hsueh i-ch'an hsuan-chi 文學遺產選集, 2 (Apr., 1957), 247-258.

Lin, Tung-p'ing 林冬平 . "Hung-lou meng te hsien-shih chu-i ch'eng-chiu" 紅樓夢的現實主義成就 , Jen-min wen-hsueh 人民文學 , No. 62 (Dec., 1954), 22-27.

Lin, Yu-t'ang 林語堂 . "P'ing-hsin lun Kao E" 平心論高 鶚 , Chung-yang yen-chiu-yuan li-shih yu-yen yen-chiu-so chi-k'an 中央研究院歷史語言研究所集刊 , XXIX:ii (Nov., 1958), 327-387.

Liu, Ping-i 劉秉義 . "Shih-lun Chia Pao-yu Lin Tai-yu hun-yin pei-chu te ken-pen yuan-yin" 試論賈寶玉林黛玉 婚姻悲劇的根本原因 , Wen-hsueh i-ch'an hsuan-chi 文學遺產選集 , 1 (Jan., 1956), 39-51.

Liu, Shih-te 劉世德 & Teng, Shao-chi 鄧紹基 . "P'ing Hung-lou meng shih shih-min wen-hsueh shuo" 評紅樓夢是 市民文學說 , Pei-ching ta-hsueh hsueh-pao (jen-wen k'o-hsueh) 北京大學學報 (人文科學) , No. 8 (May, 1957), 89-111.

————— "Hung-lou meng te chu-t'i" 紅樓夢的主題 , Wen-hsueh p'ing-lun 文學評論 , 6 (Dec., 1963), 45-63.

Liu, Ta-chieh 劉大杰 . Hung-lou meng te ssu-hsiang yu jen-wu 紅樓夢的思想與人物 . Shanghai: Ku-tien wen-hsueh ch'u-pan she, 1956.

Mao, Hsing 毛星 . "P'ing Yu P'ing-po hsien-sheng te se-k'ung shuo" 評俞平伯先生的色空說 , Jen-min wen-hsueh 人民文學 , No. 63 (Jan., 1955), 58-64.

Mao, T'ung-chai 毛桐齋 . "Lun Hung-lou meng chieh Ch'eng-i-pen" 論紅樓夢介程乙本 , Chung-kuo i-chou 中國 一週 , No. 633 (June, 1962), 16.

Nieh, Kan-nu 聶紺弩 . "Lun Yu P'ing-po tui Hung-lou meng te pien-wei ts'un-chen" 論俞平伯對紅樓夢的辨偽存 真 , Jen-min wen-hsueh 人民文學 , No. 63 (Jan., 1955), 85-91.

Pai, Tun 白盾 . "Chia Pao-yu te tien-hsing i-i" 賈寶玉的 典型意義 , Jen-min wen-hsueh 人民文學 , No. 62 (Dec., 1954), 4-13.

P'an, Ch'ung-kuei 潘重規 . "Ch'ien-lung ch'ao-pen pai-nien-hui Hung-lou meng kao t'i-ch'ien" 乾隆抄本百廿回 紅樓夢稿題簽 , Ta-lu tsa-chih 大陸雜誌 XXXIV:ix (May, 1967), 5-6.

————— "Chih-erh hung-hsueh" 今日紅學 , Hung-lou meng yen-chiu chuan-k'an 紅樓夢研究專刊 , No. 7 (Jan., 1970), 111-117.

_____ "Hsu-t'an Ch'ien-lung ch'ao-pen pai-nien-hui Hung-lou meng kao chung te Yang Yu-yun t'i tzu" 續談乾隆抄本百廿回紅樓夢稿中的楊又雲題字 , Ta-lu tsa-chih 大陸雜誌, XXXIV:iv (Aug., 1967), 4-7.

_____ "Hsu-t'an hsin-k'an Ch'ien-lung ch'ao-pen pai-nien-hui Hung-lou meng kao" 續談新刊乾隆抄本百廿回紅樓夢稿, Ta-lu tsa-chih 大陸雜誌, XXXI:iv (Aug., 1965), 1-6.

_____ "Hung-hsueh wu-shih-nien" 紅學五十年 , Hsin-ya shu-yuan Chung-kuo wen-hsueh hsi nien-k'an 新亞書院中國文學系年刊 , 4 (June, 1966), 1-13.

_____ "Kao E pu tso Hung-lou meng hou ssu-shih-hui te shang-ch'ueh" 高鶚補作紅樓夢後四十回的商榷 , Hsin-ya hsueh-pao 新亞學報, VIII:i (Feb., 1967), 367-382.

_____ "Lun Ch'ien-lung ch'ao-pen pai-nien-hui Hung-lou meng kao te Yang Yu-yun t'i tzu" 論乾隆抄本百廿回紅樓夢稿的楊又雲題字 , Ta-lu tsa-chih 大陸雜誌 , XXXV:i (July, 1967), 12-14.

_____ "Tu Ch'ien-lung ch'ao-pen pai-nien-hui Hung-lou meng kao" 讀乾隆抄本百廿回紅樓夢稿, Ta-lu tsa-chih 大陸雜誌 , XXX:ii (Jan., 1965), 1-7.

P'an, Hsia 潘夏 . "Min-tsu hsueh-lei chu-ch'eng te Hung-lou meng" 民族血淚鑄成的紅樓夢, Fan-kung 反攻 , No. 37 (May, 1951), 18-23; No. 38 (June, 1951), 19-24.

P'ei-Chih 佩之 . "Hung-lou meng hsin-p'ing" 紅樓夢新評 , Hsiao-shuo yueh-pao 小說月報 , XI:vi (June, 1920), 6-12; XI:vii (July, 1920), 5-12.

P'eng, Hui 彭慧 . "Lun Hung-lou meng te jen-min-hsing ho t'a shih-fou shih shih-min wen-hsueh wen-t'i" 論紅樓夢的人民性和它是否是市民文學問題 , Jen-min wen-hsueh 人民文學 , No. 83 (Sept., 1956), 117-126.

Shan-tung ta-hsueh shih-sheng chi-t'i t'ao-lun 山東大學師生集體討論. "Women tui Hung-lou meng te ch'u-pu k'an-fa" 我們對紅樓夢的初步看法 , Jen-min wen-hsueh 人民文學 , No. 64 (Feb., 1955), 111-121.

Shan-tung ta-hsueh wen-shih-che pien-chi wei-yuan hui 山東大學文史哲編輯委員會 . "Hung-lou meng yen-chiu t'ao-lun chuan-chi" 紅樓夢研究討論專輯, Wen-shih-che 文史哲 , 1 (Jan., 1955), 1-41.

_____ "Kuan-yu pen-k'an Hung-lou meng yen-chiu t'ao-lun chuan-chi" 關於本刊紅樓夢研究討論專輯, Wen-shih-che 文史哲 , 8 (Aug., 1955), 41-42.

Shu, Ch'ing-ch'un 舒慶春 (Lao-She 老舍). "Hung-lou meng ping pu-shih meng" 紅樓夢並不是夢 , Jen-min wen-hsueh 人民文學 , No. 62 (Dec., 1954), 1-3.

T'an, Cheng-pi 譚正璧 . Chung-kuo hsiao-shuo fa-ta shih 中國小說發達史 . Shanghai: Kuang-ming shu-chu, 1935.

Teng, T'o 鄧拓 . "Lun Hung-lou meng te she-hui pei-ching ho li-shih i-i" 論紅樓夢的社會背景和歷史意義, Hsin-hua yueh-pao 新華月報, No. 64 (Feb., 1955), 269-274.

Teng, Yun-chien 鄧允建 . "Tsai-t'an Ts'ao Hsueh-ch'in te tsu-nien wen-t'i" 再談曹雪芹的卒年問題 , Kuang-ming jih-pao 光明日報 , (June 10, 1962).
    "Ts'ao Hsueh-ch'in tsu-nien wen-t'i shang-tui" 曹雪芹卒年問題商兌 , Wen-hui-pao 文滙報 , (Apr., 17, 1962).

Ting, Yu 丁由 . "T'an Wang Hsi-feng" 談王熙鳳 , Wen-hsueh i-ch'an tseng-k'an 文學遺產增刊, 2 (Jan., 1956), 195-203.

Ts'ai, Yuan-p'ei 蔡元培 . Shih-t'ou chi so-yin 石頭記索隱 . Taipei: Chung-hua shu-chu, 1964.

Ts'ao, Tao-heng 曹道衡 . "Kuan-yu Huang Tsung-hsi, Ku Yen-wu, Wang Fu-chih teng-jen te ssu-hsiang chi ch'i yu Hung-lou meng te kuan-hsi" 關於黃宗羲顧炎武王夫之等人的思想及其與紅樓夢的關係 , Wen-hsueh yen-chiu chi-k'an 文學研究集刊 , 5 (May, 1957), 149-216.

Tseng, Tz'u-liang 曾次亮 . "Ts'ao Hsueh-ch'in tsu-nien wen-t'i te shang-t'ao" 曹雪芹卒年問題的商討 , Kuang-ming jih-pao 光明日報 . (Apr. 26, 1954).

Tso-chia ch'u-pan she 作家出版社 . Hung-lou meng wen-t'i t'ao-lun chi 紅樓夢問題討論集. Peking: Tso-chia ch'u-pan she, 1955.

Tsung, Te-kang 宗德崗 . "P'ing Hung-lou meng kao-pen" 評紅樓夢稿本, Ta-lu tsa-chih 大陸雜誌 , XXX:vii (Apr., 1965), 21.

Tun, Ch'eng 敦誠 . Ssu-sung t'ang-chi 四松堂集 . Peking: Wen-hsueh ku-chi k'an-hsing she, 1955.

Tun, Min 敦敏 . Mou-chai shih-ch'ao 懋齋詩鈔 . Peking: Wen-hsueh ku-chi k'an-hsing she, 1955.

Wang, Huang 王璜 . "Lun Hung-lou meng li te wen-hsueh yung-yu" 論紅樓夢裡的文學用語 , Tung-fang tsa-chih 東方雜誌, XL:xiii (July, 1944), 56-60.

Wang, Kuo-wei 王國維 . "Hung-lou meng p'ing-lun" 紅樓夢評論, Hung-lou meng chuan 紅樓夢卷 , vol. l. Peking, 1963, pp. 244-265.

Wang, Li 王力 . Chung-kuo hsien-tai yu-fa 中國現代語法 . 2 vols. Revised ed. Shanghai: Chung-hua shu-chu, 1955.

Wang, Li-ch'i 王利器 . "Ch'ung-hsin k'ao-lu Ts'ao Hsueh-ch'in te sheng-p'ing" 重新考慮曹雪芹的生平 , Wen-hsueh i-ch'an hsuan-chi 文學遺產選集 , 2 (Apr., 1957), 238-246.

_____ "Kuan-yu Kao E te i-hsieh ts'ai-liao" 關於高鶚的一些材料, Wen-hsueh yen-chiu 文學研究 , 1 (Mar., 1957), 166-171.

Wang, P'ei-chang 王佩璋 . "Ts'ao Hsueh-ch'in te sheng-tsu nien chi ch'i-t'a" 曹雪芹的生卒年及其他 , Wen-hsueh yen-chiu chi-k'an 文學研究集刊 , 5 (May, 1957), 217-257.

Wang, Yung 王永 . "Hung-lou meng li te shih tz'u ch'u 紅樓夢裡的詩詞曲 , Yu-wen hsueh-hsi 語文學習 , No. 75 (Dec., 1957), 16-18.

Weng, T'ung-wen 翁同文 . "Pu-lun Chih-yen Chai wei Ts'ao Yung i-fu-tzu shuo" 補論脂硯齋為曹顒遺腹子說 . Ta-lu tsa-chih 大陸雜誌, XXXIII:i (July, 1966), 6-14.

Wu, En-yu 吳恩裕 . "Kao-cheng Ts'ao Hsueh-ch'in tsu-nien wo-chien" 考證曹雪芹卒年我見 , Kuang-ming jih-pao 光明日報 , (July 8, 1962).

_____ "Ts'ao Hsueh-ch'in te tsu-nien wen-t'i" 曹雪芹的卒年問題 , Kuang-ming jih-pao 光明日報 , (Mar. 10, 1952).

_____ "Ts'ao Hsueh-ch'in tsu-nien jen-wu shuo chih-i" 曹雪芹卒年壬午說質疑 , Kuang-ming jih-pao 光明日報 , (May 6, 1962).

_____ "Tu Chih-p'i Shih-t'ou chi sui-cha tu-hou" 讀脂批石頭記隨札讀後, Kuang-ming jih-pao 光明日報 , (June 23, 1962).

_____ Yu-kuan Ts'ao Hsueh-ch'in pa-chung 有關曹雪芹八種 . Shanghai: Ku-tien wen-hsueh ch'u-pan she, 1958.

_____ "Yung-chung tiao Ts'ao Hsueh-ch'in te san-shou shih" 永忠弔曹雪芹的三首詩 , Kuang-ming jih-pao 光明日報 (Sept. 7, 1954).

Wu, Hsiao-ju 吳小如 . "Tu Chih-p'i Shih-t'ou chi sui-cha erh-tse" 讀脂批石頭記隨札二則, Kuang-ming jih-pao 光明日報 , (June 5, 1962).

Wu, Shih-ch'ang 吳世昌 . "Hung-lou meng kao te ch'eng-fen chi ch'i nien-tai" 紅樓夢稿的成分及其年代 , T'u-shu kuan 圖書館 , 4 (Dec., 1963), 45-51.
_____ "Ts'ao Hsueh-ch'in te sheng-tsu nien" 曹雪芹的生卒年, Kuang-ming jih-pao 光明日報 (Apr. 21, 1962).
_____ "Ts'eng Kao E sheng-p'ing lun ch'i tso-p'in ssu-hsiang" 從高鶚生平論其作品思想 , Wen-shih 文史 , 4 (June, 1965), 127-144.
Wu, Ta-k'un 吳大琨 . "Kuan-yu lueh-lun Hung-lou meng te she-hui pei-ching chi ch'i-t'a" 關於略論紅樓夢的社會背景及其它 , Wen-shih-che 文史哲 , 4 (Apr., 1956), 45-47.
_____ "Kuan-yu lueh-lun Hung-lou meng te she-hui pei-ching chi ch'i-t'a i-wen te pu-ch'ung" 關於略論紅樓夢的社會背景及其他一文的補充, Wen-shih-che 文史哲 , 11 (Nov., 1956), 32-36.
Wu, Tsu-hsiang 吳組緗 . "Lun Chia Pao-yu tien-hsing hsing-hsiang" 論賈寶玉典型形象 , Pei-ching ta-hsueh hsueh-pao (jen-wen k'o-hsueh) 北京大學學報 (人文科學), No. 6 (1956), 1-32.
_____ "T'an Hung-lou meng li chi-ko p'ei-ch'en jen-wu te an-p'ai" 談紅樓夢裡幾個陪襯人物的安排, Jen-min wen-hsueh 人民文學 , No. 117 (Aug., 1959), 112-119.
Wu, Yu-pai 吳羽白 . "Hung-lou meng te nien-tai wen-t'i" 紅樓夢的年代問題, Shuo-wen 説文 , 4 (June, 1944), 917-919.
Yang, Hsiang-k'uei 楊向奎 . "Ts'ao Hsueh-ch'in te ssu-hsiang" 曹雪芹的思想 , Wen-she-che 文史哲 , 3 (Mar., 1955), 36-40.
Yen, Ming 嚴明 . "Chia-hsu pen Shih-t'ou chi pu-chih shih-liu-hui" 甲戌本石頭記不止十六回 , Min-chu p'ing-lun 民主評論 , XII:xviii (Sept., 1961), 13-17.
_____ "Feng-chieh te chieh-chu i-ts'ung, erh-ling, san-jen-mu" 鳳姐的結局一從二令三人木 , Tzu-yu Chung-kuo 自由中國 , XXII:ii (Jan., 1960), 20-24.
_____ "Hung-lou meng hou ssu-shih-hui te k'ao-cheng wen-t'i tui Lin Yu-t'ang hsien-sheng te fan-an t'i-ch'u shang-ch'ueh" 紅樓夢後四十回的考證問題對林語堂先生的翻案提出商榷, Tzu-yu Chung-kuo 自由中國 , XIX:xii (Dec., 1958), 24-28.
_____ "Ts'ao Hsueh-ch'in shen-shih pien-shuo" 曹雪芹身世辨説 , Ta-lu tsa-chih 大陸雜誌 , XXIII:i (July, 1961), 20-23; XXIII:ii (July, 1961), 23-27.

Yen, Tun-chieh 嚴敦傑 . "Hung-lou meng hsin k'ao pieh-pien" 紅樓夢新考別編 , Tung-fang tsa-chih 東方雜誌 , XLI:i (Jan., 1945), 70-75.

_____ "Lun Hung-lou meng chi ch'i-t'a hsiao-shuo chung chih k'o-hsueh shih-liao" 論紅樓夢及其他小說中之科學史料 , Tung-fang tsa-chih 東方雜誌 , XXXIX:ix (July, 1943), 59-61.

_____ "Pa Hung-lou meng hsin-k'ao nei hsi-yang shih-k'o yu Chung-kuo shih-k'o chih pi-chiao" 跋紅樓夢新考內西洋時刻與中國時刻之比較 , Tung-fang tsa-chih 東方雜誌, XL:xvi (Aug., 1944), 27-30.

Yen, Tun-i 嚴敦易 . "Hung-lou meng tsa-chi" 紅樓夢雜記 , Hsiao-shuo yueh-pao 小說月報 , XV: ix (Sept., 1924), 12.

Yin, Meng-lun 殷孟倫 . "Lueh-t'an Hung-lou meng te jen-wu yu-yen" 略論紅樓夢的人物語言, Wen-shih-che 文史哲 , 4 (Apr., 1955), 45-52.

_____ "Lueh-t'an Hung-lou meng tso-che Ts'ao Hsueh-ch'in tui yu-yen i-shu te jen-shih" 略談紅樓夢作者曹雪芹對語言藝術的認識, Wen-shih-che 文史哲 , 2 (Feb., 1955), 41-43.

Ying, Pai 映白 & Sun, Chen-chih 孫慎之 . "Kuan-yu Hung-lou meng so piao-hsien te mao-tun te hsing-chih wen-t'i" 關於紅樓夢所表現的矛盾的性質問題, Wen-shih-che 文史哲 , 4 (Apr., 1955), 38-45.

Yu, Jui 裕瑞 . Tsao-ch'uang hsien-pi 棗窗閒筆 . Peking: Wen-hsueh ku-chi k'an-hsing she, 1957.

Yu, P'ing-po 俞平伯 .
_____ "Hung-lou meng chung shih-erh ch'ai te miao-hsieh" 紅樓夢中十二釵的描寫 , Wen-hsueh p'ing-lun 文學評論 , 4 (Apr., 1963), 19-56.

_____ Hung-lou meng pien 紅樓夢辨 . Shanghai: Ya-tung t'u-shu-kuan, 1923.

_____ "Hung-lou meng pien te hsiu-cheng" 紅樓夢辨的修正 , Hsien-tai p'ing-lun 現代評論 , I:ix (1925).

_____ Hung-lou meng yen-chiu 紅樓夢研究 . Shanghai: T'ang-ti ch'u-pan she, 1952.

_____ "Hou san-shih-hui te Hung-lou meng" 後三十回的紅樓夢 , Hsiao-shuo yueh-pao 小說月報 , XIII:vii (July, 1922), 1-15.

_____ "Hou san-shih-hui te Hung-lou meng" 後三十回的紅樓夢 , Jen-min wen-hsueh 人民文學 , No. 20 (June, 1951), 84-90.

———— "Kao-tso hou ssu-shih-hui te p'i-p'ing" 高作後四十回的批評, Hsiao-shuo yueh-pao 小說月報, XIII:viii (Aug., 1922), 1-16.

———— "T'an hsin-k'an Ch'ien-lung ch'ao-pen pai-nien-hui Hung-lou meng kao" 談新刊乾隆抄本百廿回紅樓夢稿, Chung-hua wen-shih lun-ts'ung 文史論叢, V (June, 1964), 395-445.

———— "Ts'ao Hsueh-ch'in te tsu-nien" 曹雪芹的卒年, Kuang-ming jih-pao 光明日報, (March 1, 1954).

———— "Ying-yin Chih-yen Chai ch'ung-p'ing Shih-t'ou chi shih-liu-hui hou-chi" 影印脂硯齋重評石頭記十六回後記, Chung-hua wen-shih lun-ts'ung 中華文史論叢, 1 (Aug., 1962), 299-339.

———— "Ying-yin Chih-p'ing Shih-t'ou chi shih-liu-hui hou-chi te pu-ch'ung shuo-ming" 影印脂評石頭記十六回後記的補充說明, Chung-hua wen-shih lun-ts'ung 中華文史論叢, 3 (May, 1963), 294.

Yuan, Mei 袁枚. Sui-yuan shih-hua 隨園詩話. Shanghai: Chi-ch'eng shu-chu, 1908.

Yuan, Sheng-shih 袁聖時. "Hung-lou meng yen-chiu" 紅樓夢研究, Tung-fang tsa-chih 東方雜誌, XLIV:xi (Nov., 1948), 47-51.

Yuan, Shih-shih 袁世碩. "Tsen-yang tui-tai Hung-lou meng" 怎樣對待紅樓夢, Wen-shih-che 文史哲, 3 (March, 1955), 41-44, 56.

IV. Western Language Materials on Dream of the Red Chamber and Chinese Literature

A. Translations of Dream of the Red Chamber:

English:

Bowra, Edward Charles. "The Dream of the Red Chamber", The China Magazine. (Translation from first eight chapters of novel). Shanghai: Christmas Number, 1868. Shanghai: vol. for 1869.

Davis, John Francis. "The Poetry of Chinese", Transactions of the Royal Asiatic Society of Great Britain and Ireland, II (1830). (Translation of chapter 3 of the novel).

Hawkes, David. The Story of the Stone. Vol. I. Penguin Books, 1973.

Hudson, Elfrida. "An Old, Old, Story", China Journal, VIII (1928), 7-15. (Translation of chapter 4).

Joly, H. Bencraft. Hung Lou Meng or The Dream of the Red
Chamber: A Chinese Novel. vol. I: Hong Kong, 1892; vol. II:
Macao, 1893. (Translation from first fifty-six chapters of novel).

McHugh, Florence and Isabel. The Dream of the Red Chamber.
New York, 1958. (Translation of the German version by Franz
Kuhn).

Thom, R. The Chinese Speaker. Ningpo, 1842, 62–89. (An
abridged English translation used for language instruction).

Wang, Chi-chen. Dream of the Red Chamber. Preface by Arthur
Waley. London, 1929.
_____ Dream of the Red Chamber. Preface by Mark Van Doren.
New York, 1958.

Yang, Hsien-yi and Gladys. Chinese Literature, No. 6 (1964),
38–42; (Translation of chapters 18, 19, 20). Chinese Literature,
No. 7 (1964), 44–75; (Translation of chapters 32, 33, 34).
Chinese Literature, No. 8 (1964), 42–95; (Translation of chapters 74, 75, 77).

Yuan, Chia-hua and Shih Ming. Hung-lou Meng and Tuan-hung
Ling-yen Chi: English Translation of Selections from Chinese
Literature. 2nd series. Shanghai: Pei-hsin shu-chu, 1933.

French:

Guerne, Armel. Le Rêve dans le Pavillon Rouge. Paris, 1957.
(Translation of German version by Franz Kuhn).

Hsu, Sung-nien. "Le Rêve dans le Pavillon Rouge", Anthologie de
la Littérature chinoise. Paris, 1933. pp. 171, 280–284, 293–302,
336–337. (Translation of stories from chapters 17, 27, 28, 31,
32).

Li, Tche-houa. Le Rêve du Pavillon Rouge. UNESCO: Paris.
(To be published).

Pao, Wen-wei. "Le Rêve de la Chambre Rouge", Etudes Françaises,
IV (1943), 67–80; 149–161; 224–237; 306–317. Pékin: Institut
Sinologique. (Translation of chapter 57 printed with Chinese
text).

German:

Kuhn, Franz. Der Traum der roten Kammer. Leipzig, 1932.
_____ "Ein Kapitel aus dem Roman Hung Lou Mong", Sinica, VII
(1932), 178–186.

Ting, W.Y. "Aug dem Roman Hung Lou Mong", Sinica, IV (1928),
83–89, 130–135.

Italian:

Benedikter, Martin. "Il Sogno della Camera Rossa", Cina, V
    (1959), 105-115. (Translation of chapter 1).
Bovero, Clara Pirrone and Carla Riccio. Il Sogno della Camera
    Rossa. Turin, 1958. (Translation of the German version by
    Franz Kuhn).

Russian:

Panasyuk, V.A. Ts'ao Hsueh-ch'in: Son v krasnon tereme. Preface
    by N.T. Federenko. 2 vols. Moscow, 1958.
Roodman, V.G. "The Dream in the Red Chamber, chapters 1, 2, "
    in Kitayskaya literatura: Khrestomatiya (Chinese Literature
    Reader), Moscow, 1959. pp. 656-683.

    B. Studies of Dream of the Red Chamber:

Published Materials:

Brandauer, Frederick P. "Some Philosophical Implications of the
    Hung Lou Meng", Ching Feng, IX:iii (1966), 14-23.
Chang, H.C. "On the Red Chamber Dream", (China Society,
    Singapore), Annual (1962-63), 1-6.
Chen, Wen-hua. rev. of Wu Shih-ch'ang's On the Red Chamber
    Dream. Tung-hai hsueh-pao, VII:i (June, 1965), 135-151.
Cornaby, W. Arthur. "The Secret of the Red Chamber", New China
    Review, I:iv (August, 1919), 329-339.
Giles, Herbert A. "Hung Lou Meng", A History of Chinese Litera-
    ture. Book VIII, chap. 1. London, 1901. pp. 355-384.
_____ "The Hung Lou Meng, Commonly Called The Dream of the
    Red Chamber", Journal of the North China Branch of the Royal
    Asiatic Society, N.S.,XX:i (Nov. 1, 1885), 1-23, 51-52.
Grieder, Jerome. "The Communist Critique of Hung lou meng",
    Harvard University Committee on Regional Studies, East Asia
    Program. Papers on China, X (1956), 142-168.
Gutzlaff, Karl A.F. "Hung Lau Mung or Dreams in the Red Cham-
    ber: a Novel", Chinese Repository, XI (May, 1842), 266-273.
Ho, Ch'i-fang. "On The Dream of the Red Chamber", Chinese
    Literature, No. 1 (1963), 65-86.
Hsia, C.T. "Dream of the Red Chamber", The Classic Chinese
    Novel, pp. 245-297. New York and London, 1968.
_____ "Love and Compassion in Dream of the Red Chamber",
    Criticism, V:iii (Summer, 1963), 261-271.

Hsia, C.T. rev. of Wu Shih-ch'ang's On the Red Chamber Dream. Journal of Asian Studies, XXI:i (Nov., 1961), 78-80.

Hsu, Min. "Dream of the Red Chamber and its Author--Exhibition to Mark 200th Anniversary of Death of Ts'ao Hsueh-ch'in", Peking Review, No. 43 (October 25, 1963), 25-28, illus.

Knoerle, Jeanne, S.P. The Dream of the Red Chamber: A Critical Study. Bloomington and London, 1972.

Koepping, Klaus-Peter & Lam Lai Sing, New Interpretations of the Red Chamber Dream, Singapore, 1973.

Mao, Tun. "What We Know of Ts'ao Hsueh-ch'in", Chinese Literature, No. 5 (1964), 85-104, illus.

Masi, Edoarda. "Nuove interpretazioni dello Hung Lou Meng", Cina, VII (1963), 68-85.

Palandri, Angela Jung, "Women in Dream of the Red Chamber", Literature East and West, XII:ii, iii, iv (Dec., 1968), 226-238.

Prušek, Jaroslav. "Neues Material zum Hung-Lou Meng Problem", Archiv Orientalni, XIII (1942), 270-277. Rev. of Heinrich Eggert, "Die Entstehungsgeschichte des Hung-lou-mong", unpubl. diss., Hamburg, 1939.

Rexroth, Kenneth. "Dream of the Red Chamber", Saturday Review, (Jan. 1, 1966), 19.

Spence, Johnathan D. Ts'ao Yin and the K'ang-hsi Emperor: Bondservant and Master. New Haven, 1966.

Teng, Shao-chi. "Ts'ao Hsueh-ch'in and his Dream of the Red Chamber", China Reconstructs, XII:xii (Dec., 1963), 30-34, illus.

Tso, Hai. "Ts'ao Hsueh-ch'in and The Dream of the Red Chamber", China Pictorial, No. 10 (1963), 16-19.

United States Department of State, American Consulate, Hong Kong. "Can We Read Books Like Dream of the Red Chamber?", Selections from China Mainland Magazines, No. 498 (Nov. 16, 1965), 29-30.

_____ "The Dream of the Red Chamber Case", Current Background, No. 315 (March 4, 1955).

Vasiliyev, V.P. "On The Dream in the Red Chamber", Ocherk istorii kitayskoy literatury (An Outline History of Chinese Literature). St. Petersburg, 1880, pp. 159-160.

Waley, Arthur. Forward to Wu Shih-ch'ang's On the Red Chamber Dream. Oxford, 1961.

Werner, Edward Chalmers. "The Translation of Chinese", The China Journal, VI:iv (1927), 175-177.

West, Anthony. rev. of Florence and Isabel McHugh's The Dream of the Red Chamber. "Through a Glass, Darkly", The New Yorker (Nov. 22, 1958), 223-232.

Wu, Shih-ch'ang. "History of The Red Chamber Dream", Chinese Literature, No. 1 (1963), 87-100.

———— Rev. of anon. mss., Chih-yen Chai ch'ung-p'ing Shih-tou chi, Revue Bibliographique de Sinologie, I (1957), 142-144.

———— Rev. of Lin Yu-t'ang's article, "P'ing-hsin lun Kao E", Revue Bibliographique de Sinologie, IV (1958), 348-349.

———— On the Red Chamber Dream: A Critical Study of Two Annotated Manuscripts of the 18th Century. Oxford, 1961.

———— Rev. of Yu P'ing-po edited text, Chih-yen Chai Hung-lou meng chi-p'ing. Revue Bibliographique de Sinologie, I (1957), 142-144.

Yang, Gladys. "The Red Chamber Dream Today", Arts and Sciences in China, I:iv (Oct. Dec., 1963), 31-34.

Yu, P'ing-po. "The Dream of the Red Chamber", People's China, X (May, 1954), 32-35.

Yuan, Shui-po. "Dream of the Red Chamber", China Reconstructs, IV:v (1955), 20-23.

Unpublished Dissertations and Articles:

Birch, Cyril. "The Riddle Poems in Chapter 5 of Hung-lou meng".

Chuang, Hsin-cheng. "Themes of Dream of the Red Chamber: A Comparative Interpretation". Doctoral thesis. Indiana, 1966.

Eggert, Heinrich. "Die Entstehungsgeschichte des Hung-lou mong". Doctoral thesis. Hamburg, 1939.

Knoerle, Sister Mary Gregory, S.P. "A Critical Analysis of The Dream of the Red Chamber in Terms of Western Novelistic Criteria". Doctoral thesis. Indiana, 1966.

Kuo, Lin-ko (French romanization, Kou Lin-ke). "Essai sur le Hong leou mong". Doctoral thesis. Lyon, 1935.

Li, Ch'en-tung (French romanization, Lee Ghen Tong). "Etudes sur Le Songe du Pavillon Rouge". Doctoral thesis. Paris, 1934.

Kunst, Richard Alan. "The Beginning and Ending of The Dream of the Red Chamber. Master of Arts thesis. University of California, Berkeley, 1969.

Lu, Yueh-hua (French romanization, Lu Yueh Hwa). "La Jeune Fille Chinoise d'aprés Hong-leou-mong". Doctoral thesis. Paris, 1936.

Mark, Lindy Li. "An Aesthetic Evaluation of Hung Lou Meng, a Novel by Ts'ao Hsueh-ch'in". Seminar paper submitted to Professor Cyril Birch, Oriental Languages 206, University of California, Berkeley, June 4, 1968.

Wang, John. "The Chih-yen Chai Commentary and the Dream of the Red Chamber: A Literary Study".

Wu, Shih-ch'ang. "Some Problems in the Hung-lou Meng", Paper read at XIIth Sinologues' Conference on Sept. 9, 1959, at Downing College, Cambridge, England. pp. 1-9. See Report of the Conference.

    C. Studies and Translations of Chinese Fiction and Related Materials:

Published Materials:

Birch, Cyril. "Feng Meng-lung and the Ku Chin Hsiao Shuo", Bulletin of the School of Oriental and African Studies, XVIII (1956), 64-83.

_____ "Some Formal Characteristics of the Hua-Pen Story", Bulletin of the School of Oriental and African Studies, XVII (1955), 346-364.

_____ Stories from a Ming Collection. Bloomington, 1959.

Bishop, John L. "A Colloquial Short Story in the Novel Chin P'ing Mei", Studies in Chinese Literature, ed. John L. Bishop. Harvard-Yenching Institute Series XXI. Cambridge, Mass., 1965. pp. 226-234.

_____ The Colloquial Short Story in China: A Study of the San-Yen Collection. Harvard-Yenching Institute Studies, XIV. Cambridge, Mass., 1956.

_____ "Some Limitations of Chinese Fiction", Far East Quarterly, XV:ii (1956), 239-247.

Bodde, Derk. "Some Chinese Tales of the Supernatural", Harvard Journal of Asiatic Studies, VI (1942), 338-357.

Buck, Pearl S. "China in the Mirror of her Fiction", Pacific Affairs, III (1930), 155-164.

Candlin, George T. "Chinese Fiction", in Miscellaneous Works on China. Chicago. 1898.

Chang, Hsin-chang. Allegory and Courtesy in Spenser: A Chinese View. Edinburgh, 1955.

Crump, James Irving, Jr. Intrigues: Studies of the Chan-kuo ts'e. Ann Arbor, 1964.

_____ "On Chinese Medieval Vernacular", Wennti, No. 5 (Nov., 1953), 65-74.

Demiéville, Paul. "Au bord de l'eau", T'oung Pao, XLIV (1956),
        242–265.

_____ "Les débuts de la littérature en chinois vulgaire", Comptes
    rendus (Nov., 1952), 563–571.

Dolezelova-Velingerova, Milena. "Vers la théorie de la littérature
    des narrateurs chinois", Cina, VIII (1964), 23–27.

Eberhard, Wolfram. Die chinesische Novelle des 17.--19.
    Jahrhunderts. Bern, 1948.

_____ "Der chinesische Roman", Universite a'Ankara. Revue de
    la Faculté de Langues, d'Historie et de Geographie, III (1945),
    203–204.

Eichhorn, Werner. Chinesische Liebes-Novellen. Bohn, 1948.

Feuerwerker, Yi-tse Mei. "The Chinese Novel", Approaches to
    the Oriental Classics, ed. William Theodore de Bary. New York,
    1960, pp. 171–185.

Gulik, R.H. van. Trifling Tale of a Spring Dream (Ch'un-meng
    so-yen). Tokyo, 1950).

Hanan, Patrick D. "The Development of Fiction and Drama", The
    Legacy of China. ed. Raymond S. Dawson. Oxford, 1964.
    pp. 115–143.

_____ "The Early Chinese Short Story: a Critical Theory in Out-
    line", Harvard Journal of Asiatic Studies, XXVII (1967), 168–
    207.

_____ "A Landmark of the Chinese Novel", University of Toronto
    Quarterly, XXX:iii (1961), 325–335.

_____ "Sources of the Chin P'ing Mei", Asia Major, X, part 1,
    23–67.

Hightower, James Robert. rev. "Franz Kuhn and his Translation of
    Jou P'u T'uan", Oriens Extremus, VIII:ii (1961), 252–257.

Ho, Shih-chun. Jou Lin Wai Che: le Roman des lettres. Paris,
    1933.

Hrdlickova, Vena. "The First Translations of Buddhist sūtras in
    Chinese Literature and their Place in the Development of Story-
    telling", Archiv Orientalni, XXVI (1958), 114–144.

_____ "The Professional Training of Chinese Storytellers and the
    Storytellers' Guilds", Archiv Orientalni, XXXIII (1965), 225–
    248.

Hsia, C.T. The Classic Chinese Novel. New York and London,
    1968.

_____ "Comparative Approaches to Water Margin", Yearbook of
    Comparative and General Literature, XI (1962), 121–128.

Hsia, C.T. "Monstrous Appetite: Comedy and Myth in the Hsi Yu Chi", Wen-Lin: Studies in the Chinese Humanities. ed. Tse-tsung Chow. Madison, Milwaukee, and London, 1968. pp. 239-245.

_____ "'To What Fyn Lyve I Thus?' Society and Self in the Chinese Short Story", The Kenyon Review, XXIV:iii (Summer, 1962), 519-541.

Hsia, T.A. "The Hsi Yu Pu As a Study of Dreams in Fiction", Wen-Lin: Studies in the Chinese Humanities. ed. Tse-tsung Chow. Madison, Milwaukee, and London, 1968. pp. 239-245.

Ingalls, Jeremy. Rev. of Franz Kuhn's translation of Jou P'u T'uan. (Reviewer's remarks based on Richard Martin's English version of Kuhn's German translation). "Mr. Ch'ing-Yin and the Chinese Erotic Novel", Yearbook of Comparative and General Literature, XIII (1964), 60-63.

Irwin, Richard Gregg. The Evolution of a Chinese Novel: Shui-hu-chuan". Harvard-Yenching Institute Studies, X. Cambridge, Mass., 1953.

_____ "Water Margin Revisited", T'oung Pao, XLVIII (1963), 393-415.

Karlgren, Bernhard. "New Excursions in Chinese Grammar", The Museum of Far Eastern Antiquities. Bulletin, No. 24 (1952), 51-80. (Study of Shui-hu chuan, Hsi-yu chi, Hung-lou meng, Ju-lin wai-shih, and Ching-hua yuan).

Kean, Vladimir. trans. Flower Shadows Behind the Curtain (Ko-lien hua-ying). (From Franz Kuhn's German translation). New York, 1959.

Kral, Oldrich. "Several Artistic Methods in the Classic Chinese Novel Ju-lin wai-shih", Archiv Orientalni, XXXII (1964), 16-43.

La-Hoai. "Le roman chinois", France-Asie, VI (1950), 454-464.

Lévy, André. "Études sur trois recueils anciens de contes chinois", T'oung Pao, LII (1965), 97-148.

Levy, Howard S. trans. The Dwelling of Playful Goddesses (Yu-hsien-k'u). Tokyo, 1965.

_____ trans. The Illusory Flame (Hsiang-yen tsung-shu). Tokyo, 1962.

_____ "Love Themes in T'ang Literature", Orient/West, VII:i (Jan., 1962), 67-78.

_____ Warm-Soft Village (Wen-jou hsiang-yuan tien). 2 vols. Tokyo, 1964.

Lin, Tai-yu. trans. Flowers in the Mirror (Ching-hua yuan). Berkeley, Los Angeles, London, 1965.

Lin, Yu-t'ang (Lin Yutang). trans. Six Chapters of a Floating Life, in The Wisdom of China and India: An Anthology. New York, 1942, pp. 964–1050.

Liu, Ts'un-jen (Liu Ts'un-yen). Buddhist and Taoist Influences on Chinese Novels. Vol. I: The Authorship of the Feng Shen Yen I. Preface by Arthur Waley. Wiesbaden, 1962.

Martin, Richard. trans. Jou P'u T'uan: the Prayer Mat of Flesh. (From Franz Kuhn's German version). New York, 1966.

Maspero, Henri. "Le Roman historique dans la littérature chinoise de l'Antiquité", Mélanges posthumes, III (Paris, 1950), 53–62.

Ono, Shinobu. "Chin P'ing Mei: a Critical Study", Acta Asiatica, No. 5 (1963), 76–89.

Průšek, Jaroslav. "Les contes chinois du Moyen Age comme source de l'histoire économique et sociale sous les dynasties des Sung et Yuan", Institut des hautes études chinoises. Mélanges, II (1960), 113–140.

_____. "The Creative Methods of Chinese Medieval Storytellers", Charisteria orientalia. eds. Felix Tauer et al. Prague, 1956, pp. 253–273.

_____. "Liao-chai chih-i by P'u Sung-ling: an Inquiry into the Circumstances Under Which the Collection Arose", Studia Serica Bernhard Karlgren Dedicata. Copenhagen, 1959. pp. 128–146.

_____. Die Literatur des befreiten China und ihre Volkstraditionem. Prague, 1965.

_____. "Liu O et son roman, le Pilerinage du vieux boiteux", Archiv Orientalni, XV (1946), 352–385.

_____. "The Narrators of Buddhist Scriptures and Religious Tales in the Sung Period", Archiv Orientalni, X (1938), 375–389.

_____. "New Studies of the Chinese Colloquial Short Story", Archiv Orientalni, XXV:iii (1957), 452–499.

_____. "Popular Novels in the Collection of Ch'ien Tseng", Archiv Orientalni, X (1938), 281–294.

_____. "The Realistic and Lyric Elements in the Chinese Medieval Story", Archiv Orientalni, XXXII:i (1964), 4–15.

_____. "Researches into the Beginning of the Chinese Popular Novel, Archiv Orientalni, XI:i (1939), 91–132.

Ruhlmann, Robert. "Traditional Heroes in Chinese Popular Fiction", The Confucian Persuasion, ed. Arthur F. Wright. Stanford, 1960, pp. 141–176.

Schumann, H.F. "On Social Themes in Sung Tales", Harvard Journal of Asiatic Studies, XX (1957), 239–261.

Semanov, Vladimir. "The Chinese Classical Novel in Russian", Soviet Literature, No. 3 (1963), 168-170.

Soulié, Charles Georges. trans. Chinese Love Tales. New York, 1950.

Vos, Frits. A Study of the Ise Monogatari With the Text According to the Den-Teika-Hippon and an Annotated Translation. 2 vols. 's-Gravenhage, 1957.

Waley, Arthur. "Notes on the History of Chinese Popular Literature", T'oung Pao, XXVIII (1931), 346-354.

Wu, I-t'ai (French romanization, Ou, Itai). Le Roman chinois. Paris, 1935.

Yang, Hsien-yi and Gladys. trans. A Brief History of Chinese Fiction, by Lu Hsun. Peking, 1959.

Unpublished Dissertations and Articles:

Bailey, Roger Blackwell. "A Study of the Sou Shen Chi". Doctoral thesis. Indiana, 1966.

Birch, Cyril. "Ku-chin Hsiao-shuo: A Critical Examination". Doctoral thesis. London, 1954.

_____ "Some Concerns and Methods of the Ming ch'uan-ch'i Drama". (Paper presented at the Bermuda Conference, Feb., 1967).

Handlin, Joanna Flug. "On the Only-Child Daughter in Chinese Hua-pen". (Paper presented to Prof. Patrick Hanan, Chinese 361, Stanford Univ., April 1, 1967).

Hsia, C.T. "Time and the Human Condition in the Plays of T'ang Hsien-tsu". (Paper presented at the Bermuda Conference, Feb., 1967).

Průšek, Jaroslav. "The Beginnings of Popular Chinese Literature: Urban Centers--the Cradle of Popular Fiction". (Paper presented at the Bermuda Conference, Feb., 1967).

Willis, Donald. "The Nieh-hai-hua and its Place in the Late Ch'ing Novel of Protest". Doctoral thesis. Seattle, 1951.

    D. Anthologies, Criticism, Histories, and Translations of Chinese Literature:

Bauer, Wolfgang and Herbert Franke. The Golden Casket. Translated from the German by Christopher Levenson. New York, 1964.

Birch, Cyril and Donald Keene. Anthology of Chinese Literature. New York, 1965.

_____ Chinese Myths and Fantasies. London, 1961.

Bishop, John L., ed. Studies in Chinese Literature. Cambridge, Mass., 1965.

Brower, Robert H. and Earl Miner. Japanese Court Poetry. Stanford, 1961.

Ch'en, Shou-yi. Chinese Literature. New York, 1961.

Eberhard, Wolfram. Folktales of China. Chicago, 1965.

Edwards, Evangeline Dora. Chinese Prose Literature of the T'ang Period, A.D. 618-906. 2 vols. London, 1937-38.

Giles, Herbert. A History of Chinese Literature. London, 1901.

Hawkes, David. "The Supernatural in Chinese Poetry", University of Toronto Quarterly, XXX:iii (April, 1961), 311-324.

Hightower, James Robert. "Chinese Literature in the Context of World Literature", Comparative Literature, V:ii (1953), 117-124.

_____ "The Han-shih wai-chuan and the San chia Shih", Harvard Journal of Asiatic Studies, XI (Dec., 1948), 241-310.

_____ Han Shih Wai Chuan: Han Ying's Illustrations of the Didactic Application of the Classic of Songs. Cambridge, Mass., 1952.

_____ Topics in Chinese Literature. rev. ed. Cambridge, Mass., 1962.

Hsia, C.T. "Traditional Chinese Literature and the Modern Chinese Temper", in Symposium on Chinese Culture, ed. Chi-pao Cheng. New York, 1964. pp. 16-20. Also in Literature East and West, VIII (Spring/Summer, 1964), 55-58.

Jung, C.G. Preface to Hellmut Wilhelm's translation of the I Ching, 3rd. edition. Princeton, 1967.

_____ "Synchronicity: An Acausal Connecting Principle", The Collected Works, eds. Sir Herbert Read, Michael Fordham, and Gerhard Adler. Trans. R.F.C. Hull. 2nd edition. vol. VIII. New York, 1966.

Kaltenmark, Odile. Chinese Literature. (Translated from the French by Anne-Marie Geoghegan). New York, 1964.

Lai, Ming. A History of Chinese Literature. New York, 1964.

Legge, James. The Chinese Classics. 5 vols. Hong Kong, 1960.

Liu, Wu-chi. An Introduction to Chinese Literature, Bloomington, 1966.

Průšek, Jaroslav. "A Confrontation of Traditional Oriental Literature with Modern European Literature in the Context of the Chinese Literary Revolution", International Federation of Modern Languages and Literature. Acta of the 9th Congress, New York, Aug. 25-31, 1963. Literary History and Literary Criticism. ed. Leon Edel. New York, 1965. pp. 165-176. Also in Archiv Orientalni, XXXII (1964), 365-375.

Průšek, Jaroslav. "The Importance of Tradition in Chinese Litera-
ture", Archiv Orientalni, XXVI (1958), 212-223.
_____ "Outlines of Chinese Literature", New Orient, V:iv (Aug.,
1966), 113-120; V:v (Oct., 1966), 145-151, 156-158; V:vi
(Dec., 1966), 169-176.
_____ "Reality and Art in Chinese Literature", Archiv Orientalni,
XXXII (1964), 605-618.
Soulié, Charles Georges. trans. Anthologie de l'Amour Chinois.
Paris, 1932.
Wang, C.C. "Chinese Literature", Chambers' Encyclopedia, III
(New York, 1950), 491-497.
Watson, Burton. Early Chinese Literature. New York, 1962.

E.   Reference Works on Chinese Civilization:

Published Materials

Briere, O., S.J. Fifty Years of Chinese Philosophy: 1898-1950.
trans. Laurence G. Thompson. London, 1956.
Chao, Yuen Ren and Lien Sheng Yang. Concise Dictionary of
Spoken Chinese. Cambridge, Mass., and London, 1962.
Chao, Yuen Ren. A Grammar of Spoken Chinese. Berkeley and
Los Angeles, 1968.
Chen Shih-Hsiang. "China--Literature", Encyclopedia Americana.
1957. pp. 541-548.
Chou, Yi- liang. "Tantrism in China", Harvard Journal of Asiatic
Studies, VIII (1945), 241-332.
Conze, Edward. Buddhist Thought in India. Ann Arbor, 1967.
Couvreur, F.S., S.J. Dictionnaire Classique de la Langue
Chinoise. Taipei, 1966.
de Bary, William Theodore. "Buddhism and the Chinese Tradition",
Diogenes, No. 47 (Fall, 1964), 102-124.
de Bary, William Theodore, Wing-tsit Chan, Burton Watson, eds.
Sources of Chinese Tradition. New York, 1960.
Dumoulin, Heinrich, S.J. A History of Zen Buddhism. New York,
1963.
Duyvendak, J.J.L. "The Mythico-Ritual Pattern in Chinese
Civilisation", (An Address delivered at the Seventh International
Congress for the History of Religions, Amsterdam, Sept., 1950).
Summary of the Address in: Proceedings of the Seventh Interna-
tional Congress (1951), 137-138.
Eberhard, Wolfram. Chinese Festivals. New York, 1952.
_____ A History of China. 2nd ed. Berkeley and Los Angeles,
1966.

Eberhard, Wolfram. Sin and Guilt in Traditional China. Berkeley
    and Los Angeles, 1967.
_____ "Topics and Moral Values in Chinese Temple Decorations",
    Journal of the American Oriental Society, LXXXVII:i (1967),
    22-32.
Fairservis, Walter A., Jr. The Origins of Oriental Civilization.
    New York, 1959.
Fung, Yu-lan. A Short History of Chinese Philosophy. ed. Derk
    Bodde. New York, 1960.
_____ The Spirit of Chinese Philosophy. trans. E.R. Hughes.
    Boston, 1962.
Goodrich, Luther Carrington. The Literary Inquisition of Ch'ien
    Lung. Baltimore, 1935.
_____ A Short History of the Chinese People. 3rd edition. New
    York, Evanston, and London, 1963.
Grousset, René. The Rise and Splendour of the Chinese Empire.
    Berkeley and Los Angeles, 1959.
Gulik, R.H. Van. Sexual Life in Ancient China. Leiden, 1961.
Herrigel, Eugen. Zen. trans. rev. and ed. R.F.C. Hull, et al.
    New York and Toronto, 1960.
Herrmann, Albert. An Historical Atlas of China. New edition.
    General ed. Norton Ginsburg. Preface by Paul Wheatley.
    Chicago, 1966.
Hummel, Arthur W. The Autobiography of a Chinese Historian.
    Leiden, 1931.
Hummel, Arthur W. et al., ed. Eminent Chinese of the Ch'ing
    Period. Washington, D.C., 1944.
Jameson, E.W., Jr. A Short Dictionary of Simplified Chinese
    Characters. 2nd ed., rev. Tokyo, 1967.
Levy, Howard S. Chinese Footbinding: the History of a Curious
    Erotic Custom. foreward by Arthur Waley. Intro. Wolfram
    Eberhard. New York, 1966.
_____ Harem Favorites of an Illustrious Celestial. Taichung,
    Taiwan, 1958.
_____ "Introduction to 'A Celestial Bedside Manual'", Orient/West,
    VIII:iv (July/Aug., 1963), 100-102.
Liu, Mau-tsai. "Die Traumdeutung im Alten China", Asiatische
    Studien, XVI (1963), 35-63.
MacNair, Harley Farnsworth, ed. China. Berkeley and Los
    Angeles, 1951.
Mathews, R.H. Chinese-English Dictionary. rev. American edi-
    tion. Cambridge, Mass., 1960.

Reischauer, Edwin O. and John K. Fairbank. East-Asia: The Great Tradition. Boston, 1960.

Schafer, Edward H. Ancient China. New York, 1967.

_____ The Golden Peaches of Samarkand. Berkeley and Los Angeles, 1963.

_____ The Vermilion Bird. Berkeley and Los Angeles, 1967.

Soothill, William Edward and Lewis Hodous. A Dictionary of Chinese Buddhist Terms. Taipei, 1968.

Takakusu, Junjirō. The Essentials of Buddhist Philosophy. 3rd ed. W.T. Chan and Charles A. Moore, eds. Honolulu, 1956.

Veith, Ilza. trans. The Yellow Emperor's Classic of Internal Medicine. New edition. Berkeley and Los Angeles, 1966.

Waley, Arthur. Three Ways of Thought in Ancient China. London, 1939.

Wang, Tsang-pao. La Femme dans la Societé Chinoise. Paris, 1933.

Werner, E.T.C. A Dictionary of Chinese Mythology. New York, 1961.

Wieger, L., S.J. Chinese Characters. New York, 1965.

Wright, Arthur F. "Buddhism and Chinese Culture: Phases of Interaction", Journal of Asian Studies, XVII:i (1957), 17-42.

_____ Buddhism in Chinese History. Stanford, 1959.

Yang, C.K. Religion in Chinese Society. Berkeley and Los Angeles, 1967.

Unpublished Materials:

Fang, Lienche Tu. "Ming Dreams". (Paper presented at ACLS Research Conference on Ming Thought, June, 1966).

Hsieh, K'ang (Sie, Kang). "L'amour maternel dans la littérature féminine en Chine". Doctoral thesis. Paris, 1937.

V. Western Criticism Useful for the Study of Dream of the Red Chamber and Chinese Fiction

A. General Critical Works:

Auerbach, Erich. Mimesis. trans. Willard R. Trask. Princeton, 1953.

Barfield, Owen. Poetic Diction. New York, 1964.

Burke, Kenneth. The Philosophy of Literary Form. revised ed. New York, 1957.

Daiches, David. Critical Approaches to Literature. New York, 1956.

Empson, William. Seven Types of Ambiguity. 3rd edition. London, 1963.

Fowlie, Wallace. Love in Literature. Bloomington, 1965.

Frye, Northrup. Anatomy of Criticism. Princeton, 1957.

Jacobs, Melville. The Content and Style of an Oral Literature. New York, 1959.

Leavis, Frank Raymond. The Common Pursuit. Edinburgh, 1963.

Lord, Albert B. The Singer of Tales. New York, 1965.

Raysor, Thomas Middleton. ed. Coleridge's Miscellaneous Criticism. Cambridge, Mass., 1936.

Schorer, Mark. The Politics of Vision. New York, 1959.

Tuveson, Ernest Lee. The Imagination as a Means of Grace: Locke and the Aesthetics of Romanticism. Berkeley and Los Angeles, 1960.

Wellek, René. Concepts of Criticism. New Haven and London, 1964.

       and Austin Warren. Theory of Literature. revised edition. New York, 1962.

     B. Allegory:

Auerbach, Erich. Scenes from the Drama of European Literature. New York, 1957.

Berger, Harry, Jr. The Allegorical Temper. New Haven, 1957.

Bloom, Edward A. "The Allegorical Principle", Journal of English Literary History, XVIII (1951), 163-190.

Curry, Walter Clyde. "Medieval Dream-lore and Chauntecler and Pertelote on Dreams", in Chaucer and the Medieval Sciences. New York and London, 1960.

Curtius, E.R. European Literature and the Latin Middle Ages. New York, 1953.

Fletcher, Angus. Allegory: The Theory of a Symbolic Mode. Ithaca, 1965.

Gunn, Alan M.F. The Mirror of Love. Lubbock, Texas, 1952.

Hanson, Richard Patrick Crosland. Allegory and Event. Richmond and London, 1959.

Honig, Edwin. Dark Conceit: the Making of Allegory. Evanston, Ill., 1959.

Ker, William Paton. Collected Essays of W.P. Ker. ed. Charles Whibley. Vol. II. London, 1925.

Lewis, C.S. The Allegory of Love. New York, 1958.

Muscatine, Charles. Chaucer and the French Tradition. Berkeley and Los Angeles, 1964.

Bibliography

Muscatine, Charles. "The Emergence of Psychological Allegory in Old French Romance", PMLA, LXVIII (1953), 1160-82.

Oulmont, Charles. Le Verger, la Temple et la Cellule. Paris, 1912.

Pépin, Jean. Mythe et allégorie. Paris, 1958.

Tuve, Rosemond. Allegorical Imagery: Some Mediaeval Books and their Posterity. Princeton, 1966.

C. Narrative Fiction:

Booth, Wayne. The Rhetoric of Fiction. Chicago, 1961.

Bowen, Elizabeth. "Truth and Fiction", in Afterthought. London, 1962.

Brooks, Cleanth and Robert Penn Warren. Understanding Fiction. New York, 1943.

Eastman, Richard. A Guide to the Novel. San Francisco, 1965.

Edel, Leon. The Modern Psychological Novel. New York, 1962.

Forster, Edward Morgan. Aspects of the Novel. New York, 1954.

Krutch, Joseph Wood. Five Masters: A Study of the Mutations of the Novel. Bloomington, 1959.

Leavis, F.R. The Great Tradition. London, 1948.

Lubbock, Percy. The Craft of Fiction. New York, 1963.

Lucas, F.L. Literature and Psychology. Ann Arbor, 1962.

O'Conner, William Van, ed. Forms of Modern Fiction. Bloomington, 1959.

Ortega, José y Gasset. The Dehumanization of Art and Notes on the Novel. trans. Williard Trask. New York, 1956.

Scholes, Robert, ed. Approaches to the Novel. San Francisco, 1966.

_____ and Robert Kellogg. The Nature of Narrative. New York, 1966.

Stafford, Jean. "The Psychological Novel", Kenyon Review, X (1948), 214-227.

Van Ghent, Dorothy. The English Novel: Form and Function. New York, 1953.

Watt, Ian. The Rise of the Novel. Berkeley, 1957.

D. Symbolism:

Barfield, Owen. Saving the Appearances. London, 1957.

Bays, Gwendolyn. The Orphic Vision: Seer Poets from Novalis to Rimbaud. Lincoln, 1964.

Beebe, Maurice. Literary Symbolism. San Francisco, 1960.

Bodkin, Maud. Archetypal Patterns in Poetry. London, 1965.

Bowra, Cecil Maurice. Primitive Song. New York, 1962.
      The Romantic Imagination. New York, 1961.
Caillois, Roger. The Dream Adventure. New York, 1963.
      and G.E. Van Grunebaum, eds. The Dream and Human
   Societies. Berkeley, 1966.
Campbell, Joseph. The Hero with a Thousand Faces. New York,
   1961.
Cassirer, Ernst. Language and Myth. trans. Susanne K. Langer.
   New York and London, 1946.
Eliade, Mircea. Images and Symbols. trans. Philip Mairet.
   London and New York, 1961.
      The Myth of the Eternal Return. trans. Willard R. Trask.
   New York, 1954.
      Myths, Dreams, and Mysteries. trans. Philip Mairet.
   London, 1960.
      The Sacred and the Profane. trans. Willard R. Trask. New
   York, 1961.
Flugel, John Carl. The Psychology of Clothes. London, 1930.
Jacobi, Jolande. Complex, Archetype, Symbol in the Psychology
   of C.G. Jung. trans. Ralph Manheim. New York, 1959.
Jung, C.G. "The Archetypes and the Collective Unconscious",
   Collected Works, eds. Sir Herbert Read, Michael Fordham, and
   Gerhard Adler. trans. R.F.C. Hull. 2nd edition. Vol. IX,
   part 1. New York, 1966.
      Psyche and Symbol: A Selection from the Writings of C.G.
   Jung. ed. Violet S. de Laszle. Garden City, New York, 1958.
      "Two Essays on Analytical Psychology", Collected Works.
   eds. Sir Herbert Read, Michael Fordham, and Gerhard Adler.
   trans. R.F.C. Hull. 2nd edition. Vol. VII. New York, 1966.
Raymond, Marcel. From Baudelaire to Surrealism. New York,
   1950.
Shumaker, Wayne. Literature and the Irrational. Englewood Cliffs,
   New Jersey, 1960.
Starkie, Enid. Baudelaire. London, 1957.
      Arthur Rimbaud. New York, 1961.
Symons, Arthur. The Symbolist Movement in Literature. New
   York, 1958.
Tindall, William York. The Literary Symbol. New York, 1955.
Yeats, William Butler. Essays and Introductions. London, 1961.

Glossary

The Allegorists. A school of Chinese critics of the late nineteenth and early twentieth centuries who interpret <u>Dream of the Red Chamber</u> as a book of hidden meaning.

Beware Illusion Fairy 警幻仙子 . Goddess in charge of lovers and their fates.

Buddha Dharma 佛法 . The teaching of the Buddha. Ultimate reality. In popular Buddhism it signifies wizardry and magic.

Buddhist and Taoist Celestial Clerics 一僧一道 (茫茫大士, 渺渺真人). Two Immortals in the guise of a Buddhist monk and a Taoist priest who transport the Stone to earth.

<u>chen-chia</u> 真假 . "Real"-"Unreal"; "True"-"False". The theme of complementary opposites.

Chen Pao-yu 甄寶玉 . The "true" (chen) Pao-yu who in appearance is the mirror image of "unreal" (chia) Pao-yu but who in personality is the opposite of the novel's hero.

Chen Shih-yin 甄士隱 . A retired official who experiences suffering and embraces Buddhism. He is the character "opposite" of Chia Yu-ts'un. His name is a homophone for "true affairs hidden".

Chia Cheng 賈政 . The father of Chia Pao-yu.

Chia Lien 賈璉 . Husband of Wang Hsi-feng.

Chia Pao-yu 賈寶玉 . The incarnation of the Stone in the Red Dust and the hero of <u>Dream of the Red Chamber</u>.

Chia Yu-ts'un 賈雨村 . A young scholar who becomes an official through the help of Chen Shih-yin. He is the character "opposite" of Chen Shih-yin. His name is a homophone for "fictive language and vulgar vocabulary".

Chih-yen Chai 脂硯齋 , "Master of the Red Ink-slab Studio". Commentator on early manuscripts of the novel.

Ch'in Chung 秦鐘 . Brother of Ch'in K'o-ch'ing. Schoolmate of Chia Pao-yu.

Ch'in K'o-ch'ing 秦可卿 . Wife of Chia Jung. Chia Pao-yu's niece.

Crimson Pearl Sylph Herb 絳珠仙草 . A weeping plant in the creation myth which is reborn as Lin Tai-yu.

Divine Crystal Page 神瑛侍者 . Mythic name of Chia Pao-yu. In the creation myth, the Divine Crystal Page waters the Crimson Pearl Sylph Herb with dew.

Feng Yuan 馮淵 . Man who is killed by Hsueh P'an in dispute over buying Ying-lien.

fu 賦 . Prose-Poem. Rhymed Prose. An Exhibitory Essay.

Hao-liao Ko 好了歌 . The "Sweeter-Over Song". A lyric sung to Chen Shih-yin by an insane Taoist which enlightens the former as to the meaning of life.

Hsi-jen 襲人 . Chia Pao-yu's favorite maid.

Hsiang-ling. See Ying-lien.

Hsueh P'an 薛蟠 . Brother of Hsueh P'ao-ch'ai.

Hsueh P'ao-ch'ai 薛寶釵 . Girl Pao-yu marries.

hua-shen 化身 . "Transformation". From the viewpoint of allegory, a fictional event, location, or character is a transformation of some real-life counterpart.

hung-hsueh 紅學 . "Redology". Native Chinese textual, biographical, or bibliographical studies of Dream of the Red Chamber.

Hung-lou meng 紅樓夢 . Chinese title of printed editions of Dream of the Red Chamber.

Jung-kuo 榮國 . One branch of the Chia clan.

kalpa. An aeon of incalculable duration. A fabulous period of time.

Kao E 高鶚 . The editor of the 120 chapter printed editions of Dream of the Red Chamber who claims to have discovered missing manuscripts of the novel.

karma. The operation of retributive justice (reward or punishment) determined by deeds or action.

lai-li 來歷 . "Background" or "provenance" which explains a
   character or event.
Leng Tzu-hsing 冷子興 . A curio dealer from the Capital and
   friend of Chia Yu-ts'un.
Lin Ju-hai 林如海 . Father of Lin Tai-yu.
Lin Tai-yu 林黛玉 . Pao-yu's beloved.
Liu Lao-lao 劉姥姥 . A country bumpkin who befriends the
   Matriarch.
Madame Wang 王夫人 . Mother of Chia Pao-yu.
Matriarch 賈母 . Grandmother of Chia Pao-yu and head of the
   Jung-kuo branch of the Chia clan.
Ning-kuo 寧國 . One branch of the Chia clan.
nirvana. The extinction of consciousness and desire.
Nu-kua 女媧 . A goddess of the heavenly realms. In refining
   stones to repair the vault of heaven, she rejects the Stone that is
   to become the hero of the novel, the "precious jade", Chia
   Pao-yu.
pao-yu 寶玉 . "Precious jade". The mysterious jade amulet
   found in Chia Pao-yu's mouth at his birth; the source of his
   name, "Pao-yu".
Penumbra Mechanics 玄機 . "Key to the arcane". Esoteric
   knowledge.
Pervading Fragrance. See Hsi-jen.
Precious Clasp. See Hsueh P'ao-ch'ai.
Precious Jade for Penetrating the Numinous 通靈寶玉 . Words
   inscribed on the jade amulet Pao-yu wears around his neck.
Red Dust 紅塵 . This changing conditioned world.
Reverend Taoist Kosmo Kosmos 空空道人 . While in search
   of enlightenment he discovers the Stone Record.
samsāra. The endless ebb and flow of life.
The Stone 石頭 . A divine stone rejected by the goddess, Nu-
   kua. It undergoes earthly experiences in the Red Dust in the
   form of Chia Pao-yu.
Stone Record 石頭記 (Story of the Stone). One of the
   original names of Dream of the Red Chamber.
Synchronicity. Meaningful chance. The principle of acausality
   according to which the configuration of a particular moment in
   time and space is considered significant.
tao 道 . Ultimate reality. Metaphysical truth.
Two Breaths Theory. Chia Yu-ts'un's cosmological theory that
   human good and evil originate in two universal breaths, the
   "Upright" 正氣 and the "Perverse" 邪氣 .

tz'u 詞 . Lyric.

Wang Hsi-feng 王熙鳳 . Wife of Chia Lien. Chia Pao-yu's aunt.

yin-kuo 因果 . Buddhist principle of moral causality. Cause and effect.

Ying-lien 英蓮 (Hsiang-ling 香菱). Daughter of Chen Shih-yin. Concubine of Hsueh P'an.

ying-shu 影書 . "Shadowbook". A book with a hidden allegorical meaning.

ying-tzu 影子 . "Image", "shadow", or "reflection". According to allegorical interpreters, each character in the novel is a mimic or "shadow" of another.

Index

Index

Cause and effect, 69, 93. See also
    Yin-kuo
Censorship, 13, 14n, 207n, 263,
    264-265, 274
Chance, 8-9, 78, 107, 109, 141. See
    also Synchronicity
Chang Hsin-chih, 7
Chang Tai, 20n
Chao Kang, 20, 21, 113n, 207, 263,
    269, 272-273, 274, 275-276, 277
Characterization, 18n, 29, 56, 62n,
    88, 111, 134n, 155, 177, 243, 284,
    285-286; reflection technique, 7, 8,
    155-156, 176, 177; names, 113n;
    opposites, 155-156, 178, 285;
    parallelism, 281, 285
Chaucer, Geoffrey: Canterbury Tales,
    13; Troilus and Criseyde, 14-15,
    230n, 243
Chen family, 156
Chen-chia (true-false) theme, 16n, 75n,
    81n, 87, 115, 117, 121, 137, 146,
    165, 173, 176, 177, 178, 181, 183,
    205, 211, 218, 227, 244n, 256, 284
Ch'en Ch'ing-hao, 21n
Ch'en Chung-i, 20n, 207, 274, 275
Chen Pao-yu, 78, 92n, 111n; and Chia
    Pao-yu, 135-136, 155-161, 165-166,
    172-180, 255, 282, 285, 292, 295
Chen, Shih-Hsiang, 46n, 96
Chen Shih-yin, 79, 281; dream-vision,
    27, 29, 30, 35, 41-46, 53, 54, 62,
    64, 65, 66, 67, 69, 70, 73-74, 76,
    77, 78, 80, 83, 89, 90-97, 146,
    182, 198, 217, 265, 266; song,
    56-57, 100-108, 293-297; and Chia
    Yu-ts'un, 71, 72, 109, 111-115,
    117, 118, 121-123, 125-127, 132,
    137-138, 141-150, 153, 155,
    243-244, 251, 253, 255, 282, 285;
    enlightenment, 88, 89, 91, 92, 94,
    95, 97, 103, 104, 105, 108, 109,
    111, 126, 198, 281
Ch'en Yu-p'i, 16n, 206
Cheng Chen-to, 267, 268
Ch'eng Wei-yuan edition, 33, 76n, 219,
    258, 263, 269, 276, 277
Chi-hu, 20n, 33, 207, 274
Chia. See Chen-chia theme
Chia-chen manuscript, 270, 273

Chia Cheng, 90, 109, 133, 147, 156n,
    157, 166, 230, 231, 279, 292, 296
Chia family, 11, 39n, 90, 91, 109,
    131, 134, 136, 148, 156, 187n,
    227, 228, 243, 263, 280, 283-84,
    288, 290, 295, 297
Chia-hsu manuscript, 6n, 33, 177,
    206, 208, 219, 274, 294
Chia Pao-yu, 78, 91, 108, 132-33,
    147, 194, 223, 230-32, 255, 278-79,
    280-81, 282, 290, 291, 292;
    enlightenment, 15, 63-64, 92,
    130n, 145, 146, 174, 178, 244,
    255, 256; mythic origins, 18n, 21,
    41, 46, 68, 83, 134, 135; dream-
    visions, 22, 34n, 61n, 65, 103, 137,
    145, 156n, 157-58, 159-61, 165,
    166, 172, 176, 178, 179, 226,
    229, 288, 291; identification with
    Stone, 37n, 39n, 58, 71, 81-82,
    93, 94, 114, 142, 143, 144, 228n,
    267; and Lin Tai-yu, 54-55, 60,
    121, 226-27, 243; and Hsueh Pao-
    ch'ai, 90, 233, 234, 289; and
    Chen Pao-yu, 111n, 136, 155-59,
    165-66, 172-80, 285, 295
Chia Yu-ts'un, 29, 68, 74n, 78, 79n,
    233, 255, 279, 287, 288, 293,
    297; and Chen Shih-yin, 27, 30,
    54, 71, 72, 73n, 87-88, 89-92,
    108-109, 111-18, 121-28, 130,
    137-38, 141-50, 243, 282, 285;
    and Leng Tzu-hsing, 37n, 131-36;
    enlightenment, 44n, 137, 141, 142,
    149, 150, 153-55, 244, 245, 249-
    50, 252, 253, 256, 292
Chiang Ho-sen, 20n
Chien (glimpse) formula, 44n, 71-72
Ch'ien Hsing-ts'un, 264
Ch'ien-lung manuscript, 6n, 269, 271-
    72, 275-76, 277
Chih, use of, 80, 81, 82, 251-52
Chih-yen Chai: identity, 20-21n,
    206, 274; commentary, 25n, 30,
    31, 32, 33, 34n, 38n, 40n, 45n,
    53, 54, 55n, 56, 57n, 58n, 59,
    61n, 62-63, 64, 65, 66-67, 77,
    78, 79n, 81n, 84n, 92n, 96n, 104-
    105, 107, 111-13, 114n, 123,
    126n, 128, 130, 131n, 156-57,
    176-77, 178n, 183, 189, 193, 194,